Empty Phantoms

INTERVIEWS AND ENCOUNTERS
WITH JACK KEROUAC

EDITED BY

PAUL MAHER JR.

THUNDER'S MOUTH PRESS
NEW YORK

EMPTY PHANTOMS
INTERVIEWS AND ENCOUNTERS WITH JACK KEROUAC

Published by
Thunder's Mouth Press
An Imprint of Avalon Publishing Group Inc.
245 West 17th St., 11th Floor
New York, NY 10011

AVALON
publishing group incorporated

The author gratefully acknowledges everyone who gave permission for material to appear in this book. He has made every reasonable effort to contact copyright holders. If an error or omission has been made, it can be brought to his attention at pm2005@lycos.com.

Excerpts from "An Interview with Allen Ginsberg" from *Composed on the Tongue* by Yves Le Pellec, copyright © 1980 by Yves Le Pellec. Excerpt from *Guilty of Everything* by Herbert Huncke, copyright © 1990 by Estate of Hebert Huncke. Excerpt from *Nobody's Wife: The Smart Aleck and the King of the Beats* used by permission of Joan Haverty Kerouac. "First Reader of *On the Road* Manuscript: An Excerpt from the Journals of John Clellon Holmes," "The Great Remember," and "Gone in October" used by permission of Sterling Lord Literistic. Excerpt from "Neal & Allen [notes on conversation about Kerouac]" by Allen Ginsberg, August 1954 from *Journals Mid-Fifties 1954–1958* copyright © 1996 by Estate of Allen Ginsberg. Used by permission of Harper-Perennial. "Kerouac at the Village Vanguard" by Dan Wakefield, copyright © 2000 by Dan Wakefield. Used by permission of the author. "Kerouac on Kerouac," "Kerouac in Lowell," "Conversation with Kerouac," "Kerouac Leaves Lowell," "On the Road with Marty and Jack," "Kerouac, Joyce, Proust," and "Kerouac Remembers Them All" used by permission of *Lowell Sun*. "St. Jack" copyright © 1998. Used by permission of the Estate of Al Aronowitz and Michael K. Dorr of LitPub Ink. "A Strange Game of Baseball with a Legendary Writer" and "Playing Baseball with Jack Kerouac" copyright © Stan Isaacs. Used by permission of the author. "Excerpts from Interview with Miklos Zsedely" used by permission of Northport Public Library. "Interview with Jack Kerouac" from *The Paris Review* copyright © 1968 by *The Paris Review*. Reprinted with permission of The Wylie Agency. "Firing Line with William F. Buckley" used by permission of Stanford University and Hoover Institution Archives. "Off the Road: The Celtic Twilight of Jack Kerouac" by Gregory MacDonald. Used by permission of *The Boston Globe*. "David Amram Remembers" used by permission of the author. "Is There Any End to Kerouac Highway?" copyright © 1994 Estate of Ken Kesey. Permission granted by Sterling Lord Literistic.

Library of Congress Cataloging-in-Publication Data is available

ISBN 1-56025-658-3
ISBN 13: 978-1-56025-658-8

9 8 7 6 5 4 3 2 1

Book design by Maria Elias
Printed in the United States of America
Distributed by Publishers Group West

To my daughters, Chloe Jane and Rachel Leigh . . .

Contents

Acknowledgments   *xv*

Introduction   *xvii*

Excerpt from an Interview with Allen Ginsberg, Part 1
—Yves Le Pellec, *Composed On the Tongue*
(Grey Fox, 1980)   *1*

Excerpt from *Guilty of Everything*
—Herbert Huncke
(Paragon House, 1990)   *9*

Excerpt from *Nobody's Wife:*
The Smart Aleck and the King of the Beats
—Joan Haverty Kerouac
(Creative Arts Book Company, 1990)   *11*

First Reader of *On the Road* Manuscript: An Excerpt from the
Journals of John Clellon Holmes
—*Moody Street Irregulars* No. 5,
(Summer/Fall 1979)   *15*

Neal & Allen: Notes on a Conversation about Kerouac from the
Journal of Allen Ginsberg, August 1954
—Allen Ginsberg, *Journals—Mid-Fifties 1954-1958*
(Harper Perennial, 1996)   *18*

An Interview with Carolyn Cassady on Kerouac
—Andrew O'Hagan, BBC Online
(Undated)   *20*

Witless Madcaps
—Dan Balaban, *Village Voice*
(February 13, 1957)   *38*

Writing Novels by the Foot
—Luther Nicholls, *San Francisco Examiner*
(June 1957)   *41*

Back to the Village
—Jerry Talmer, *Village Voice*
(September 18, 1957)   *44*

Beat Generation: Roadster
—Maurice Dolbier, *New York Herald Tribune*
(September 22, 1957)   *48*

Trade Winds
—Jerome Beatty, *Saturday Review*
(September 28, 1957)   *50*

Trade Winds
—John G. Fuller, *Saturday Review*
(October 4, 1957)   *52*

Off the Road, Into the Vanguard, and Out
—Howard Smith, *Village Voice*
(December 25, 1957)   *54*

Kerouac at the Village Vanguard
—Dan Wakefield, *The Nation*
(January 4, 1958)   *58*

Interview with Jack Kerouac:
Lowell Author Gives His Version of the Beat Generation
—Mike Wallace, *New York Post*
(January 21, 1958)   *63*

He Scorns Beatniks
—UPI, *Detroit News*
(August 24, 1958)   *67*

On the Road Back: How the Beat Generation Got That Way According to Its Seer
−*San Francisco Examiner*
(October 5, 1958)   *71*

Interview with Ben Hecht
−Ben Hecht, *The Ben Hecht Show*, WABC-TV
(October 17, 1958)   *74*

The Beat Debated−Is It or Is It Not?
−Marc D. Scheifer, *Village Voice*
(November 19, 1958)   *87*

The Age of Unthink
−James Weschler, from *Reflections of an Angry Middle-Aged Editor*
(November 6, 1958)   *92*

Interview with Kenneth Allsop
−Kenneth Allsop, *Lilliput*
(January 1959)   *104*

Kerouac On Kerouac
−"Pertinax," *Lowell Sun*
(April 17, 1959)   *107*

Interview with Steve Allen
−Steve Allen,
The Steve Allen Pontiac Show
(January 16, 1959)   *110*

The Great Rememberer
−John Clellon Holmes, from *Gone in October*:
Last Reflections on Jack Kerouac
(Limberlost Press, 1985)   *113*

St. Jack (annotated by Jack Kerouac)
−Al Aronowitz, *New York Post*
(March 30, 1959)   *137*

A Strange Game of Baseball with a Legendary Writer
–Stan Isaacs, www.TheColumnists.com
(2002)   *173*

Playing Baseball with Jack Kerouac
–Stan Isaacs, *Newsday*
(February 16, 1961)   *177*

Beat Bard Denies He's the Daddy-O
–Alfred Albelli, *New York Daily News*
(December 14, 1961)   *181*

Dialogues in Great Books
–Charles E. Jarvis and James Curtis, WCAP Radio Interview,
Lowell, Massachusetts
(October 1962)   *184*

Kerouac in Lowell
–"Pertinax," *Lowell Sun*
(September 19, 1962)   *203*

Conversation with Kerouac
–"Pertinax," *Lowell Sun*
(September 20, 1962)   *206*

Kerouac Leaves Lowell
–"Pertinax," *Lowell Sun*
(September 25, 1962)   *209*

On the Road with Marty and Jack
–"Pertinax," *Lowell Sun*
(October 2, 1962)   *212*

Kerouac, Joyce, Proust
–"Pertinax," *Lowell Sun*
(October 24, 1962)   *215*

Kerouac Remembers Them All
–"Pertinax," *Lowell Sun*
(October 25, 1962)   *218*

Book News from Farrar, Straus & Cudahy, Inc.
—Press Release for *Visions of Gerard*
(1963)   *221*

Jack Kerouac Reads, etc., at Lowell
—*Harvard Crimson*
(March 25, 1964)   *225*

Excerpts from Interview with Miklos Zsedely
—Northport Public Library Oral History Project
(April 14, 1964)   *228*

Kerouac Revisited
—Val Duncan, *Long Island Newsday*
(July 18, 1964)   *253*

Beat Is Rhythm, Not an Act
—Robert E. Boles, *Yarmouth Port Register*
(Undated)   *260*

Radio-Canada Interview
—Fernand Seguin, *Sel de la Semaine*
(March 7, 1967)   *265*

Excerpt from an Interview with Allen Ginsberg, Part 2
—Yves Le Pellec, *Composed on the Tongue*
(Grey Fox, 1980)   *277*

Interview with Jack Kerouac
—Ted Berrigan, *Paris Review* No. 43
(Summer 1968)   *282*

Interview with Ted Berrigan
—Ted Berrigan, from *Talking in Tranquility:*
Interviews with Ted Berrigan
(Avenue B, 1991)   *322*

***Firing Line* with William F. Buckley**
—William F. Buckley, *Firing Line*
(September 3, 1968)   *328*

Off the Road: The Celtic Twilight of Jack Kerouac
—Gregory MacDonald, *Boston Globe*
(August 1968)   *356*

Jack Kerouac—End of the Road
—Larry Vickers, from *Kerouac at the "Wild Boar"*
and Other Skirmishes edited by John Montgomery
(Beat Books, 1986)   *368*

Jack Kerouac Is on the Road No More
—Jack McClintock, *St. Petersburg Times*
(October 12, 1969)   *374*

This Is How the Ride Ends
—Jack McClintock, *Esquire*
(March 1970)   *376*

Jack Kerouac: Off the Road for Good
—Carl Adkins, *Story: The Yearbook of Discovery*
(1971)   *385*

Jack Kerouac: Beat Even in Northport
—Mike McGrady, *Long Island Newsday*
(October 25, 1969 and April 19, 1973)   *399*

Strange Gray Myth of the West
—Richard Hill, *L.A. Free Press*
(August 7, 1970)   *409*

David Amram Remembers
—David Amram, *Evergreen Review*
(October 24, 1969)   *419*

Gone in October
—John Clellon Holmes, from *Gone in October:*
Last Reflections on Jack Kerouac
(Limberlost Press, 1985)   *424*

Jack Kerouac: He Wrote the Great Lowell Novel
–Charles G. Sampas, *Lowell Sun*
(October 26, 1969)   *470*

Is There Any End to Kerouac Highway? The Demise of Conformity
–Ken Kesey, *Esquire*
(December 1983)   *473*

Notes   *479*

Appendix
Excerpts from Official Military Personnel File,
National Personnel Center   *489*

"We're all just empty phantoms."

–Jack Kerouac to Mike Wallace

Acknowledgments

Many thanks go to John Oakes and Thunder's Mouth Press for bringing this project to fruition. Also a gracious thanks to Johnny Saunders for his time and superlative effort to help turn this manuscript into a finished book. I would also like to extend gratitude to John Sampas and the Kerouac estate for bringing Jack's posthumous work into the world with competence and care and for doing so with an eye toward Jack's intentions.

Also, warm graciousness to Dave Moore for helping me locate the bulk of the interviews found in this book. The progress of this project would have been a lot more laborious and time-consuming had Mr. Moore not already keyed many of the interviews into text files. Thanks to Northport Library, the *Paris Review*, the Estate of John Clellon Holmes, and a slew of newspapers and magazines that gave permission for reprint.

And last, a warm and loving thank-you to my wife Tina for supporting my interests.

Introduction

D espite his photogenic appearance, Jack Kerouac did not possess that ease of social grace that interviewers love. Nor on taped interviews did he fare so well. His manner, though impassioned, was awkward, straining both Kerouac's sensibilities and at times the interviewer's patience. Kerouac committed the social faux pas of simply being *too* honest. Whether he was telling the world that he was waiting for "God to show his face" or expressing his casual attitude toward drugs or that he thought the violently accelerating war on Vietnam was being fought "just to get jeeps in the country," his views expressed an earnest volition that never failed to amuse (though seldom enlightened) his contemporary audience.

Such was the tenor of his perceived cluelessness that Kerouac was publicly insulted on live television, when he was parodied by Jack Paar. Kerouac had attended a *Tonight Show* taping with his host, comedian Steve Allen. Allen suddenly yelled, "And now, presenting Jack Kerouac!" According to Kerouac, he was "rushed onstage before millions of viewers." When Paar's writer, Jack Douglass, asked Kerouac on camera, "What is the Beat Generation?" Jack simply responded, "Nothin'." Kerouac then casually reached for Douglass's lighter to light his cigarette. Douglass quipped, "Oh, I use morphine myself." Kerouac responded, not realizing that he was being toyed with condescendingly, "Haven't you tried H[eroin] yet?" The next night, Kerouac was spoofed as a fumbling goof, lighting numerous cigarettes whilst spouting "nothin'" nonsensically. Later, Kerouac was again brutally satirized as "Jack Crackerjack" on television.

One month earlier, Kerouac had been harshly insulted in the *New York Times* by J. Donald Adams in his "Speaking of Books" column: "Reading Mr. Kerouac's *On the Road or The Subterraneans*, I am reminded of nothing so much as an insistent and garrulous barroom drunk, drooling into your ear." That Kerouac often behaved publicly in this manner made many critics and scholars take him less seriously than they did other writers, much to his disdain. In a sense, Kerouac did himself in by *being* himself.

Kerouac's growing fear of making a fool of himself paralyzed his will. For this reason, he shied away from the numerous opportunities that *On the Road*'s fame brought him. Despite this, he entertained several film adaptation offers (even though he regretted that the offers were less than what he and his agent thought he deserved). It gave him a heightened sense of self-importance and literary celebrity. He even took the desperate step of writing a letter to actor Marlon Brando, suggesting that he costar in a film version of *On the Road* with him. Unsurprisingly, Brando never responded. The one film adaptation he did accept an offer on was for his novel *The Subterraneans*. Its result was a disgrace; the black love interest was changed to a white woman and it was rewritten with somewhat of a more uplifting, happy ending. This defeated the lead character's emotionally charged conflict with his love Mardou Fox. Kerouac never again courted Hollywood with such unbridled optimism.

Compared with the sheer body of written work created in Kerouac's lifetime, his interviews are few. In July 1958, Kerouac wrote to friend and poet Philip Whalen that he had temporarily begun to turn down interviews. The anxiety they induced in him often made him physically ill (as occurred during his 1959 television appearance with Steve Allen). Around the summer of 1958, Kerouac had also turned down an offer to appear in a film in which he would have been superimposed over a Benny Goodman recording session. Even John Wingate, host of *Nightbeat*, asked him back to be interviewed, not because he was interested in Kerouac's literature but for the thrill of seeing him "ad libbing with a stripteaser." Acknowledging his ill-advised tendency to speak his mind honestly ("I would say anything that was on my mind, any moment," Kerouac told novelist John Clellon Holmes on July 21, 1958), Kerouac realized that there was an intrinsic value in simply staying quiet.

Kerouac's common sense, what little he had of it, was bested by his frequent imbibing of alcohol. Yet, Kerouac reasoned, this imbibing defeated his social "awkwardness." Kerouac's logic was that in order to write honestly—or speak honestly, for that matter—one had to defeat the awkwardness of inhibition and the disabling fear of pretension. Alcohol, sadly, was the mechanism through which he overcame his introversion.

He had strengths, though. The hypnotic power of his reading, his grasp of semantics, and the linguistic blend of his Lowellian, Franco-American, Western cowboy, Atlantic seaman, railroading brakeman, earthbound Okie, and streetwise Manhattanite accents brought his reading to life and resonated well over airwaves. His Lowell accent, his clipped tongue, his remarkable range of tone and inflection, and the sincerity of his voice lent Kerouac a unique approach toward his recitations. Recognizing the power of his reading abilities, Kerouac accepted some offers to record his reading both with accompaniment and solo. Ultimately, three long-playing records would emerge in Kerouac's lifetime. The engaging dispatch of his readings keeps these legendary recordings in music stores to this day.

Unwittingly, when Kerouac accepted interview requests, he didn't realize that some were intending to do a hatchet job on him and his work. Such was the intention of the *New York Post* when the paper sent journalist Al Aronowitz to his home (Aronowitz declined to treat Kerouac poorly and interviewed the author with dignity and respect). Writing to poet and pal Gary Snyder in June 1958, Kerouac explained, "When a book comes out people don't leave you alone, you end up panting in bed at night wondering if you're going to die."

He envisioned himself a modern-day Thoreau, and in 1960 he wrote his girlfriend Lois Sorrells of his plans finally to acquire a driver's license and buy a Volkswagen so that he could travel and buy a cabin. It was a vain attempt to hug his "will" after "being caught by surprise in 1957 with on the road [*sic*] success." Kerouac sensed that he had been doing nothing for the past several years but "following everybody"; in a vain attempt to extract himself from this predicament, he foresaw the formidable impulses his own "will" would ultimately exact upon him mentally and physically. The excessive alcoholism, he theorized, was brought upon by being "dragged around" to places he despised and being forced to "drink" in order to fit in. Unwittingly, despite his yearning to fit in, Kerouac remained out of sync with America's dulled edge of conformity: "I drink by myself always sensibly, always eat right, it's only when I'm overwhelmed by bores and non-bores I don't wanta see that I get myself sick" (Kerouac to Lois Sorrells, January 19, 1960).

During his interviews, Kerouac became for America's television-watching public the prototypical "beatnik." It was a pejorative term he deeply detested, for it made a mockery of him and, more important, his life's work. Repeatedly, Kerouac defined and restated his philosophy of Beat to interviewers over and over in order to dispel their skewed understanding of the term. The spiritual associations connected to being Beat were distorted; the public's concept of Beat identity stubbornly remained that of Bohemian layabouts, sinister street hoodlums, and beret-wearing, coffee-house pseudo-intellectuals spouting shallow poetry. By the early 1960s, Kerouac had fled New York City to suburban homes in both Northport, Long Island, and Orlando, Florida. At the former, he was harassed by rock-throwing youths—and by determined journalists who kept on turning up on his doorstep despite being turned away by Gabrielle, Kerouac's mother. In Orlando, Kerouac feared that his books would drop in sales without his presence in the North; Kerouac beat down a path along the eastern seaboard, never completely comfortable in the North or the South.

In negotiations with editors, Kerouac feared the "castration jobs" they inflicted on his completed manuscripts. And when the novels and poetry were finally published as he intended them to be read, it was the book critics who misunderstood his methodology. Ignorantly or intentionally, they mistook his prose and poetry for Bohemian slapdash. When *Time* magazine wrote a disparaging review of Kerouac's novel *Big Sur*, poet and publisher Lawrence Ferlinghetti wrote a letter in defense of the work. The letter, however, was never published.

As Kerouac sank deeper into literary oblivion during the mid-to-late 1960s (much like his literary hero Herman Melville after the publication of *Moby-Dick*), Kerouac's defenders gradually diminished. Even Ferlinghetti, who had valiantly arisen to defend Kerouac, was dismissed by Kerouac as a "mediocrity" during a 1962 radio interview broadcast in Lowell, Massachusetts. Later, in 1968, during an appearance on William F. Buckley's *Firing Line*, Kerouac would accuse Ferlinghetti of "jumping on my back" when the term "Beat" had become disparaged by the press. Kerouac refused to ride the coattails of the term "Beat." He derided the more sensational aspects of the word in his private correspondence and in public.

Another constant target for Kerouac's barbs in letters and interviews was Allen Ginsberg. Though Ginsberg did not overtly do anything to earn his disrespect, Allen's vehement public protests during the 1960s clashed with Kerouac's conservative politics. Kerouac's stoic patriotism and empathy for the American soldier clashed with Ginsberg's impassioned political activism. Unpublished documents, such as Kerouac's stirring prose piece observing the death of Robert F. Kennedy and mid-to-late journal entries about the dissolution of America, underscore his devout patriotism. To see an old friend tread the worn path of futile activism stirred his vitriol; Ginsberg's first duty to the world, thought Kerouac, was as a poet, not as a crusader for legions of disenchanted youths.

Kerouac, too, was above all a poet. This he held before him as his banner and shield. Refining his public image was not part of his chemistry. It is in these interviews and encounters that we see evidence of a man constantly out of step with his times. With a flawed idealism expressed in earnest, Kerouac remained stubbornly inclined to state and restate his beliefs and ideas even against the swelling tide of public opinion. Here he remains most pure. It is on these pages that he is revealed—not completely but enough to penetrate one of the twentieth century's most perplexing literary personalities.

–Paul Maher Jr.
Fitchburg, Massachusetts, June 2005

Excerpt from an Interview with Allen Ginsberg, Part 1

Yves Le Pellec, *Composed on the Tongue* (Grey Fox, 1980)

Poet and liberationist Allen Ginsberg (June 3, 1926–April 5, 1997), born in Newark, New Jersey, was the author of Howl and Other Poems, *published in 1956. Ginsberg, like Kerouac, attended Columbia University from the fall of 1943, intent on earning a degree to become a labor lawyer. However, these plans were thwarted as Ginsberg became rapidly acquainted with William S. Burroughs ("the intelligent aristocrat"), Lucien Carr (the "angelic-looking kid"), and Jack Kerouac ("the romantic seaman who writes poem books"). These new companions evolved their individual aesthetic into the New Vision, a precursor to the intellectual philosophy of the Beats. The New Vision provoked a line of questioning concerning art, philosophy, and morality under the daunting shadow of the atomic bomb and World War II.*

YLP: Could we speak of the early days in New York, the mid-forties, when you were at Columbia? From what I read and heard I found that many of Kerouac's friends considered him as the intellectual, almost the scholar. Neal, for instance, regarded him as a man who had a university culture. Yet he had spent only one or two years at Columbia?

AG: And then in forty-nine he went to the New School for Social Research. He had already written *The Town and the City*. By his standards that was a very great piece of prose, traditional prose, but it was like the last possible gasp of such orchestral bildungsroman prose, as in Thomas Wolfe. It was a great contribution to that actually. It's still a very valuable book and there are great prose passages in it. I think the description of Times Square is prophetic. It leads on to the whole hippie movement twenty years later.

Kerouac was always sort of an exile in the university community. He was a football player but when he quit I think the football bureaucracy got mad at him and took away his scholarship and he was not able to pay for his housing there. He was very brilliant in class, he got good marks from Mark Van Doren,[1] who was a Shakespeare scholar and a poet.

YLP: He was your professor too?

AG: I had him for one term, in fact I had six or seven professors each term. The one professor who had good relations with me and Jack and who respected Jack's prose then, the only one was a man named Raymond Weaver. He was the first biographer of Melville and the discoverer of the manuscript of Billy Budd. He wrote a book called *Herman Melville, Mariner and Mystic*. At Columbia he was a considerable intellectual presence, like an old-fashioned scholar and at the same time a very modern soulful intellectual. He was sort of mystic, Gnostic, he had lived in Japan and used some Zen for teaching. So Kerouac had written a manuscript the name of which I don't remember . . . . It was before *The Town and the City*. . . .

YLP: Wasn't it *The Sea Is My Brother?*

AG: I think it's in between, it was another little thing, a little romance about angels coming down fire escapes [laughs]. He took it to Weaver and Weaver recommended that Jack read the Egyptian Gnostics, Jacob Boehme, Blake, *The Egyptian Book of the Dead*, perhaps *The Tibetan Book of the Dead* and I think some Zen classics. So Weaver perceived immediately the magical aspect of Kerouac's character and his mystical potential. Everybody else around that scene was very materialistic in the sense of "If you write a story it should have a middle, a beginning, and an end, and you shouldn't have too many fancy words because you know it's not in the tradition of realism that might grow out of the older proletarian novel and make sense in the new American facing the postwar future . . . ." Everybody was writing sort of rationalistic discourses putting down the communists and very heavily political in a very negative way, in a very status quo way, and most of them were writing about manners, and good manners were Henry James and Jane Austen in those days. Whereas Kerouac was writing about the descent of angels in workman's overalls, which was basically the really great American tradition from Thoreau through Whitman . . . .

YLP: Was Whitman taught at Columbia?

AG: He was taught but he was much insulted. I remember, around the time of the writing of *On the Road*, a young favored instructor at Columbia College told me that Whitman was not a serious writer because he had no discipline and William Carlos Williams was an awkward provincial, no craft, and Shelley was a sort of silly fool! So there was no genuine professional poetics taught at Columbia, there was a complete obliteration and amnesia of the entire great mind of Gnostic Western philosophy or Hindu Buddhist Eastern philosophy, no acceptance or conception of a possibility of a cosmic consciousness as a day-to-day experience or motivation or even sort of cranky pathology. So Whitman was put down as "a negativist crude yea-sayer who probably had a frustrated homosexual libido and so was generalizing his pathology into oceanic consciousness of a morbid nature which had nothing to do with the real task of real men in a real world surrounded by dangerous communist enemies" [laughs] or something like that . . . .

YLP: The same things were said about you and Jack in the first reviews you got. The term "narcissistic" recurs very often.

AG: Sure, it's just typical of the Pentagon to call anybody that criticizes their policy narcissistic and unrealistic.

• • •

AG: Kerouac was literally banned from physical presence on the [Columbia University] campus because he quit the football team and had strange Dostoyevskian friends! It takes a Russian police state to conceive of such a stupid social situation. Because we all knew everybody, it was a small campus, four hundred students, and everybody knew everybody. And you banned somebody who was a writer, a poet! So, I remember, Kerouac came and stayed with me one night in 1946. He had spent the evening with Burroughs, talking; Burroughs had warned him against his mother, he thought Kerouac would never be able to get away from her if he didn't make a break, and Jack was all disturbed, so he came to my room in the residence hall, Livingston Hall, I think, and said "I have been talking to Burroughs and he said the most interesting thing," so we started talking about that. I had written a long poem modeled on Rimbaud's "Bateau Ivre" and the

Baudelaire voyage theme, it was called "Le Dernier Voyage," a very stupid poem, fifteen pages of rhymed couplets or something, and I read it to him. Then we went to bed, in the same bed, in underwear; at the time I was a virgin though I was in love with Kerouac, but I was very afraid to touch him . . . .

YLP: And what about him?

AG: Well, let me finish the story. So we slept very peacefully. But I had written on the windowpane, which was very dirty, like this window out here (rubbing dust off the windowpane), lot of dust here, "Butler has no balls"—Butler was the president of the university—and "Fuck the Jews," and drawn a skull and crossbones, thinking that the chambermaid would look at it and wash it off and clean the window. But instead she looked at it and reported it to the dean. So about eight in the morning, the assistant dean of the student faculty relations burst into the room and saw me and Kerouac in bed. Now it turned out this man was formerly the football coach that Kerouac had worked with. So naturally the football coach assumed the worst. And Kerouac saw the situation and did something very characteristic of him: he jumped out of bed, ran into the next room, jumped into my roommate's bed, pulled the covers over his head and went to sleep [laughs] and left me to face the situation. The assistant dean said, "Wipe that off the window," so I wiped it off the window, and when I went downstairs after about an hour I found a note in my box charging me two dollars and thirty-five cents for having an unauthorized visitor overnight and a note saying the dean of the college wanted to see me. So I went down to Dean McKnight an hour later. I sat down in his office and he looked at me very seriously and said: "Mr. Ginsberg, I hope you understand the enormity of what you have done." These were his opening words. Burroughs had just given us *Voyage au Bout de la Nuit*.[2] Do you remember that scene when Céline is in the middle of the battlefield and realizes he is in a place surrounded by very dangerous madmen? So I looked at the dean and remembered that phrase and thought "Watch out, he's a dangerous madman." [laughs] The "enormity"! The word itself is incredible! So I said, "yes I do, sir I do!" cringing and crawling, "I do," thinking "what can I do to get out of this situation, how can I apologize?" The dean was mad and Columbia College was mad! Well, what I am trying to point out is the difference between the private consciousness was the camaraderie and common sense of talking very late at night, showing poems, sleeping, having the personal subjective relations we had, the public sense was "Mr. Ginsberg, I hope you realize the enormity of what you had done!" I mean, to have banned Kerouac from the campus to begin with was an act of such great hysteria and stupidity and desensitivity and, I think, so unacademic! I mean, imagine Socrates trying to ban Alcibiades from conversation![3] It just wasn't proper, it just wasn't classical. And those people were posing as the inheritors of tradition and the guardians of learning and wisdom. In fact just at that point they were putting themselves in the service of the military and were building an atom bomb, secretly making the biggest political decision of the century without consulting the democratic populace, and by later examination one saw that the entire university had been turned over to capitalist vocational training.

YLP: Did this awareness lead you to a political expression?

AG: I personally, and I think everybody around, immediately questioned the whole structure of Law and immediately apprehended the basic principles of philosophical anarchism. Kerouac had been a communist already, I even think he had been a member of the party. As a member of the National Maritime Union, before it had been taken over by the right-wing types and the CIA, so to speak, and the government—he was very overtly communistic for several years, from thirty-nine to forty-one, forty-two.

YLP: I didn't know that. I'm surprised. From what he wrote I would never have imagined him as a Marxist! And he had read Marx?

AG: Certainly, sure. Kerouac was very learned, you know, he was always very learned. I don't think he read it with any formal scholarship but I'm sure he read in and out of *Das Kapital* and read through the *Communist Manifesto* and maybe a few other things and he read the *Daily Worker*. It was not a phase that lasted very long, it was only two or three years. When was he born, in 1924?

YLP: 1922.

AG: Well, it was 1940, forty-one when he was a communist. He was nineteen, twenty years old, he was still like a very vigorous seaman. It's proper. Like any young man now. Just normal, quite normal. I think he got to dislike communist ideology later on because the Marxists in general now feel that we were some sort of helpful, hopeful, useful, prerevolutionary something, they've fitted us in somehow. But at the time there was a large attack by the left against the idea of revolution of consciousness, sexual revolution particularly, and psychedelic revolution involving chemicals and dope, even involving marijuana which is after all an old folk-culture tribal totem. You would have thought they were smarter than that, but they had very little anthropological training. There were two aspects that Kerouac objected to. First, the tendency among the Marxists to deplore our Bohemianism as some sort of petit bourgeois angelism, archangelistic tendencies, and to deny the existence of God, to deny the existence of the great empty universal consciousness. And also the left attempted to make the cultural revolution we were involved in, which was a purely personal thing, into a lesser political, mere revolt against the temporary politicians, and to lead the energy away from a transformation of consciousness to the materialistic level of political rationalism. But the Marxist rational interpretation of the psychological situation we saw in America was not sufficiently understanding, delicate, tender, to really apprehend the full evil of American society as far as its psychic effects on ourselves and, say, Dean McKnight were concerned. It was too linear, as they say now, an interpretation of the economic causation of the mass stupidity. Around 1948 we began having definite visionary experiences. We had been reading Rimbaud by this time, especially his letter to Georges Izambard about *"un long, immense et raisonné dérèglement de tous les sens."*[4] Under the influence of Burroughs we already had had the experience of some of the opiates, on and off, and by 1952 we already had had the experience of peyote, partly as a result of translations of Artaud's *Voyage au Pays des Tarahumaras*, which appeared in *Transition* magazine in the forties, and (Aldous) Huxley's *Doors of Perception*. Some of Kerouac's writings of fifty-two, particularly his *Visions of Cody*, are some of the most brilliant texts written about the psychedelic experience, especially the descriptions of him and Neal on peyote. So I am talking about the development of a new consciousness, as they say now. I think the phrase is used in *The Greening of America*. . . .

Excerpt from *Guilty of Everything*

Herbert Huncke (Paragon House, 1990)

Herbert Huncke (January 9, 1915–August 8, 1996) was born to hardworking (but miserable) parents in a middle-class household in Greenfield, Massachusetts. The boy soon ran away from home, resenting his familial discomforts, and fell into a habit of petty hustling by the age of twelve. From 1934, the gentle Huncke spent the next six years adrift in pre–World War II America; his camaraderie was now marginalized by narcotics, thievery, and male prostitution. In 1940, Huncke arrived in Times Square and at once became comfortable with the milieu of intellectual misfits that would come to be known as the "Beat Generation."

T he first time I met Kerouac was on a day not long after I had first met Bill [Burroughs]. I was hanging out in Washington Square Park when Bill and Jack walked by. Bill introduced me, and then told me he'd picked up something in the way of a narcotic and asked me if I knew anything about it. I can't recall what the drug was but I had not heard of it. I didn't think it was something I wanted to fool with, simply because I did not know what it was.

I remember thinking Jack was green, but he was taking everything in and making little comments to Bill—mostly about the scene in general. His eyes were flashing around. Kerouac was a typical clean-cut American type. He looked to me like the Arrow-collar man. They always had these clean-cut progressive American businessmen in their ads with the hair cut neatly and a twinkle in the eye. That was Jack.

Bill invited us up to his room over on Waverly, where we decided this drug was something that should be shot up intramuscularly. We did shoot it that way, and nothing happened. Bill tried to talk Kerouac into shooting up, but Jack said no, he would pass on it, though he was obviously curious about it. At that time Jack would smoke a little pot, but he was leery of the needle.

We went back outside and split up. They wanted to go and get coffee but I had a habit and I knew I was wasting time with them, because I'd already sounded them down for money. Neither had any bread on them, so I went on about my business alone.

Excerpt from *Nobody's Wife: The Smart Aleck and the King of the Beats*

Joan Haverty Kerouac (Creative Arts Book Company, 1990)

In November 1950, Jack Kerouac met twenty-year-old Joan Haverty at a New York City loft formerly inhabited by Bill Cannastra. Cannastra had just died from a tragic accident on October 12, 1950, leaving his roommate, Haverty, temporarily alone. When she met Kerouac, they were immediately love-struck. Kerouac had thought of getting married again in his letters to pal Neal Cassady. Kerouac's impulsive decision to marry Joan Haverty ("because she was beautiful" Kerouac told journalist Al Aronowitz in 1959) coincided with his dis-covery of a new prose style (influenced by the confessional tell-all writing style of Cassady) which preoccupied him immensely. Ill-advisedly, Kerouac and Haverty were married by a justice of the peace on November 17, 1950, mere days after meeting. Shortly thereafter, Kerouac's sporadic joblessness and creative preoccupation ground their honeymoon period to a halt. Also, there was the looming presence of Ker-ouac's mother, Gabrielle Kerouac, with whom they lived tem-porarily after moving out of Joan's loft. They eventually rented an apartment of their own in January 1951 at 454 West 20th Street in Manhattan. In April 1951, Kerouac began and ended the typing of his legendary scroll of On the Road. *But the conception of this new writing style also coincided with the conception of his first and only child, Janet Michelle Kerouac, born on February 6, 1952. Kerouac chose not to acknowledge paternity, for he was stubbornly insistent that the girl was conceived through Joan's infidelity with a Puerto Rican dishwasher. Haverty eventually separated and divorced Kerouac. She died in 1990 after a long bout with breast cancer. This excerpt begins as Kerouac is typing the* On the Road *scroll in a three-week manic blast.*

O n a sloppy wet evening in early April, I came home from work tired and worn, to find Jack staring unhappily and silently at his typewriter.

I had found a better waitressing job at the new Brass Rail on Park Avenue and 41st. All the help was new, including Puerto Rican bus boys just off the plane, some speaking no English at all. For two weeks prior to opening we were trained in heavy silver service, tray on the shoulder. I laughed aloud on the night of the grand opening when the first two letters on the neon sign failed to light up. From that night on, I would always remember that restaurant as the "Ass Rail."

Jack seemed to have been locked in some struggle with *On the Road* through my whole training period. He wasn't writing, and he wasn't talking much, either. He asked broad, grasping questions about style, about structure. They seemed thoroughly irrelevant to me. Neal was spontaneous. The words should simply come out. They should spill out onto the page without control, finding style and structure in the telling.

I sat down across from Jack and looked tiredly at him. "What was it like, Jack?" I finally asked, after a long silence.

"To be on the road with Neal?"

"Yes, what happened, what really happened?"

I started asking questions. Questions about Neal, about traveling, cities, trains, New York, Mexico, cars, roads, friends, Neal, Neal, Neal, and Neal.

"Jack," I asked him again, "what really happened? What did you and Neal really do?"

The questions after a time, seemed to ignite some spark in Jack. He went back to his typewriter, and now he typed with accelerating speed, pounding keys, late into the night. When I got up in the morning, I saw that the clothes he had dropped on the floor were soaked with sweat. And I saw that there were feet and feet of the teletype roll, filled with dense typescript, hanging off the back of the typewriter now.

I was glad that Jack was writing again. It improved his mood immeasurably. I knew it was ironic that I acted as his muse and his inspiration when his writing had always been so unimportant, even unreadable, to me. But it was such a relief to have him focused on something other than his own boredom and selfish needs.

For the next few weeks, I became accustomed again to sleeping while Jack typed. I only woke if it stopped suddenly. That happened one night, May 10, 1951, and the consequences would change both our lives forever.

Jack was in his bathrobe, behind the screen that surrounded his desk, typing furiously. The typing stopped. I opened my eyes, and almost immediately he emerged.

"Quick!" he said, dropping his bathrobe and pulling down the covers off me. A brief argument ensued: spontaneity vs. preparedness.

Spontaneity won, and the diaphragm stayed buried with the socks.

Two minutes later, Jack rolled over and went to sleep. I knew I wasn't responsible for his arousal, and I got up to see what was in the typewriter. I found my answer in his description of Terry, the Mexican girl he knew in California, and the pity he felt for her. Remembering other occasions when I hadn't been able to understand what precipitated his sudden inspiration, it all hung together. There was always an element of the pathetic, or the downtrodden, or abject poverty and misery, either in the conversation or in something or someone he'd seen. I had never allowed him to see anything of that sort in me. I would not acknowledge my own weakness or pain and I never cried. So I had nothing to do with his arousal. I was merely the receptacle. This was the time, though, that the receptacle turned out not to be empty.

First Reader of *On the Road* Manuscript

An Excerpt from the Journals of John Clellon Holmes

Moody Street Irregulars No. 5 (Summer/Fall 1979)

Novelist John Clellon Holmes, born in Holyoke, Massachusetts, on March 12, 1926 (the same day but not the same year as Kerouac, who was born in 1922), remained a lifelong friend and colleague of Kerouac's after they first met at a Manhattan party in 1948. The pair ignited their strong friendship based purely upon their mutual interests in literature and writing. The result was an impressive body of correspondence and a number of insightful journal entries authored by both.

Note: Kerouac, exhausted after the prodigious effort of its composition at white heat, gave me the now-notorious "scroll" a few days after its completion. He, himself, could not bring himself to read it. What follows is an entry I made in my work-journals soon after finishing the book.

I read Jack's book a few days ago. He wrote it in twenty days,[5] and it is one long strip of tracing paper, one hundred and twenty feet long, it seems. It has much wonderful material in it.

And, surprisingly enough, the style is straightforward, genuine, simple, still as lyric, but not as curlicue as it once was. If anything this book is, in most important aspects, more mature than *The Town and the City*. It needs work. The transitions are weak. There is, perhaps, too much of it. The character of Neal around which it gradually centers itself needs to be focused a little more clearly. Those sections where he does not appear might be thinned out, pointed in his direction. It comes close to being a developed study of Neal, with his gradual changes from energetic juvenile delinquent to the kind of W. C. Fieldsian wanderer that Jack feels he is. The love in the book is charged and clear and masculine and good . . . . Jack's knowledge of this subject [speaks for] itself from every line . . . with the necessary work, it will make a very exciting and important book indeed. All the material is here, it only needs to be sharpened, brought out, smoothed a bit. The writing, with only occasional, minor exceptions, doesn't need any alteration . . . . The descriptions are fine, clean things, filled with Jack's old power, without the plethoric wordage that sometimes used to dull the glass. He has made a decided improvement here, I believe, and now has his own style. There will certainly be no comparisons to Thomas Wolfe this time. He simply let the style take care of itself, I feel, and it did just that. It is simple, moving, evocative, and filled with real perceptions. He could cut down some of the extraneous intellectual-type conversations that occur at various periods at terminal ends of his zigzagging routes across the country. A little of them go a long way, and like all of us he makes his point long before he believes he has done it. Also I felt that some of the characters could be removed. They are unnecessary. I speak of myself, some of the people here in New York, who only wander through, have no lines and no real effect on the action. But this is all just carping, and does not dent what is a fine straight narrative that moves with incredible rapidity, has scenes of unusual power that dredged me dry, and has straight-forward clean American writing and a new recognition of the depth of the American experience that should set the critics squabbling.

I was the first human eye to read the book. Even he hasn't read it straight through, and I went down to visit he [*sic*] and Joan a nite ago to take the ms. back to him and tell him my impressions. We had a nice evening, with beer, a spell at a water-front bar, and even fifteen dark, cool minutes out on a cluster of pilings at the end of a pier watching a huge, lovely liner, all crusted with warm lights, steam slowly out of the harbor, her pinkish smoke-stacks lit up. A beautiful, silent giant, dwarfing even the Jersey coast beyond. I told Jack that I could not entirely be objective about the book (which is very true, even now that I have had several days to think about it); told him this because I know all the people, and have lived so close to the conception and execution of all the drafts through which *On the Road* has passed. But I did, I think, communicate to him my enthusiasm about it, and my feeling that it will make exciting and stimulating reading when the few minor faults are wrestled out, and the line of it honed just a bit. The book had cleaned me out, exhausted me, because I had read it straight thru without stopping for anything but cups of coffee. It took me a little over eight hours. The sections in Mexico are faultless, lovely, sad. There is much, much else. I want to read it again, and see if I can give him more help. He said: "You know, kid, your book and mine constitute a new trend in American literature!" I said "amen" to that.

Neal & Allen

Notes on a Conversation about Kerouac from the Journal of Allen Ginsberg, August 1954

Allen Ginsberg, *Journals–Mid-Fifties 1954–1958* (Harper Perennial, 1996)

N: "Nothin' is nothin' except every little thing that affects *him*. Well Jack is really sort of a fool. The reason he always disliked me is that I kept calling him on it. But the real trouble is you could never make him believe that, i.e., he's always being *misunderstood*. Fundamentally because. . . .

There's always a black hair in his tea, it's never any good unless you find a hair in it.

A: I didn't realize that Jack's self-pity was so akin–so imitative–of Wolfe's which fucks up Wolfe's books. Even to the very language of brooding, mysterious swirls and red October afternoons.

N: No one feels as much as they do when they're alone.

A: Death of Father and end scene in *Sax* is so naturally very true and full of feeling; where does he get off being a fool?

N: But I don't think we've put the finger on his foolishness. For one thing, it comes to downright eccentricity at times, bullheaded.

A: As Bill and you often complain, [Jack says] "Oh don't bother, I'll build a little gas jet through the wall and get a hot plate."

N: He refuses to receive graciously. What the hell do I care about his shyness? I'm afraid he's too old now, too set in his ways. His only hope is to really convince himself that nothing is nothing. But I don't think he'll be capable of doing that.

A: "It requires a great effort—"

N: Besides he's too smart. Deep down he knows everybody loves him but he just can't accept it because he knows that would put demand on him so he acts surly and he's a bore—just like me. I can receive all day but I can't give back. He knows he can't give back consistently so he doesn't want to receive. Well he really did in Denver there that time. (Start the blankness.) Misunderstanding. I don't remember. What does Jack need, that's the important thing. Nothing haw haw after all "nothing is nothing." Well I don't know anybody could ever penetrate that lard ass. Even if nothing is nothing, it would still be quite a struggle. I'm just wondering how many incarnations ago I was a woman. Oh sure I've been a woman, all of us have been a woman. Next lifetime, in 3 lifetimes, I'll be a female whore. You've already been a real queer. I want to beat the 97 times.

A: Then he (Mel) and Jack got into a conspiracy against mc; I've always found it hard to forgive of Jack, though easy to Mel, since so much was expected of them both, but with Mel the road was much more bitter.

An Interview with Carolyn Cassady on Kerouac

Andrew O'Hagan, BBC Online (Undated)

AO: I was looking again this morning at that rather well-known interview that Kerouac gave to the *Paris Review*. He is very clear about his debt to Neal Cassady as far the writing style goes. He said he really got it from that long letter, which is an excellent letter. Can you talk about that and tell us what he meant?

CC: Well, yes, that was only one, but I suppose was the longest and maybe the most excited. Well, Neal just totally unself-consciously wrote him the story of . . . Jack and Allen were always asking him to write them letters about sex, so unfortunately there is quite a lot of those, and he just would rip them off. However, it came to him without any self-consciousness—one of Jack's problems was being aware of the audience when he was writing, so that was one of the things he wanted to get away from, you know. Finally the letters book Ann Charters edited—there are four or five letters that Jack wrote to Neal that were never mailed, which she did not mention, but he was really trying to write straight to Neal and forget the audience, and that was quite a struggle, but those letters are actually closer to the man I knew than any of his books, because he is not so aware of somebody else listening and he could only really be himself with Neal and or his mother, I guess.

AO: More about that sense that you have just expressed of him, you know, feeling the pressure of his audience, who he was writing for–what did that do to him?

CC: Well, that's why it is difficult for me to read his books, because I can tell when he is being bombastic or show-offy or silly, and, you know, it's embarrassing. That's why I enjoyed those letters so much, because that was really how he was when he was unself-conscious, and so that's about it. Well, another aspect of that is, whenever he was reading, as in the little tape I have is–and even when we were all together–he would go into W. C. Field's accents or Major Hoople or something. He was always so terribly self-conscious.

AO: What you say slightly suggests someone who was divided as a character, someone who had, as it were, a public persona or who had at least a sense [of] who the writer should be in the world, how he should perform for the world.

CC: No, I think it was just that he was so self-conscious and embarrassed and shy, so he turned to drink. There is not a single interview anywhere that he had not had something to drink, even the Steve Allen one, where he is as straight, I guess, as he ever was, but even then he had to drink because he was just so shy.

AO: Can we shuffle backward and look at some of the earlier shaping influences, especially Lowell and his mother. Going about America interviewing people, it never ceased to surprised me just to the extent to which Lowell and his mother–he was endlessly traveling back to them in some sense. Can you tell me about that?

CC: Well, that's my feeling about his mother as well. People keep saying he was dependent on her and tied to her apron strings, which it does not seem so to me, because he was leaving her all the time, but what I do think might have been a tremendous draw was the fact that with her he could be completely himself and say anything all the time, totally unself-conscious. I gather they exchanged very frank conversation, but he did not have to worry at all about any audience or what people would think, and to me I think that is one of the biggest draws—to be with her, to really relax. Very seldom could he otherwise.

AO: It's surprising in a way, the person he could relax most with is his mother, given that he had tendencies you know, as a drinker, as a drug taker, as you know . . .

CC: Well, he was not in the beginning. It was not till fifty-seven when *On the Road* came out that he started drinking heavily. When he was with us he did not drink, you know, a little bit of well Poor Boy [Kerouac refers to his taste for alcohol in *The Dharma Bums*: "soon we headed into another siding at a small railroad town and I figured I needed a poor-boy of Tokay wine to complete the cold dusk run to Santa Barbara"]. Do you know how much that is? A glass and a half, that would last him all day. But he did not drink during the day, anyhow. He and Neal would have a beer or so, but, you know, it was just, like, refreshing lemonade, it was not—he did not drink.

AO: Do you think he would have been in a position to feel free to smoke pot in front of his mother?

CC: See, I don't know really, I don't know her well enough for that but I . . . one of the interesting things to me was that Neal knew her very well and he must have known what she was really like and yet never ever did he say anything about her except that she was the perfect, lovely, little old lady mother, you know. When I learned from the Charters books how feisty she was and the language she learned, I was just horrified because we used to write little notes to each other on the bottom of Jack's letters and Neal never said a word, always indicated she was this lovely mummy, and, God, I was so stunned. So in that case, perhaps he could have done anything in front of her. I don't know.

AO: Could you give an account of how he seemed to change to you over the years, say over the time that you knew him, both physically and, if you like, emotionally. What happened to him?

CC: Oh well, what happened was that he was so misunderstood and misrepresented but he was just so sensitive that he was absolutely crushed; he expected to be accepted as a serious literary figure, and that first review in the *New York Times* was gratifying, then to have that just destroyed with the most vicious, horrible condemnation and not anything that he had intended. And then as it went on and he got the credit for the Beat Generation and then the Father of the Hippies, he just was tortured, so that's what happened to him. It was obvious to us, and, of course, I did not see him once, when he came to the house with a gang and he was thoroughly drunk, and then in 1960, we were seeing him every year before then. And he did come to California a couple of times but he was too ashamed to come and see me, so . . .

AO: Why too ashamed?

CC: Because he was drunk and disorderly. [laughs]

AO: Is it true that he viewed your household at that time as a sort of haven? One gets the impression from the letters that he looks upon your household as a sort of . . . always with envy certainly, with a sort of yearning as something that he would like to have, stability.

CC: Well, that's what he wanted, but he finally began to realize he would never be able to be a husband and father, although he talked about homes with me all the time, and Neal kept telling me about how hung up he was with the idea of home. But he had it then with us—we were his family, and he just loved the children, and he always wrote about my children when he wrote to us. He would explain how he had never learned to work and keep a job as Neal had, and that's why Neal could take care of this family, but he knew he couldn't. Of course he dreamed that he would make enough money writing, that he could get married and have a home and children, but little by little that became less and less likely, and so we were his family and his home. That was the way he thought of it, and he could relax and be himself with us as well.

AO: Do you think that given that situation that it was difficult for him to confront you later when he was more disappointed?

CC: Yes, definitely, well, then he'd write that I would see him, so he was not coming, and he would write about how disappointed I would be, too. But it was interesting he hardly ever wrote a letter that did not mention the children—Jamie was his special favorite, always asked about her, and Neal would send him notes about her, and so . . .

AO: Can you identify the contradiction there, someone who would kiss and watch for other people's children but would not recognize his own?

CC: Well, to me that's simple, I could be wrong, but everyone says he was so irresponsible but I think his, it was the reverse, his ideal father was something he knew he could not live up to because he could never have a home, he could not establish it. The idea of being a poor father, he just could not face it, so he just denied that he was one because he could not stand it, and, of course, she had already been rather damaged later on when he met her—in the beginning he thought it was someone else's. He still kept the jealousy of Joan's infidelity for a long time, so he kept insisting it was someone else's, but I think he must really realize that there is no way he could bring up a child without constant guilt, which was a big factor. Anyway, you know he had enough of that already.

AO: You have given a detailed account off the road in your own book but I wonder if you could give us a sense of just the sort of daily round, what life was like for you when you were living together and he was working with Neal and so on. Can you give us a sense of what kind of life you had at that time?

CC: As far as I was concerned, it was wonderful, you know. I had the best of both worlds, but it was mostly when they were both there, it was just lots of fun, and the other thing is, it was mostly intellectual, our relationship. It was sitting around reading from books and talking about books, or reading Shakespeare's plays, we'd all take different parts, and Jack would read his work aloud, and Neal would read aloud, and lots of other books and great discussions about authors and whatnot, all the time. It was just, the noise level was so high, and the tape recorder is going all the time, and then the jazz, they discussed music and of course sports, so there was always really something going on all the time, except when Jack was writing. He had a room in San Jose as well, and so he had been hours writing and he spent hours and hours scat singing with pots and pans for drums and things—just hours doing that.

AO: Did you get on with your work?

CC: No, no, well, the San Jose house was enormous, so there was never any conflict in that, and the San Francisco one was so

many levels, it was three levels, and he was on the top, and all
that went on, with the children and our domestic thing, on the
bottom levels, so it was fine.

AO: What did Jack see in Neal?

CC: Well, they had a mutual thing. He of course admired Neal's
poise and lack of self-consciousness and his ability to get along
with everybody, and of course Jack admired all that as well as
his brilliant mind. I think one of the most appealing things is
that both of them were the most compassionate men I have ever
run across and they were also very macho, which is a rare thing
to find in another man, so that that was really a big bond. Now,
Jack had been taught by a traditional father to defend yourself
and fisticuffs, which he only indulged in when he was very very
drunk, but Neal had not had that, and there was no way he was
going to . . . you know, the ordinary coward meant nothing to
him—it's just stupid to stand there and get hurt or hit somebody—so when he had altercations with Hell's Angels and
things, he'd run. That's the only sensible thing to do. So that was
funny, because Neal was totally nonviolent not only in action
but also he never criticized or condemned, so there were things
in common they had which were very rare, and then the other
was the opposite, Neal's poise and Jack's self-consciousness.

AO: Do you think the mythological view of Jack and Neal veers from
reality to some extent. In what ways would you say it does, if so?

CC: I think in this, the intellect and that heartfelt compassion sort of
thing, I don't think they were interested in that because they were
so joyous and energetic and active. All the things they seemed to
admire or want to imitate or want to turn round to have
[inaudible]. I think they had more of a purpose than their fathers.

AO: Do you think there was a sort of case of mistaken identity when it comes to both Jack and Neal, inasmuch as they were mistaken as products of the sixties or as sixties figures when really, if anything, they were Depression-era kids?

CC: Oh yes, same thing altogether is the set of values that we were all raised with, which if you had not had them you can't imagine I guess. You know, perhaps it's easier to stereotype Victorian values somehow, but when your whole consciousness and your whole world's consciousness is about the same with these sort of values—like every man in the fifties and forties just assumed that you get married and have a family and home, I mean that was just the given—even Allen Ginsberg expected to have a family and children and a home, and I just ran across one of his letters lately when he was describing in great detail what his wedding is going to be like and who is going to be there and, you know, this was part of his nature. So there they were, perfect gentlemen, they were, they never swore in mixed company at all, I never heard them swear, and all these attitudes that are very unpopular now, that was part of that nature, it was hard to believe they were such gentlemen and so polite, and both of them were.

AO: What was that about Kerouac that made him less willing than was Neal to take part in this sort of sixties business?

CC: Well he did not approve, for one thing, but Neal did not either, until he lost it all, and then a lot of it was machismo, and he just, you know, gave up, and we always think it was after he died that he had it easy because he did not care any more. He had the name and he played the game, he did a lot of stupid things trying to get killed and yet, unfortunately, as I say, the most footage is of him then, and a lot of the memories were influenced by that, whereas to him this was despicable. He did not like *On the Road*

because he did not like the side of his character that was celebrated, that was the side of himself that he was trying so desper-
ately to change and overcome, so he was totally misunderstood
as far as his real feelings.

AO: He didn't like to see himself pictured as a hedonist?

CC: No, nor that sort of irresponsible life tearing around. Yes, he
spent the rest of his life trying to get straight, which nobody wants
to hear, you know [laughs].

AO: Both together and individually, you and Neal seem to represent
a sort of authenticity for Kerouac. It comes through more
strongly in the letters, I think, than anything else. Why do you
think he needed two half figures of authenticity, why did he need
to look on you in that way? Was there something about himself
that he was uncertain about?

CC: Kerouac? Well, yes, I mean, there was not . . . I think he was
certain about his writing ability, he really believed in that, but
for himself of course he had a large dose of guilt and the church
and so, you know, he was a miserable worm, obviously, but I
don't see that as any more of a problem than it was for everybody else.

AO: That uncertainty we were talking about—I'd like to proceed on
that question. The point I have been trying to make is that that
uncertainty plays into the book so much, it plays into his letters
so much in a sense that he is divided, he is troubled, he is finding
it impossible to square this, you know, expectation of him as a
writer with his sense of who he actually is, where he comes from,
and I just want to try and focus on that.

CC: Well I think it was such a general thing and certainly . . . with
heavily Catholic families it was like second nature to be
unworthy, but it's not just Catholics, a lot of people feel that way

... um, I was trying to think of something specific that he did not like in himself—can't really think of anything, except perhaps that he was not good enough. He was sort of a perfectionist, and physically he began deteriorating anyway, and he did not exercise or anything, he was such a klutz anyway, that was another thing that he admired in Neal, who was so together and energetic and surefooted, and Jack was clumsy, so little things like that—I don't really know why he felt inferior specifically.

AO: Do you remember how he would feel—those late-night phone calls when he was going on in that way and obviously in some deep, deep distress—do you remember what you thought to yourself then?

CC: Well, yes, how awful it was, all he wanted to do was talk about sex anyway, and that was bad enough because he had always been modest, you know, overly modest, which everybody else thinks is so funny, and he would just become so gross and revolting, and it was awful. Of course, that's why it's so hard for Neal to watch him go under with alcohol, since he had already had to go through it with his father, and it just broke his heart—for all of us it's such a disease that you just can't help, and of course near the end he was just repulsive, it was too sad, and . . .

AO: Can you tell us what you thought when he announced his intention to climb that mountain, Desolation Peak.

CC: Well, we all knew he was crazy. He was always going on about getting away by himself. Of course, he was an escapist anyhow in whatever way he could, so it was not so surprising to us that he was always talking about "Oh I must go off by myself sometime." But we knew that that would be a disaster. It seemed that he was not into self-analysis as Neal and I were, so there was not any way we could tell him, of course, but we could not really say that that was not what he was like, and then he would be very unhappy and he was . . . it's funny he could not see that in himself.

AO: When you say he was not into analysis, was it perhaps a part of his folly or part of his misfortune that he felt that he could analyze himself and that was partly what his writing was about? Would he have scoffed if we had suggested that he speak to an analyst, for example?

CC: Oh yes, well, he had a different kind of mind, he had a much more . . . I think he responded to everything emotionally first, and that's why he will say with some very heavy opinion one minute and then two minutes later he's just as adamant about the opposite views, and we could never pin him down as to what it is he really believed, because it changed every five minutes. That's why he went into Buddhism, I am sure it was, that lovely imagery and so forth, whereas Neal and I are more of a logical and analytical mind, and you have got to show us, you know, and prove it—it has to be practical, and so we analyzed everything. The why, the causes of everything, was what we were after. Fortunately both of us agreed on this, but Jack was not at all . . . and every time you'd get close to analyzing or, you know, bring it home, he'd throw up "Oh everything is an illusion" or, you know, go off in some poetic something. He did not like standing still and facing things anyway, really, so whatever you asked, I think that's what he does.

AO: When he came down from that mountain, what had happened to him?

CC: Oh, I think he describes that wonderfully in the book, I mean he really tells exactly how he felt. To that extent he could be objective and stand outside and look at himself often and be an observer of others and in himself. In lots of his books he stands outside and to that extent he could be self-analytical, but just to that extent, so in the book he realizes that he can't be alone that long and that was a mistake. He still has the yearning, but that's the escape thing, to get away from, because he was so self-conscious, so confidence is what he needed—self-confidence physically and personally—and he always seemed to think he could find it, but that's why he behaved as he did with the drink. He was all up-front and boisterous and bravado and whatnot, so I think when he came down the mountain he was relieved, but it did wise him up a bit on that.

AO: To people that did not know him and who read the letters, for example, the impression that you get of the young person that he was . . . as a young man he was kind of very keen for fame, he wants to be renowned, and yet when he gets it . . .

CC: No, he wanted respect, he was notorious, not famous, and he did not get the literary respect or even the understanding from the readers that he had expected, and from publishers of course. His letters are full of condemnation of the publishers and how [inaudible] there . . . yes, he wanted to be a respected academic or at least establishment writer like Tom Wolfe or anybody. His letters are full of the writers that are making the best-seller list. I was reading one the other day where he was complaining about all the ones who are making it, and that's the kind of life he envisioned—that he would be looked up to, and not by kids who are all misbehaving by not doing what . . . they just steal his books off library shelves, and that's what he got instead of best-sellers.

AO: And did you have a sense at the time, as far as you can recall, that the success or the kind of success that *On the Road* enjoyed, as it were, would reckon?

CC: Well, he did not think that any of that was going to happen, anyhow; we thought he was a great writer but we thought he was going to get the kind of attention he should have done. But it was easy to understand why it had, because I had never ever read anything so awful and vicious and wondered what these journalists were so afraid of. It seemed as though they were terribly threatened—they could not say enough horrible things, and the only thing I could think of was the hypocrisy of our generation. I suspect they were doing a lot of these things themselves, or something, and had some real fear that they would be exposed. It could have been subconscious, or something, but that is one thing that did happen in the sixties, it did break up that hypocrisy we were all so smug about. I don't know, I really did not think of it because even lots of other writers have said that never in the history of literature has anyone been so viciously attacked, and so, of course, that, for a sensitive soul like Jack. it was just murder.

AO: Can you tell us a sense of how that notoriety, as you have described it, actually works in real life? Was it hard to be around them?

CC: Oh yes, all these girls that were running after him and that was hard to take, except that was the reason for it, I think, and yes, they had the paparazzi problem, too. It was just awful, you know—in several letters he writes how he can't get away from them, then when he moves to Northport and whichever one of those places, and he would build big fences, and there were kids who would tie him to fences and just harass him all the time, and again, for the wrong reasons, see that's what hurt—it was not what he had hoped to attain.

AO: Can we go back to that business and work. Could you give us a sketch of the part that played with his relationship with you, because it is different with his relationship with many people, because he actually had a job from time to time when he was around you?

CC: Well, don't forget he was a seaman off and on and, I think, when he first started running around. Didn't he go down to North Carolina and Washington and work at things like dishwashing and stuff like that? I mean he was not allergic to working. Neal's pressure on him rose more from Neal wanting to keep Jack with him. Neal pushed the jobs.

AO: What sort of jobs?

CC: Well, what Neal did, you know—railroading and parking lots. Because Neal was happy when Jack was writing. He believed that was what he was about, so it was not that he was pushing him because he felt that he should be—well, we wanted him to earn money as well, so that he would be more independent, and Neal certainly did not resent supporting him as everybody would like to think. And any little remarks he made were only jealousy or dissatisfaction, but Jack was then willing to try anything Neal would put forth, and since he loved the railroad so, it was exactly right for him, and he felt that it might be for Jack, because there was a lot of time where you just sit and think or you could sit and write. But again, Neal had that physical prowess and was so swift and sure, and Jack was so clumsy and also not as focused. His mind was more like to wander and, of course, there were some funny old men that called him Caraway Seed and things that his self-consciousness objected to. He just felt clumsy and not with it, so he was not happy, but I was always surprised that he kept going back to it and coming back to it and even going to work on the railroad in the East Coast. I am not sure that he ever did, but he planned, so it was not something that he made himself do, no matter how uncomfortable, but as far as parking lot jobs, of course that was out of the question, because he could not drive and certainly not like Neal. He was going to try that too, but I think Neal wanted to keep him with us, and he would try to get him nailed down to a job as a writer—he could write anywhere so . . .

AO: This business of not driving, that's the deepest and somehow most hilarious irony of them all, isn't it?

CC: Well, you know, you live in New York you don't need a car, so he never actually needed one.

AO: But not everybody in New York writes a twentieth-century classic about driving across America.

CC: Yes, but he did not drive, he rode and observed. You should see what Neal writes about driving—he'll tell you all the details of the motor and what's in it. Not that he could fix it at all, but he could tell you all about it and all about all the pieces of the car and so on, but Jack could not have cared less, it was just, you know, a seat that Neal was carrying him around in.

AO: It was a 40 Hudson, wasn't it?

CC: It was the only new one that we ever had, Neal went through a couple of other people's new ones. I think a newish one. but here was one that he could actually . . . but that was newer than his. All the others, the eighteen we went through in two years or whatever, had all been used cars, until I got to the point where I was never ever going to push another car and I went out and bought myself a new car, and said "Don't you touch it." So that I would never have to do that again. Luckily we lived on a kind of a sloping street, so in the morning, I thought "Ooooh, here we go again," and he'd say "Ma, come out and push the darn thing down the hill so we could go". Oh so embarrassing, everywhere all his sandwiches go down the hill so it's easy there. It was hysterical, these cars which he'd say was just waiting to come round and con into fixing them, because he did not know which end of the wrench. Cars are his things and car racing and so forth, as far as Neal was Jack's thing, the car [laughs].

AO: Would it be part of your estimation of that scene that you have said how guilty he was and how natural it was for someone from his background to be guilty, do you think it was a possibility that he was also guilty about his background, about the sunniness of his childhood, in a way, and Neal had a sort of low-life childhood that was not Jack's, and he sort of in some strange way admires it and thinks it's authentic and it's closer to the ground?

CC: The Western of course fascinated everybody, especially easterners. Neal was really sad–he was a cowboy, he rode horses, but when he came to our farm in Tennessee, I could not get near a horse, I mean, I had a horse and we had a couple of others and I could not get anywhere near it, so I have always wondered how much a cowboy he was. He worked in Neal's ranch but he could have just been fixing [inaudible]. I know he could not have done either, I don't know what he could have done–fed the chickens– but I can't think . . . I never asked him, either: "What did you do?" All those stories you have to take with some grains of salt, but Jack saw him as a Wild West cowboy, because he was from way up in New England and Canada so it was quite different.

AO: Do westerners represent something else, something–the frontier and so on?

CC: Oh yes I was brought up with that too. I had read all [inaudible] by the time I was eleven and I think everybody was in love with the Wild West, which it was still, when I traveled around the country in the thirties. They were still two-lane roads and cowboys and what not, Indians. I think everybody romanticizes about that, and Jack must have especially. He loved all the

American ethnicities, you know, the pioneers, and all the
Appalachians, and all the various Indian tribes and all the wonderful names of everything that the pioneers and the Indians gave
the whole American ethic, it was . . . just loved it.

AO: He did sometimes give the impression that he was part Indian,
didn't he?

CC: Well he was, just as I learned Neal's grandmother, one of his
grandmothers, was Cherokee, I guess we all . . . I don't think I
can claim it but . . . there seemed to be quite a lot of Indian mix-
tures along the way everywhere, so he was. I think he had ancestors, I forget the tribe, it says somewhere but . . .

AO: Can you tell us the story about the episode of the car?

CC: Oh, in Big Sur, Neal had ordered a hot bath or something, and
Jack himself had said in the letter that the only two who wouldn't
take their shorts off were Neal and Jack. He said here we are,
these beatniks, and we are the only ones who would not take off
our shorts. It's very telling, I think, actually.

AO: Of what?

CC: Well the fact that they were influenced by their background and
their modesty, that was partly the Church and partly the culture,
and later on we both got over that. But Jack was always . . . our
bathrooms were always inconvenient in both houses, and so he
had an awful time with that—embarrassment in the bathrooms—
and I think I mentioned in the book—I am not sure if it is still in
there—but anyway the bathroom in San Jose had two doors and
one that was in our bedroom, and I happened to open it and Jack
was leaning over the bathtub doing something and he only had a
short on, oh he was so embarrassed. Oh my God, me already, so
there we never took our clothes off—it's always in the dark. It's
hard to believe, but it's the truth.

AO: There are a clear number of people who are really happy to say, both on the record and off, that you were essentially the true love of Kerouac's life. Does that come as any sort of surprise to you?

CC: Well I don't think it's true, for one thing because in his case, well, Neal too, they were both so compassionate and Neal was an Aquarian and typical. He loved everybody, everybody, and so Jack, too, I think, sincerely loved the women that he was with— it's just that they kept loving the next one as well. So I think he was involved with me longer than the others, and may have been more relaxed, because of Neal and because I was safe, for one thing, and then I never asked anything of him. I think some of the others may have wanted him to be as interested in them as they were in him, whereas they did not need that with me. I had Neal and realized early on that it was more satisfactory to listen to him, more or less talk about him, and so that was easy for me because I did not want anything from him, so I think he appreciated that and the fact that I was always there, and the children and so forth, and he noted the correspondence with me was the longest of any he had, so he was a sort of another mommy in some ways, aside from the romance, but I don't think that he had any one love of his life, really. He saw us in different roles, like he saw Edie Parker as perhaps . . . or someone like Edie as maybe the ideal wife, because he kind of liked the craziness as well, and, you know, a little bit of everything, but I don't think he ever found that one, and then Neal just really did, so interested in everybody not just women. Of course he had the sex problem but often he had sex with really ugly girls because he thought they would never have it any other way [laughs]. Talk about compassion. So I am afraid they were not anywhere near as stereotypical as they are portrayed.

Witless Madcaps

Dan Balaban, *Village Voice* (February 13, 1957)

A little over half a year before the publication of Kerouac's second novel, On the Road, *in September 1957, Kerouac had already become somewhat of a celebrity with the publication of the short prose excerpt from* On the Road, *"Jazz of the Beat Generation" in* New World *magazine. Coupled with Kerouac's new turn of literary success after years of abject poverty and despondency, was Allen Ginsberg's poetic breakthrough,* Howl and Other Poems, *published by City Lights Press, a San Francisco poetry press founded by poet Lawrence Ferlinghetti. Jailhouse poet Gregory Corso (March 26, 1930–January 17, 2001) had met Kerouac and Ginsberg in 1950 after his release from the notoriously brutal Clinton State Prison in New York.*

T hree itinerant poets came home to roost last week, but not for long. The "San Francisco Poets"–Jack Kerouac, Allen Ginsberg, and Gregory Corso–told The *Voice* they were off to Tangiers to pursue their exciting destiny. "We are witless madcaps," they announced, "who sing little insensible ditties."

"We want everyone to know that we had to leave the Village to find fulfillment and recognition," said Allen Ginsberg.

"There is no room for youth and vitality in New York," said Gregory Corso. "It is a city full of guilty academicians."

"Too big, too multiple, too jaded," chanted Jack Kerouac.

"We want to take everything in," continued Corso, "and to write about it. That's why the academicians feel guilty. They want to experience sensation too."

"We were saints and Villagers and we're beautiful," said Kerouac. "And we went to San Francisco and did beauty there."

"Beauty, beauty, beauty," harmonized Corso.

"We wanted to get away from cliques and snobbery here," said Corso. "The poets in the Village are disorganized and isolated."

He went on to describe how they went to San Francisco three years ago. They got together with some of the poets there—Kenneth Rexroth, Gary Snyder, Philip Whalen, and others. "We gave a series of readings in a big art gallery.[6] People would bring jugs of wine. Everybody would talk; we had to shout to be heard."

First they attracted citywide and then national attention. "I was thrown into jail for vagrancy the first week we were there," recalled Ginsberg. "The cops apologized after the poetry readings." Soon afterward the City Lights Pocket Bookshop of San Francisco published a collection of Ginsberg's poems entitled *Howl*. In New York it is on sale at the Eighth Street Bookshop.

Richard Eberhardt, poet and teacher at Dartmouth, wrote about them in the *New York Times Book Review*, where Harvey Breit followed up with a piece some two months later. *Mademoiselle* mentions them in a story on the lively arts in San Francisco, and carries a poem by Corso. As they sat in the office of the *Voice*, they were fresh from being photographed by *Life* for a proposed picture story.

"I told them people should read more poetry magazines than *Life* magazines," said Corso. Louise Bogan, they asserted, will include them in an article she is writing on San Francisco poetry for the *New Yorker*. "*Partisan Review* is reading our poetry now."

Grove Press and New Directions are preparing collections of their work for publication. Grove will also bring out a novel by Kerouac called *The Subterraneans*. Viking Press plans to publish another novel of his, *On the Road*.

"Right now," Corso summed up, "we are hot."

Before departing, each poet left with us a statement for cogitation by the multitudes.

Corso: "Don't shoot the warthog."

Kerouac: "Pity dogs and forgive men."

Ginsberg: "Everybody is a big mystical shear—snip, snip, snip."

Writing Novels by the Foot

Luther Nicholls, *San Francisco Examiner* (June 1957)

The period of his life preceding On the Road *was especially prolific for Kerouac. Living in the cottage of fellow poet Philip Whalen in Berkeley, California (where he had hoped to make a home for himself and his mother), the thirty-five-year-old Kerouac wrote haiku, drafted an early version of his 1958 novel* The Dharma Bums *called* Avalokitesvara, *wrote a spontaneous prose poem called "Lucien Midnight" and a short story, "A Dharma Bum in Europe," pieced together his planned* Book of Dreams, *and compiled the typing from his sketching notebooks into typescript for his grand prose poem,* Book of Sketches. *Kerouac also painted paintings while he impatiently awaited the galleys of* On the Road *to arrive in the mail.*

I n the better little magazines, such as *Paris Review, New World Writing,* and *New Directions,* in the places where writers gather to gab around Russian, Potrero, and Telegraph Hills, and nationally wherever people try to keep up with the literary current, you increasingly notice a new name: Jack Kerouac.

Kerouac is usually identified as a promising young novelist of the "Beat Generation"—this being a sort of equivalent in its affinity for jazz and disillusionment to the "Lost Generation" of the 1920s.

The other day at Bardelli's I had lunch with Kerouac, in the course of which he lived up to his reputation for being Bohemian, darkly handsome, outspoken, occasionally naïve, and a nice guy with an unusual approach to writing.

Mechanically, his approach is to paste art papers together until he has a roll about 100 feet long, wind the roll into his typewriter, and then peck away at full speed, getting the thoughts down as fast as he can.

"I write about ten feet in a good day," he says. He never edits, because "Whatever you try to delete from a manuscript, that's what is most interesting to a doctor."

To forestall those who will say, "Is he writing for readers or doctors?" Kerouac doesn't give a hoot about either. He's a "pure'" writer who has dedicated his life to nothing but gathering experience and getting his impressions of it unadulterated on paper.

Since his birth in 1922 as a French-Canadian in Lowell, Mass., his rage to live and write has taken him to school at Columbia University, where he was a star football prospect until he simply "got tired" and quit; to the North Atlantic as a merchant seaman; to Tangier, Marseilles, Paris, London, Mexico City and all over the United States as a vagabond. Now he's off again from Berkeley to Mexico City to write. (Yes, girls, he's had two marriages, but neither stuck.)

His first idol was Thomas Wolfe, of whom he says, "Nobody's paying any attention to him today because they're jealous." Now his idols are Joyce and Proust. Two writers more different than [sic] Kerouac in their meticulous techniques would be hard to find. But he says, "I'm not interested in their methods, only in their concerns. Joyce was interested in language, Proust in memory. I'm interested in both."

So far Kerouac has written about ten novels, but only two have been published. The first was *The Town and the City*, a critical success if not a commercial one of 1950. The second, *On the Road*, will be published by Viking on September 5.

What I've written here—written at turtle speed and much befouled—is only a bit of what could be said about Jack Kerouac. But it's better to get it straight from the man himself. For that you have only to read his books. "All my novels," he says, "belong to one story—the story of my life. When I'm through you'll have the whole thing on one shelf. That's the grand scheme."

Back to the Village

Jerry Talmer, *Village Voice* (September 18, 1957)

Numerous articles began to appear immediately after the pub-
lication of On the Road *in September 1957. Kerouac, by nature*
an introvert, was not equipped for the media onslaught that
relentlessly hammered his time, energy, and psyche. Though
the publicity subsequently helped Viking sell a lot of books, it
took its toll on Kerouac. His already apparent dependency on
alcohol accelerated after On the Road's *publication.*

J ack Kerouac, the Greenwich Village writer who (with Allen
Ginsberg and Gregory Corso) had to go to San Francisco to
become a San Francisco writer and get famous, sat in Goody's Bar,
off 10th Street, the other night, in a battered royal-blue polo shirt,
his white T-shirt showing beneath, the bright red top of a cigarette
package projecting from the pocket on his chest, his strong arms
reaching perpetually for the bottle of Schlitz before him on the table,
his dark rakish face and glistening black hair more handsome than
Cary Grant's or Wally Reid's. "Man," he said, "I can't make it. I'm
cutting out."

He was talking about the whirl of TV and radio and cocktail parties they've had him in, the Viking people, ever since he returned from Europe and Tangiers just a few days ago. He was talking about the publicity, the success, the rave reviews, the terrifying half-hour with Wingate on *"Nightbeat,"*[7] the girls, the bars, the lionhunters, the whole bit.

"Someday," he said, "if I can write it. If anyone could write it. They have a little girl there, sitting by you, while you wait to go on the TV."

"Just to keep you happy?"

"Just to keep you happy. One of those cute little uptown chicks. If I could write it . . ." He muzzily flagged the waitress for another beer and told how he and Wingate had gone out on the town after the show. The show itself had come as quite a shock to many of his friends and the general public. Kerouac had clammed up almost totally, giving terse, noncommunicative answers and looking like nothing so much as a scared rabbit. One of the few young authors of (inversely) the Big Yes, he had sat there like a stump, saying no.

"What was it? Were you scared?"

"Yeah, man, plenty scared. One of my friends told me don't say anything, nothing that'll get you in trouble. So I just kept saying no, like a kid dragged in by a cop. That's the way I thought of it—a kid dragged up before the cops."

The conversation switched to poetry readings. Could Kerouac go on stage to read some of the San Francisco poetry, his own and Corso's and Ginsberg's? "No, not me. I can't do that. I get stage fright. Wait till Allen comes back—he's great. He loves that."

To what did Kerouac attribute his sudden recognition on the West Coast, after years of the opposite here in the East? "One thing," he said. "Rexroth. A great man. A great critic. Interested in

young people, interested in everything." But presently, when the subject had drifted to jazz—its decline and fall this past half-decade—
Kerouac talked of a California jazz concert which Kenneth Rexroth
hadn't dug at all. "What a square!" Kerouac cheerfully hooted.
"What a square!" And then it emerged that, some time since,
Rexroth had kicked Kerouac out of his house as an objectionable
loafer—just to be an artist, he had said, wasn't enough. As Kerouac
recalled the incident, he seemed to derive great pleasure from it and
to hold no grudge against his mentor.

About *On the Road*, the novel now making such a splash everywhere, Kerouac insists on dismissing it as "my potboiler." He wrote
it six years ago, in 1951, allegedly "to amuse my wife"—the wife he
had then, anyway.

"I'm a serious artist," he said, lightly but intently, downing the
beer without a break, "a serious artist . . . like James Joyce. I've
written eight books since *On the Road*. Viking's going to start
bringing them out."

"What's your best one?"

"A book called *Doctor Sax*, a kind of Gothic fairy tale, a myth of
puberty, about some kids in New England playing around in this
empty place when a shadow suddenly comes out at them, a real
shadow. A real shadow," he said, stressing the image, his black eyes
flashing. "Then there's *The Subterraneans*. That's about an affair
with a colored girl. And then there's . . ." But he let it drop as something weird popped back into his head and he said: "Man, man, on
that TV they make you up!"

"And what's happening to you next? Beside the TV and all that?"

"I'm cutting out. They don't know it, but I'm cutting out. I'm going
down to my mother's in Orlando. Always go back to my mother.
Always." He grinned widely, dangerously, but not altogether freely.

"And if we want to get in touch with you tomorrow? For a picture or something?"

"Call this chick. Wonderful kid—really important. She'll know where I am." He gave a telephone number and a name which for our purposes here can be Elizabeth Jones. We did in fact want to get him for a picture later, and when I called that number the next day, a girl answered, but she drew a blank. "I'm not Elizabeth Jones," she said, doubtfully.

"Oh? Is there any Elizabeth Jones at this number?"

Long pause. "No," she said, "but maybe it's me. I'm Harriet Jones."

Beat Generation: Roadster

Maurice Dolbier, *New York Herald Tribune* (September 22, 1957)

In an October 31, 1957, letter to Allen Ginsberg, Kerouac remarked about the period immediately following On the Road's *publication: "Unbelievable number of events almost impossible to remember including earlier big Viking Press hotel room with thousands of screaming interviewers and* Road *roll original 100 miles ms. rolled out on carpet, bottles of Old Grandad, big articles in* Sat. Review, *in* World Telly, *everyfuckingwhere . . . ." The result, Kerouac states, was a nervous breakdown, which he alleviated by a concentrated rereading of Dostoyevsky's novel,* The Idiot.

J ack Kerouac had been showing a previous interviewer the manuscript of his "Beat Generation" novel *On the Road* (Viking), and when I came into the room he was rolling it up again. It took a long time. The manuscript was closely typed on a single roll of thin drawing-paper that when unrolled was as long as a football field (or almost as long—a black cocker spaniel, behaving like an outraged reviewer, had chewed up some of it).

Mr. Kerouac, who was born in Lowell, Mass., was at one time a star on the Columbia football team, but left when Lou Little assigned him a position that in Mr. Kerouac's opinion, involved too much traveling about. His career since then has not displayed much distaste for travel. *On the Road* reveals how extensively he has wandered over the North American continent, and when his publishers sent him proof-sheets, his address was Tangiers.

On his first trip abroad, he found that the Beat Generation was not a purely American phenomenon. England's Teddy Boys are a part of it, and the young patrons of Paris's existentialist cafés, and jazz enthusiasts behind the Iron Curtain, and blue-jeaned youth in North Africa. Does it have a goal? "Certainly," says Mr. Kerouac, "The goal is ecstasy."

He sees it as all part of a religious movement, "the Second Religiousness that Oswald Spengler[8] prophesied for the West," and when one's mind begins to boggle at the vision of Presley's sideburns and Jean-Paul Sartre and Brando on a motorcycle as units in a religious revival, you are reminded of the posthumous adoration of James Dean and the trance-visions induced by drugs, and you wonder. Mr. Kerouac hammers out the case with anonymous instances of strange manifestations, foreshadowings of the end of the world and the Second Coming, hipsters who have seen angels and devils, and reports quite casually that he too has heard the heavenly music while speeding along a California highway. The Gothic Age is upon us again, and Mr. Kerouac, a man of his age, is writing a novel called *Doctor Sax*, which he describes as "a Gothic myth set in New England."

Asked about his favorite writers, Mr. Kerouac said: "Among English writers, Aldous Huxley is my man. In France, there are two: Céline and Genet. And in America . . . Thomas Wolfe, I guess, but maybe I'd better read him again."

Trade Winds

Jerome Beatty, *Saturday Review* (September 28, 1957)

Presumably everyone is reading *On the Road* and talking about Jack Kerouac, the author. The book's all about the "Beat" generation, the young people who are rushing around like crazy in cars or on the streets in the middle of the night, having parties ("orgies"), and going to Paris, or Mexico, or San Francisco. Don't get 'em mixed up with delinquents, nor with Bohemians. They're different. I guess you have to read the book to figure it out.

Kerouac says there's such a thing as "respectable Beatness," too, so there is hope for the Ivy Leaguers as well. "Even Billy Graham," he told me, "is very hip. Hip and Beat mean the same thing, you know. What's Graham say, 'I'm going to turn out spiritual babies'? That's Beatness. But he doesn't know it. The Beat Generation has no interest in politics, only mysticism, that's their religion. It's kids standing on the street and talking about the end of the world."

Jack Kerouac says that this is a period of Caesars, where a few great families turn out the leaders, and that the Beat Generation has a feeling of great corruptness in Washington. Therefore the only attitude to take is one of noninterference: "Don't assert yourself and nothing happens to you. The only thing that matters is food and drink. And I write to celebrate that."

He has done a lot of celebrating: there are six other novels waiting to be published. One, *Visions of Neal*, is about the same guy who is the main character in *On the Road*. It's "the greatest I've done," says Jack, "but the world isn't ready for it, and it won't be published for twenty years."9

We had to wait a long time for *On the Road*. It was done in 1951. Here's how: "I wrote it for my wife. She'd come home from her four-hour waitress job and she'd always want to know all about Neal and what we'd done. 'What did you and Neal really do?' she'd ask, and I'd write it for her, and she'd come home and laugh at what I'd written. I'd sit behind a big screen and yell 'Coffee!' and her hand would come around the corner holding a cup of it."

Kerouac got art paper, which comes in twenty-foot rolls, and pasted it together. Then he'd start it in the typewriter and begin writing. He could write 18,000 words without changing paper. Now things are a little different. He's divorced and lives with his mother in Orlando.

"I just sit in the yard and think and eat ice cream. I start writing at midnight. I'm really a quiet fellow; shy. It's only when I come to New York that I got to start drinking and talking."

Kerouac is only one member of what's known as "the San Francisco group." My "Trade Winds" colleague, John G. Fuller, is out there right now, and next week he will report in this space on this interesting bunch of poets, writers, and people.

Trade Winds

John G. Fuller, *Saturday Review* (October 4, 1957)

Before leaving New York for the coast, we talked to Jack Kerouac, author of the new novel *On the Road*, mentioned briefly in this column last week. Kerouac is a peripatetic member of the San Francisco group, a slight, intense young man who is convinced that you've got to embrace life completely if you want to dig it.

"I guess I was the one who named us the 'Beat Generation,'" he said. "This includes anyone from fifteen to fifty-five who digs *everything*, man. We're not Bohemians, remember. *Beat* means *beatitude*, not *beat* up. You *feel* this. You feel it in a beat—in jazz, real cool jazz, or a good, gutty, rock number." He demonstrated this with a fairly acceptable hand-drumming exhibition on the table in his hotel room.

"The Beat Generation loves everything, man. We go around digging everything. Everything means something; everything's a symbol. We're mystics. No question about it. Mystics."

Kerouac has bummed his way back and forth across the country a half dozen times. *On the Road* is based mainly on these experiences. He wrote the book on a continuous scroll of mechanical drawing paper,* banged out on a typewriter in single space with no paragraphs whatever. He showed us the scroll—started nearly ten years ago, about a foot in diameter, and looking a little as if it was one of the originals from the Dead Sea. We had to leave before we could find out from Kerouac just how he was able to go about digging life with full emotional abandon—while also fostering the discipline to turn out the thousands and thousands of words a novelist must produce.

---

* The material used for the 120-foot scroll was not teletype paper. Kerouac taped together 12-foot strips of architectural drafting paper he had found in the West 20th Street loft he had shared with his second wife, Joan Haverty Kerouac.

Off the Road, Into the Vanguard, and Out

Howard Smith, *Village Voice* (December 25, 1957)

Kerouac's appearances at New York City's Village Vanguard was ill-advisedly suggested to him as a way of promoting On the Road. *Relying on alcohol to give him the edge he needed to perform, Kerouac's run at the Vanguard was short-lived. Packed-house audiences on opening night gradually dwindled to a few by week's end. In his "biographical résumé," written in 1957, Kerouac remarked: "In recent reading appearance at Village Vanguard I was universally attacked, but all I did was stand there and read my heart out, not caring how I looked or what anybody thought, and I am satisfied because the dishwasher (an old Negro named Elton Stratton) said: 'All I wanta do is get 2 quarts of whiskey and lie down in bed and listen to you read to me.' Also, the musicians (Lee Konitz, Billy Bauer, Wilbur Little) said I was 'singing' when I read and said they heard the music, and since I consider myself a jazz poet, I am satisfied with that. What intelligentsia says makes little difference, as I've always spent my time in skid row or in jazz*

joints or with personal poet madmen and never cared what
'intelligentsia' thinks. My love of poetry is love of joy."

O ut front the J. J. Johnson Quartet heats up the buzzing, jammed-in, packed house to a supercharged, pregnant pitch. In a back alcove, near the men's room, sits Jack Kerouac, who has come off his road into the spotlight of the literary world and his sometime home, Greenwich Village, for a stay at the Village Vanguard that was supposed to be indefinite. It lasted seven nights.

His receding hairline tousled, sweating enough to fill a wine cask, Kerouac looks like a member in good standing of the generation he called "Beat." Anxious drags on cigarette after cigarette, walking around in tight little circles, fast quick talk to anyone nearby, swigs from an always handy drink, gulps of an always handy coffee, tighten Paisley tie, loosen tie, tighten tie.

"What am I going to read?" . . . and he leafs through a suitcaseful and suddenly realizes no one remembered to bring a copy of his own *On the Road*. His combination manager–literary agent talks slowly and carefully in the assuring way they get paid to talk in, but the girl jazz singer is lilting a flip version of "Look to the Rainbow," and Jack knows he's on next.

He leafs through lots of little pads filled with the tiniest hand-lettered notes. "When I write I print everything in pencil. My father was a printer. He lost his shop on the horses. If he didn't, I'd be a printer today. I'd probably be publishing the fresh, young poets . . . ."

He's getting more nervous, but his speech comes easy in answer to certain questions. "You don't know what a square is? Well, old Rexroth says I'm a square. If he means because I was born a French-Canadian Catholic . . . sometimes devout . . . then I guess that makes

me a square. But a square is someone who ain't hip. Hipness? Him"
(pointing to me) "and I, we're hip."

Trying to keep up with the questions, he goes on at an even
faster rate. "I was sitting with Steve Allen out front for a while; he
said he wished he had his old *Tonight* show, so he could put me
on. I told him he should wire Jack Paar . . . . Jazzmen and poets
are both like babies . . . . No, I decided not to read to music
because I feel they don't mix . . . . Well, maybe Allen* will sit in
on the piano for a while, though . . . . Yair, whatever I write about
is all true . . . . I think Emily Dickinson is better than Whitman,
as a wordman, that is."

The drink, the sweat, the smoke, the nerves are taking effect.
It's time for him to go on. He grabs some of those pads and begins
making his way through the maze of tiny nightclub tables. They
all came to see him, a few tieless buddies from the old days, a little
proud and a little jealous, the fourth estate, the agents, the hand-
shakers, the Steve Allens, the Madison Avenue bunch trying to
keep ultra-current; all treating him like a Carmine DeSapio or
Floyd Patterson.[10]

He's shorter than they expected, this writer who has been likened
to Sandburg[11] but looks like a frightened MC on his first job. They
applaud wildly for this thirty-five-year-old who was drunk for the
first three weeks that his book made the best-seller list and now

---

* Kerouac and *Tonight Show* host Steve Allen first met at Kerouac's reading at the
Village Vanguard. Allen sat in on piano with him for the second show. Afterward,
they decided to collaborate on a spoken-word album. When it was eventually
placed on acetate, the reading session was recorded in one take. Dot Records,
which was scheduled to release it, canceled the long-playing album at the last
minute, after review copies had already been sent out. Soon afterward, it was reis-
sued by Hanover; its liner notes were written by Gilbert Millstein of the *New York
Times*, who also wrote Kerouac's first rave review for *On the Road*.

stands before them wearing an outfit of fair middle-class taste, but with a thick, hand-tooled, large-buckled leather belt.

"I'm going to read like I read to my friends." A too-easy murmur of laughter; the crowd is with him. He reads fast, with his eyes untheatrically glued to the little pad, rapidly, on and on as if he wants to get it over with. "I'll read a junky poem." He slurs over the beautiful passages as if not expecting the crowd to dig them even if he went a little slower. "It's like kissing my kitten's belly . . . ."* He begins to loosen up and ad lib, and the audience is with him. A fast fifteen minutes and he's done.

The applause is like a thunderstorm on a hot July night. He smiles and goes to sit among the wheels and the agents and pulls a relaxed drag on his cigarette.

He is prince of the hip being accepted in the court of the rich kings who, six months ago, would have nudged him closer to the bar if he wandered in to watch the show. He must have hated himself in the morning—not for the drinks he had but because he ate it all up the way he never really wanted to.

As I was leaving, I heard some guy in an old army shirt, standing close to the bar, remark: "Well, Kerouac came off the road in high gear . . . I hope he has a good set of snow tires."

---

* From Kerouac's *Mexico City Blues*—"230th Chorus": "Like kissing my kitten in the belly / The softness of our reward."

Kerouac at the
Village Vanguard

Dan Wakefield, *The Nation* (January 4, 1958)

*Like Kerouac, Wakefield studied with Mark Van Doren, Eng-
lish professor at Columbia University. However, it wasn't
under this auspice that they encountered each other. Wakefield recalls in his book,* New York in the Fifties *(Houghton-
Mifflin, 1992): "Romero's wasn't known as a literary bar, yet
that first time I went there Sam spotted a writer he knew at a
table in the back and took me over to meet him .... Wearing
a red-and-black checked flannel shirt, with mussy hair and a
day's growth of beard, Kerouac seemed more lumberjack than
literary man as he quickly offered to buy us a drink. He was
celebrating an advance he had gotten for another novel. We
sat down at a table with Kerouac and several of his friends,
and Jack talked in the rather grumpy, desultory way he had,
evidently his customary manner with people he'd just met. I
took him to be a heavily serious sort of person, one who
seemed more weighted down than elated about the sale of his
novel to Viking Press, a prestigious publisher of fiction. What
most impressed me about Kerouac, though, was that he paid*

for our drinks by pulling a wad of bills from a money belt he
wore around his waist that contained some of the cash from
his $1,000 advance from the publisher."

J ack Kerouac opened at the Village Vanguard in New York on the Thursday night before Christmas, as part of a holiday bill which included the J. J. Johnson Quartet and Beverly Kenny. J. J. Johnson is an old pro, a trombone man of dignity and distinction. Beverly Kenny is a redhead who sings a deep-throated, swinging style, and Jack Kerouac is the "spokesman" of the Beat Generation by merit of his recent novel, *On the Road*. Kerouac, the uncompromising hipster, was billed as reading from his own "works," to the background accompaniment of a jazz pianist. A beer at the Village Vanguard goes for a $1.25, and the minimum for sitting at a table is $4 per person, so it was understandable that not too many "Beat" characters were able to enjoy Kerouac's debut on the nightclub circuit. There were, however, one seaman, one poet, and one blonde in Kerouac's corner (the dimly lit corner at the back) for Friday night's performance.

An agent of the *Nation* showed up late, ordered a beer at the bar, and turned to face the stage, where Kerouac stood beneath the several smoky beams with large sheaf of manuscript in his hands and recited to a cold (as distinguished from cool) audience from a piece about life in the famous Cellar bar in San Francisco. Kerouac wore his hair in need of a cut; brown slacks, brown shoes, cotton argyles, and a gold-thread open-neck sport shirt that glistened in the dark and hung over his belt.

Kerouac was reading a passage about his friendship with the bartenders at the Cellar. A gentleman known as Lou, tending bar at the Vanguard, turned to his clients and remarked quietly, "He won't make many bartender friends if he keeps on usin' *that* stuff." Lou was a man in his late forties, and no doubt unfamiliar with the Beat Generation.

There were, however, signs of genuine liberal tendencies from the audience. A table of what looked to be the leftovers of an office party from around Times Square was shuffling restlessly when one of the gentleman "sshhed" them and explained, "Some people like this stuff." Back in Kerouac's corner, the blonde explained to the newly seated *Nation* agent that Jack didn't like the idea of this nightclub business but thought it might help *On the Road*. "If it gets back on the best-seller list, they may make it as a movie. If he sells it as a movie, he won't have to do *this* sort of thing anymore."

Kerouac finally finished with "this sort of thing," and retired to the back room where J. J. Johnson and his pros were taking their break. Johnson and his sidemen were supremely sober, and Kerouac came back drunk to sit at the edge of their table. He was at first politely ignored and was finally recognized after asking Mr. Johnson, "What did you think of what I read?" Johnson looked at him, the lion-tamer in the circus looking at the kid who had just won the amateur hog-calling contest, and asked him if he had written it. Kerouac admitted he had written it, and Johnson, after a pause, judged that "it sounded very deep." Kerouac said how much he enjoyed Johnson's trombone and said that he personally had always wanted to be a tenor sax man.

"Man, I could really work with tenor sax," said Kerouac.

Johnson looked up without expression and said, "You look more like a trumpet man to me."

Kerouac's next "set" opened with a reading called "The Life of a Sixty Year Old Mexican Junkie." It seemed this junkie had been picked up while a young man by an American female junkie and finally got the monkey on his back. The story was sad indeed. It met with applause from the audience of the Village Vanguard. After that episode, Kerouac looked out blinking from beneath the spotlights and asked, "Has anyone here ever heard of Allen Ginsberg?"

Kerouac's corner clapped, and a few scattered claps came from across the floor. Kerouac then announced that he had Ginsberg's latest poem right there with him and that he would read it. He raised the sheaf of manuscripts before him, pointed his finger to the smoky ceiling, and began to proclaim. In the dark, it was impossible to note down all the verses, but the key refrain seemed to be, "Mother, with your six vaginas."[12]

Kerouac did not share where Ginsberg is at present, and for all we know he is still in San Francisco. It seems only reasonable, though, that he soon will be opening at El Morocco. If Kerouac has made the nightclub circuit, Ginsberg should not be far behind.

It seems only yesterday that Ginsberg was sitting on a deserted railroad tie in California with Jack Kerouac, writing poetry about his Beat friends who challenged the status quo and bewailed the rape of American letters by Philistine forces. Was it only yesterday that Ginsberg dedicated his almost-banned book of poems, *Howl*, to Jack Kerouac, "the new Buddha of American prose," whose eleven books were "published in Heaven"? And now one is published by the Viking Press and the others are being read at the Village Vanguard by the Buddha himself. The glow-in-the-dark, gold-threaded shirt worn by the Buddha in his Vanguard readings seems to be the principal symbol of his "protest" still remaining. One recalls the lines of Kenneth Rexroth's poem dealing with the death of Dylan Thomas: "You killed him, in your goddam Brooks Brothers suit." We can only shudder at the genocide that could be wreaked by Kerouac's haberdashery.

But all is not beat. It so happened, by one of those wonderful plots of the Muse, that on the same night Kerouac was reading from his testament at the Vanguard, a young poet named Richard Wilbur was about four blocks across the Village, reading from his work at New York University.

Richard Wilbur[13] was born in 1921 and is thereby entitled to inclusion as a member of the Beat Generation. He wears, however, a Brooks Brothers suit, has never recited from his work in the Village Vanguard, quotes heavily from Greek and medieval philosophers, and is currently teaching a Shakespeare course at Wesleyan University. Richard Wilbur is thirty-six years old and Jack Kerouac is thirty-five. The painful difference is that Wilbur is a man and Kerouac is a kid.

To go from the university lecture hall to the Village Vanguard the Friday night before Christmas was to realize that there is no such thing as a "generation"; that there are born each year a certain number of men and a certain number of boys; that out of each era in our national history there come a few poets and few poor boys who wander with words, and that no grand generalization can tie them together. Jack Kerouac sweats beneath the spotlights of a nightclub to bring his novel back to the best-seller list. He is now "On the Town." Lo and behold—it is Richard Wilbur who is on the road; who has been, all along.

Interview with Jack Kerouac: Lowell Author Gives His Version of the Beat Generation

Mike Wallace, *New York Post* (January 21, 1958)

The year of 1958 saw a glut of Kerouac works published: a new Viking novel, The Dharma Bums; *a Grove Press paperback of* The Subterraneans; *and also a string of smaller works placed by his agent, Sterling Lord, in such publications as* Esquire, Playboy, Pageant, *and* Holiday. *For his interview with journalist Mike Wallace, Kerouac remarked to Allen Ginsberg in a January 8, 1958, letter written from Orlando, Florida, about making "big Marian[14] nervous speeches to Mike Wallace tape." In Florida, he was miserably annoyed by his sister and her husband, Caroline and Paul Blake. Anticipating a trip to New York City to record a poetry album with Steve Allen, Kerouac wrote on January 13, 1958, to his girlfriend Joyce Glassman (who wisely advised Kerouac to be discreet after mentioning his drug use in his Wallace interview) that he planned to search for a house in Long Island (he also apologized for the possibility of leaving crab lice on her toilet seat that he suspected were lifted from the "back toilets" of nightclubs and bars: "If so I'm sorry").*

I n twentieth-century America, a new kind of mystic has appeared—the Beat Generation visionary. He doesn't eat locusts, wear hair shirts, sleep on nails, or perch on pillars. He uses the strange modern techniques of jive, junk, and high speed to achieve his special ecstasy. Here we interview Jack Kerouac, author of *On the Road* and chronicler of the Beat Generation. A tattered, forlorn young man with the chronic exhaustion of one who eats and sleeps infrequently, Kerouac gives us a glimmering of the hope and despair of the Beat in their search for the Beatitudes.

MW: What is the Beat Generation?

JK: Well, actually it's just an old phrase. I knocked it off one day and they made a big fuss about it. It's not really a generation at all.

MW: It's a type of person?

JK: Yeah. It starts with rock 'n' roll teenagers and runs up to sixty-year-old junkies, old characters in the street . . . it really began in 1910.

MW: Well, what links the junkie and the eleven-year-old and Jack Kerouac? What *is* it to be Beat?

JK: Well, it's a hipness. It's twentieth-century hipness.

MW: Hip to what?

JK: To life.

MW: What kind of life are they hip to?

JK: . . . to religion.

MW: What kind of religion?

JK: Oh, it's weird. Visions. Visions of God.

MW: You mean Beat people are mystics?

JK: Yeah. It's a revival prophesied by Spengler. He said that in the late moments of Western civilization there would be a great revival of religious mysticism. It's happening.

MW: What sort of mysticism is it? What do Beat mystics believe in?

JK: Oh, they believe in love. They love children . . . and, I don't know, it's so strange to talk about all this . . . they love children, they love women, they love animals, they love everything.

MW: They love everything? Then why is there so much violence? Why do they *drive, drive, drive*? Why do they *go, go, go*? Why the rush?

JK: Oh, that's just lyricism. Wild motorcycle rides under the moonlight . . . A lyrical thing. It's not so unusual.

MW: Why is jazz so important to this new mystique?

JK: That's the music of the Beat Generation.

MW: What's mystical about it?

JK: Jazz is very complicated. It's just as complicated as Bach. The chords, the structures, the harmony, and everything. And then it has a tremendous beat. You know, tremendous drummers. They can drive it. It has just a tremendous drive. It can drive you right out of yourself.

MW: How about dope?

JK: Same thing. You can escape. You can have visions with dope.

MW: Have you ever taken dope yourself?

JK: Sure. A lot. But I have never got in the habit because I'm allergic to it.

MW: Have you had visions with it?

JK: I'll say.

MW: Do you remember any clearly?

JK: I fainted. I passed out, fell flat on my back on the grass. During that time, I saw Paradise. I saw—well, I wasn't there any more. There was only one thing . . . there was a great golden light, and I wasn't there . . . but it was like, I suppose, God . . . but it was blissful, because I didn't have to worry about being myself any more. That was all over with.

MW: Sounds like a self-destructive way to seek God.

JK: Oh, it was tremendous. I woke up sick about the fact that I had to come back to myself, to the flesh of life . . .

MW: You mean that the Beat people want to lose themselves?

JK: Yeah. You know, Jesus said to see the Kingdom of Heaven you must lose yourself . . . something like that.

MW: Then the Beat Generation loves death?

JK: Yeah. They're not afraid of death.

MW: Aren't you afraid?

JK: Naw . . . What I believe is that nothing is happening.

MW: What do you mean?

JK: Well, you're not sitting here. That's what you *think*. Actually, we are great empty space. I could walk right *through* you . . . You know what I mean, we're made out of atoms, electrons. We're actually empty. We're an empty vision . . . in one mind.

MW: In what mind—the mind of God?

JK: That's the name we give it. We can give it any name. We can call it tangerine . . . god . . . tangerine . . . But I do know we are empty phantoms, sitting here thinking we are human beings and worrying about civilization. We're just empty phantoms. And yet, all is well.[15]

MW: All is well?

JK: Yeah. We're all in Heaven, now, really.

MW: You don't *sound* happy.

JK: Oh, I'm tremendously sad. I'm in great despair.

MW: Why?

JK: It's a great burden to be alive. A heavy burden, a great big heavy burden. I wish I were safe in Heaven, dead.

MW: But you are in Heaven, Jack. You just said we all were.

JK: Yeah. If I only knew it. If I could only hold on to what I know.

"You must meet my friend, Philip Lamantia," said Kerouac casually on departing. "He was knocked off a bench by an angel last week."

He Scorns Beatniks

UPI, *Detroit News* (August 24, 1958)

As the phenomenon of the Beats began to pick up steam in American culture, Kerouac was noticeably disconcerted by Hollywood's sidestepping him and adapting his ideas for film without his knowledge or consent. The word "Beat" was now paired with the suffix "-nik" in the wake of Sputnik's launch; "beatnik" came to be a pejorative term describing a lifestyle that rejected intelligence in favor of kicks, drugs, and a lackluster Bohemian existence that was corrupting America's youth–who had already been "poisoned," it was thought, by the advent of rock 'n' roll. Despising the inferred association with beatniks, Kerouac wisely began to shun the press. Intuitively, Kerouac foresaw Ginsberg's involvement with politics and feared that he would "get me and everybody in hot water." The high press profile, the Beats' associations with narcotics, and Neal Cassady's arrest for selling marijuana cigarettes to undercover police officers in April 1958 implanted a new paranoia in Kerouac. Nevertheless, he remained staunchly implanted in mysticism and poetics: "Beautiful fullmoon

*Augustcool night the other night when my 2 rows of corn
looked like a throng standing behind Jesus who is pointing up
at the moon to show their upward gazes the entrance-light of
the Angels" (JK to Philip Whalen, Northport, New York,
August 4, 1958).*

J ack Kerouac, thirty-six-year-old author who coined the term
"Beat Generation" to describe a wild, jazz-loving segment of
American youth, has been hailed by some literary critics as among
the most significant new U.S. novelists since Ernest Hemingway and
dismissed by others as a "barbaric yawper." In the following interview, Kerouac comments on charges that he glorifies hoodlumism.

New York, August 23 (UPI)

"This 'Beat Generation' stuff is beginning to beat me," novelist Jack
Kerouac said today. Kerouac, whose choice of subject matter in his
much-publicized books has led some critics to picture him as a sort
of apostle of drug addiction, promiscuous sex, and auto theft, denied
suggestions that his writing encourages juvenile immorality or defiance of law. "Youthful criminals of today may be using the 'Beat
Generation' tag as an excuse for their actions, but the term as I
meant it has nothing to do with crime," Kerouac said.

"What I meant when I thought of the phrase was this: when
you're young and you're a deadbeat, you drift from job to job and
bum around, you believe in art and friendship but no one believes
in you because you haven't got a cent to show for it," Kerouac said.

"Comes a day when you suddenly raise your eyes to Heaven in
despair and you feel a wave of beatitude flowing through you, especially in church. This feeling is as old as time."

Kerouac's recent best-seller, *On the Road*, is a powerfully written novel describing the deeds and misdeeds of a group of twenty-year-olds during a frenetic trek back and forth across the United States in stolen and borrowed automobiles.

"It's a humorous, sentimentally flavored–type shot of life as it's lived," according to the author, not a recommendation for conduct.

"Youth in the past has frequently been called wild, or flaming, or what you will," Kerouac said. "In the 1940s, when I was in my twenties, the term 'beat' seemed to apply to me and the people I knew. But we were individualists compared to the wolf packs of today."

"There is no relation between the pranks of that lonesome, talkative Beat Generation of the forties and the concerted desecrations of this new delinquency-hounded generation of the fifties," he added.

Kerouac feels no sense of leadership toward those groups of young Bohemians in New York and San Francisco who have been identified with his Beat Generation term.

"The so-called 'beatniks' of San Francisco wouldn't even talk to me when I was wailing there in the late forties," he says. "Why, those guys who picketed the Giants coming to San Francisco in the name of the Beat Generation don't realize that I used to be a center fielder for the Boston Braves in my dreams.

"When I was in high school, I used to be like DiMaggio after deep or short flyballs. I was a wrist hitter, fourteen home runs in ten games. I even had a tryout with the Woonsocket Sputniks, or somebody."

A lover of rock 'n' roll music, which he plays on the radio "every day" at the newly purchased house where he lives with his mother and two cats outside New York City, Kerouac mentioned the recent rock 'n' roll riot in Boston.

"Blaming juvenile delinquency on my books is about like blaming the Boston rioting on the music," he said.

"There is no relation between rock 'n' roll, which is very beautiful oral jazz, if you'll listen, and the handful of hoodlums who give it a bad name—as though love song ever spelled footpad."

The author says he is no expert on juvenile crime and does not like to see lawbreaking any more than the next man.

"I'm as completely in the dark about all this new cruel ganging-up business as you or Freud or anyone else," he said.

"There have always been the criminally insane and whether they blame their actions on alcohol, heroin, possession by the devil, marijuana, or 'Beatness,' the fact still remains that they are criminally insane, young or old."

Kerouac, who is deeply interested in Buddhism, indicated that his forthcoming literary efforts will move on from the Beat Generation "hipster" characters that brought him to public attention.

"In my new novel, *Dharma Bums*, which is coming out this fall, there isn't even one sentimental hubcap stolen," he said with a chuckle.

"It's really a book about religious vagrants—young guys wandering around smiling, with rucksacks on their backs, drinking wine in the moonlight like Li Po, the Chinese poet, climbing mountains to pray for the final safety of all living beings.

"Why? What more decent activity?"

On the Road Back: How the Beat Generation Got That Way According to Its Seer

San Francisco Examiner (October 5, 1958)

Drum major for the Beat Generation, setting the wild, free, jazz tempo by which it marches out of step with society, is Jack Kerouac, a onetime San Franciscan who now lives on Long Island. His novels about the hopped up, way out, nomadic cool cats of that generation, *On the Road* and *The Subterraneans*, have excited both cheers and boos from the critics and a hubbub of controversy throughout the nation. Kerouac's latest novel, *The Dharma Bums*, is reviewed in this section. Here he answers some questions fired by *Highlight* [*Editor's note: "Highlight" refers to one of the* San Francisco Examiner's *chief entertainment columns*].

H: Would you tell us your version of the origin of the term "Beat Generation" and why San Francisco happens to be its most fertile ground for growth?

JK: In 1948 I said to John Clellon Holmes, "This is really a beat generation." He agreed and in 1952 published an article in the *New York Times* entitled "This is the Beat Generation" and attributed the original vision to me. Also, I had already called it the Beat

Generation in my manuscript of *On the Road* written in May
1951. San Francisco is the last great city in America, after that no
more land. It was there where poets and bums could come and
drink wine in the streets before the recent crackdown by police
who spend too much time watching *San Francisco Beat* on TV
and not enough time reading books in the library.

H: What would you say is the chief difference, if any, between the
"lost" generation of Fitzgerald-Hemingway and the "beat" generation of today?

JK: The Lost Generation, from what I can tell from the books, was
based on an ironic romantic negation. "Beat" generation is
sweating for affirmation, and yet there is an irony, almost a cynicism, involved, a kind of lip service about the "greatness" of life.
And, of course, Romanticism is dead: In its place, the search for
Gnosticism,[16] absolute belief in a Divinity of Rapture. I believe
God is Ecstasy in His Natural Immanence.

H: The young rebels of the 1930s found their means of striking back
at an objectionable society through political action. Today's generation seems disinclined to take any action at all. How do they
hope to improve things if they don't take action, and if they don't
take action, can't they rightly be accused of irresponsibility and
futilitarianism?

JK: The political apathy of the Beat Generation is in itself a "political" movement; i.e., will influence political decisions in the
future and possibly transfer politics to their rightful aims, i.e.,
sense. "So long as he governs his people by the principle of
nonassertion, things naturally arrange themselves into social
order." For "when a country is in confusion and discord, ideals of
loyalty and patriotism arise" (Tao).

H: What do you think have been the main achievements of the so-called "Beat" writers, and what do you think their influence is or may be on younger writers?

JK: Neal Cassady, although never published, wrote the greatest piece of the Beat Generation, a 40,000-word letter addressed to me in New York in 1950,[17] which was the greatest story ever read by any American writer in American history. Gregory Corso is a gigantic poet ("Gasoline" is only a hint). William Seward Burroughs is the secret shadow hovering over world literature. Al Ginsberg is, of course, a poet's poet. Gary Snyder and Philip Whalen are the magicians of West Coast poetry. [Kenneth] Rexroth appeals to me as a poet of great grandeur, I don't care if he doesn't like me. Mike McClure is wild. Naturally the younger kids will pick up from them.

H: To some it appears that the days of the Beat Generation in San Francisco are numbered. You've gone to Long Island, Ginsberg and Corso to Europe, Snyder to Japan, Whalen to the East Bay. How do you view what seems to be the end of the literary Beats here?

JK: Originally I came from New England and Long Island, anyway. San Francisco was my mad, wild playtown. Ginsberg's home is in Patterson, Corso's in Manhattan. Snyder was actually born in S.F. Whalen is Oregonian. The literate Beats will make it just the same (there are some hidden geniuses in S.F. yet to speak), and of course you have your Rexroth and [Lawrence] Ferlinghetti and Robert Stock and Ronny Loewinson and others. When Stan Persky of Chicago hits S.F., you will have your new poet. Who cares about geography? But yes, San Francisco is the poetry center of America today.

Interview with Ben Hecht

Ben Hecht, *The Ben Hecht Show*, WABC-TV (October 17, 1958)

*Ben Hecht (February 28, 1894 – April 18, 1964) was himself
an author of some radical notoriety. The sexual subject matter
and illustrations of his novel* Fantazius Mallare *caught the eye
of post office censors when it arrived in bookstores in 1922.
Later on, federal authorities charged Hecht and his illustrator
with obscenity, to which they pleaded no contest. During the
1920s, Hecht also published the* Chicago Literary Times, *an
eclectic collection of parody and commentary on Chicago's
artistic and literary personalities and mainstream cultural
institutions. Commenting on the quality of Chicago journalism, Hecht wrote: "The reading matter of the newspaper is
not the voice of the people but the comforting assurances of
the institutions within which people hide from themselves and
one another." Hecht's interview with Kerouac comes across as
sympathetic when compared to the scathing treatment he
received at the hands of other critics and journalists.*

BH: Hello Jack.

JK: Hello Ben.

BH: You're the fellow that invented the word, or the phrase, "Beat Generation," aye?

JK: Yeah.

BH: Well I'm gonna' ask you some questions, don't mind not answering if you don't want to. First, I read in one of your books a very interesting statement. You said that "everyone feels like a zombie and somewhere at the end of the night the great Dracula figure of modern disintegration and madness, the devil if you will, is running the whole thing." Now I like that because that's the way I felt about the world often but I'd like to know if our devils are the same. Who's this devil?

JK: Well that's a quote from . . . a character says that.

BH: You don't believe there's a devil running the world? I'm very disappointed.

JK: No. The devil is defeated.

BH: By the Beats?

JK: No, no, by God.

BH: God licked him.

JK: Sure.

BH: Well about God you made a statement that also fascinated me, you said that . . . let me get this, put my glasses on and get it accurate. You said that, um . . . your philosophy you described as being "Catholic . . . Catholicism mixed with gin." In what proportions?

JK: Gin? G-I-N?

BH: G-I-N, and that's what it said on a tape recording interview I heard of yours. In what proportions, Jack? Is the gin improved by this mixture? What did you mean by liquor and religion? Reality and spirituality? Or what?

JK: Well I don't understand your question. How is the mixture improved?

BH: Well let's jump to another question.

JK: Does the gin get better?

BH: Does the gin get helped by being religious or does the religion get helped by being full of gin? Which is improved?

JK: [laughs] I don't know. That's a non sequitur.

BH: Non sequitur, right . . . now let's go back. You boys, I gather from having read your very fine book, which I bought because I thought it was about drama critics, it's not *drama* bums, it's *dharma* bums.

JK: Ooh, *The Dharma Bums*.

BH: In this book you seem to have a wonderfully good time and you seem to have it by turning your back on all the things that the bourgeoisie have to contend with. One of the things you most like to turn your back on, though you say the devil has been defeated, who are the devils that make you turn your back? Do you like politics?

JK: No.

BH: Do you like the Republican Party?

JK: I like Eisenhower as a man . . . as a man, great man.

BH: You do, huh? Is he a great man?

JK: Nice man.

BH: Why do you think he's a nice man?

JK: He's a kind of man you would like to shake hands with. He's a *nice* man. *You* know he's a nice man.

[Hecht laughs]

JK: I don't know anything about politics.

BH: I adore Mr. Eisenhower but I don't think he's a great man or even an intelligent man.

JK: He probably is, you know the American people probably don't realize what he's doing.

BH: What's he doing?

JK: I don't know, we'll figure it out in fifty years. In years you can look back.

[Hecht laughs]

BH: I think he's one of the leaders of the Beat Generation, huh? I think he's turned his back on us just as you boys have . . .

JK: [laughs] No, no . . .

BH: [continues] . . . for probably the same reason. Are you gonna vote the next election?

JK: I've never voted.

BH: Well how can you think any one politician is better than another? Wouldn't that lure you into casting a ballot?

JK: I shouldn't be proud of never having voted, but I never have. I don't know what's the matter.

BH: I can understand. I only voted once and under protest.

JK: You too?

BH: Yeah once . . . for the wrong guy.

JK: Where? When? [laughs]

BH: Roosevelt.

JK: [laughs]

BH: You like Ike? You think he's adorable? What do you think of his pals? There's a fellow called Dulles who creates . . .

JK: Well you spend a whole lifetime learning all the techniques of . . .

BH: He's great too?

JK: He's a great technician.

BH: Yeah . . . at what?

JK: Running the secretary of state office. Running the, uh . . .

BH: You boys have had your backs turned . . .

JK: No, no I don't agree with my confreres, you know, about politics.

BH: They're against and you're . . .

JK: They have the same ideas you have.

BH: They have, huh? Bad ones, huh?

JK: No, no. There's no reason to criticize anybody, actually. We're all gonna go to Heaven.

BH: We are?

JK: All of us.

BH: Me too?

JK: Everything, even the microphone.

BH: I like that.

JK: You too, and your cigar.

BH: I couldn't do without it. Jack, have you ever been in trouble with the government forces that you like so well? I gather not, because you seem too full of human kindness. Has the government ever gotten sore or interested in the Beat Generation? Do you think there will ever be a time when you boys will be hailed up and you'll have to swear that you never belonged to the Beat Generation or belonged to it now? Do you think they'll get after Buddha?

JK: Gee, you can't get to him.

BH: They can't? They keep trying to get to a lot of things that they can't get to.

JK: Buddha, you know, in his lifetime, nobody ever laid a hand on him.

BH: You think he's safe. Do you think its safe worshipping Buddha? Do you think you boys are out of reach of our law enforcers by worshipping Buddha?

JK: I don't only worship Buddha.

BH: Whom else?

JK: I worship Christ, I worship Allah, and I worship Yahweh who is
    the father. I worship 'em all.

BH: Where did you get this worship instinct? Because I read your
    book and I think it's real. I think it's really worship.

JK: I was born in a religious home.

BH: I see.

JK: My father was very sensitive and . . .

BH: I was pleased to read in your book that sex didn't exist outside
    of the realm of worshippers, too.

JK: What?

BH: I said worshippers don't . . . do not necessarily *not* go in for sex
    which is usually the rule.

JK: Well they shouldn't.

BH: They shouldn't. Do you think sex helps worship along?

JK: No, I mean, *both* are necessary . . .

BH: But they're not separate?

JK: . . . including the gin.

BH: The gin, huh? You boys love life providing that you don't have
    to be hurt by it. Is that one of your ideas?

JK: No, no, we've been hurt.

BH: Who hurts ya?

JK: Hunger. I've been starving many times on the road.

BH: You've written a lot of books haven't ya? I hear that you got
    about four or five books that haven't been published yet?

JK: That's right.

BH: And you write ten hours a day?

JK: No, I wrote . . . I've been writing since I was eleven.

BH: Eleven.

JK: But I mean . . . I just went through a furious three years when I thought I'd be like Shakespeare and write three masterpieces in a year.

BH: Well that's not being very back-turning when you write ten hours a day, three masterpieces a year. What makes the Beat people, if they are the people in your last book, *The Drama Bums* . . .

JK: Dharma. *The Dharma Bums.*

BH: Okay. What makes them climb mountains, look at their navel and yell "OM! OM!" Why do they go in for mysticism?

JK: They don't look at their navels.

BH: They don't? Whose navel do they look at?

[Kerouac laughs]

BH: I read in your book there's a new cult called, not *cult* but a new phrase called—or word—called *yam*. What's that?

JK: Yabyu*mmm*.

BH: Yabyum.

JK: That comes from Tibet. It's an ancient ceremony.[18]

BH: It pleased me to be reminded of this thing, because I remember it in my youth, a lot of boys and one girl. Is there any . . . ?

JK: No, no, one man and one girl and priests chanting around beating on drums.

BH: One man and one girl?

JK: Yeah that's all, in the middle.

BH: I read a party that you described, I think it was *five* men and one girl.

JK: Well it was a sloppy yabyum.

BH: "Sloppy." It should just be one on one?

JK: Yeah.

BH: That's depressing.

JK: It is?

BH: Because I figured out being an amateur psychiatrist that that had something to do with homosexuality.

JK: Oh no.

BH: It hasn't?

JK: No.

BH: This is not a personal attack, I've gotten a good look at your puss, I wouldn't even think of making such a suggestion.

JK: That's one thing I'm not is homosexual.

BH: Have you an opinion or attitude about homosexuals?

JK: They can do what they want. They should.

BH: Are they productive and constructive people like the rest of the world?

JK: I could name you names . . .

BH: Yeah.

JK: . . . who were great and creative, including Socrates.

BH: Socrates. Who else? Julius Caesar?

JK: [laughs] Julius Caesar.

BH: Lycurgus, the head of Sparta. I knew them all.

JK: [laughs with rest of crew]

BH: What do you think about people who don't climb the mountain, don't have mysticism? What do you think about a fellow like me who is on a treadmill, always trying to make a little money?

JK: Nah, you've lived a wonderful life.

BH: I have?

JK: Yeah, I could write a book about the way you've lived, a newspaperman traveling around, writing scripts, plays, people throwing roses at you.

BH: It looks like I was fishing for something but I wasn't.

JK: Oh no, no.

BH: What turned you boys to the Buddha? Was it your thought that the Christian civilization was a pretty silly thing? And that a religion, the *Christian* religion, which has possibly produced maybe eight hundred million murders, crucifixions, wasn't quite as spiritual?

JK: That's one thing that I've thought of, because in Buddhism there's not been one crusader . . .

BH: Not one, not one . . .

JK: . . . not one crusading war.

BH: Buddhism never hurt anyone.

JK: Never.

BH: Christianity has torn the world apart, there'd been almost . . .

JK: Yeah, but that was because of charlatans who came in and took it over from Peter.

BH: Who's to judge? They don't seem like charlatans when they're in the box. They just seem like people in charge. Later they turn out charlatans.

JK: An awful lot of people.

BH: The fellas that burned Joan didn't seem like charlatans to Joan, I bet you.

JK: Peter was a fisherman.

BH: Yeah. One thing I've noticed in the writings of you and your pals, Mr. Ginsberg particularly, is that you have an affinity for Negroes. Is it that the Negro is an authentic, automatic *Beat* without having to put on it a title?

JK: Yeah, he *is* the original Beat character.

BH: He is the original Beat, he's the one that starts, he's outside. He's born with it.

JK: He's full of glee, if you noticed—he has fun.

BH: Glee over what?

JK: He has a lot of fun! You've noticed the way the Negroes have a lot of fun. They also suffer.

BH: I'm afraid I only heard professional Negroes talk lately, I didn't hear the boys we used to hear in Chicago.

JK: That's right.

BH: They were very happy.

JK: They're happy. They still are.

BH: They still are. I remember . . . did you ever hear of a place called Sunset No. 1 in Chicago? The Black-and-Tan joints? They were very happy there. There was no Negro problem.

JK: Yabyum?

BH: Yes. Not the *yabyum* you wrote in your book. Another thing in your book fascinated me, you wrote about drugs very charmingly and honestly as a sort of holy water for the Beat Generation. What drugs did you use and where did you get 'em and how much did they cost?

JK: Well . . .

BH: Are they expensive?

JK: I know a lot of people who take 'em and I know all the facts about it. Yeah, *now* they're expensive.

BH: Are drugs as vicious and horrifying as the propaganda make out?

JK: Yeah the drugs that you take through the needle *are* vicious and horrifying.

BH: You gotta smoke 'em, sniff 'em or what?

JK: Well, uh . . . also sleeping pills are vicious and horrifying, worst of all.

BH: Yeah, I take those. I'm the worst offender. I can't stand them but I take 'em.

JK: Never take three.

BH: No, not unless you want to say "good-bye."

JK: No, in a way . . .

BH: *Six* are good-bye.

JK: Well, actually fifty.

BH: Fifty are good-bye?

JK: Fifty.

BH: We had a lot of Beats in our time that didn't wear that title. Did you ever hear of the Dill Pickle Club in Chicago?[19]

JK: No I never have been to Chicago.

BH: My fame gets around. Jack Jones, have you ever heard of him?

JK: Jack Jones?

BH: Yeah.

JK: I thought you were gonna say Jack Reed.

BH: I knew Jack Reed, yes, he was a great reporter who preferred Russia to the United States. God knows why.

JK: Who's Jack Jones?

BH: Jack Jones ran the Dill Pickle Club. He was an ex-sailor, he assembled maybe three hundred people in a little barn, gave them a place to sleep and a podium from which to recite their poems.

JK: They're doing that now.

BH: They're doing that now. We did that in Chicago in 1920. Tell me, is this mysticism really a religious training? Or is it a ruse to avoid the slings and arrows of our time? Most mystics put a hat on right over their ears so they wouldn't see what's going on.

JK: It's hard to say.

BH: You like the world? Not the people . . .

JK: I like the *essence* of the world, but not the world itself.

BH: Do you like its organizations, its advertising factotums, its automobiles, its assembly-line souls? Is it bad?

JK: Well it's silly.

BH: Let's remove it, huh?

JK: Well it feeds me, it brings me cans of pork and beans and stuff.

BH: Briefly, you're gonna' starve after this new book *The Drama Bums* runs its course, you're gonna' be dying from hunger. Authors never get fed, they have to beg and plead. I asked you this before: how do people get involved in your group, and is it growing? How does one qualify?

JK: Yeah, I was gonna say . . .

BH: How do you qualify as a Beat fellow?

JK: . . . it's not a *Bohemian* generation. It's like a lost generation, it contains millions of people. There were millions of bathtub gins and flappers and raccoon coats. Now there are millions of black slacks and ponytails and . . .

BH: You're ahead of those?

JK: No! I'm saying the Beat Generation . . . the Bohemian has always been with us, even in the days of Walt Whitman.

BH: That's right.

JK: There's been only a few thousand Bohemians *ever*.

BH: But usually the *Bohemian*, or the *Beat*, or the *Lost* Generation came *after* a war, and you boys seem to have beat the gun. You're *before* the next war.

JK: Was Rembrandt a Bohemian?

BH: Rembrandt? No, he was an artist and a painter.

JK: And the people that hung around him were Bohemians?

BH: Kibitzers, kibitzers.

JK: Were they Bohemians?

BH: They were maybe soft touches for a good painter that the painter lives on. Are you boys afraid of the next war? Worried about it? Do you look forward to it?

JK: I don't think there'll be one.

BH: Why not?

JK: Because things are in good hands.

BH: Do you think that if there were enough Beats who conducted a spiritual sit-down strike for civilization to be spared another war, that nobody would attend?

JK: No, that's too hysterical.

BH: You don't believe in asserting yourself?

JK: History will work its way out and everybody will come together. The whole world will come together, east and west.

BH: You think so, huh?

JK: If it doesn't come out, you can crawl up to me in a pit and . . .

BH: Who shall be the little child that leads them? Mr. Dulles?

JK: The little child will lead them in a cart drawn by two white lambs.

BH: You think God is working in us, Jack? You thinking he's working our politicians? Or does he concentrate on Beats?

JK: Maybe he'll work on Mao.

BH: Mao? What's he got to do with him? He's already a Buddhist. He hasn't got far to go with Mao.

JK: Mao is no Buddhist.

BH: What is he, a Shintoist?

JK: He used to be a Taoist poet.

BH: Who do you love, Jack? Mother, father, child, wife? Who is it you love in the world?

JK: My mother.

BH: Your mother. Thank you Jack for talking about the Beats. I'm gonna send them my dues soon as I get enough money.

The Beat Debated–
Is It or Is It Not?

Marc D. Scheifer, *Village Voice* (November 19, 1958)

This scathing attack on Kerouac's aesthetic is typical of the late-1950s attitude, still weaning from traditional forms of novel writing. Rather than participating in the debate, Kerouac chose to read his essay "Is There a Beat Generation?" thus facing the academicians and journalists with indifference, if not disdain. It was Kerouac's impression that he was brought to Hunter College Playhouse to read poetry. He would fall for the same lure from William F. Buckley in 1968. Instead of the reading Buckley asked of him, Kerouac was set up in a debate about "hippies" with a sociology professor and the prototypical "hippie."

L et the cats in!" someone shouted, while an overflow crowd of hundreds pushed against the doors barred by anxious college girls. The place was Hunter College Playhouse on November 6, where there was a debate scheduled on the theme "Is There a Beat Generation?"

Sponsor of the affair was Brandeis University, whose dean, Joseph Kauffman, peered at the audience and looked uncomfortable, glanced at guests Kingsley Amis, Ashley Montagu, James Weschler, and then looked more uncomfortable. When the evening's festivities of hoots, cheers, insults, and poetry were over, Dean Kauffman's discomfort was so great that I feared for his supper. *But he was still smiling.* And after all, isn't discomfort a small price for enlightened academicians to pay when they carry the creative process into lecture-hall operating rooms on a stretcher and then dissect it as they would a bloodless corpse?

Thoughts, somewhat excerpted, in order of their appearance:

Kerouac (dashing offstage a dozen times, clowning with a hat to the final stumble and wild dragging of poet Allen Ginsberg onstage toward the end of the "debate"):

Live your lives out, they say; nah, love your lives out, so when they come around and stone you, won't be living in any glass house—only your glassy flesh. What is called the "Beat Generation" is really a revolution in manners . . . being a swinging group of new American boys intent on life. James Dean was not the first to express this. Before him there was Bogart and the private eyes. Now college kids have started to use the words "hung up" . . . I'm hung up, you know . . . words I first heard on Times Square in the forties. Being Beat goes back to my ancestors, to the rebellious, the hungry, the weird, and the mad. To Laurel and Hardy, to Popeye, to Wimpy looking wild-eyed over hamburgers the size of which they make no more; to Lamont Cranston, the Shadow, with his mad heh-heh-heh knowing laugh. And now there are two types of beat hipsters:

the Cool, bearded, sitting without moving in cafés, with their unfriendly girls dressed in black, who say nothing; and the Hot, crazy, talkative, mad shining eyes, running from bar to bar only to be ignored by the cool subterraneans. I guess I'm still with the hot ones. When I walk into a club playing jazz, I still want to shout: "Blow, Man, Blow."

Kingsley Amis (author of *Lucky Jim*, wearing a conservative light-brown suit, perplexed by the mad audience, but in a friendly way trying to understand the madness):

There is a general impression that the Beat Generation has opened a branch in England, or at least made an alliance with a group called the Angry Young Men. Thus a Detroit critic says: "America's Angry Young Men are called the Beat Generation." Is there a group of young English writers united and unique in protesting about creative stagnation in contemporary life? No, emphatically, no. "The Angry Young Men" is an invention of literary middlemen, desperate journalists who thrive on classifications and clichés, who put writers in pigeonholes and save people the trouble of reading. This nonsense can also be traced to the Anglo-American cult of youth. In England, anybody who writes and is under pensionable age is put under the title of AYM. Any day I expect to see Boris Pasternak so labeled. Yes, Osborne is angry, that's his privilege. But all the English writers who have been so categorized are doing what writers have always done—they are going about the job of writing. There is no Angry Young Men movement. There may be a Beat Generation, but I doubt it.

James Weschler (editor of the *New York Post* and author of *Revolt on the Campus*, looking angry if not young, vigorously chewing his gum with open-mouthed liberal sincerity, staring at Kerouac with incomprehension whenever Jack mentions God, Poetry, or the Cross):

I am one of the few unreconstructed radicals of my generation. Much of what has happened in the past twenty or so years has challenged my basic beliefs, but I still adhere to them. [turning to Kerouac] Life is complicated enough without having to make it into a poem. I am convinced that ethical values will reemerge. What gives meaning to life is the survival of these values. It is a sad thing for America that this Beat Generation is supposed to represent rebellion and unorthodoxy. After listening to Kerouac, I understand less about what they stand for than before. I see no virtue in organized confusion. The Beat Generation as a symbol is sort of a joke. The issue is not whether civilization will survive. There is no valor in their [the Beats'] kind of flight and irresponsibility.

Ashley Montague (Princeton anthropologist, author of *Immortality* and *Man, the First Million Years*, white-haired, calm, slightly amused, and slightly sleepy-looking just the way the Ladies League thinks a professor should look):

James Dean symbolized the Beat Generation. His death was consistent with the BG philosophy—life is like Russian Roulette. Their only conformity is nonconformity. The Beats give personal testimony to the breakdown of Western values. These are the children who were failed by their parents. Compassion, not condemnation, is called for. The BG is the ultimate expression of a civilization whose moral values have broken down. While not everybody born in the past thirty years is Beat, and while there were Beat people born more than thirty years ago, the Beat writers are describing their generation.

The Age of Unthink

James Weschler, from *Reflections of an Angry Middle-Aged Editor*
(November 6, 1958)

O n the evening of November 6, 1958, I took part in a symposium on the Beat Generation at Hunter College. The event,
if it may be so described, was sponsored by Brandeis University; the
other participants were Jack Kerouac, author of *On the Road* and
self-proclaimed voice of the Beat Generation; Kingsley Amis, the
talented, witty, British writer who admits to being neither young nor
angry but has been so labeled on two continents; and Professor
Ashley Montagu, the noted anthropologist.

I almost missed the meeting, proving that books, like other productions, are prey to the accident of history. It occurred just two
days after the state elections of that year; I was still tired, if not beat,
and the prospect of a long evening of recitation and listening
seemed less congenial than, say, watching a basketball game at
Madison Square Garden.

But I had a certain curiosity about Kerouac, whom I had never
seen, and about the subject, which I had heard discussed with
increasing frequency and earnestness by my son (then sixteen) and
some of his friends. In fact I had begun to feel out of touch. So,

though ill-prepared to deliver a speech (and even less prepared for what happened), I reached the auditorium a few moments after Kerouac had begun what turned out to be a forty-minute rendition, and there was more than one reprise.

My first astonishment was the size of the audience. As one apparently addicted to public speech since an early age, I have grown accustomed to addressing empty seats as well as uplifted drowsy countenances. I had steeled myself for the sight of unoccupied leather. Instead, on arrival at the entrance, I discovered that this was what is known in the trade as an SRO affair, with scores of young people milling around outside the auditorium in the vain hope that the capacity of the hall would be expanded by the rhetoric inside.

Having forgotten there was a stage entrance, I proceeded at once to the main door, where a strong-minded young woman effectively barred the way. The meeting had begun, and I tried, perhaps impatiently, to tell her I was one of the scheduled performers; at first this evoked almost no reaction except massive resistance. I could not tell whether she thought I was an impostor or whether she had been intimidated by the Fire Department; anyway, after producing my press card and adopting a tone of entreaty rather than insistence, I was finally admitted.

As I walked a trifle uncomfortably down the center aisle to the stage, I got my first view of the leader of the Beat Generation. He was attired in a lumberjack shirt unadorned by tie, but there was nothing especially ostentatious about his lack of dress. A little more flabbergasting was the discovery that he was holding what proved to be a glass of brandy, and throughout the evening he made several trips to the wings for a refill. Kerouac acknowledged my arrival by observing, "You ruined my sentence," and then resumed a discourse which I am obliged to describe as a stream of semiconsciousness.

The audience was predominantly, if not exclusively, young, ranging from high-school students to college seniors, with a sprinkling of the middle-aged and the old. With due reverence for Messrs. Amis, Montagu, and myself, a large proportion of those present had obviously come to see and hear Kerouac, which, after all, explained my own belated presence too. There was plainly a bloc of the committed Beat reveling in each of his mischievous irrelevancies and with whom he used a kind of sign language mystifying to outsiders; there were also what might be called the fellow travelers of the Beat, some of whom manifested bewilderment and even impatience with the Leader by the time the evening had ended. There were also, no doubt, some who had just come for the show.

I cannot recall as large an assemblage of young people, except for the captive audiences of school assemblies, since the radical heyday of the thirties. The Beat, of course, do not carry membership cards, and one has no way of knowing how many true disciples were recruited or disaffected by Kerouac's chaotic exhibition. But the size of the turnout was extraordinary.

Having listened to a recording of the evening's proceedings and pondered a transcript, I still find myself largely out of Kerouac's reach. I am, admittedly, eight years older than he, forty-three to his thirty-five the night of the symposium at Hunter—but such a gap is not normally considered prohibitive among adults. I was on speaking terms with a lot of men some years younger than Kerouac. Moreover, I brought no instinctive hostility to the occasion (toward the end, in one of his most coherent thrusts, he cried, "You came here prepared to attack me," but in fact I had come, as previously indicated, utterly unprepared—period).

There were times when he sounded like a jaded traveling salesman telling obscene bedtime stories to the young; there were

others when the melancholy of his cadences achieved a mildly hypnotic effect, so that one listened to it as if hearing an obscure but
appealing fragment of music. There were also many intervals that
can only be described as gibberish. Thus at one point he was
chanting (and I quote from the transcript):

In fact here is a poem I've written about Harpo Marx:

Harpo, I'll always love you.
Oh Harpo, when did you seem like an angel the last and
played the gray harp of gold?
When did you steal the silverware and buckspray the guests?
When did your brother find rain in your sunny courtyard?
When did you chase your last blond across a millionaire's
lawn with a bait hook on a line protruding from your
bicycle?
Oh, when last you powderpuffed your white flower face with
a fish barrel cover?
Harpo, who is that lion I saw you with? . . .

Without questioning the place of Harpo Marxism in history, I
find little rhyme or reason in these observations, and the Leader
drooped to the dimensions of ham. The totality of his performance,
brightened as it was by flashes of imagery, was a union of madness
and sadness; by the end, the occasional vivid or moving phrase
seemed like an isolated line of poetry surrounded by vulgar ram-
blings on a latrine wall.

Kerouac is dark-haired and sturdily built (he played football for a
year for Lou Little at Columbia, and when he quit, the coach said
prophetically that the "boy was tired"). He has rather graceful gestures;

he alternates murmurs of flirtive sexuality with intimations of high piety. He deftly evokes the emotional loyalty of those who feel that they too are Beat. It is no irreverence, I trust, to say that at moments he might have been called the Billy Gloomy-Sunday of our time.

Did we ever establish any communication? I think we did; at least there is no other way I can explain the furious feeling he exhibited in the exchange that took place after the allegedly prepared recitals had occurred.

JK: . . . James Wechsler . . . Who's James Wechsler? Right over there. James Wechsler, you believe in the destruction of America, don't you?

JW: No. [The transcript added "laughter."]

JK: What do you believe in, come here, come here and tell me what you believe in . . . You told me what you don't believe in. I want to know what you do believe in. [Cries from the audience: "That's right."] This is a university, we've got to learn . . . I believe in love, I vote for love [applause].

It was rather difficult to avoid a pretentious reply:

JW: I believe in the capacity of the human intelligence to create a world in which there is love, compassion, justice, and freedom. I believe in fighting for that kind of world. I think what you are doing is to try to destroy anybody's instinct to care about this world.

JK: I believe, I believe in the dove of peace.

JW: So do I.

JK: No you don't. You're fighting with me for the dove of peace. You came here prepared to attack me.

It went on for a little while longer, and then the chairman merci-
fully explained that it was very late, and in truth it was a few minutes after ten.

There is no point in indefinitely prolonging the reportorial agony.
This was hardly a debate in which anyone could have scored the
points; I was grappling with a man in outer space, and it was only
for the briefest of intervals that we even seemed to occupy the same
mat. I shall never quite understand why he assumed I had come
there with a plot, or even why he responded so angrily to a minor
quip I made at President Eisenhower's expense, this being a time
when even Republican newspapers were ceasing to regard Eisenhower as above criticism.

Kerouac had observed, if that is the proper term:

Well, Mr. Wechsler, I was sitting under a tangerine tree in
Florida one afternoon and I was trying to translate the Diamond Sutra from Sanskrit to English and I said shall I call it
a personal god or an impersonal god, and at that moment a
little tangerine dropped out of the tree and they only drop
out of a tree about once every six weeks and landed right
square in the middle of my head. Right, boing; I said, okay,
personal god.

Somewhat testily I interjected: "I just want to say, Mr. Kerouac,
that as an editor I have to write about Dwight D. Eisenhower's press
conference every week."

JK (interrupting): He's very witty—
JW: . . . and it's possible to reduce life to an area of so little sense
     that there would hardly be any reason for all these people to have

come here tonight, or for us to be here. I don't think we render any service by doing that.

JK: Education is education.

JW: Well, as Eisenhower would say, government is government.

JK: And as Dulles would say, statesmanship is statesmanship.[20]

For that small moment we seemed like two quarreling editorial writers occupying the same planet.

Dr. Joseph Kauffman, the soft-voiced moderator, gently interpolated that "the point which Mr. Wechsler makes is one which is fairly commonly held among people who are considered activists in the sense of social and political action."

In what I must characterize as a growl, Kerouac responded: "Don't give me that stuff. I'm going out of this atmosphere."

In a sense, that is the last I saw of him.

What I had tried to say was embodied in an earlier statement that evening; since it is rather awkwardly relevant to the conception of this book, perhaps some words of it should be published here:

It is a strange thing to participate in this symposium because I guess that I am one of the few unreconstructed radicals of my generation, and much of what has happened in the last twenty and twenty-five years has challenged many of the things that I believe in deeply. Yet my basic sense about what I care about in the world, what I fight for, what I believe in, is remarkably unaltered.

I have to say to you that, with due respect to Mr. Kerouac, I see no really major point in this kind of organized confusionism . . . . To me the astonishing thing, after all these years of our time and our century which have been brutal, cruel and difficult years, is that we can still find, if I may say so, a Boris Pasternak, and he is only a name and a symbol; but that all over the world there does seem to be a sense of the survival of human values and decency which seem to me to be the only things that give meaning to life . . . .

The impressive fact is that there survives and that there recurs and is renewed among young kids all over the world the sense that there are values of decency worth fighting for and even giving one's life for.

There was a man named Felix Cohen who died when he was forty-six. He was the son of Morris Raphael Cohen and he wrote a great essay which has meant a great deal to me in my life in which he argued that the astonishing thing about our world is that, given all the travail and the turmoil and the sadness, it does seem to be true that certain ethical values do reemerge and that children grow up sensing them and understanding them.

I do not happen to be a religious man in any conventional sense but I do have the sense that what gives meaning to life is the survival of these values. And so it is that there are people all the time all over the world who, when they see cruelty and injustice and intolerance and bigotry, often risk many things to fight against these incredible conditions. Now I know there is a view that this is probably because they were dropped on their heads when they were small children. But I thought Arthur Koestler answered that point rather well when he said that if we really believed that the only people who have any decent instincts in the world are those who were dropped on their heads when they were babies, it's very hard to make any sense out of life . . . .

I think there are values that have transcended these difficult and complicated conditions of human existence. It is a
sad thing about America now that what is regarded as the
great revolt and the great representation of dissent and
unorthodoxy is what is called the Beat Generation. Because I
guess it has very little meaning to me and, after listening to its
spokesman tonight, I must say that I find myself groping in the
darkest confusion as to what the hell this is about [from audience: "Shame on you"]. [Laughter and applause.] There is the
right, thank God, for all of us to scream and shout and do anything we damn please in public. There is also, I think, the
responsibility for us to try to give to the people in our society
some sense of what matters and what is important and what
we care about.

People say so often that there are no issues any longer, that
everything was settled by the New Deal and the Fair Deal, and
that there really aren't any great differences in political life. To
some extent that's true. Yet we live in a time when there are two
things that seem to me to be worthy of everything within us.

One is the fact that there is something called the hydrogen
bomb which can make a mockery of anything we call civilization. The other is the quest for human equality which has
become the dominant and decisive issue of our lifetime in
America. So it never has seemed to me really that there is
nothing left to fight for or that there is nothing worth arguing
about in our society.

There were far better words spoken that evening by both Dr.
Amis and Professor Montagu than any recited by Kerouac or myself.
Dr. Amis suggested amiably but pointedly that there was no

genuine union between the so-called Angry Young Men of Great Britain, who had at least voiced a certain definable—and not monolithic—protest against the grayness of life, and the rambling wrecks from American Tech who had ostentatiously proclaimed themselves the Beat Generation.

Professor Montagu, perhaps because he had not been accused of being angry, perhaps because an anthropologist acquires a certain occupational patience with the eccentricities of man, spoke with the greatest compassion:

> What I am trying to say is that it is not condemnation or contempt that is called for, but compassion and understanding, that the Beat Generation is not something either to bemoan or disown but a suffering confusion of human beings crying out for sympathetic understanding. The Beat Generation represents the ultimate expression of a civilization whose moral values have broken down and in many ways, what is even worse, a civilization with little faith or conviction in the values it professes to believe [from audience: "Right!"].

> Its ideal values are one thing. But its real values—the values by which it lives—are quite another. Our ideal and our real values are in conflict. The Sermon on the Mount and the principle of competition are simply not compatible with one another. And this fact gives rise to the great hypocrisy of a society that preaches the one and lives by the other, and it gives rise, among other things, to a demoralization of the sort which results in beatniks.

> Human beings living in a society in which such mutually irreconcilable, such conflicting and false values that are dominant are likely to be confused and confusing. Those who

subscribe to such values damage not only themselves but wreak havoc upon their children, many of whom constitute members of the beat generation.

The beatniks know that there is too much that is wrong with the non-beatniks, but they are thoroughly confused as to why it is that what is wrong is wrong. Their cult of unthink is of no help, nor is resort to esoteric cults and Eastern religion.

Whatever it is they're in revolt against, we must take care that the anarchy that is so apparent in the Beat Generation is not mistaken for anything oilier than it is, namely a signal of distress, a cry for love, a refusal to accept defeat at the hands of the unloving lovers who made them what they are.

We owe a debt of gratitude to the Beat writers for so forcefully articulating what the less vocal members of this generation feel and think.

In the anarchy of the evening, these were the most generous and thoughtful phrases and they were plainly addressed to an audience beyond the gathering of the moment. They created a stillness and reserve that had been lacking throughout the previous recitations, as if even the most frenetic Kerouacians had been persuaded for the instant to think of themselves in a larger context. But I suppose there were also those who whispered to themselves and their neighbors that Professor Montagu was an amiable square who just wasn't getting enough kicks.

At the end there was the usual flurry around the platform, and I did not get a chance to talk to Kerouac again. We probably would not have had much to say to each other. I felt both very young and very old: young, in the sense that it seemed to me I found life less overwhelming than Kerouac did, and old because I knew I could not offer any simplicities comparable to his platform of raucous hedonism.In the aftermath of the Kerouac episode, what struck me most as we met was that the youngest man in this room was Arthur Schlesinger, Jr., who had just passed his fortieth birthday.

The beatnik proclaims his alienation and his irresponsibility, and his contempt for those who have the effrontery to seek to influence the affairs of men or establish order in the gone universe. But no single voice really speaks for him. Kerouac at Hunter was a caricature of the breed; on another evening in a different setting at Columbia, Allen Ginsberg (whom Kerouac had dragged onto the stage like a circus donkey the night of our meeting) recited poetry in a fashion that Diana Trilling found extraordinarily moving and intelligible and led her to feel pity rather than disdain for him and his cohorts. She added: "Whatever one's view of the poetry, the manners, the compulsive disreputableness, and the sometimes ostentatious homosexuality of those who term themselves Beat, it is perhaps most noteworthy that their form of protest is almost wholly nonpolitical, and at moments a rebellion against politics itself."

Interview with Kenneth Allsop

Kenneth Allsop, *Lilliput* (January 1959)

Kenneth Allsop (1920–1973) was the host of Britain's BBC television program, Tonight. *In America, Allsop was known for his nonfiction series,* The Bootlegger, *which detailed the United States' prohibition era. Allsop died of a drug overdose in 1973.*

T he first Beat I met in the United States grunted at the waiter for a double. Then he propped his jeaned legs on the table and sprawled back in his seat. His copper-haired chest bulged through the cleavage of his lumberjack shirt.

This was Jack Kerouac, writer, mystical bum, and prophet of America's Beat Generation. He looked it all right, but the double when it came was neither heroin nor even Scotch on the rocks. It was a double coffee ice cream with pistachio nuts.

While he shoveled in the goo and crunched the wafers, he talked about the meaning of the Movement, about Zen Buddhism, narcotics, antimaterialism, cool jazz, new sex concepts, and royalty returns. In the Seventh Avenue soda-fountain, I matched coffee with nuts with a double Rainbow, and sat back to listen to the Voice of the Beats.

"We don't correspond with your Angry Young Men," Kerouac said. "Their equivalent here is our Silent Generation, the conformist college crowd, very elegant, milquetoast creeps. You can line us up with your Teddy Boys. That's where your next great literary movement is going to come from. You'll have a great Teddy Boy literature."

"The phrase Beat Generation," he went on, "really started with [John] Clellon Holmes's novel *Go*, published back in 1952. That was about a bunch of real crazy hipsters who rushed around shouting Yes! Yes! to everything that was happening to them. That's how you gotta be. Ecstatic. Dig me?"

"The phrase didn't take hold until my *On the Road* came out. Beat doesn't mean necessarily beat-up. It may mean that. But it can also mean beatific. Beats are mystic vagrants, always penniless but not necessarily uneducated. Holmes was being supported by his wife when he wrote his book. I was being supported by my mother. I wrote it when I was twenty-nine, but it took me years to get it published. I was bumming around as a hobo, working as a seaman or a forest worker. Intermittently I'd dash down to Mexico, where a dollar's worth eight dollars, and write.

"Now things are really whirling. Everyone's taken up the phrase. *On the Road* is going into a paperback edition, which means all the high school kids will read it. That's just great. What we Beats are against is technique and efficiency. Everyone in this country is a slave to the Deepfreeze and the hi-fi. They're too rich—a kind of sinister luxury. But we Beats are in spiritual revolution. We believe in the pulse of the heart.

"It's all about putting a rucksack on your back and walking off to mountain tops and praying for the salvation of all of us. It's lots of cheap wine and lots of girls who think like you do, and living in shacks and eager discussions of poetry, and listening to Charlie Parker or Gerry Mulligan. Jazz is very important. This movement came up at the same time as rock-and-roll. I think a movement like this can affect the minds of the mass of the people, make them less afraid of one another, more joyful. It's a kind of anarchy-existentialism, not political socialism. We want to stay out of politics.

"They've said I'm a hoodlum. Actually I'm not. I'd never start a fight. I'm alone in my Buddhist-Catholic-contemporariness. I don't really want to do anything except stare at the ceiling. You know, meditate. You gotta live simply. Not consume. Everyone in America just consumes. My motto is: Love, suffer, work. I work in spurts—prepare myself, then I really go, man. I put a roll of teleprinter paper in my typewriter and type ninety words a minute."

Afterwards Rexroth, a middle-aged man in velvet jacket and string tie who has the face of a bleached Eartha Kitt, added to Kerouac's definition:

"Beats? Well, you could say we're like anonymous messengers from another planet just roaming around in the electric-razor age. One way I figure we can communicate with each other is through this poetry-jazz workout. This isn't just a gimmick for the unwashed cats and chicks on the marijuana network. We're trying to evolve a new dimension."

Kerouac on Kerouac

"Pertinax," *Lowell Sun* (April 17, 1959)

"Pertinax," the pseudonym of Mary Sampas, Kerouac's future sister-in-law, was also the title of a Lowell Sun *newspaper column. Being the wife of Charlie Sampas, who had a column of his own in the* Sun, *gave her ample opportunity to be in constant contact with Kerouac.*

I f you kept our rendezvous yesterday, Friend, you know we were entangled with what some Lowell State Teachers collegians had to say about Jack Kerouac.

Today, a scoop. What Kerouac has to say about Kerouac.

In a letter postmarked New York City, a continent away from the North Beach haunts of the generation that he himself christened "Beat," Jack denies, unequivocally, bitterly, and passionately, that he is—or ever was—of the Beat brotherhood himself. (In effect, does writing murder mysteries make Clarence Buddington Kelland a mysterious murderer?)

In his first book, our native novelist dealt kindly with Lowell in *The Town and the City*, although some portraits were certainly etched in acid. Consider now his newer work, written in 1952 when he was "in exile" in Mexico, to be published next month by Grove Press:

"It will probably be banned in Lowell, and Boston, too. It's all about my French-Canadian boyhood in Pawtucketville, touches of earlier days in Centralville, playing at Textile Field and along the banks of the Merrimack. The big flood of 1936. Strange work—the end is a phantasm in the boy's mind, whereby a hundred-mile-long snake is made to emerge from below the Castle of the World (the Centralville hump hill that you see from the bridges). All the forces of world evil are gathered there and Doctor Sax, with the help of the boy, prevents world destruction.

"It's wild . . . the first real vision in America since *Moby-Dick*. The flood river foams and lunges like a snake through my hometown. Full title is *Doctor Sax and the Great World Snake*—subtitled *Faust, Part III*. It is the completion of the Faust legend, and also a Gothic New England, with roots in Melville and Hawthorne. You'll see, in any case. It has nothing to do with the Beat Generation . . . .

"After *Sax*, I will never dare to visit Lowell again, but it is my deepest vision of the world, which, to me, was and still is Lowell. The Lowell of my mind, satisfying my need as I get older, Lowell—a kingdom and the river is central. After I go to Japan and India and everywhere, I'll wait ten years before sneaking back there, with my black slouch hat, to hear the laugh of Dr. Sax by the river.

"That one will be followed by two more books on Lowell. One, about my Centralville childhood and the death of my brother, *Visions of Gerard*. The other, my Lowell High School love affair, titled *Maggie Cassidy*."

Will Success Spoil Jack Kerouac? The handsome lad with the black-fire eyes has been enslaved almost nonstop by his typewriter, from which his manuscripts emerge in yards-long rolls of paper. Last year, he had written us that he had already completed "twenty novels, for which the world is not yet ready." He has been discussed, maligned, admired, and reviewed on several continents, but he remains bitter:

"I don't even have the money that people think I have, as the movie sale of *On the Road* was stalled by another studio coming out with a picture on the same Beat theme, so I lost out. I don't need much money for myself, but the awful abuse I have taken from some critics resulted in complete neglect of *The Dharma Bums*. I have never, personally, had anything to do with "the bearded beatniks," and I am angry now . . . .

"I go to Paris again this spring, and hope to write something beautiful about that beautiful city. When I am an old man, I'll at least have my jug of wine, and my loaf of bread, and my Lowell kingdom-of-the-mind."

He writes as he must, and scorns compromise. If Lowell will not forget, perhaps it will forgive.

Interview with Steve Allen

Steve Allen, *The Steve Allen Pontiac Show* (January 16, 1959)

The critically acclaimed NBC series The Steve Allen Pontiac Show *ran from June 24, 1956, until some time in 1960. This Sunday night show had a neck-to-neck ratings battle with Ed Sullivan's Sunday night CBS show that saw Allen in the lead one week and Sullivan ahead the next. Regulars on the* Steve Allen Show *were Tom Poston, Pam Garner, Louis Nye, Pat Harrington, Don Knotts, Dayton Allen, Gabe Dell, Skitch Henderson, and announcer Gene Rayburn. On the night of Kerouac's appearance, singer Frankie Laine and actress Pamela Garner also appeared, William Bendix spoofed* Life of Riley, *and Mr. Answers answered people's questions. Kerouac shirked his rehearsal; instead he chose to read his selection on the fly before dashing offstage and vomiting from nervousness. The text he read was a paragraph from* Visions of Cody *pasted to the front dust jacket flap of his hardcover reading copy of* On the Road.

SA: Jack told me a little earlier he was nervous. Are you nervous now?

JK: No.

SA: No? Good. Jack, I got a couple of square questions but I think the answers will be interesting. How long did it take you to write *On the Road*?

JK: Three weeks.

SA: How many?

JK: Three weeks.

SA: Three weeks? That's amazing. How long were you on the road itself?

JK: Seven years.

SA: Seven years . . . I was on the road once for three weeks and it took me seven years to write about it. It was the other way around. I've heard that you write so fast that you don't like to use regular typing paper, but instead you prefer to use one long roll of paper. Is that true?

JK: Yeah. When I write narrative novels and I want to change my narrative thought, I keep going . . . [Kerouac gestures his arm in a backward sweeping arc suggesting continuity].

SA: You don't want to change the papers at the end you mean?

JK: Foot-long teletype paper.

SA: Oh, teletype roll. Where do you get it?

JK: Huh?

SA: Where do you get the paper?

JK: Teletype paper.

SA: Where do *you* get it?

JK: In a very good stationery store.

SA: I see . . .

JK: When I write my symbolistic, serious, impressionistic novels, I write them in pencil.

SA: Oh yeah?

JK: [nods in the affirmative].

SA: I've seen a lot of your poetry written in pencil, but I didn't realize that's how you worked on the prose stuff.

JK: For the narrative it's good.

SA: I got the most hard question of all, but everybody always puts it to you, I'm sure, *because* everybody always puts it to you. How would you define the word "Beat"?

JK: Well, sympathetic.

SA: Sympathetic? Alright, I asked. Well, about this point, naturally, we planned to have Jack read some poetry, and while looking again [Allen picks up and opens a hardcover edition of *On the Road*] through his book the other day, it struck me, it occurred to me all over again, that his prose is extremely poetic. I think it's probably more poetic than . . . who else writes poetic-type prose? Thomas Wolfe I guess.

JK: Walt Whitman.

SA: Uh-huh [laughs].

JK: [seriously] His *Specimen Days*. Walt Whitman's *Specimen Days*.

SA: I see, I thought you were putting me on there.

JK: No, no . . .

SA: Alright, we'll look into that. And right now we'll look into Jack Kerouac's *On the Road*, and he'll lay a little on you and then maybe you'll buy these pages. Want to try it? [Allen hands Kerouac the book]. I'll play the blues like we did in the thing and see how it works out.

[Kerouac proceeds to read a lengthy excerpt merging *Visions of Cody* and the closing paragraph of *On the Road* together as one text].

The Great Rememberer

John Clellon Holmes, from *Gone in October: Last Reflections on Jack Kerouac* (Limberlost Press, 1985)

A great rememberer redeeming life from darkness": thus Kerouac, self-described. But he is, as well, an American phenomenon as indigenous as a gas station in the Grand Canyon: the athlete-artist, the tramp transcendentalist, the renowned recluse. And despite all the public nonsense about "the King of the Beats," he remains as unique, primal, and obscure as Niagara Falls, which has been looked at so often it can no longer be seen.

Though he has already created a larger body of work than any of his contemporaries, to most people his name summons up the image of a carefree do-nothing sensation-hunter. Though that body of work creates a dense, personal world that is as richly detailed as any such American literary world since Faulkner, he is continually thought to be nothing but the poet of the pads and the bard of bebop. And though he is a prose innovator in the tradition of Joyce, whose stylistic experiments will bear comparison with any but the most radical avant-gardists of the century, he is constantly ticketed as some slangy, hitchhiking Jack London, bringing a whiff of marijuana and truck exhaust into the lending libraries. In short, the kind of writer that only America could produce and that only America could so willfully misunderstand. One has only to remember Melville, "the writer of boys' sea stories," and Whitman, "the author of 'O Captain My Captain,'" to recognize what legacy of national neglect Kerouac has fallen heir to. For ours is a benevolent society. Not for us to doom our Mark Twains to a garret. No, instead we praise them as vaudevillians and later wonder why they gnashed their teeth.

The life "redeemed from darkness," which Kerouac's books describe, is nothing less than the whole of his *actual* life, and if the man (and it's the man I am concerned with here) can be approached through the work, it is primarily because that work is not so much concerned with events as it is with consciousness, in which the *ultimate* events are images. A montage of that consciousness might unreel like this:

Redbrick alleys of New England. Brown 1930s suppertimes. Loam-rank cellars full of shadows. The boom of sneakers on trackmeet boards. Love's choked throat under the wheeling prom lights. Times Square wartime bars. Hip sneers in neon flicker. October intersections, Butte midnights, Denver glooms. The awesome prairie from a fatalistic truck. Generation parties whooped on beer. Wino flophouse mattresses. Lost reds of twilight on Mexico adobe walls. A junkie's crucifix. Intersections, further intersections. Pacific immensities by the kerosene cabin. Mad hobos of rainy Susquehannas. Then all of it again. Intersections, lofts, bars, woodsy musings. Until God is no more a superstition, and Truth lies in the Buddha' blessed emptiness, and our portion is to moan for man, and meanwhile wait.

That is the burden of the consciousness that invests Kerouac's books (sixteen so far), and to read them straight through leaves you exhausted, bowed down, baffled, roused, depressed, exulted, riled, amused, but above all *silenced*—silenced by that immensity of distance and that eternity of time, which most religious visions and all hallucinogenic drugs hint at as the true nature of Reality. An odd emotion stirs in your throat, the emotion you would experience if, from some great height, you saw a lone figure walking across an empty plain in the dusk. A pang of creatureliness, intensified by awe, would reconcile you at the exact moment that it saddened. Or as Kerouac puts it, daring to use those orphaned accents that actually murmur behind most modern bravado:

I'm writing this book because we're all going to die—In the loneliness of my life, my father dead, my brother dead, my mother far away, my sister and my wife far away, nothing here but my own tragic hands that were once guarded by a world, a sweet attention, that now are left to guide and disappear their own way into the common dark of all our death, sleeping in me raw bed, alone and stupid: with just this one pride and consolation: my heart broke in the general despair, and opened up inwards to the Lord, I made a supplication in this dream.

That paragraph could stand as the key to the man. But what sort of man is he? Though few modern writers have embedded themselves more solidly in their books, there is far more to Kerouac than the books suggest, and I have to admit to the difficulties of my writing about him, so much is my adult life entangled in our friendship.

He has awed me with his talents, enraged me with his stubbornness, educated me in my craft, hurt me through indifference, dogged my imagination, upset most of my notions, and generally enlarged me as a writer more than anyone else I know. We have wrangled, and yelled, and boozed, and disliked, and been fond of one another for almost twenty years. He has figured in my books, sometimes directly on the page, but most often standing just off it; and I appear here and there in his, under various names, though usually as a snide, more fortunate, migraine-headache intellectual who borrows his ideas, makes money from his perceptions, and is always trying to involve him in stifling ego dramas. And yet only one part of his complicated nature thinks of me this way. For the rest of it, we are curiously close. We represent something to one another: everything we are *not* ourselves.

Our minds, which work in opposite ways, have never been entirely compatible. He is freely contradictory, I tend to be trapped by my own consistencies; he absorbs, I analyze; he is intuitive, I am still mostly cerebral; he muses, I worry; he looks for the perfection in others and finds existence flawed; I am drawn *toward* the flaw and believe in life's perfectibility. But there is and was from the beginning a real and generous affection between us, based on a peculiar sense of kinship—puzzling, maddening, indescribable—that has made our relationship oddly fateful for both of us. For his part of it, I think he believes my heart is in the right place, but I bore him after a while. For me, what follows may suggest a little of what he has meant to me.

We became friends more quickly than I have ever become friends with anyone else. Everything about him was engaging in those days. He was openhearted, impulsive, candid, and very handsome. He didn't seem like any other writer that I knew. He wasn't wary, opinionated, cynical, or competitive, and if I hadn't already known him by reputation, I would have pegged him as a poetic lumberjack or a sailor with Shakespeare in his sea locker. Melville armed with the manuscript of *Typee* must have struck the Boston Brahmins in much the same way. Stocky, medium-tall, Kerouac had the tendoned forearms, heavily muscled thighs, and broad neck of a man who exults in his physical life. His face was black-browed and firm-nosed, with the expressive curve of lip and the blue, somehow tender eyes that move you so in a loyal, sensitive animal. But it was the purity in that face, scowl or smile, that struck you first. You realized that the emotions surfaced on it unimpeded. Mothers warmed to him immediately: they thought him nice, respectful, even shy. Girls inspected him, their gazes snagged by those bony Breton good looks, that ingathered aura of dense, somehow *buried* maleness.

He was moody; there were always weathers in his soul. You would see the clouds pass over his sun; you would see the light go out of his face; he would become dismal as November and sit there with an odd heaviness about him, saying only the perfunctory least, ungiving, dour beyond help of a joke, as gloomy as an old New England house on a rainy afternoon. But, when it came, his smile was as dewy, radiant, and optimistic as the first hour of sun on a May morning. He beamed with an irresistible belief in the equity of things, laughing at himself under his breath, playful, warm and giving off warmth, his mind flowing impetuously out of his mouth, his eyes flashing with humors: everything about him exuded his pleasure in you, simply because you were there.

Above all, he had that quality of charisma, presence, undivided flow of being that is neither character nor charm but something more elusive and more rare: call it certainty, or demon; call it a hint of the integrity of the soul that some people give off like an aroma. Lawrence had it, they say. Love him or hate him, he was always *there*—as a cataract is there, or a snake. Kerouac had it too. You always felt the strong pull of his special view of the world. The uniqueness of his ego was magnetic. He was as genuine as a hand-crafted weather vane—one of a kind, continually veering in the wind. Such people can be as exhausting as they are fascinating, and this is not because they live at a different pitch but because they *always* live at it. Still, this quality of thereness is hard to resist, and I responded to it in Kerouac as you respond to a recognition which you do not realize you have been awaiting until it comes. For I had been waiting, and was more dissatisfied with the attitudinizing of most of my other friends than I knew. I opened up his exuberance without a moment's thought.

And meanwhile I read his novel alone one night at Alan Har-rington's dim, lofty room on East 60th Street (mysteriously full of old newspapers), reaching into that yawning black bag for the suc-ceeding notebooks, all of different sizes and all filled to the margins with that angular, flowing rush of print that is his handwriting. I read on for hours, enthralled as only fiction, moving deeply and surely toward the achievement of its imagined world, can ever enthrall the reader. I was drawn down into the book, as you are drawn into a volume of Thackeray, or Dickens, or any of those huge, life-size novels of the nineteenth century that simply burst with innumerable, fascinating events—for *The Town and the City* was just such a crowded, essentially idealistic chronicle of many people living furiously, despite the sorrow that tinged its end.

Amazed by the energy of the book, I was also secretly relieved to discover (being an overly critical young man just then, unsure of his own creative gifts) that it wasn't really *contemporary* in the fashion-able sense of that term—not soured, anxious, existential, or Euro-peanized, and thus "posed no threat" to the bleakly allegorical novels the rest of us were trying to write. This foolishness was, of course, mainly a sop to my sophomoric preconceptions of the time, which, once thrown, freed me to the excitement that flowed out of the book like rainwater from a spout. Similarly conflicting reactions on the part of the people who should know better still haunt most of the reviews of Kerouac's work with the unspoken complaint: "Why isn't he something other than what he is?"

But more than the work, it was the man who attracted me. He was sympathetic, changeable, unsophisticated, quixotic, canny, and madly imaginative. Whenever we were together, we always seemed to end up at dawn on a street corner somewhere, still talking. He was at ease in all the myriad worlds outside my stuffy, bookish rooms and was already absorbed in capturing, or being captured by, the vision of our generation that would become uniquely his. In little more than two months after our meeting, we were close enough friends for him to entrust his work journals to my eye.

I responded instinctively to the Kerouac I encountered there: the Kerouac who noted down each day's hoard of completed words, and then figured up his overall batting average; who zealously recorded his slumps along with his streaks, and just as zealously pep-talked or remonstrated with himself; the Kerouac, dizzied by the odors of the spring but chained in solitude by the mad endeavor that is the writing of a novel, who actually tried, with frustrated defiance, to *screw* the earth one night, to simply thumb-hole into the loam, and mate with it, so that he could get on with the task; the Kerouac who wanted to blow a lot of Spenglerian wind into the sails of a book that was already under full canvas on its own; who, in those doldrums of midpassage, those horse latitudes that one reaches in the second half of a long, exhausting project, wondered pensively whether his book was "intellectually substantial," after all, but who, nevertheless, could write at the end:

Sept. 9. Tonight I finished and typed the last chapter. Last sentence of the novel: "There were whoops and greetings and kisses and then everybody had supper in the kitchen." Do you mean the folks of this country won't like this last chapter? Or would it have been better if I had said, "Everybody had dinner in the dining room . . . ." But the work is finished.

In these journals, I saw the very work problems that were defeating me shouldered toward solutions; I saw my own confusion about the times spelled out, grappled with, forced to its crisis, and clarified in the art of fiction; and, above all, I saw a man, no more fortunate on the surface of it than myself, tirelessly clutching at his special truth as any writer must.

When I had finished the last notebook, I felt an emotion unfamiliar enough in me to demand immediate expression, and longed to call him up (though he had no phone, just then, in Ozone Park), for I was filled with prideful idealism in our common craft; a keener sense of what must be given to it than I had ever had before; admiration for the stubborn, tender, lonesome, angry spirit that spoke from those pages; and something else I neither knew how to recognize nor handle: something almost familial, as if in this account of his consciousness my own had recognized a still-unexpressed fragment of itself; as if the impulsive reflex in him, and the wary reflex in me, were responses to an identical feeling about the world; as if he was an older, wilder brother, utterly unlike me, but sharing the same blood, shaped by the same life in the same house, and embodying the other half of a strong and ambivalent family trait. I wrote him a long, meandering letter, trying to tell him this, but lost the feeling in chagrin.

I mark that night as the start of the curious interaction between

my nature and his. I mark it, as well, as the night when I began to be
a writer in all seriousness. For something had been summoned out of
me: I had glimpsed the potentials and the costs of the vocation; I had
been articulated what was still inchoate in my own mouth; I had
taken a first step outwards by acknowledging (against my own timidi-
ties) that this man's view of the task was a view through which I
might somehow come into my own best self as a writer.

In one of Kerouac's books, "Duluoz" writes to "Cody" that he is
"haunted in the mind by you (think what that means, try it reverse,
say, supposing you referred all your sensations to somebody and
wondered what they thought . . . supposing each time you heard a
delightfully original idea . . . you immediately slapped it over to
check with the CODY THING)." For some years, I did just this with
Kerouac, checking my ideas, my perceptions, my emotions, and
even my braver sentences with the Kerouac, uncannily astute and
inexhaustibly creative, who always looked over my shoulder in my
imagination. Every young writer has a catalyst, and he was mine.

Later, his vision and his style would prove as contagious to others
as they did to me during those apprentice years. Later, he would be
parroted with a literalness that was anything but flattering. What *I*
got from him, however, was not a voice, but an eye. "Reality is details,"
he would say, and you cut so close to the bone of the detail as words
would go. A decrepit bureau was infinitely creakier, and emptier, and
older than an ancient one. Rueful was sadness plus regret. Punctua-
tion was the movie-music of prose. Form should be poetically satisfying rather than mechanically demonstrable. And ultimately the
writer's task was to write the book that he, himself, would most want
to read, and to amass "a daily heap of words" toward that end. Beyond
those rudiments, I tried to develop his instinct for the moment when
gravity becomes pretension, and emotion turned to sentiment.

"Always pull back," he would suggest, "and see how silly it all must look to God."

Once I gave him a chapter of which I was very proud at the time, an intensely Dostoyevskian confrontation between two over-wrought young men, each of whom finally expresses a truth about himself which the other fails to notice. I was worried about the ending of this chapter because, no matter how I rewrote it, I couldn't seem to erase the tone of false solemnity that turned it ludicrous. Kerouac read the last paragraph several times—impatiently, almost indifferently—and then scribbled down the simple exclamation "Goodness me!" as the final comment by the weariest of the two. "That's what he'd say . . . . See, now he retreats, he feels embarrassed, he sees how funny they are, talking like a couple of Raskolnikovs that way." It was precisely the right note, it restored the perspective in a flash, and this kind of warm canniness, this eye for the sad nonsense of life, has gone mostly unnoticed by Kerouac's critics (busily reacting to his material, as most of them are), but it is an essential part of his view, because his compassionate interest in humankind is grounded, at the bottom, in a fond awareness of its follies.

But if my writing was under his spell in those days (the four years difference in our ages put me four years behind him in experience and skill), my life was not. Though our New England backgrounds were somewhat similar, we were drawn in different directions. I was married, and rooted in New York. I was ambitious for fame and money, and had not yet come upon my own themes. Kerouac, on the other hand, was trying to find a fate to which he could consign himself. He was trying to make soul-choice, for once and all, between the cozy nest of love and work the boy he had once been longed to build (particularly when in revulsion against cities, and city-centerlessness), and the Wild Road of freedom and possibility to which the man he was becoming was so powerfully attracted.

These were the years of his obsession with Neal Cassady (the "Cody" of the books); the Neal he had met a few years earlier, whose raw energies drew Kerouac back and forth across the continent time and time again; in whom he invested for a while all his deep, and deeply thwarted, fraternal emotions; and from whose vagabond joys and woes he created his most vivid portrait of the young, rootless America, high on life. For in the "Cody" books, Kerouac expresses most clearly his vision of America, "an Egyptian land" at once cruel and tender, petty and immense; and in "Cody" himself, he embodies both the promise of America's oldest dream (the unbuttoned soul venturing toward a reconciliation of its contradictions) and the bitter fact of its contemporary debauching (the obscenely blinking police car that questions anyone "moving independently of gasoline, power, Army or police"). As Americans always have, Kerouac hankered for the West, for western health and openness of spirit, for the imme-morial dream of freedom, joy, communion, and Oriental Oneness that even Concord-bound Thoreau always sauntered toward, and his peevish indictments of New York (and New Yorkishness) were symp-tomatic of his feeling that a certain reckless idealism, a special ven-turesomeness of heart, had been outlawed to the margins of American life in his time. His most persistent desire in those days was to chron-icle what has happened in those margins.

But he was not always of one mind. Once, leaving my apartment with two Negro hipsters at dawn, off again across "all that," he glanced ruefully at my crowded bookshelves, my littered desk, the copy of *Doctor Faustus* I had been reading when he'd rung the bell hours before to say good-bye (all the conventional props of the author's room), and said with plaintive earnestness: "When I come back this time, I'm going to settle down for a while . . . you know, and read everything again. Like this Thomas Mann, for instance . . . . You'll see, John. That's just what I'll do." Then he went away, somehow reluctant to depart (I felt), as if he was already living ahead into all the sore-foot, dispiriting complications of penniless travel (for he never romanticized it, and always spoke of "the essential shame of hitchhiking"), half wondering, in the very moment of setting out, *why* in God's name he was doing it. But though he hesitated (and I always fancied that I saw the horror of being stranded for long from the roaming, searching side of his nature, and the shifting tensions in his books result from the balancing nature of these ambivalences.

As a passionate believer in his talent, I felt that his ceaseless wandering was only putting off his "proper" work. I was always adjuring him to sit in one place long enough to write another *Town and City*; I lectured him about responsibility; I pelted him with letters detailing *my* vision of the books he should be writing. For a time, my surprising empathy for him deluded me into thinking that I knew him better than he knew himself, and I squirmed with querulous concern every time he came back from another harrowing jaunt to Mexico, his face haggard, his spirit somehow stretched taut, his feet unfeeling in his battered shoes—for all like a man staggering away from a debauch. I never fully understood the hunger that was gnawing in him then, and didn't realize the extent to which the breakup of his Lowell home, the chaos of the war years and the death of his father, had left him disrupted, anchorless; a deeply traditional nature thrown out of kilter, and thus enormously sensitive to anything uprooted, bereft, helpless, or persevering: a nature intent on righting itself through the creative act. But though I was often mystified by the unfoldings in his work during those years, I knew that his temperament was entirely too obstinate, too unique, and too driven to be corralled by anyone. He simply had to dowse wherever his forked stick led him, no matter how parched the acre seemed. And somehow he always found a spring.

But that spring was in himself, not (as I thought) in the outside world he seemed intent on swallowing in a single, Gargantuan gulp; and tapping it was not (as most people still think to this day) simply a matter of sinking down a pipe and letting the water gush. When off the road in those days, he was mostly trying to write *On the Road*, finding, through all his successive attempts, that the traditional, "novelistic" form of *The Town and the City* was not fluid enough to contain the formlessness of the experience he was attempting to set down. "It's all an overlay," he kept insisting stubbornly. "It's added on afterwards. That isn't the truth . . . . I want deep form, poetic form—the way the consciousness *really* digs everything that happens."

When he came by on the late afternoons, he usually had new scenes with him, but his characters never seemed to get very far beyond the many-layered New York milieu a well-made novel seemed to demand as a contrast to all the footloose uprootedness to come. He wrote long, intricate, Melvillean sentences that unwound adroitly through a dense maze of clauses; astonishing sentences that were obsessed with simultaneously depicting the crumb on the plate, the plate on the table, the table in the house, and the house in the world, but which (to him) always got stalled in the traffic jam of their own rhetoric. To me, on the contrary, the writing was the acme of brilliance—cadenced, powerful, cresting toward an imminent beach, and I could never understand why it dissatisfied him so. I would have given anything I owned to have written such tidal prose, and yet he threw it out and began again, and failed again, and grew moody and perplexed.

Then one day (he was married at the time, living in a large, pleasant room in Chelsea, doing book synopses for 20th Century Fox, and more remote from the road than I had ever known him), he announced irritably: "You know what I'm going to do? I'm going to get me a roll of shelf paper, feed it into the typewriter, and just write it down as fast as I can, exactly as it happened, all in a rush, the hell with these phony architectures—and worry about it later."

Though anything I wrote off the top of my head was only fit to wipe shoes on, this method of composition sounded like good therapy at least, and when I visited him a few days after that, I heard his typewriter (as I came up the stairs) clattering away without pause, and watched, with some incredulity, as he unrolled the manuscript thirty feet beyond the machine in search of a choice passage. Two and a half weeks later, I read the finished book, which had become a scroll three inches thick made up of one single-spaced, unbroken paragraph 120 feet long, and knew immediately that it was the best thing that he had done.

It was not another *Town and City*. The warmth, the hope, the youthful melancholy of that book had darkened, toughened, and matured. The eager chronicler of family suppers had become the fatalistic shambler after a carfull of horizon chasers, and the lyrical, Wolfean tone had grown as urgent and discordant as the times. Though I loved the book, though it awed me, though I felt as protective about it as if it had been my own (and later helped a little with getting it to sympathetic eyes), it disturbed me too, for in it I caught my first glimpse of the Kerouac to come, a Kerouac for whom I was oddly unprepared: a lonely, self-communing, mind-stormed man—still devout, though in a ruin of faiths; persistently celebrating whatever flower had managed to survive our bitter, urban weeds; indefatigable of eye and fumy of mind; haunted by a reflex of love in the very pit of rude sensation; and, above all, hankering—hankering for an end: for truth to finally end the relativism, for harmony to somehow end the violence, so that peace would come to the young of this era, who were the heirs of both—and, failing that, for death. Something murmured behind the reckless onrush of the prose. It wasn't quite audible, but it accounted for the note of distant, fleeting sibilance that reverberated within the book's headlong syncopations. And for the first time, I suspected that underneath his youthful energy and jubilant thirst for life, this man was immeasurably old in his soul.

It is difficult to articulate, but as the years have passed he has seemed more and more an old spirit to me; folk-old, poet-old, not of this world; like a ragged, tipsy old Li Po, thrashing around down there in the river marshes, muttering verses to himself by his fire of twigs in the dusk, allowing reality to pass through him unobstructed, writing messages back from solitude. Perhaps this is why his evocation of every gas tank, rail yard, skid row, and street corner that he has ever seen is so hallucinatory, so charged with feeling, and yet so strangely muted by the perspective of our common destination. In any case, it has always struck me as curious that no one hears the old man's garrulity, nostalgia, sense-pleasure, stubbornness, and resignation behind his work, because in a special corner of his mind he always appears as an old vagabond going West alone.

I think I first spied this inmost Kerouac in *On the Road*, but he did not come into view until that book failed to find a publisher, despite the lionizing, evenings at the opera, and good reviews that had greeted *Town and City*, and Kerouac's hopes for a quick career seemed to vanish (as surely as Dreiser's did when *Sister Carrie* was suppressed by the very house that printed it), and there was nothing left for him to do except consign himself, without a lifeline, to that "huge, complicated inland sea they call America," to sink into despondency, like Dreiser, or somehow swim.

Swim he did, though from the shore his efforts sometimes looked like the flailings that help to drown a drowning man. He took a deep plunge into the continent (and himself), a plunge that lasted almost five years, during which he regularly surfaced in San Francisco (for work on the railroad), Mexico City (for writing and kicks), and New York (for the quiet days and drowsing nights of home life with his mother). Stubbornly, he kept writing during this impoverished time. Ironically, he came into full and unique voice precisely during this half-decade of anonymity. Paradoxically, it constituted the most fruitful period of his life—a period of explosive creativity (an average of two books every twelve months) that is perhaps unequaled in contemporary American literature, except by the four years during which Faulkner wrote *The Sound and the Fury, As I Lay Dying, Sanctuary*, and *Light in August.*

I saw less of him during those years, but his letters were absorbed in the struggle to throw his net wide enough to snare the feverish vision of his own life that was maturing in his imagination:

When I get to be so pure you won't be able to bear the thought of my death on a starry night (right now I've nothing to do with stars, I've lied of it, in every conceivable mask) and yet digress from that to my lyric-alto knowing of this land . . . a deep-form bringing together of two ultimate and at-present-conflicting streaks in me. (July 14, 1951)

This feeling that he had "lied so far" had driven him to write *On the Road* as he did; rejection of the book by the publishers made it seem that there was no one to write for but himself, and little sense in writing "novels" that were not wanted anyway; and so he proceeded to dismantle all his hard-learned "artistries," seeking to free the whole range of his consciousness to the page—the consciousness that was one continuous, vivid flow of sense-data, associations, memories, and meditations—until by the spring of 1952, he could write to me exultantly:

> What I'm beginning to discover now is something beyond the novel and beyond the arbitrary confines of the story . . . into realms of revealed Picture . . . *wild form*, man, wild form. Wild form's the only form holds what I have to say—my mind is exploding to say something about every image and every memory . . . . I have an irrational lust to set down everything I know . . . at this time in my life I'm making myself sick to find the wild form that can grow in my wild heart . . . because now I KNOW MY HEART DOES GROW.

Though I didn't always comprehend what he was driving at, I always encouraged him (as did all his friends), because there was simply no distrusting a man who burned as purely as he was burning then.

The letters kept arriving—tortured, angry, pensive, triumphant, bitter with complaints, insistently creative; letters from west coast Mexico, from L.A. slums, from rusty tankers and Washington State lumber towns; letters that traced (for me) the progress of a man gradually sinking out of sight, down into the darks of life and Self, below "literature," beyond the range of its timid firelight. Manuscripts kept arriving too, sent haphazardly across thousands of miles of road, wrapped in brown paper bags, unregistered, uninsured, often with no carbon copy at the other end in case of loss.

I read them eagerly. I read each one at a single sitting. And I
always had the same reaction. I was overcome each time by a
strange mixture of exhilaration and depression. Some linchpin had
been pulled in these books, some floodgate had been opened, and
Kerouac wrote like a man unhinged by his own prescience, as helpless as someone under LSD to control the movement of his consciousness backward and forward over his life. I imagined him (a
lightning typist since his youth) sitting at the machine, staring into
the blankness of the space in front of him, careful not to will anything, and simply recording the "movie" unreeling in his mind.
Somehow the words were no longer words, but had become things.
Somehow an open circuit of feeling had been established between
his awareness and its object of the moment, and the result was as
startling as being trapped in another man's eyes.

For me, reading those books was like recklessly diving through a
surf you have underestimated. At first, the green shimmer of the sub-
terranean world beneath the waves intoxicates you with the daring
of your own species; then all at once the power and the reality of
the element in which you are trespassing comes home to you, and
for one moment the danger and the joy are so absolutely intermin-
gled that something in you shrinks back from Kerouac's books. I
feared for his mind out there, and sometimes for my own. His eye
was like a fine membrane vibrating between the intolerable pressure
of two walls of water: the consciousness flowing outward to absorb
everything in the drench of thought; and reality flooding inward to
drown everything but the language to describe it. My eerie sense of
kinship with him gave his work a reality for me that always seemed
to overwhelm my own life for a while.

This curious reaction was intensified by my hope that he would
write something that would earn him a settled life. But every new

book he sent me seemed to beat more obstinately against the literary currents of the time, and I found myself in a paradox that was distinctly uncomfortable for a serious man: so passionately did I long for his work to be given the recognition it deserved that sometimes I caught myself wishing he would blunt the edge of it a little toward that end. Also, I must confess, I did not always have the courage of my own tastes. I remember, for instance, reading *Visions of Cody* one muggy afternoon and then going out to walk by the East River, cursing Kerouac in my head for writing so well in a book which, I was firmly convinced, would never be published. To this day, whenever I grow complacent about my own good sense, I recall that river walk. I recall that I cursed *him*, rather than the publishers, or the critics, or the culture itself that was excluding him. Some years later, I reread *Cody* with a feeling of amazement at my own confusion that was fully as great as my shame, for it was immediately apparent that it contained prose of an eloquence that was Elizabethan, in an accent that was indelibly that of our postwar generation.

Notoriety came suddenly in 1957, and with it money, adulation, TV appearances, interviews, scandals, and another sort of crucible (the crucible of the public eye) than any Kerouac had survived already. That notoriety was mostly based on *On the Road*, a book six years old, written by a man he was only second cousin to any longer, and yet people invariably looked at him, spoke to him, and deferred to him as if he *was* that other man, for the Beat Generation was news by then, and Kerouac (they thought) *was* the Beat Generation.

They tended to drive their cars more recklessly when he was with them, as if he was "Dean Moriarty," and not the Kerouac who hated to drive and whom I once saw crouching on the floor of a car in a panic during a drunken, six-hour dash from New York to Provincetown. They plied him with drinks, they created parties around him, they doubled the disorder in the hopes of catching his eye, and so never glimpsed the Kerouac who once confessed to me: "You know what I'm thinking when I'm in the midst of all *that*—the uproar, the boozing, the wildness? I'm always thinking: What am I doing here? Is this the way I'm supposed to feel?" They peeked at him as if he was the Petronius Arbiter of cool, detached hipness, and saw, to their confusion, a man who always turned the volume up, who tapped his feet and exulted, and loathed the hostility for which cool-ness was a mask. They saw the seeker after continuity who, no matter how rootless his life may seem, has always known that our anguish is uprootedness. Wherever he went, he was confronted by that other man. Once in L.A., alone in a coffeehouse, he tried to strike up a conversation with the guy behind the counter, saying, "Hey, I'm Jack Kerouac. Let's have a talk or something," to which the guy replied, with hip disdain: "Sure you are, they all say that." A few such encounters produce the bizarre feeling that one is invisible, and there were many such.

On top of this, he heard his writing praised as "rollicking" or damned as "typing," knowing that both opinions were probably based on a reading of no more than *On the Road*—in some ways his most carelessly written work. *Doctor Sax, Cody, Tristessa, Lonesome Trav-eler*—all the books in which his voice is most assured and his vision clearest—were either dismissed or ignored, because they did not easily jibe with the image of the adolescent, kicks-hungry yawper that has dogged Kerouac's career as relentlessly as the image of the South Sea Island tale-teller dogged Melville's. He saw the Buddhist reverence for all sentient life, which months alone on mountaintops and years in the glut of cities had only reinforced in him, repeatedly labeled "gibberish" and "nonsense" by men who relegated "reverence," without a qualm, to the religion shelves of their libraries and then called *him* uneducated. And the man who wrote me fifteen years ago, "Life is drenched in spirit; it rains spirit; we would suffer were it not so" (and believes it still), lived to see the books which embodied this credo on page after page used as bibles of hipness by the beatniks, derided as incoherent mouthings by the critics, and treated as some kind of literary equivalent of rock 'n' roll by the mass media.

The years went by; the books appeared one by one; he moved ceaselessly back and forth between Long Island and Florida; and he went on writing just the same.

In 1960, it became a mystery to me why he did it: he seemed to carc less and less about things like "career" and "reputation." All of a sudden, I couldn't understand any longer what made him continue. I remembered Melville (the American writer Kerouac most resembles in temperament); I remembered that something had abandoned Melville in midlife—some unexamined faith, some fruitful illusion, which had cohered in him long enough for the early novels to get written. I remembered, as well, that Hawthorne, sensing its absence in 1856, had sadly reported that Melville had "pretty much made up his mind to be annihilated." And suddenly I felt, with a shiver, that Kerouac would not live much beyond forty. Such voracious appetites, such psychic vulnerability, such singleness of purpose, must (I felt) ream a man out at the end, and the Kerouac I knew was as incapable of turning away from his own consuming consciousness as he was of living for long once he had been burned out by it. Still (I told myself), eight years after Hawthorne's insight, he himself was dead of the very abandonment he had felt in the other man, while Melville, living on into that quiet obscurity that comes to men who have passed through themselves, turned as naturally to poetry as aging men turn to gardening. Perhaps with Kerouac it would be the same.

Whenever we got together, however, I was not so sure. We always seemed to sit and drink—sometimes for a week. In the beginning, we would sit and talk and talk and talk, but then we would grow strangely silent, as if there was no more need to say certain things. During these silences, I caught myself looking at Kerouac, as you look at all tremendously gifted, tremendously complicated men, wondering where in God's name the damned vision comes from.

I saw a man, often quarrelsome, sometimes prone to silly class resentments, as defensive as a coyote on the scent, and as intractable as a horse that will not take a saddle; a man who sometimes seemed positively crazed by the upheavals in his own psyche, whose life was painfully wretched between the desire to know, for once and all, just *who* he was, and the equally powerful desire to become immolated in a Reality beyond himself. I saw a man who (for as long as I had known him) had undeviatingly pursued his vision of the dislocations and attritions of his generation's experience "in great America," undeterred by failure or despair, so selflessly enlisted in its service that the man and the vision were inseparable; the process by which one fed the other (and vice versa) too organic and too mysterious to comprehend, and the only word inclusive enough to contain the full range of all the gifts, and all the flaws, that vague word, "genius." Looking at Kerouac, I realized he was the single writer I had ever known for whom no other word would do. And yet I could not shake off the premonition that he would vanish suddenly.

Then one day an odd thing happened. A few miles up a bad stretch of road, imperiled by an autumn flood, a few years ago, I drove into Marquette, Iowa, under the bleak Mississippi palisades, in a dismal rain, and there, at the end of the street, saw Burke's Hotel—grimy, plain as coffee grounds, soot-enlayered, in need of paint, redolent of iron bedsteads, damp sheets, forlorn unopened Gideons, smoke-blackened paneling in the shadowy lobby, and corrugated tin ceilings of 1930s cobwebs. There it was, decrepit as a bureau under the forbidding, wild escarpment in the river drizzle, with its steamy lunchroom full of greasy smells, and its barbershop of rusty fans: an end-of-the-road hotel marooned in that rainy Saturday afternoon, in that town of woeful beer taverns and hardware stores—the huge bluffs of the awesome river looming over it.

Instantly, I thought of Kerouac, for the place was quintessentially *his* America, the America he knows down to its last stained mattress ticking and its final broken bottle in the railroad weeds; the America he taught me how to see, full of the anxious faces in which his eye had spied an older, more rooted America (of spittoons, and guffawing, and winter suppers), now vanishing bewilderedly behind the billboards and TV antennas; an America whose youths stand around on the street corners, undecided, caught in the discrepancy between the wild longings they feel and the tame life they get; a land (now in its sour time) which Kerouac goes on evoking in the accents most native to it: "I loved the blue dawns over racetracks and made a bet Ioway was sweet like its name, my heart went out to lonely sounds in the misty springtime night of wild sweet America in her powers, the wetness of the wire fence bugled me to belief. I stood on sandpiles with an open soul." (There's all our uprootedness in that, and all our hungering for roots—what another American writer called our "complex fate": even truer of us now, in a century severed from its faiths).

The special Kerouac-mood was on that town, and, as I waited for the stoplight, realizing again how eloquently he has spoken for the pang of being young in America in this time, I imagined him there in Burke's Hotel, having a coffee behind the blurred plate glass, baseball-hatted and crepe-soled for the road, weary and intent, something spectral and unnoticed about him down the counter there as the waitress gossiped—passing through, years ago, toward the promise of another coast.

I caught myself thinking: he has given this way of seeing to all of us. Then I missed him keenly, and knew for sure he would survive.

St. Jack
(annotated by Jack Kerouac)

Al Aronowitz, *New York Post* (March 30, 1959)

He was dressed in one of those heavy, flannel work shirts, tails hanging loose, that he always seems to wear on the jackets of his books and that makes it seem as if only his books have jackets. He was dressed in baggy pants and old shoes and his hair, uncombed and black, was blowing in the silent February sunlight. He looked as if he had just stepped out of one of his novels, or was about to step back into one, picking cotton, perhaps, in a California field next to his girl friend, of Mexican amber, and her little son, who picked cotton faster than he could as he cut his fingertips trying to earn a day's food for the three of them and a night's love for the two, a love that had brought him to a life only a poor Mexican could know and that was both as fierce and tender as all his other loves and as restless and as short.[21] Or maybe rushing in clunker shoes,[22] he calls them, to catch his train as a brakeman on the Southern Pacific, running like the football star he once had been,[23] or maybe just to catch it as a hobo going nowhere, seemingly, but always, really, going someplace, riding in a box car or an open gondola in summer heat or bitter cold, catching the cold, sometimes, but never the bitterness. Or perhaps smoking marijuana, in the same clothes, at a Denver society party, confounding the society at the party with a drunkenness that is so much less sophisticated than the liquored drunkenness of themselves but so much more knowing, or perhaps smoking it in a brothel on the way to Mexico City, the smoke of it turning the brothel from a place of crawling flesh to a place of fleshy enchantment. Or maybe sitting as a forest ranger, alone for two months on a desolation mountain peak called Desolation, shouting Frank Sinatra songs at the stars above or the canyons below, and hearing the canyons and even the stars answer him.[24] Or perhaps racing from one of these places to the other, from the East Side to the West Coast, sometimes in 90-mile-an-hour cars, sometimes in slower buses, and once on the back of an Okie's truck, standing with other hitch-hikers, laughing , urinating into the wind, and he says woe unto those who spit on the Beat Generation, the wind'll blow it back. He was on the road in front of his house, not so symbolic as other roads he had traveled, perhaps, but certainly as unpaved, and he walked through the mud carrying a shopping bag a head taller than himself.

"Beer," said Jack Kerouac. "Refreshments for the afternoon. Come on in."

He pointed the way with a quick toss of the chin that sent his hair flying into a new state of disorder, and he walked toward a rear kitchen door, staggering, somewhat prematurely, under his load. At the door was his mother, smiling and cheerful in an unexpected cliché, with eyeglasses, an apron, long, woolen stockings and a housewife's bandana tied around her head.

"Dorothy Kilgallen wrote in her column that I live in a thirty-thousand dollar mansion on Long Island," he said, his voice, like his face, youthful and tenor and full of strange, friendly gusto. "Does this look like a thirty-thousand-dollar mansion? If I paid thirty thousand dollars for it, I sure got cheated, huh? I only paid fourteen," and for the word fourteen, he dropped his voice, like the price of the house, to a near-baritone, making the fourteen sound even lower and even mysterious.

The house was like many other older generation houses in Northport,[25] members of the Weatherbeaten Generation, perhaps. It was large and wooden with porches, front and rear, and a sag but no swing. It was surrounded by trees, hedges and other surviving marks of rusticity and it was covered by a recent, but unsuccessful, coat of camouflage, battleship gray.

"This isn't even our furniture" said his mother, a short, not yet rotund woman of sixty-four, who spoke with that distinct but almost indefinable accent that the French-Canadians have. "This furniture came with the house. They're always printing things about Jack that aren't true—you know, about the Beat Generation and all that juvenile delinquency. Everybody says, "Beat Generation!—He's a juvenile delinquent! But he's a good boy—a good son. He was never any juvenile delinquent. I know, I'm his mother."

"Yeah," he added. "We're Middle Class, we've always been Middle Class. We're Middle Class just like you," and he offered to conduct a sight-seeing tour through the house. The furniture clearly was Middle Class, with overtones of mahogany and over-stuffing of couches and if it hadn't been theirs to begin with, it certainly seemed to have come from the past he wrote about in Dr. Sax, his childhood and his adolescence in the big tenement flats of Lowell, Massachusetts, where, son of a printer who was also a pool hall and bowling alley operator, he played with marbles, traded comic books, imitated The Shadow, and didn't miss any of the most important films of the Thirties, not realizing until long afterwards that what he laughed at in Harpo Marx delight was really Kafkaesque commentary on contemporary civilization.

"We got the house through an agent, a real estate agent," he said. "We saw an ad in the *New York Times*, and we bought it," and he pronounced the *ought* in bought somewhere between *ought* and *ott*, a legacy, too, of Lowell, although other aspects of his speech, his animation, his accents, his undulating rhythms, were strangely Far Western. "We bought it from the Eddys—George Eddy and Mona Kent Eddy, you must have heard of her. She wrote the radio serial— *Portia Faces Life*. She's very famous," and there was a factualness to his very famous that sounded as if it had come from two thousand quarter-hours of listening. "She paints, too. She gave me that picture for Christmas."

He walked toward a small framed canvas above the server in the dining room, with its early American chairs and tables and all looked down upon by a modern plastic bubble lamp that hung from the ceiling, and he surveyed the painting for a moment, commenting, "Look at that, ehh?" Then he turned back and continued walking through the house, saying: "Everybody thinks I've got a couple of my books published I'm a millionaire. I've only made, maybe twenty thousand dollars, and bought this house. And all those years, and didn't get anything published, and now all of a sudden I'm supposed to be a millionaire. But nobody says anything about those eight years I didn't make any money at all, except what I made when I was working on the railroad."

In the kitchen, his mother, with an affability that apparently had endured for years, was unpacking the contents of the shopping bag, transferring the cans of beer into one of the many cabinets beneath the long counter tops that had never been imagined when the house was built. Quickly, he salvaged what he could from the bag, filling both hands. "I owe everything to her. Come on upstairs. We'll have some beer and talk."

"You go ahead," his mother said. "If I watch television, will that interrupt you?" and she sat down in the parlor to the still unexorcised thrills of an afternoon quiz show.

"I watch television," he said, leading the way up the front step. "*San Francisco Beat*—you know that television show with the two big cops. Two big plainclothes cops running around grabbing these bearded beatniks. On television, yeah. And the bearded beatniks always have guns and they're beatin' the cops." He chuckled and, still chuckling, added: "I never knew beatniks had guns. And I saw Truman Capote. He said"—and he mimicked in a high-pitched voice, easy for him—"he said, 'Oh, they don't write, they typewrite.'"

He entered an upstairs bedroom that, with a desk, a typewriter, a tape recorder, books, papers, all in neat piles on the upstairs bedroom furniture, had been turned into a study. It overlooked the road.

"I don't sleep here," he said, motioning toward the bed. "I sleep in another room with the windows wide open, winter and summer. We have plenty of rooms, so we use them all. I like to sleep late sometimes . . . Don't get up till noon, one o'clock . . . I never thought I'd make money writing, either . . . Initially, art is a duty.[26] It's an old theory of mine in teenage notebooks and was culled from Dostoyevsky's holy diary. In other words, when I wrote these books, I did it as a 'holy duty' and thought my manuscripts would be discovered after I was dead, never dreamed they'd make money . . ."

He offered a can of beer, punched one open for himself, took a long swallow, sat back in a chair at the desk and suddenly became engrossed in a rush of thoughts, phrases, ideas, the poetry of his brain, mouthing some of it silently to himself, his lips moving, mumbling, as he looked out the window, alone, to himself, in the room, and in his pocket a notebook and a pencil, always there, ready to catch these droppings of his mind, but he didn't take them out of his pocket, he returned to the conversation. It was about one of those nights in 1957, a year before, when he had been reading his poetry in a cellar night club, the Village Vanguard, and the newspapers, with the verbal sneers that are journalese for satire, had laughed at him. He walked over to a dresser near the bed and pulled open a drawer. The dresser turned out, like the whole bedroom, to be nothing but a front for his literary activities. Inside there were none of the bed-clothes or underclothes or other garments that might be expected in a dresser drawer but rather several piles of manuscripts, all of them quite naked, and an old, thick scrapbook, which although not quite naked, too, was losing its covers. He pulled out the scrapbook and began leafing through its pages, stopping several times but only momentarily. On one page there was a clipping from the *New York Times* of November eighteenth, 1939 . . .

"Point-starved by Tome for two straight years, Horace Mann's football squad yesterday shook off the jinx personified by the Maryland team, as Jack Kerouac a shifty, flat-footed back from Lowell, Mass., and the spearhead of the Maroon and White attack made a touchdown dash . . ."

On another page, there was a clipping from another New York newspaper, unidentified . . .

". . . Lou Little is basking away up at Cape Cod and dreaming about those long runs from reverse that Jack Kerouac, sophomore wingback, is going to gear off for the grid Lions next fall . . ."

He continued leafing and now there was something of an incongruity between the clippings at the front and the clippings at the back, the incongruity of sports reviews and book reviews. He opened the scrapbook, finally, to a page which contained an article about him reading at the Village Vanguard.

"Oh, it was all right," he said. "But I guess I was feeling morbid . . . drunk . . ." and his voice suddenly took on that mood. "I just can't take this kind of stuff anymore"—and now, without a pause, his voice brightened with a bright idea—"I'm going to move to Florida. I'm going to get a house in the country . . . In the country near my sister's . . . Oh, about ten miles out. I'm too close to New York here. I get telegrams . . . I'm supposed to call *Life* today. I'm sick of dealing with brainwashed journalists who think that facetiousness is funny or that bad news better be better than good news or they'll lose their jobs. They build their own Hells."[27]

"That time at the Vanguard? I was drunk on pernod. That was a Sunday afternoon. They made me read something over again that I didn't want to repeat. I also read a thing where I had to sing from *On the Road* . . . What was horrible about that afternoon, what really upset me, you know, I had an old prep school buddy from Horace Mann, Dick Sheresky who owns restaurants around New York—you know Sheresky? Hadn't seen him for millions of years and he comes up to me and instead of saying 'Dick—there you are!' I was so decadent by this time with all these cops coming in back and saying I had to join the police union or something—police card— and big gangsters coming in or something to make me join the union, and kids pulling at my sleeves, I say"—and his voice assumed a whining wise guy's voice in an imitation of himself—"I say, 'ah Dick the Schmick,' I said to Dick. He said 'That's a good one.' He was the wit at school, he was the funniest guy. He bought me a pernod. But I wasn't polite to him or his friend. His friend turned to me and said, 'Do you think that *On the Road* is a joke? I said"—and the disgust in his voice now seemed as much as disgust with himself as with the question—"I said, 'Ahhh, everything's a joke!' and I walked away . . .

"Was I a Buddhist then? Well, I couldn't be, a Buddhist has got to be alone." He laughed at the thought. "A night club Buddhist!" Then he reflected for a moment. "Ahhh, I was a Buddhist, yeah . . ."

He had also read that afternoon at the Village Vanguard a selection from *The Evergreen Review*, one of his stories called "October in the Railroad Earth."

"I can write like that," he said with a quick and sure enthusiasm. "In fact, I have a nice method for that. That's spontaneous writing. Spontaneous and before breakfast in the morning. That's when you're real fresh. You got to have a good typewriter. I could hardly sleep when I wrote that. I could hardly talk. One Friday. Fifty-three. That part in the *Evergreen Review*, that's only half of it. I have the other half of it untyped—I have to retype it double spaced for the publishers." He laughed to himself again. "Ol' Truman Capote," he said—and once more he mimicked—" 'It isn't writing, it's typewriting.' But it's hard to do it fast, spontaneous . . . You don't do it sentence by sentence. Sentences are stumbling blocks to language! Who in the hell started this sentence business? Like, John Holmes, I've watched him write. He writes on a typewriter so fast, but he gets stumped—he can't think of the proper word. I don't do that. If I can't think of the proper word, I just do *bdlbdlbdlbdlbdlbdlbdl*. Or else, *bdlbdlbluuu-uuuh*. Right now, I'm typing up another one of my novels. . ." and he pointed into the drawer again toward the largest mass of manuscript . . . "*Visions of Neal*—Neal Cassady . . . he's a friend of mine in California. *On the Road* was all about him. He's a brakeman on the Southern Pacific . . . *Visions of Neal*, that's a huge one—that's this one here. We're going to publish thirty-eight pieces of it. Seven dollars and a half. Limited edition. You see, in my serious writing,

I'm Jack through it all. But everybody else, their names are changed. I always had the same names, but the editors changed them, the publishers changed them. Ray Smith is Jack, Sal Paradise is Jack, Leo Percepied is Jack . . ."

His mother smiled through the doorway.

"Am I disturbing you?" she asked.

"No!" he answered. "No! Come on in and say something."

"What should I say?" she asked, "What should I tell you? I have two children. A daughter. She's married and she lives in Florida. And Jack. He's not married. I had another son, older than him, but he died. Gerard."

"I was four," Jack said. "He was nine. That's another book I wrote. *Visions of Gerard*. In *On the Road* I wrote I had a brother, but that was really my brother-in-law. When you're writing true stories about the world you simply have to throw everybody off for the sake of the law. The rest is fiction, idle daydreams."

"There's a lot of things he wrote in *On the Road*," his mother said, "that really don't belong in there."

"No," he insisted. "It's all true. Neal knows it's true. Only the names are changed."

"Well," his mother said, "I'll tell you right now, he's always lived with me, outside of when he travels. He wanted to write a book, to write something different, so he asked me and he took off one day and he did. So, anyhow, after they read the book, they write an awful lot of things about him that's not so—I know, I'm his mother. He lives with me all his life. Once in a while, he takes off, he goes on a trip, he sails away to Spain, he visits all his friends, you know, for a few months, but he comes back, he always has his home with me—unless he gets married and goes away someplace. But as long as he wants to live with me, it's all right. But when he did travel, I was working, you know, while he was away. I was making good money, he never wanted for anything. He would say where to send it, and there was always money there, I used to send it any time he needed it, for food, shoes, clothes—I was working . . ."

"She was working in a shoe factory." he said.

". . . Oh, I was making good money," she continued. "We're Middle Class—we've always been that way . . ."

"We're *bourgeois*," he said.

". . . We never had luxuries or many elaborate things," she added, "but we always had a good home, plenty to eat—"

"Sunday roasts!" Jack interrupted.

"—New clothes to wear," she continued. "He don't wear it, but it's true. We're just like any other ordinary people, working people, go to shows once in a while, travel a little bit. As far as I know of him, he's never been a delinquent or anything. You know, because he travels around a lot, that doesn't mean anything, he's really a nice boy. And kind. He's kind to everybody . . ."

"I used to be, anyway," he interrupted again.

". . . And that's all I can say," she concluded. "He never had a beard in his life, although I think he'd be better off myself if he had one."

"Yeah," he said. "Clifton Fadiman had on TV—a guy with a beard on a motorcycle with a portable typewriter typing as he rode along."

"Two years ago, he took me to California," she said, "and he took me all around—"

"I took her to Berkeley," he said. "I used to live in Berkeley."

"And I met some of those fellows there," she said. "They didn't look bad to me—none of them acted really bad, and one of them, Philip Whalen, he was very nice.[28] Well, they were polite. You know, when he wrote this book, *Town and the City*, he used to dress up like a bank robber . . ."

"I didn't make any money on *The Town and the City*," he said. "Just two, three thousand dollars."

"Oh, more than that," she said, "Four, anyhow. When you went to Denver."

"You know, I spent three years writing *Town and the City*," he said. "I spent twenty-one days writing *On the Road. Town and the City*, that was my first book, that was a novel-type novel. It had characters and development and all that. It was mostly fiction. Fiction is nothing but idle day dreams. Look what I did with *Town and the City*—I gave my father a nice big house, I gave my mother three daughters to help her wash the dishes, I gave myself four brothers to keep me company, protect me. Baaaaah! Idle day dreams! The way to write is with real things and real people. How else are you going to have the truth!"

"When he was writing *Town and the City*," his mother said, "my husband was very sick at the time and I had to work to support the house. So he stayed home and took care of his father. He could handle his father—I couldn't. You know, he had to carry him around and take him to the bathroom and clean him and all that and the things I couldn't do. And I was making enough money to support everybody because I had a good job."

"I was writing a chapter when he died," Jack said, "and I thought he was snoring in the next room, you know, a loud snore—"

"It was not a snore," she interrupted, "it was a . . ."

"Death rattle," he said. "But I was typing away, and so I missed out on it. And you know, that . . . that was terrible. I went around to go see him because he had stopped snoring, and I thought he was sleeping . . ."

"He was fifty-five." she said.

"Fifty-seven." he corrected.

"Honest?" she said. "I thought he was fifty-five."

"Cancer of the spleen." he said.

There was the quiet of sadness unwillingly remembered, of thoughts buried in the mind ten years before, but the mind is a shallow grave.

"Well, anyhow," his mother said, "I want to show you something. It's very simple. It'll only take a minute."

She walked six steps out the door and through the upstairs hall into her son's open window bedroom. "If he was so bad," she said, pointing toward a silver crucifix over the headboard, "would he have that? And that?"—and she pointed to a string of rosary beads on his night table—"He wore that around his neck, but they broke. They were blessed by Trappist monks."

Jack stood watching, holding his beer can, his second or his third, something like a sponsor, perhaps, listening to a commercial and then he pointed, beneath the crucifix, showing off with the same pleasure that it gave him, a night-light with a pull chain attached to the headboard and a sheaf of notepaper in a clipboard hanging from the adjacent wall.

"I just fixed this up," he said, pulling the string to light the bulb and taking the clipboard from its hook, from which also dangled a pencil, "I use them to write down dream thoughts. I hear them in a dream and wake up and turn the light on and write them down. You know, like *Old Angel Midnight*."

He read what was written on the top sheet, the previous night's message "Go, tell the ash with the fish, all he needs is illuminating . . . Man's will, which is already recorded in heaven—strange will . . . Death makes a stand in its own darkness. I can get more grace from a snot nose wart brain . . ."

"These are what I call bedside sheets," he said, "you know, sheets hanging by the bedside."

"Who ever heard of anything—is that what you have hanging in the window there?" his mother asked. "Is that where you got the idea?"

"Huh?" he said.

"Those are bed sheets Mrs. Eddy put up—" she said.

"No," he corrected, "bedside sheets, pieces of paper hanging by the bedside!"

"Oh," she said, "explain yourself."

"I did," he chuckled. "You don't listen. You're airing sheets."

He walked back into his study and, looking at the clipboard, read again, this time slowly, so it could be copied: "Man's will, comma, which is already recorded in heaven . . . dash . . ." and then he added, almost as if it were an afterthought, "strange will!" saying *strange will* as if it were a whistle of amazement, whew-whew! "period . . ." and liking the sound of it, he repeated "strange will!" again in tune to whew-whew! but this time more softly, "Death makes a stand in its own darkness"—and he chuckled again, and, still chuckling, continued—"I can get more grace from a snot nose wart brain."

"Oh, God!" his mother said.

"I can get more grace from a snot nose wart brain," he repeated, chuckling all the way through, "—I can tell I was doubtful with that!"

"Who understands these things?" his mother said. "I don't."

"Well," he said, "it means I'm mad, I'm not getting enough grace, I can get more grace from a snot nose wart brain than I can from heaven . . ."

"Well, what's that mean?" she said.

"It's just a religious thought," he said, and he chanted to himself: "'Snot . . . nose . . . wart . . . brain . . .' Those are dream thoughts. I hear them in a dream and I wake up."

"You're worse than I am," she said. "When I dream about something, it's always cute."

He swallowed some beer, and, voiceless, began forming phrases with his mouth again, more thoughts, dream thoughts perhaps in the middle of the day. He looked out the window, his eyes on the road, his face as abstract as what was behind it. It was a visitation, if not of *Old Angel Midnight* or of *Old Angel Daylight*, then certainly of the Muse. But then, he seemed to have many angels and, judging by the number of drawers in the dresser and by what they contained, he seemed to have many visitations. He mumbled, with a sound intelligible only to himself, several phrases of this private imagery, which, once written, would be intelligible to so many others—others who, in the coffee shops of New York's Greenwich Village, in the bars of San Francisco's North Beach, even now had beatified him, calling him, with the same spontaneity of his typewriter, St. Jack.

"Oh, sure," he said, returning to the conversation, "they're going to write lots of books about me . . . After I'm dead? Like Hemingway . . . Criticisms . . . they have some about Hemingway already . . . Biographies. I mean before he dies? . . . I'm kind of sensitive."—and there was a conveyed embarrassment in his sensitivity—"I used to be a naive, overbelieving type."

"I haven't read all his books," his mother said. "He told me one time that if I read the book, *On the Road*, I'd get mad at him, so I read up to Page Thirty-Four—I quit. I didn't get mad at him that far back, but I will read it some day when I quiet down."

"She can read *The Dharma Bums*," he said, "That's nice. But I told her not to read *The Subterraneans* at all . . . My sister read it. She likes everything I do, my sister."

"She's a cute girl," his mother said, "wonderful girl. She's not at all like he is. Day and Night!"

"She's a bookkeeper," he said, and he took another drink of beer. "*The Dharma Bums*," I wrote that after *On the Road* came out. I said to Viking, 'I'll get you another book.' And Malcom Cowley, my editor, said 'Please write another book like *On the Road* with adventures about people. Stop talking about yourself.' It's got good sentences, *Dharma Bums*. I spent five hundred dollars having it restored to my original way I wrote it. They . . . they took *Dharma Bums* and changed it—made three thousand commas and stuff, type changes, rearrangements, sentence rearrangements. I rearranged everything back to the way I wrote it . . . and got a bill for five hundred dollars. The bill said 'alterations'. But what it is is restorations! The way they fixed it was awful. They said 'That's our house style here at Viking'" and he said it sweetly, "'That's our house style here at Viking.' Did you ever hear of a house style?—Well, that's all right for newspapers, or whore houses, but not publishers. *On the Road* sold twenty thousand hard cover copies. And now, five hundred thousand soft covers are being sold . . ."

"Paperbacks, they're called." his mother said.

"Paperbacks, yeah," he said. "Five hundred thousand. A penny a copy for me. But we sold *Dharma Bums* to soft cover people for ten thousand. I get five. *On the Road* and *Dharma Bums* are almost even, I think now. *The Subterraneans* made more money than the others because MGM took it—fifteen grand! . . . . I should have settled for ten times that much . . ."

"You know," his mother said, "when you look in the papers and read about these fellows that the movie people take their books, one hundred thousand . . ."

"A hundred and sixty-five!" he said, his voice in imitation of a headline. "I don't know anything about business . . . But it was a beginning. *The Subterraneans* is all over the world—Japan, Argentina, everybody's taking it"—and there was a surprise in his voice, which he quelled with another beer. "I had sold the movie rights to *On the Road*, too, but then they reneged. Two thousand option money. Yeah, that was Mort Sahl and Joyce Jamison and a bunch of guys. They should have taken it . . . it's a good production. Now, nobody has it. Jerry Wald keeps writing a letter every six months, saying 'I'm thinking about it—it's a tough plot.' Everybody thinks it's sold, so they don't ask for it. In fact, I thought of making an ad in *Billboard—ON THE ROAD*—NOT SOLD!' Then if I got a big chunk of money, you know what I'd do with it? Five percent in something, five percent, you know, check every month. That'd be nice. Then I could, you know, bring fellows to India and all that stuff, go out and do things, and all that money's free, see? And you'd have your check," he said, turning toward his mother.

"Well, I'm going downstairs now," she said, "and I'll make you some little sandwiches, they're not meat but I think you'll like them . . ."

"Well, finish your story," he said.

"Which story?" she said. "I haven't got much of a story to tell, outside that I was your benefactor all my life," and she laughed. "I'm sixty-three now, I'm going to be sixty-four next week . . ."

"And we're going to go to Radio City," he said.

". . . . Time flies!" she said. "God! The years go by so fast after sixty. But I don't care. If I keep healthy, that's the main thing. I got fat now, you know, I wasn't always this fat. But I stopped wearing girdles, you know, and I'm spreading . . ."

"You know, her favorite is Genevieve there on television," he said, then repeating, with a half-French pronunciation: "Genevieve. How do you spell her name?"

"Genevieve," she said. "It's G-E-N-E-V-I-E-V-E."

"Well, that's pronounced Gen-e-vieve, isn't it?" he said.

"In French, let me tell you," she said, "in French, JAN-VIEVE! JAN! JAN-VIEVE!"

"Say something in French," he said.

"Qu'est-ce-que tu veux savoir?" she said.

"She tutored you," he said, and then he added, turning toward her and correcting her: "Tu tutoye. Qu'est-ce-que VOUS voulez savoir?"

There was a pride in her French as well as a difference. It was the pride of a French which the French-Canadians believe is a preservation of the language of France before Louis XIV, when German and Moorish influences began to shape it to its present sounds. It was the language which the *emigrés* had brought to Canada with them, just as they had brought the name Kerouac.[29] Now, of course, the name was returning to France on book covers. And when G. Claude Gallimard, the French publisher, had visited America some months before, he had said: "I must meet him. I must meet your Jacques Kerouac." And so Barney Rosset, the head of Grove Press, had arranged a dinner at his home.

"That afternoon there," he said, reminding his mother, "when the Filipino butler . . ."

"Oh, yeah," his mother said, "oh, my goodness! They gave me a couple of drinks and they made them so strong. I don't know what happened."

"We talked French," he said. "We had a big, screaming dinner, all talking French. Don Allen and Barney Rosset—you know, from Grove Press—they were quiet. They didn't know what to say. Michel Mohrt announced I was speaking pure Eighteenth Century Norman French."

"It was delicious, though," she said. "We had a wonderful dinner. I was all over the place. I had to leave the men by themselves, you know. And I played the piano, though I don't play very good, and then I went downstairs and I kidded with the butler, the little butler . . ."

"Then we started," he said, "then my mother and I started roaming up the street, hitting all the bars, Fifth Avenue, Schmifth Avenue . . . And then I was supposed to go to *Holiday Magazine* to meet an interviewer and we got there late . . ."

"I'll never do that again," his mother said. "Well, I had just come back from Florida, and we had settled down here, and I hadn't been to New York in quite a while, and we were having a ball out there, and . . . I overstepped my line," and she laughed. "Oh, I had too much, might as well come out with it, I had too much to drink, although I should at my age, you know, be careful. But I was having a big time. I was with him . . . Yeah, he drinks a little, I think a little too much for his own health, his own good health."

"Yeah," he said, "If I was away from home, I'd drink too much. I don't drink much here."

"In Florida, when we lived there," she said, "he didn't drink at all, only sometimes on a weekends he would go and get a little bottle if we had company—my son-in-law would come, you know. We had beer and wine. But over here, there's always somebody coming in and out and he's been to parties around here, and, oh, my! One drink after another!"

"I wanted to come here and hide out, you know," he said, "and the guy that owns this house insists on having me meet every-body—George Eddy, you know, like Nelson Eddy. Mona Kent Eddy's husband . . ."

"I like them," his mother said, "but all their friends they want me to meet! Jack's friends, there's one I can't stand. That's right. Allen Ginsberg. Because there's something about that man I just can't stand. And I'm afraid of him. And then one time, I read a letter he sent to Jack, and he was insulting a priest, a Catholic priest that had befriended him . . ."

"He was telling Franciscan monks," Jack said, "to take their clothes off, in Italy, on a lawn outside the monastery in Assisi."

"That burned me up," she said. "And then my husband couldn't stand him, either. And when my husband died"—

"He's one of my closest friends," Jack said. "She doesn't like my girl friend, either."

"And before my husband died," she continued, "he made me promise, never to let . . . to try to keep Allen Ginsberg out of the house. It's the only one he didn't like . . ."

"She likes Neal Cassady." Jack said.

"Neal's all right," his mother said. "He is all right. No fooling. He's a little eccentric and he loves to play the horses—that's what makes him so nervous, I guess. He used to come to our house in Richmond Hill, and that fellow couldn't stay put on the chair more than a second. He would jump from one place to another. He was always active. I never met his wife and children, though I'm told they're very nice."

Jack's mother rose off her seat on the edge of the bed and suddenly hurried from the room.

"I got a letter from Henry Miller, two or three days ago," Jack announced. "See what it says here? He says," and he turned about, picked up a sheet of paper from this desk top and began reading in a rapid, chirping style: "'Dear Jack, Right-o for all your ills, laughter. So said the master, Rabelais. Northport sounds even more remote than Big Sur'"—and he interpolated, "That's not true." Then he continued reading: "'But no matter where you are now, you'll be pestered. I don't worry about you. You're tough, resilient, gay and suicidal in a healthy way. Carry on! *Allez-y! Au bout du monde, Baudelaire.* et cetera.' He says, 'One day, I'll just quit, probably with pen in hand. All the best now. *Du courage, quoi!* Henry.' See, he's going to write the preface for the soft cover edition of *The Subterraneans*."[30]

In a moment, his mother had returned, carrying a book that was leather-bound.

"This is *The Town and the City*," she said. "This is the first book that he ever came out with. Read what it says there. That tells the whole story," and she opened the book to its inside cover and a message, written in ink:

To my dear mother, Gabe–

"That's for Gabrielle," she said. "That's my name."

"–From your loving son, your humble son. No mother could have given stronger support over the harsh years to her son, without which no book would have been written at all. And no mother in this world was ever so wise, so good, so dear, and so sweet as you are. Here's hoping this book will help repay you at last for a life of toil, humility and true piety and gladden your heart, and Pa's, which will gladden mine. All my love, Jean."

"That's my real name." Jack said.

"Isn't that cute?" his mother asked, and she hurried out of the room again, returning seconds later with another book. "Here's a funny one. This is *The Dharma Bums*–look at that," and again she turned to an inscription inside the cover.

"To Ma, Timmy and Tyke–

"Aaaah," Jack said. "Timmy's gone. Got run over."

"The cat." his mother said.

"Two cats." he said.

"–A third adventure to pay for the house, the cat food, the brandy and the peaceful sleep. From Dharma Bum Jack, Ti Jean. Mom, you're on Pages One-thirty-two, one-thirty-three, one-forty-eight."

"Isn't that sweet," she said, laughing, and he laughed, too. Then she went for another book, also leather-bound.

"Here's another one," she said, "this is *On the Road*. That's a cute one."

"It's a special bound copy," Jack said. "They only make one."

"He gave it to me," she said, and she opened it, too, to the inscription.

"To ma—This book, which will buy you the little cottage you always wanted where you'll find—"

"It bought this house," Jack said, with another chuckle. "Just about paid cash for it. Gave them seven thousand and then six months later gave them another seven. That doesn't include the furniture . . ."

"Oh, no," his mother added. "They're going to come and get that stuff out of here."

"That's their chair," Jack said, motioning toward one.

"They took some furniture out and left some in," his mother said. "There's some more they have to take, like this mirror and the stuff downstairs . . ."

"—complete peace and happiness for the first time in your long and helpful life. From Ti Jean, your son, the author. Jack Kerouac. January fourteenth, 1958."

"See, I get them all," his mother said. "Now I got to read them."

"She hasn't got *The Subterraneans*," Jack said, and then, after she had gone downstairs to prepare the sandwiches, he added: "You know, *The Subterraneans*, it's about a love affair with a Negro girl!"

He leaned back with his beer can again, his fourth or fifth. "I can take it," he said. "You know, as I say, Li Po and all those other guys drank. Li Po, the Chinese poet"—and chuckling: "I don't mean Edgar Allen! I remember James Wechsler—he said I didn't believe in peace. Awww, he's a politician. As Allen Ginsberg says, I'd hate to be a poet in a country where Wechsler is the Commissar of Poetry.[31] I'm not interested in politics. I'm interested in Li Po. He was a

Dharma Bum type. You know, a poor poet, roaming China. You know, I have some eighteen-year-old writings that are pure Buddhism. I'm thirty-seven now. My birthday's March twelfth. So I've always been a Buddhist. When I was a little kid, I used to lock myself in the toilet whenever company would come. Once they couldn't open the door—I was locked in. But all this angry hipster stuff, it's all just an overjoyed bit of life . . . you know what this is like? It's like *Citizen Kane*. Remember the guy in *Citizen Kane* going around, getting all this, seeing old Joseph Cotten at the hospital. That's me. Then he goes to see the old Jewish publisher, remember that? Everett Sloane. There was a guy going around—who was it? You know when I saw it? I saw it Pearl Harbor day. I came out of the theater and saw the headlines about Pearl Harbor. It was a Sunday night . . ."*

There were lines on his face now that darkened it, no more the picture of handsome beauty that once had adorned a page of *Mademoiselle* magazine but the reflection of his own verbal images, with his voice constantly playing the different roles, imitating the tones of others and himself, sometimes light, sometimes broody—broody now, but even in its broodiness, still mellow.

"I was in the Navy in World War II,"** he said. "A few months—six months. I was discharged. Schizoid personality," and he chuckled. "They gave me a rifle and they had me marching out on the drill field, right turn, left turn, and I said, 'Awww, I don't want to do this,' and I dropped my rifle and I went into the library and I started to read. I told them, 'I don't want discipline and I'm not

---

* Kerouac saw *Citizen Kane* in Lowell, Massachusetts at the Royal Theater when he first saw the *Lowell Sun* headlines he is referring to here.
** See appendix.

going to have discipline.' So they put me in the hospital. Then I went into the Merchant Marine. It was during the war, but I didn't get shot at. I mean, no torpedoes were fired at us. It was in 1940 I went to Columbia to play football. I played wingback. That's in the single wing, before the T—the guy who comes around, gets the reverse and comes waaay around the other end. I only played in my freshman year. I quit twice—quit the football team twice.

"See, I played football at Lowell High. Horace Mann High, for me it was a prep school to make up credits. To make up math and French. At Columbia, broke my leg in the game, third game of the year. I was out all the rest of the season with crutches, sitting in front of the fire in the Lion's Den, eating big steaks and hot fudge sundaes. It was great! And that's when I started reading Thomas Wolfe. I had the leisure, see, to read. I went back in the fall of 'Forty-One for the season. Now I was a sophomore and I was going to be on the varsity. And, I don't know, I was getting very poetic by that time, and I'd get black and broody and everything. Packed my suitcase and walked right out in front of Lou Little. He said, 'Where you going?' I said 'Oh, this suitcase is empty. I'm going to my grandmother's house to get some clothes.' I walked out with a full suitcase.

"Then I was a big poet and wanted to go down to Virginia and see the moon shining in Virginia. I went down to Virginia." and he laughed at himself. "Then I came back to work in filling stations and everything and went to sea, went to the North Pole, in the Merchant Marine. Got back in October, 1942. And Lou Little—there was a telegram there saying, 'You can come back on the team if you want to take the bull by the horns.' I went back. Worked out a week, and the Army game came up—my great enemy, Henry Mazur, was making long runs for Army, captain of Army. Told Lou Little, 'Let me in there, man! I'm going to get him!' He's the guy in *The Town and the City* who pushed me out of the shower when I was a little kid. He played for Lowell High, too—he was a senior and I was a freshman. He was mean—I was going to get him in that game. And Lou didn't put me in that game, the Army game, so I said pooh"—and he pooh-spit—"and I quit.[32] But the reason why I quit is deeper than that. I was just sitting in my room, and it was snowing, you know, the dorms, snow was falling, time to go to scrimmage, time to go out in the snow and the mud and bang yourself around. And on the radio, it started, you know—'Dum dum dum dummmmmmmmm'—Beethoven!—'Dum dum dum dumm-mmmmmm'"—and he hummed the opening bars of Beethoven's *Fifth Symphony*. "I said," and now he whispered, "I said 'I'm going to be an artist! I'm not going to be a football player!' That's the night I didn't go to scrimmage. And I never went back to football, see?

"And shortly after, a month or so, I left the whole college. Because it was hard to keep going to an Ivy League school if you quit your football. They make it hard for you. The Ivy League is hypocritical, you know. Oh, I flunked in chemistry. I hate chemistry. Gee, I kept cutting it, I never went to class anyway. But I had an A in Shakespeare. With Mark Van Doren. And flunked chemistry. Well, after all that, yeah, I quit college and then back to sea. Got an apartment on the campus, the Columbia campus with my first wife before we were married. And all the students used to come in with books and bottles, hang around. My apartment was a hangout for the young intellectuals of the campus. My wife, her grandmother lived right there. Her grandmother was an old friend of Nicholas Murray Butler's, and they lived in an old house next to Butler's. She was supposed to be living with her grandmother, but was living in sin with me in an apartment. And in walks Ginsberg, and in walks everybody else. Ginsberg, sixteen years old with his ears sticking out at that time. The first thing he said to me was, 'Discretion is the better part of valor'—and he imitated Ginsberg with mock freshman earnestness, and then he laughed. "He was a freshman. But after a few years of that, Ginsberg really began to develop and became a hipster—whooooh! the influence of Huncke. Herbert Huncke.

"Well, Ginsberg and I, there we are. And then there's this great figure we hear about, this great evil figure from St. Louis, Bill Burroughs. We go over, and he's just great! We sat at his feet and, well, Burroughs went around and found Huncke and found everybody else. We had a gang of friends from St. Louis. It was a St. Louis clique of rich guys from St. Louis, decadent intellectual types, *fin de siècle, enfants terribles* types, ugh! Allen and me? Well, we were poets together. I like the way he told long stories about New Jersey and everything. I've always had a friend like Allen. In Lowell, I had a friend, Sebastian Sampas, who was just like him—you know, always a weird, poetic, Latin type. I always had a Latin friend somewhere who was a poet, somehow. Latin? Well, I mean dark, dark, mysterious, you know . . . Sebastian died on Anzio beachhead . . .

"But, you know, Allen and I got our start forming a circle around Burroughs and the guys from St. Louis—the whole thing really begins in St. Louis. And Harvard. Yeah, Burroughs went to Harvard. And Huncke's very important, you know, might be just as important as Neal, almost. He's the greatest story teller I ever met. I don't like his ideas about—a mugger and all that stuff. Of course, he doesn't do the mugging himself—he gets mugs to do it for him. He has a mug with him to do the mugging—he doesn't do it himself, he's just a little guy, you know. Bitter . . . or used to be, he's fine now . . . Allen and I started out among petty criminals, but we weren't criminals.[33] We were students in school—I was a seaman and he was a student. We were studying their personalities for poetic reasons, like Villon.* We never did anything, except that Allen didn't know how to throw them out of the apartment. Yeah, he didn't know how to throw them out–they foisted themselves on him. And there was this big, tall, six-foot redhead there, Vicky.** And she's the later Liz Martin in *The Town and the City*. The Liz Martin starts out as my little sister and grows up into a big evil Vicky. That wasn't a well-done book, but it was a great idea. The fascination was, as Norman Mailer would say, Hip. We had been to college, we had heard all that bull, and this was a new philosophy. And it found its most beautiful flower in Neal, who wasn't a petty criminal, you know, he wasn't a criminal. Yeah, a large natured man, much too much of a nature to be a criminal. Besides, Neal's a Jesuit. You know, he used to be a choir boy. Priests cried on his shoulder . . . ."

Jack's mother bustled in with a trayfull of Friday sandwiches, tiny, tasty, prepared with housewife expertness and arranged in a display meant to be too pretty to eat but too appetizing not to. He asked her to get him another can of beer.

"I had two wives," he said. "Twenty-two years old I got married, and I got married again at twenty-eight. Each time the marriage lasted six months. The first wife was a rich girl from Michigan, and we didn't have any money or anything. We kept eating mayonnaise sandwiches. Well, 'Go back home to your family and eat good!' Yeah, I was writing then. I was writing essays on Yeats. Early novels, juvenile novels I have all over the place. She was nice, and I actually sent her home because it would be better for her. But the

---

* Francois Villon (1431 – 1474): French poet born in Paris.
** Vicky Russell was an acquaintance of the Beat circle in the mid to late 1940s and notorious for her criminal exploits of drug dealing and thievery.

second–I didn't like her! She didn't like any of my friends, none of my friends liked her. She was beautiful. I married her because she was beautiful . . . Did they tell you about Bill Cannastra? The guy that jumped out of the subway? He climbed out a subway window, said, 'We'll get one more beer at the Remo.' Well, he had a loft. After he died, she moved into his loft. I met her in the loft. I would wake up in the morning and look at her and how beautiful she was. And then we would have to get out of bed and go to work. She's remarried and has twins. She's alright, but she's always sending cops after me for non-support. That's why I ran away to California . . .

"My girl's name is Dody. She's a widow, she's the one that my mother doesn't like. Because she has long, long hair, she doesn't tie it up. Because she likes to go barefoot. Because she's an Indian. She's ninety-five percent Indian. My mother calls her *la sauvage*– the savage. You know, she's a very Bohemian painter, a very good painter. I just met her. All of us, you know, the gang, just met her. They love her, too. Allen likes her. Everybody loves her."

His mother brought him another can of beer and he punched a hole in it.

"Beat?" he said. "Yeah, I remember the scene. John Holmes and I were playing jazz records and drinking beer alllllll day on a gloomy"–and he pronounced gloomy as if he were saying *ugh!*– "afternoon, and we were talking about the Lost Generation and 'What's this sad generation?' And we thought of various names, and I say"–and he half whispered it–"I say, 'Ah, this is really a Beat Generation!' And he leaped up and said, 'That's it! You've got it!' see?" and Jack chuckled. "John says no? I remember, he forgot that. He went 'Ahhhhh', you know. He's a very nice kid, he's always enthusiastic. But anyway, then I put it in the *On the Road* manuscript–the expression. But he publicized '*Beat Generation*' first before *On the*

Road was published. *On the Road* wasn't published for seven years. He publicized the expression in the *New York Times*. And I got angry. Well, because the article he wrote for the *New York Times* was a *precis* of the plot of *The Town and the City*. And nobody seemed to want to believe that I made up the term, 'Beat Generation'.

"I was going to use *The Beat Generation* for the title of *On the Road*, but my editor, Malcolm Cowley, didn't want to. He said, 'Oh, *On the Road* is a better title.' That was my original title. Then I changed it to *Beat Generation* and then back to *On the Road*. But I could write another novel and call it that—my next novel. I'm going to call it *The Beat Generation** before I lose any, you know, lose out on that. I'd like to write a novel about getting published. You know, start off with me tramping along with a rucksack, all the way up to making a speech at Hunter College with James Wechsler, who accused me of not believing in peace.[34] Could end it there. And, you know, include all the cocktail parties, publishers' parties, wild weekends, TV appearances, nightclubs. That'd be a funny book, huh? Call it *The Beat Generation* cause that's what they're all talking about. Now they're making a movie, now MGM's making a movie with that title, something about beatniks beating up housewives. But that's my title—they don't own that title! They didn't get it. We're going to sue 'em. My lawyer's going to sue 'em. My agent's lawyer. Sue 'em for the title . . .

"Allen . . . Allen said that Huncke said it first . . . 'Beat' . . . But Huncke didn't say 'Beat Generation.' He just said 'beat.' We learned the word from him. To me at first it meant being poor and sleeping

---

* Kerouac did indeed write *Beat Generation*—only, as a play. It was published in October 2005 by Thunder's Mouth Press.

in subways, like Huncke used to do, and yet being illuminated and
having illuminated ideas about apocalypse and all that. It was quite
different then. Then I went to Lowell, Massachusetts, in 1954. Got
a room in Skid Row near the depot. Walked twenty miles around
Lowell every day. Went to my old church where I got my first confirmation. Knelt, all alone, all alone in the church, in the great
silence of the church . . . And I suddenly realized, beat means
beatitude! Beatific! I was beatific in the church . . . See? It doesn't
apply to anybody else, I don't think, the remembrance of your
first vow."[35]

"What does it mean today? Beat Generation . . . Well, there was
an article in the paper yesterday. A young kid with a beard said
that Johnny Jones of East Islip, Long Island, over here, went to
San Francisco to be a beatnik. Stayed there, lived in a cold water
pad, he wrote poems and he hung around with Negroes and jazz
musicians. Finally he gave up in despair and called his mother
long distance and cried and now he's coming home and shaving
off his beard. You see, this is silly, it has nothing to do with the
serious artists who started the whole thing just by, you know,
writing the poem, writing the book. It's just a fad, just like the Lost
Generation. I really think it's just a generation fad. *On the Road*
was about what happened ten years ago. Today it's become
famous and popular . . ."

He rose up from his chair with an invitation to follow him and
walked into another bedroom, this one almost bare of furniture but
with several large, recent canvases leaning against the wall and with
a smaller one on an easel.

"I'm just starting to learn." he said, picking up a brush and dab-
bing at an indistinct brown figure against the vast green background
of the canvas on the easel. "My girl friend is showing me how. She's

a very good painter.* Her husband was a famous young German Expressionist. She has a loft full of his paintings, must be worth thousands of dollars."

He stood there a short time, displaying the canvasses and talking about painting with a relish as green, perhaps, as the canvas on the easel, surprised that he could paint at all, surprised that anyone would compliment his paintings, surprised almost, that talent could be universal. But his business was with literature.

"See," he said, returning to the study, "Allen and Gregory—Gregory Corso—like they come up to me at midnight and say"—and he imitated Allen with an excited half-whisper—"and say, 'Look, we've done all this, we've made great literature. Why don't we do something REAL great and take over the WORLD!' And Gregory says, 'I'll be your HENCHMAN!' You know, half joking. I say, 'Yeah,'"—and his voice cracked in innocent simplicity as he imitated himself saying Yeah—"but I just want to be Cervantes alone by candlelight.' And they both say 'What would you do if you conquered the world, what would you do with it? It'll cough and won't let you sleep all night,' you know, quoting from *Howl*. And I really do want to go away, you know, in the country and spend long, long times just being an old Japanese haiku poet. An Emily Dickinson-type man. I can't stand the hectic, public eye, you know. I like to go out and get stoned Saturday night with a gang of guys and girls, but I don't like the official connotations. But Allen and Gregory, they just love that. They'd love to be big . . . to be riding in green Chrysler squads and all that stuff. They'd love that. Gregory, he's kidding all the time . . . when he says that. And Allen . . . Allen is the sweetest man in the world! And I've thought about him for years as being the devil,

---

* Jan Müller (1922 – 1958): painter and husband of Dody Müller.

see"—and he dropped his voice to mimic an inner one, speaking in a nervous, ominous undertone—"see, he's the devil, he's the devil"—and then he raised it again, saying: "Sometimes I thought,"—and he dropped it once more—"No, I'm the devil. But now we've both got older and I realize he's not the devil at all. I used to tell him, 'You're the devil.' He'd say, 'Don't talk like that!' Now I realize he's the sweetest . . .

"He doesn't drink much. He's had a lot of dope, you know. That guy's had more dope, heavy dope, you know, in the arm, than anyone I know that didn't become a dope addict. Great will power! Great will power! Experiments. I've had a lot, too. But I didn't have to use will power because I have an allergy to it. I keep throwing up. Yeah, I've had a lot. Not now, though. Like, I'll go to Tangier and see Bill Burroughs and he'll say, "Well, boy, how about kicking the gong around tonight and get some opium!' Or else I go to Mexico City and see old Bill Garver. He'll say, 'Well, I'll give you a shot of morphine.'"—and he imitated Bill Garver with a Mid-Western twang and then he imitated himself: "'Okay, Bill.' . . . Well, what happens when you take it is you throw up. But after you throw up, you lay in the bed for eight hours, great for your mind. Great to get rid of your liver bile, too. Burroughs, he was 'Old Bull Lee' in *On the Road*. Actually, there was none of that gang who was really bad, except one guy named Phil. He was "Mad Killer' in 1945. He used to kill storekeepers, but we didn't find out about that until later when he was arrested. He hanged himself in the Tombs."

He arose again from his chair and stepped to the dresser, where he pulled open another drawer. Inside were piles of notebooks, small, five-cent, pocket size, like the one protruding from his back pocket now, each pile with fifteen or twenty notebooks bound together with rubber bands, the piles in neat rows, one next to the other, filling the drawer.

"Novel," he said, tapping a pile, "novel," he said tapping another, "novel," he said, tapping a third, "novel," he said tapping a fourth, "novel, novel, novel," and he waved his had over the rest of the piles. "That's the way I write 'em—like that! See, Truman Capote said I always typewrite. I wrote half of them in pencil. Like *Visions of Neal*, my greatest book, right there. *Visions of Neal*. All in pencil. Here's *The Dharma Bums*"—and he pointed to a manuscript type-written on a roll of teletype paper. "It's a hundred feet long. I wrote *On the Road* on another roll—on Cannastra's paper, a roll of Cannastra's drawing paper that you draw through.[36] For *Dharma Bums* I could afford the teletype roll. Three dollars," and he laughed. "*On the Road*, I gave that roll to Viking. It was all no paragraphs, single-spaced—all one big paragraph. I had to retype it so they could publish it. Do people realize what an anguish it is to write an original story three hundred pages long?

"See, I changed my style from *The Town and the City* because of Neal—Neal Cassady. Because of a forty-thousand-word letter that Neal wrote me. He wrote me a forty-thousand-word letter! But Allen lost the letter, or Gerd Stern did, actually. Gerd Stern, he lived on a barge in Sausalito. He lost that great letter, which was a work of literary genius. Neal, he was just telling me what happened one time in Denver, and he had every detail. It was just like Dostoyevsky. And I realized that's the way to tell a story—just tell it! I really got it from Neal. So I started to tell the story just the way it happened, too. *The Town and the City* was fiction, you know, mostly. But in spontaneous prose, you just tell what happened. You don't stop, you just keep going. That's the way Neal wrote me the letter. You get excited in telling a story, like Homer probably did. Spontaneity is also in Shakespeare, you know. His publishers say that all his manuscripts were brought in—he brought them in clean, without a mark, without a change, without an addition, without an erasure. They said that he was such a perfect writer, that he just flowed right along. I believe it. Nobody can prove it, but that's what I think. I can tell by the swing and rhythm of his speeches. So, I get this from Neal, I wrote *On the Road* about Neal. He was the prototype for Dean Moriarty in *On the Road*.

"Neal . . . Neal was discovered by Denver Doll, by the guy who was the prototype for Denver Doll in *On the Road*. But Malcolm Cowley made me take him all out of the book," and he laughed. "Because he's a lawyer. He's the guy who developed Neal, see? He discovered Neal. Neal was an urchin. It's a real Charlie Chaplin story, and he's a real Charlie Chaplin. Yeah! Justin W. Brierly"—and he pronounced Justin W. Brierly as if he were sitting in a Mid-West Elk's Club with a large cigar in his mouth. "He's a lawyer. That's why they were afraid of him at Viking. He went to one of his clients who was a drunken Indian. Knocked on the door, and the door was opened by a fifteen-year-old boy with a big hard-on. Neal. Screwing the maid upstairs. Denver Doll said, 'Well, what is this?'"—and he imitated the voice with the cigar in his mouth—"He said, 'My dear fellow,' he said, 'your ears aren't washed.' Took him home and made him wash his ears. Made him go to school. Made him read literature. Made him read Schopenhauer.* See? Wrote long letters to Neal's warden in reform school. We see now that he was a wise, perceptive man to believe in Neal.

"So this guy, who is a member of the Columbia Alumni Association, see, this Denver Doll, the old lawyer, he was going to get Neal

---

* Kerouac's marginalia for his copy of *The Philosophy of Schopenhauer* (Modern Library, 1928) suggests his fascination that "the cosmic will is wicked . . . and the source of all endless suffering." This philosophical ideology is pervasive throughout many of Kerouac's works.

into Columbia. And Denver Doll kept coming to New York on big trips to see Hall Chase, Ed White and all the Columbia boys, and there was Ginsberg and Kerouac hanging around Hall chase and Ed White, the Phi Beta Kappa scholar. So, rumors of Neal began floating around, and he finally came. Quite a story, at that! Completely complicated by Dostoyevsky."

Outside the sun was ice and twilight, and he began changing his clothes, putting on a pair of slacks, a sport shirt and a jacket. He walked downstairs and his mother made him put on a tie as well, a Continental bow tie, the latest style then, and she had bought it for him as a gift.

"See," she said, "I told you he has new clothes. He wears them sometimes," and she smiled again.

He kissed her goodbye, it was time to go, he had an appointment in New York, and he was getting a ride. The author of *On the Road* didn't own a car.

"See," he said outside, "I'm going to move to Florida, close to my sister. I want my mother to be close to someone when I'm not home, when I'm traveling. When I'm traveling. When I'm on the road. Like tonight, I'll go away, I'll be away all weekend, and my mother will be home alone in that big house. She gets frightened. I don't like to think of her home alone there . . ."

He fingered his bow tie. Later, when he got to New York, he took it off in a barroom.

"But Neal," he said, "Neal knows me better than anybody else. Neal knows way down deep what I really am. See, Neal is more like Dostoyevsky, he's a sex fiend like Dostoyevsky, he writes like Dostoyevsky. I got my rhythm from Neal, that's the way he talks, Okie rhythms. Like"—and he imitated, perhaps Neal Cassady, perhaps himself—"Like, 'Now, look h'yar, boy, I'm gonna tell you what see?

You hear me boy?'—That's the way he talks. I've written three novels about Neal and a play—*On the Road*, *Visions of Neal*, and *Desolation Angels* and *Beat Generations*, that's the play, we're making a little movie out of the third act called *Pull My Daisy*. Neal . . . Neal was a great Midwest Poolroom Saint. Neal Cassady and I love each other greatly."

Final note, "In any case, apparently what Allen wants you to do is to abandon this project entirely but it's too late. So in putting in these inserts, corrections, additions and deletions I'm doing the best I can do to promote a hopelessly committed venture. I want you to know that in discussing Cassady, Ginsberg, Burroughs, myself, Orlovsky and Corso you're dealing with some great American writers, the greatest since the Transcendentalists (Thoreau, Emerson, Whitman, Dickinson) and your name will go down with us or up with us. You will go 'up'! You must realize that what we mean by 'shallow journalism' is simply the failure to give complete tragic detail to your facts for the sake of 'sensational' touches. These 'sensational touches' are only sensational today, not tomorrow, when a posterity will want to know every detail and fact of this our sad life today. You know for instance that I, as author of *Doctor Sax* am no clown-drunkard merely. That I am a man of stature which will be recognized when the dust settles. A lot of jealous critics hate us, you know that. Corso and Burroughs have produced tremendously great work. You've got to give them your loving attention when you talk about them. A Certain Party does seem to put poor Allen Ginsberg in a silly light. If he grabbed a Harper girl by the neck I'm sure there was a certain charm in the way he did it, which you don't mention at all. You make him look like a hood. Why? Did Wechsler ask you to do a hatchet job on the beat generation on account of I called him a shit at Hunter College? Is that why? Are you truly sad and repentant when you come into Allen's kitchen and apologize or is that just your technique to get the story? Are you just buttering these young struggling artists (including myself) in order to make fools of them? If so, your reward will not be huge. In fact I can expose you in my Escapade column any time. But I think you're sincere and what you say about journalistic stringencies is accurate. I don't know. The whole thing has been a sad mess, that young kids in this country instead of yearning to be jet pilots should have turned their attention to Rimbaud and Shakespeare and struggled to draw their breath in pain to tell a brother's story.

–Jean Louis

A Strange Game of Baseball with a Legendary Writer

Stan Isaacs, www.TheColumnists.com (2002)

Stan Isaacs is a former Newsday *sports and feature columnist and wrote the popular column "Out of Left Field," which won a National Headliners Award. He also had a one-year National Endowment for the Humanities fellowship at Stanford University and wrote a column for the ESPN page on the Internet. The first article here by Isaacs, "A Strange Game of Baseball with a Legendary Writer," was written for ESPN in 2002. The second article, from which the first one quotes, is printed in its entirety. It reveals Kerouac and his passion for his fantasy baseball game, which he had invented and maintained since his childhood. A modified version of such a game is currently popular on the Internet.*

A n item in a newspaper caught my attention. The story was about a literary exhibit in the Berg Collection of the New York Public Library that featured, among others, artifacts of the beat writer Jack Kerouac.

The exhibit, winding up next week, includes some of the homemade cards fashioned by Kerouac as a kid into a baseball game which he played even as an adult. The *Newsday* story by Aileen Jacobson quoted Kerouac's brother-in-law, John Sampas, saying "It was a very complicated game" and that "he didn't think Kerouac ever played the game with another person."

Well, it so happens that I played Kerouac's homemade baseball game with him.

This was on a frosty afternoon in the winter of 1961, when Kerouac, who coined the term, "Beat Generation," was living with his mother in a Cape Cod house on a nondescript street in Huntington, deep in the heart of Suffolk County suburbia on Long Island. I had read about the game and Kerouac living on Long Island. I contacted him, and, recognizing a kindred spirit, he invited me out to his house to play the game.

Kerouac manipulated the game with the home-made cards, some hundred in all. A player-manager might turn over such cards as "infield tap," "miss," "off i.f.'s glove," "way up out of park," and "pop foul."

Many a youth made up such baseball cards. The charm of Kerouac's cards was the imagination he brought to them, creating wondrous personalities, keeping records, writing stories about the action.

Kerouac brought to life such players as El Negro of the St. Louis Whites, the leading home run hitter ("He's a big Negro from Latin America," Kerouac said. "El Negro means 'The Negro'") There's Wino Love of the Detroit Reds, the league's leading hitter with a .344 average. ("He's called Wino because he drinks, but he's still a great hitter.") Big Bill Louis is everybody's favorite. ("I patterned him after Babe Ruth; one day I had him coming to bat chewing on a frankfurter.") Pic Jackson, the league's best hitting pitcher, "likes to read the Sunday supplements; his name 'Pic' is short for Pictorial Review."

I was fascinated by the name Burlingame Japes. "Where did you ever come up with the name, Burlingame" I asked. He said, "It's the name of a town just outside of San Francisco." (Some twenty years later I became friends with a man I met in San Francisco; he lived in . . . Burlingame).

Kerouac grew up in Lowell, Mass. There is a picture of him as a high school football star at Lowell High in the library exhibit. He went to Columbia on a football scholarship, broke his leg as a sophomore, and didn't play again. He is a cult figure today whose books are expensive collectors' items.

The archives include a grade-school notebook for April 16, 1936, when Kerouac was fourteen. It reads: "Pop says he may bring me to a baseball game, Bees-Giants, Sunday. Hotcha. Home run leader is now [Mike] Kreevich of the White Sox with two today. Today it's $10 each, Don Doll and Naval Cadet at Ol' Grow."

"Ol' Grow" was his way of referring to the old Maryland race course, Havre De Grace. The entry was for a "mind" or fantasy bet he was making for the day.

Kerouac and I played his baseball card game through the late afternoon hours. I grew heady from the Petri wine we sipped through the innings. His white-haired mother would pop into the living room, chastising him not to make a mess. He was thirty-nine at the time and would die eight years later in 1969.

He conducted a running commentary about the players as the game proceeded. His Blues scored a run in the first inning, my Browns took a three-to-one lead in the third, matched his run in the sixth with a pair of runs, and we wrapped things up with a four-run rally in the seventh inning.

This rally started when his shortstop, Francis X. Cudley ("an Irishman from Boston who stood up at the plate very erect, like a Jesuit"), fumbled a grounder by Johnny Keggs. ("Keggs is an old guy;

his neck is seared from the Arkansas sun. He has a brother named Earl who used to be a ball player but who now is back in Texarkana selling hardware.")

The rally continued with Ron Melaney's second hit and a two-run double by Lefty Murphree that knocked out Larry Hooker and brought on Hugh Nesbitt, a six-foot-seven relief specialist. An error by his first baseman, Sugar Ray Simms ("he looks like Sugar Ray Robinson"), "trying to showboat a grounder" and a third hit by slugger Herb Jangraw upped the Browns lead to its final margin of nine-two.

My pitcher, Ron Melaney, ended the game striking out three of the last five Blues. When I visited the library and was shown some of Kerouac's papers by archivist Isaac Gerwitz, I learned that Jack had written a story centering on his baseball game that was published in the May 1958 *Esquire*. In the story, called "Ronnie on the Mound,"[37] he free-associated the action much as he had when playing with me. And I noted, too, that the Ronnie of the story was the same Ron Melaney who beat Kerouac's Blues for me that 1961 afternoon in Northport, Long Island.

Footnote: Kerouac was disillusioned by Columbia football coach Lou Little because Little lost interest in him once he didn't play football any more. Years later, after Kerouac's novel *On the Road* became a best-seller and established his reputation as the most celebrated of the Beat Generation writers, I ran into Little at a pro football game at Yankee Stadium. I mentioned to him that I had seen Jack Kerouac recently.

Little said, "Oh, yes, he was a good boy. What's he doing now?"

Playing Baseball with Jack Kerouac

Stan Isaacs, *Newsday* (February 16, 1961)

Kerouac had first written Isaacs in November 1958, expressing an enthusiasm for the sports reporter's interest in him. On November 12, he wrote in a postcard: "I'm extremely honored to've heard from a sports writer and a good one at that—I've always wanted to be a sports reporter and now that I could be one (offers everywhere) I haven't even got time to go to Paris and see a horse race, or time to p." Later that month, Kerouac wrote him once again, apologizing for a "5-day bender" that caused him to miss an appointment with Isaacs. To avoid committing further irresponsibility, Kerouac instead invited Isaacs to his home.

T he snow was a few feet deep outside, but the cry of the hot dog vendor and the crack of the warm-up ball against the catcher's mitt sounded inside writer Jack Kerouac's house in Northport recently as the Pittsburgh Browns prepared to take the field against the visiting Chicago Blues in a battle for fifth place.

Chicago manager Cracker Jack Kerouac chose the Blues'

curveballing righty, Larry Hooker, to protect the Blue's one-game lead over the Browns. Pants Isaacs, sometime reporter filling in for ailing Pittsburgh manager Pie Tibbs, countered with his young ace, hard-luck Ron Melaney.

"Melaney has a blazing fast ball," Kerouac said. "I created him the same night I unveiled Bob Gold of the league-leading Cincinnati Blacks. Gold is the fastest pitcher in the league, with an eleven-to-four record, with a two-point-three-six earned-run average." While the fans in the Plymouth Stadium awaited the cry of "play ball," Kerouac—the low priest of the Beat Generation—sketched in some background on his baseball game.

He manipulates it with a set of homemade cards. It is a game he has used in some of his short stories, and he hopes to put it on the market some day. "I usually play it alone when I'm in the woods," he said as he made up a box score in the official league stenographic notebook.

Kerouac's league is full of great players. There's El Negro of the St. Louis Whites, the leading home run hitter. ("He's a big Negro from Latin America," Kerouac said. " 'El Negro' means 'The Negro.'") "There's Wino Love of the Detroit reds, the league's leading hitter with a .344 average. ("He's called 'Wino' because he drinks, but he's still a great hitter.") Big Bill Louis is everybody's favorite. ("I patterned him after Babe Ruth; one day I had him come to bat chewing on a frankfurter.") Pic Jackson, the league's best hitting pitcher, likes to read the Sunday supplements and his name "Pic" is short for Pictorial Review."

Kerouac turned over the first card and Melaney's first pitch was a strike. Ron quickly retired Chicago's first two hitters, the Simms brothers. "Sonny Simms, the center fielder, is like Willie Mays," Kerouac said. "His younger brother, Sugar Ray, was just brought up from the minors. He's called Sugar Ray because he is a flashy character and looks like Sugar Ray Robinson." With two out, Melaney walked Byrd Duff, and Earl Morrison, a tall left-handed batter with eyeglasses, sent him home with a double to left.

Pittsburgh came back with a run in its half. Burlingame Japes celebrated his return to the lineup by starting the rally with a walk. "Japes," Kerouac said, "is forty years old now, a little left-handed hitter who in his younger days was the league base-stealing champ. I put him in for Joe Boston, who broke his leg sliding and who wasn't helping the team anyway." Slugger Herb Jangraw singled Japes to second. Then a walk to catcher Herm Bigger loaded the bases. ("Bigger is a Roy Campanella type. He thinks there's nothing better than comfortable shoes and a good mattress.") The run scored as Hooker walked John Gronning on four pitches.

Manager Isaacs talked to Melaney before the second inning, and Ron proceeded to pitch four scoreless innings. In the meantime, the Pittsburgh Browns peeked away at Hooker for a three-one lead.

Chicago scored again in the sixth as Morrison singled, stole second, and scored on a triple by Francis X. Cudley. ("He's an Irishman from Boston. He stands up at the plate very erect, like a Jesuit.")

Pittsburgh came back in its half on a two-run homer by Gronning. ("That's what makes this game so good; he's only a .200 hitter but even he can come through.") The Browns then added four more in the seventh on a rally that started when Cudley messed up a grounder by Keggs. ("Keggs is an old guy; his neck is seared from the Arkansas sun. He has a brother named Earl who used to be a ball player, but who now is back in Texarkana selling hardware.")

The rally continued with Melaney's second hit and a two-run double by Lefty Murphree that knocked out Hooker and brought on

Hugh Nesbitt, a six-foot-seven relief specialist. An error by Sugar Ray, trying to showboat a grounder, and a third hit by Jangraw upped the Browns' lead to nine-two.

Simms atoned for the error by homering in the eight, but Melaney bore down after that, stroking out three of the last five hitters. The last out was a grounder to shortstop by pinch-hitter Hophead Deane. "Some people think he's called 'Hophead' because he takes pot, but actually it's because he wears his hat askew and does silly things," Kerouac said.

It was a good game.

Beat Bard Denies He's the Daddy-O

Alfred Albelli, *New York Daily News* (December 14, 1961)

Joan Haverty Kerouac, still married to Jack in the middle of the 1950s, made desperate attempts to collect both paternity payments for their daughter, Jan, and later his signature on divorce papers. Kerouac, still maintaining his belief that the girl was not his, made it a habit to hide from Joan. Writing to Allen Ginsberg in 1957, he said:

I was feeling so good because no lushing and happy thoughts of concentrating on Duluoz Legend, damn her, she's like a snake snapping at my heels . . . . She got some doctor to prove she couldn't work and support her child, because of TB . . . . She made sneaky calls to Sterling who dug her right away without my telling him and kept mum . . . . So what I'll do Allen, when I get their roundabout letters, is answer them, mail the letter to you to mail from Casablanca, as tho I was there.

Kerouac retained Eugene Brooks, Ginsberg's brother, as his attorney after he was served a summons demanding a back payment of $17,500 in child support. The stress of the case turned him into a self-described "ugly ghoul" as his drinking accelerated.

J ack Kerouac, the bard of the beatniks, flatly denied yesterday that he was the father of a nine-year-old daughter borne by his former wife, and claimed instead that years ago, when he tried to effect a reconciliation, she barred him from their apartment because "another man was in bed."

Kerouac made the charge in Supreme Court in asking for a blood test of himself, ex-wife, and daughter that "might exclude me as the father." Justice Samuel Gold set down a hearing for tomorrow.

Brunette Joan Kerouac, thirty, former actress and model, of 163 Avenue B, has sued the author of *On the Road* for $17,500 maintenance and support for herself and the child, Janet Michele, saying that she, the nine-year-old, and four-year-old twin daughters by a subsequent marriage are "completely destitute and dependent on relief payments from the city."

Trial of her suit for support was scheduled by Gold for January 17.

Tells of Separation

In denying responsibility, Kerouac said: "Now, some nine years after the birth of the child, she has brought this action. I am not the father of this child."

Kerouac said that in April 1951, "I was compelled to leave the apartment in which we were living at my wife's insistence."

"Some weeks after I was kicked out of our apartment, I attempted to make a reconciliation, but she met me at the outer door and told me I could not come in because another man was in bed," Kerouac charged. He added: "I did not even learn through her that she was pregnant, but only through a mutual friend. She later remarried and moved to Missouri and had twins by her second husband. Then, at the end of 1960, she separated from her second husband and returned to New York."

Her Side of Things

Joan, who is represented by attorney Lewis B. Stackwell, has charged that she even had to pay the maternity bills after the child was born. She said that Kerouac recently sold a book to a Hollywood company, while she is forced to support herself and the child at "menial jobs including that of a waitress."

The Kerouacs were married in November 1950, and she charges he abandoned her in June 1951, which he denies. Kerouac lives in Northport, Long Island.

Dialogues in Great Books

Charles E. Jarvis and James Curtis, WCAP Radio Interview,
Lowell, Massachusetts (October 1962)

*Kerouac spent a four-day-long drunken debacle at John
Clellon Holmes's Connecticut home in late summer 1962. In
his journal, Holmes writes:*

*Jack sits in torn blue pajama bottoms, a rank tee shirt,
grimy socks and Japanese slippers, unshaven in nearly a
week, his hair never combed till 5:00, growing headier &
headier in the armpits, smoking his little Camels, fixing
his brandies & soda, padding around with stiff, faltering
old man's steps, talking in torrential gusts . . . . He drinks
a fifth of Courvoisier every day, plus rations of Scotch,
beer & wine . . . . Sweet & tentative when sober, he
becomes truculent, paranoiac, garrulous, stiff-jointed,
wild-eyed, exhaustless, and amnesiac when drunk.
Booze alone can seem to produce in him the "ecstasy" he
needs to get thru time.*

For many years, Kerouac had longed to revisit his hometown; he impulsively decided to make the trip after tiring of Holmes's home.

Professor Charles E. Jarvis, an instructor with Lowell Technical Institute (now the University of Massachusetts at Lowell) witnessed the writer's entrance at a Market Street bar: "When I saw him I was startled. I hadn't seen him for years. The once dark-maned, clear-eyed, Endymion youth had become somewhat soggy. His face was booze-lined. He was bombed, and he was raucous." Though the booze did little to erode his imaginative mind, it was also a false euphoria. Though he exuded genuine glee to see some of his old friends and acquaintances, he must have felt a twinge of disappointment and regret knowing that they felt pity for him. Jarvis, confronting Kerouac in a bar, professed his admiration for Kerouac's work. Before the end of a long night, Jarvis proposed that Kerouac sit for an interview with him and his cohost, James Curtis, for WCAP, a local radio station.

Kerouac agreed to be interviewed by Jarvis and Curtis, an attorney. Accompanying Kerouac was his future wife, Stella Sampas. During the course of a half-hour, Kerouac rambled from topic to topic, wittily evading Jarvis's attempts to reign him in with an intellectual discourse regarding his work. Preserved on tape by WCAP, the interview is published here in its entirety.

CJ: Good morning, ladies and gentlemen. Once again we're here with "Dialogues in Great Books," and this morning we feel that we have reached a milestone in our program. We've been on the air now for six years, and we've discussed many, many books, many essays, many philosophical treatises. But this morning we feel that we have reached an excellent milestone in our radio career. This morning . . . all right.

JK: Lewis Milestone.*

CJ: This interruption by the way was by the internationally famous Jack Kerouac of Lowell. We have done Jack's books over the air here over the years and we've had some fine responses from our listeners and as I've said, this morning we have the distinct pleasure and privilege to have Jack Kerouac here with us and we intend to talk with him about many things. And, of course, my colleague, Attorney James T. Curtis, is here . . . and Jim, how do you feel about this?

JC: Well, I think this is, to be trite about it, quite momentous . . . like thunder.

JK: Why are you staring at each other?

JC: Good morning, Jack. You're in good form this morning.

CJ: You certainly are.

JC: I heard thunder last night and as I walked down Market Street, I looked at the right and there he was.

JK: You heard what?

JC: Thunder.

JK: Thunder?

JC: Thunder. Now, Jack, tell me about this thunder. What are you doing in Lowell?

JK: Lewis Thunder is my name.

CJ: I thought it was Milestone.

JK: Lewis Milestone,[38] Gallstone, Death.

CJ: All right, fine. Jack, how did you happen to all of a sudden come to Lowell after an absence of about eight or nine years, as I recall you were telling us.

---

* Boyhood friend of Kerouac.

JK: Let me see. Why did I come to Lowell? Oh yeah. I came here to see George Apostolos.

CJ: George Apostolos is a boyhood friend, if we might say. Have you been keeping in touch with him all these years?

JK: Oh yeah. We don't write. He doesn't write. *I* write. I write to him; he never answers. He's giggling right this minute. George Apostolakos is his real name.

CJ: Is he one of your chief characters in your first book, *The Town and the City*, as I recall?

JK: Yeah.

CJ: He was.

JK: What did I call him in the book?

CJ: I think it was Rigopoulos. Was it J. G. Rigopoulos?

JK: Yeah, J. G . . . . Yeah, Rigopoulos . . . G. J.

CJ: G. J. How did G. J. become a chief character in your book?

JK: We grew up across the street from each other. We threw small crab apples at trees.

JC: Jack, in reading your books, many times when we were discussing *Dr. Sax* . . .

JK: When were we discussing *Dr. Sax?*

JC: Well, Charles and I; when we were discussing *Dr. Sax*, many people wrote to us or called in. They wanted to know whether or not we felt . . . we . . . now, we didn't write the book . . . there was any connection between "The Shadow" as we used to hear him on the radio, and [the character of] Dr. Sax.

JK: Yeah.

JC: They were right. There was a connection.

JK: The Shadow is a creation of Lamont Cranston's. No, what was the name of the guy who wrote the book—*The Shadow* magazine? Lamont Cranston.

CJ: Wasn't he the chief character . . .

JK: No, that was The Shadow's other name. He'd be riding in a cab and he was Lamont Cranston, wearing a tuxedo, and all of a sudden he'd go, "Hee, hee, hee," and he'd sneak out of the cab and he'd go off and blast the New York underworld. I forget the name of the author though.

CJ: Well, I was going to ask you this . . .

JK: Must've been Lamont Cranston.

CJ: Yes . . . why is this Dr. Sax such an important character? Is this a collective, a syncretic character? What kind of character is this? Will you give us symbolism? What does he stand for?

JK: In Pawtucketville [a section of Lowell bordering the Centralville section and the Merrimack River, the Kerouacs moved from Centralville to Pawtucketville in 1934], there are big trees and the wind blows through them in October and we're all hiding there and playing basketball and everything, and G. J. Apostolakos, Apostolos, George Apostolos, is coming down the stairs, and I'm hiding in the shadows and I grab him and break his arm . . . I didn't break his arm. I almost broke his arm, and he gave me a headlock and almost killed me [laughter].

CJ: You were playing.

JK: We were playing.

JC: Is there supposed to be any symbolism about this, Jack?

JK: It's glee.

JC: Just glee.

JK: It's glee. Lowell glee, in fact.

CJ: Local glee. Now, Jack . . .

JK: What did you say? Local? I said Lowell.

CJ: Okay, Lowell.

JC: There's a difference between Lowell and local . . .

JK: Incidentally, I want to make an announcement.

CJ: Yes, sir.

JK: In my opinion, Lowell, Massachusetts, is now the most interesting city in the United States of America.

JC: Well, thank you very much.

JK: It is.

CJ: Well, that's an accolade, and I certainly . . .

JC: Why do you say . . .

JK: I saw a thousand guys yesterday, from Moody Street all the way to the Greeks and the Portuguese and everybody. I gave my cross away to a Portuguese guy whose name I have to get later.

CJ: You feel Lowell is a city full of interesting people and . . .

JK: Terrific. Sweet people.

CJ: Has it provided you with a lot of material?

JK: Even the police are sweet here. What?

CJ: The sources. The city of Lowell has provided you with many sources for your literary works. Is that it? It has. If I may ask you this, Jack, what about these other books, for instance? Now, *On the Road* is a departure, let's say, from your Lowell books in a manner of speaking.

JK: Eliopoulos?

CJ: Isn't it?

JK: Eliopoulos is sitting and listening.

CJ: Yes, he is.

JC: Yes, he is present. We might say that's Chris Eliopoulos who is present, and also Miss Stella Sampas who is present . . .

CJ: I was going to ask you, Jack . . .

JK: Who hasn't said a ding-dong word.

CJ: These books here . . . books like *On the Road, The Dharma Bums*, they're kind of . . .

JK: All true stories.

CJ: Are they a departure from the Lowell type books that you've had?

JK: Yeah. When I took off West, you see. California.

JC: Let me ask you this, Jack. Now you wrote *The Dharma Bums*, and we enjoyed reading it. You said you lived up on a mountain all alone for all those months.

JK: Yes, as a Forest Service lookout.[39]

JC: I see. I mean, you were up there alone looking for fires.

JK: Well, it was my job—and I had a fire-finder—and I found a few fires.

JC: Now, there was a good scene I liked there when you described running down the mountain.

JK: You know, it's not true what Smokey the Bear says.

JC: Why?

JK: What does he say? "Only you can prevent forest fires." Most forest fires are started by dry lightning. In other words, it's lightning but no rain.

JC: Not the cigarette butts.

JK: Nah, there's very few fires started . . . maybe a few pyromaniacs. Most of them are started by lightning without the rain.

CJ: Jack, would you say in a way nature is at fault also for some of the fires.

JK: Nature starts most of the fires.

CJ: It does.

JC: On purpose.

JK: On purpose [laughter].

CJ: On your literary style—so much has been said about your literary style and there've been so many things written about it. Some people have said that you write with some kind of demonic, animal energy. That once you begin writing, you just don't stop until you feel that you've completed what you were to say.

JK: I write in vast, eighteen-hundred-words-a-night bursts for about six nights, and the book is done. I use teletype paper; I put a sixteen-foot strip of teletype paper through the typewriter and blast away, single spaced, saying, "I'm going to tell you what happened," because it's all true stories and all I do is change the names, for libelous reasons, although I have never insulted anyone in my literature.

CJ: I'm sure you haven't, I'm sure you haven't.

JC: Jack, you never go back . . .

JK: That's what Balzac[40] did, you know, with a little twist. Balzac did a few other things [laughter].

JC: Jack, you said last night you never go back to revise and correct . . .

JK: Never what?

JC: Because . . .

JK: Once God moves the hand, you go back and revise, it's a sin!

CJ: That's it.

JC: What if your thought can be improved upon by revision; it might hang better logically; it might hang better in harmony.

JK: Every time I turn on the faucet in the toilet . . . wait a minute [laughter].

JC: In the kitchen . . .

JK: My thought went into the river. Deep river you got here. There's a lot of water in Lowell.

CJ: Yes, a lot of falls, canals.

JK: My thought does not have to be improved because I got it from Heaven, just like you got yours.

CJ: You feel that it's perfect, Jack, once it leaves you? Is that it?

JC: He's smiling again.

CJ: Do you feel once this thought . . . [laughter] . . . once this thought leaves you . . . [more laughter].

JK: Hey, Dave. By the way, ladies and gentleman, the engineer is . . . Dave Cate?

JC: That's right.

JK: How do you spell that?

DC: C-A-T-E.

JC: He is a fine engineer.

JK: What kind of name is that—Roman?

CJ: That's an English name.

JK: English? Birmingham?

CJ: No, Cornish.

JK: Cornish?

DC: London.

JK: A-a-ah. I used to be a footpad in London in my previous lifetime.

JC: Ladies and gentleman, we will now give you an interview between Jack Kerouac and Dave Cate.

CJ: I think that would be very interesting, I'm sure. Let me ask you this, Jack. How do you create all these fantastic word pictures? You seem to create words, you combine words, you have words that . . .

JK: No, wait a minute now. You're asking me about my prose.

CJ: Exactly.

JK: Now, I read all the *Remembrance of Things Past* by Marcel Proust, and I decided to do just like he did—but fast.

CJ: Fast.

JK: Fast. Marcel Proust had asthma and was lying around writing and eating in bed. Once in a while he'd get up feebly, put on a coat, and go down to a bar in Paris. He'd say, "Where's the head waiter?" And the head waiter had died. He had to go back and write that. That was a great writer, you know. I mean, he *is* a great writer.

JC: Jack, you will sit down and sustain writing for many hours in one day?

JK: Aside from all this—now wait a minute, I'm finishing this.

JC: Okay, all right, all right . . . go ahead.

JK: Shakespeare—William Shakespeare—is known to have written spontaneously, but I have arguments with guys at the University of California and at the University of Oxford in England. They claim that he was a craftsman and he revised. He wrote *Hamlet* in one night.

CJ: This is your opinion.

JK: This is my opinion.

CJ: My I ask you this, Jack . . .

JK: And *King Lear* the next night.

JC: Jack . . .

CJ: Was the fact that he was an actor . . .

JK: First he started off as the guy holding the horses in front of the theater. Little boy, twelve years old, holding horses. Then he became an actor.

CJ: The fact that he was an actor, you feel this in a way helped his writing and this is why you say it was so spontaneous and . . .

JK: All I know is he died of drinking in Avon when Ben Jonson and Philip Massinger came to visit him. They were very sad about that. These are all Englishmen.

CJ: What do you think of this other opinion that a lot of Shake-speare's works were written by Christopher Marlowe? This has been . . .

JK: No, no, no, no. You know how Francis Bacon died? Incidentally, he was one of the greatest lawyers–in fact, the greatest lawyer of all time. His real name was–you know what his real name was? What was it? Lord what? Ends in "m." Bum, rum. What his name, Dave? Well, anyway, that's his real name.

JC: Well, Jack, while you're here . . .

JK: Lord Verulam! And his greatest opponent in the law courts in England, when the jurisprudence of the United States of America was established, was Sir Edward Coke.

JC: Now, let's discuss your new book. The new book that's hit the presses . . .

JK: They backed up the Magna Carta, however you call it . . . .

JC: Mr. Kerouac.

JK: What?

JC: Let us discuss your new book, *Big Sur*, which has just hit the presses, and we intend to review it here. Tell us . . .

JK: There's a few typos in it, by the way.

JC: Tell us about . . .

JK: Typographical errors

CJ: Will you tell us about this book?

JK: I told my mother. I said, "Listen, there's some awful typographical errors in this book," and she said, "When I was working in the shoe factories in Lowell and I made a mistake skiving shoes, I had to pay."

JC: Well, tell what the book is about. What are you saying in this book?

CJ: What's your purpose here, Jack? Is there a message in this book? Is there any kind of special . . .

JK: No, no. Yeah, of course there's a message. The message is . . . ooh, that goes too far back. It goes back to a vision I had of Heaven.

CJ: We'd like to here about it.

JK: My job is to describe Heaven just a little bit. There's a thousand guys in this town that know more about Heaven than I do, including George Akakos, who's one of the sweetest guys that I've ever met, really.

CJ: And do you feel you accomplished this in the book that you just finished?

JK: I accomplish anything.

CJ: You did . . .

JK: I'm dead? What?

CJ: No, I said "you did." No, you're not dead yet.

JC: What about the sea. You make a reference to the sea and the poetry of the sea. I think in your last . . .

JK: Yeah, you see James Joyce, who's also—well, you see, Proust and Joyce are the greatest twentieth-century writers.

JC: No question about it.

JK: Proust, I mean Joyce, was gonna' sit by the sea. He's blind, remember? He's gonna sit by the sea and write the sounds of the sea, and he died and didn't do it, so I did it for him.

CJ: That's marvelous.

JK: And this is only the beginning. That's Part One. That's the Pacific. I'm gonna sit off the end of Land's End, Cornwall, and write the sounds of the Atlantic. And then I have to go all the way down to the mouth of the Ganges and write the sounds of the . . . what's the name of that one . . . the Indian Ocean? Whew! And then I have to go all the way up to Hokkaido and write the sounds of the North Pacific.

CJ: You've written the sounds of the Merrimack very well, Jack, haven't you?

JK: [laughs] I'm doing good, eh?

JC: I like the–there's one line that goes–the wave sounds like this: sh-h-h-h weee . . . whistling in Dixie.

JK: You ain't just whistling Dixie. You know where I got that? From Sam Snead, the golfer.

CJ: Oh, you saw it on television somewhere?

JK: Yeah, that commercial where he's shooting his golf and he's saying, "This is the greatest, this weather . . ." and the guy says, "Really?" and he says, "I ain't just whistling Dixie."

JC: I think it was Alka Seltzer or something.

JK: Yeah, Alka Seltzer [much laughter]. I threw a bottle of Alka Seltzer at a doorway on Moody Street yesterday because I was lost. I had bought an Alka Seltzer for a guy who had heartburn or something. I couldn't find my way back, so I threw the Alka Seltzer at the doorway of a bar that was closed. In fact, I think it was the Flamingo Lounge.

JC: Oh, that's been closed for some time.

CJ: Can I ask you this, Jack. You said you have some more books that you are . . .

JK: I have three books already written.

CJ: And they're not published yet? Is that it? Or are they going to be?

JK: They're going to be; of course they're going to be.

CJ: Could you give us some idea as to what . . .

JK: *Visions of Gerard.*

JC: Who's Gerard?

JK: My brother. He died when he was nine years old and I was four.

JC: You mean you remember him?

JK: Do I *remember* him?

CJ: Sure he does.

JK: He's the one who's doing all this. When he was on his deathbed, nine nuns of St. Louis de France filed into his room and said,

"Gerard, repeat what you told us about Heaven." You know, he could hardly repeat it [at this point Kerouac's voice trembles with emotion], but he did. And they took down their notes and went away.

CJ: This is one of the best books that you just . . . .

JK: Then Father Labossiere came to the house and put his foot under the kitchen table and all that, and said, "Don't worry Mrs. Kerouac."

CJ: I think that was very tender. Could you tell us . . .

JK: He told my mother before he died he was going to build her a little white cottage in Heaven [Kerouac's voice trembles on the word "Heaven."]

CJ: That's a very beautiful thought, Jack, very beautiful thought.

JK: And that's Gerard Kerouac. Gerard *François* Kerouac.

CJ: Could you tell something about the other books you have?

JK: The other one is something called *Desolation Angels*, which is a sequel to *The Dharma Bums*, which is all about all the drunken degenerate poets going around all over the world doing every-thing, you know. And there's another one; I haven't named it yet. It carries the story a little further.[41] Actually, I don't know what to write next.

JC: Write about the sea.

CJ: Jack, do you feel you can still write books about Lowell? You haven't exhausted . . .

JK: Well, *Visions of Gerard* is about Lowell.

CJ: About Lowell, of course. Do you think you have other books in you about Lowell?

JK: Yeah, coming, oh yeah.[42]

CJ: Well, we're certainly looking forward to all of them, I'm sure. You mentioned *The Dharma Bums*. You know, there's been a lot said about *dharmakaya*.

JK: Dharmakaya?

CJ: Could you tell us something about this philosophy? Few people understand this philosophy.

JK: First of all, I will tell you where Buddhism comes from. It comes from Persia, from the Mithridatic Light. And he came all the way from India, Buddha. Dharmakaya? That means . . . I knew it yesterday! *Dharma* means *truth*. *Kaya* means *body* in Sanskrit.

JC: On the way to the radio station you mentioned that you do practice somewhat of a yogi by standing on your head three times a day.

JK: No, no. Three minutes a day. Yes, all the doctors are gonna' go out of business.

JC: What does it do for you? First of all, I notice your hair is still black. You still have all your hair.

JK: It keeps your hair, it's good for your teeth, good for the eyeballs. It's not good for your sinuses, though. It's good for your glands, it's good for your pituitary gland and the other one, and it's good for your stomach. You never get an ulcer; it's good for the liver, you never get liver trouble. It's good for the pancreas and good for the extremities . . . hands and feet; and you're never sick, never. All you do is drink.

CJ: May I ask about some people like Ginsberg and Ferlinghetti? Did you know these people well?

JK: I'm charmed.

CJ: I'd love to hear about them.

JK: All right. Frame your question.

CJ: My question is this: one of the most famous poems that has come out now, the past three, four years . . .

JC: Which we did on this program.

CJ: . . . is the poem "Howl" by Allen Ginsberg. Could you tell us something about its creative reasons–the way Ginsberg might've been inspired by it. What his talent . . . what force motivated him to create this poem?

JK: "Ashcans and unobtainable dollars."[43]

CJ: Really? This was the motivating force?

JK: Yeah.

JC: You think if he obtained dollars, he would not be motivated?

JK: He's from the Ukraine–you know, the Jews of the Ukraine.

CJ: He's of Jewish extraction.

JK: So is Norman Mailer by the way. All the literary intellectual Jews of New York are all from West Russia; the Lower East Side. They're always talking 'bout unobtainable dollars.

JC: What do you think of Norman Mailer as a writer?

JK: I don't know. I haven't read him. Who cares? I think he stinks.

JC: I noticed *Time* magazine lumped you and Jimmy Jones together.

JK: Well, now, Jimmy Jones . . .[44]

JC: There is a writer.

JK: No. He's a tough man.

CJ: He's hard? In what way?

JK: He's a big, tough guy, physically strong.

CJ: Does he have literary strength?

JK: I haven't read him yet. See, I'm reading such things as Cervantes. I'm very busy, really. I'm reading Petronius.

CJ: Oh, marvelous. Have you read anything by Plato or Aristotle?

JK: That Greek guy? Oh yes. I know all about 'em. All the Fordham priests told me about Plato.

CJ: Excellent, fine.

JK: I haven't read Plato yet.

JC: Jack, have you done any teaching, like guest lecturing at many universities and colleges?

JK: I'm invited to lecture everywhere . . . Oxford, Cambridge, Tokyo, Vienna.

JC: Have you gone, have you accepted, have you contemplated on going?

JK: Well, I'm so busy. First I have to investigate one thousand guys waiting for me right this very minute out there in that bar. What's the name of that bar? Oh, it's a good one. Cuckoo O'Connell's. What a bar! That's the best bar I ever went to.

CJ: Could I ask you this, Jack. Could you give us something about Ginsberg and Ferlinghetti. Have you talked much . . .

JK: Ferlinghetti is a mediocrity . . . mediocrity. In fact, he imitates me. Ginsberg and Kerouac are good, too, you know.

CJ: Of course, of course.

JK: The genius is William Seward Burroughs, who's an Englishman. I wrote him a letter recently and I said, "Are you the crumbling Burroughs or the rotten Burroughs?" Well, you know . . .

JC: Didn't he write *Big Table, No. 1*?

JK: Yes. *Naked Lunch.*

JC: Now, Jack, we have about three minutes. Why don't you tell us about some of your newest . . .

JK: He's a brilliant linguist, brilliant linguist . . .

JC: In the last three minutes . . .

JK: Brilliant linguist. Had to say it three times: Father, Son, Holy Ghost.

JC: Yes. Now tell us in the next few minutes we have—we're almost out of time—what your future plans are, your impressions, et cetera We'd like to hear you.

JK: W-e-l-l, probably Tony Sampas will drive me into Boston and I'll fly to New York and go get drunk with some Scotch.

JC: Are you planning to go to Florida?

JK: Yeah, I have to get there. My mother's there. I live in a house with my mother. It's a monastery, and I'm a monk, and my mother is the Reverend Mother.

JC: Are you planning to ever return to Lowell?

JK: I wouldn't mind moving back here.

JC: Why don't you? Are you planning to?

JK: Well, don't you think that everybody'd get drunk every day?

JC: We'd have a party every day.

JK: We'd all be in Lowell and get sick.

JC: I suppose so—if we stood on our heads.

CJ: Jack, a lot of people ask about Lowell . . . could you give us some closing statement on, let's say, what you actually see in the city of Lowell which has given you so many sources for your famous books?

JK: It's a vast collection of Christians.

CJ: Christians.

JC: Do you see any visions here, any visions of God. Do you see God wherever you go—in a pantheistic way?

JK: No—in a Deistic way, in an Gnostic way, in a Jesuitical way. I'm a Jesuit!

JC: Are you a Jesuit, Jack? All right. Well, our time is up, isn't it?

JK: How'd you like that, Mike?

CJ: I'd like to thank Jack Kerouac sincerely and very cordially for coming here and speaking to us for this . . .

JK: In a pantheistic way . . .

CJ: . . . half-hour.

JK: I'm only making fun of you two. You're all right. I'm just trying to bug you. Pull your leg a little bit.

JC: I understand. I'll tell you, you're my good client and we're gonna do something.

CJ: And we want to thank you very much, Jack, and we certainly hope you'll come back again . . .

JK: What's your name—Arapaho Rappaport?

CJ: No, it's Charles E. Jarvis.

JC: You've heard of him. Would you like to meet him? This is Jack Kerouac, Mr. Jarvis.

CJ: And now, until next week, we bid everybody a pleasant Sunday.

Kerouac in Lowell

"Pertinax," *Lowell Sun* (September 19, 1962)

*Kerouac made a splash in his hometown during the early fall
of 1962. Writing to John Clellon Holmes on October 9, 1962,
he describes his raucous visit:*

> *My adventure in Lowell was fantastic: I stood poor
> Lowell on its head: when asked to go onstage of rock 'n'
> roll club to be introduced instead did a 7-second cos-
> sack dance—held up traffic they tell me one night on
> Moody Street as I recited poetry with a jug in my hand
> (this I don't remember)—when I left, my original favored
> bar of 8 bookies was suddenly a bedlam of 250 people
> of all kinds including photogs, teenage girls, whores,
> musicians, garage mechanics, elderly interview ladies,
> lawyers, took off fast with two new Lowell buddies and
> drove to Lucien's in the Village . . . .*

Mary Sampas of the Lowell Sun *reported on Kerouac's visit to
Lowell over several days.*

S o there I was Sunday night sitting next to royalty, but it was all very, very informal, for this was the world's most casual monarch: This was Jack Kerouac, King of the Beatniks. (Once he'd put it in writing that though he'd originated beatniks, he wasn't one himself . . . but now he was saying proudly, "I've changed my mind. I'm, yes, I'm the King of the Beatniks.")

The King of the Beatniks came to Lowell by taxi. By taxi from New York.[45] The driver's name was Bartalucci (Kerouac pronounced it dramatically, very Italiany), and the trip cost sixty-two dollars, but it wasn't much because he'd just been given a $10,000 advance on his latest book, *Big Sur*, and he was rich, yes he was rich, and he had an airplane ticket to somewhere, he wasn't sure just where.

It was a little unnerving to think that at the very moment the New York Sunday papers were being readied for their readers with the full-page ads for *Big Sur* and the reviews of *Big Sur*, that *Big Sur*'s daddy didn't care enough to stick around there but was rushing to the old hometown Lowell in a taxi, whizzing up to a Christian Hill house on Sunday at 3 A.M. Undoubtedly, Kerouac was ready for Lowell, but was Lowell ready for Jack Kerouac?

He spent Sunday whipping boisterously, roisterously through the city, so that by late evening he was what a non-Kerouac-type author would daintily call "feeling no pain." Kerouac, in fact, was having a very LARGE time, and if there was any truth in *Big Sur* (that the hero, Kerouac himself—no false modesty, he's ALWAYS the hero—was cracking up) then he was making a crack-up seem like a FUN thing to have.

He talked incessantly and athletically, jumping up and down, waving his arms, sometimes leaning over to play make-believe POP gun. He was full of a kind of REHEARSED restlessness (kept biting his nails but when he put his hand down, I saw the nails weren't bitten at all . . . he chain-drank beer but, like a trick glass, the glass was always the same: Half-full) and he was tanned, heavier, not at all dissipated-looking, tousle-haired, yes, but the blue eyes were clear. Kind of a beatnik.

He talked about: guardian angels (everyone has one) . . . his Lowell high school love—the thinly-disguised *Maggie Cassidy* from the book so titled—whom he'd been to see that day and who was still beautiful and whom he still loved ("I still love ALL the girls I loved") and who was going to be married soon . . . and he quoted from Hamlet, immediately after which he sang a snatch from "A Pretty Girl Is Like a Melody." . . . He thought it would be grand if we could all go somewhere right then, right THEN, like maybe maybe to the Bartlett school, and drink to it by the light of the moon.

Through *Big Sur* is the home of that other very controversial writer (*Tropic of Cancer*) Henry Miller, Kerouac hasn't met him yet. Miller has written glowingly of Kerouac, but Kerouac is "night people" and Miller "who's 99 years old, goes to bed too early for us to make connections." He was interested—but not too much—in his big N.Y. reviews that day, and only mildly irked by *Time* magazine's cavalier treatment of *Big Sur*. What angered him was that they roasted James Jones's *The Thin Red Line*; Jones wrote about how Company C took Guadalcanal . . . Guadalcanal . . . and some pantywaist on *Time* doesn't think that's enough.

The writer had left this city a strange, dream-enchanted boy, and was now back a strange, exciting, dream-haunted man known worldwide, translated into many languages. It was not, however, the kind of literary light return that could ever conceivably lead to, say, an address before the PTA. He talks the way he writes, though he apologizes for his candor after he's been too "candid" . . . and what he is, mostly, is an enigma: Is he for true? For more Kerouac, come back tomorrow . . . .

Conversation with Kerouac

"Pertinax," *Lowell Sun* (September 20, 1962)

I t is the city's open secret that—while reviewers (like *Saturday Review*'s this week) are mostly heaping praise on Jack Kerouac's new book *Big Sur*—the King of the Beatniks has come home to hold court in one continuing, monumental pub crawl, trailed by admirers and hangers-on . . . dispensing bizarre beatnik philosophy and sketches . . . leaving the nativeniks shocked or gaspingly titillated.

Sunday evening, between reminiscing (his memory for Lowell names and places is staggering if you don't discount the nightmare miles and dissipated years between the then and now) and table-thumping and jumping up to crow or bark or laugh, Kerouac had such as this to say:

Let's GO . . . let's go to Paris and visit Cocteau—Cocteau's door is ALWAYS open. Ah, but my favorite French writer is dead, he's dead.* In Vienna there's a Viennese, no, he's a

---

* Kerouac is referring to Louis-Ferdinand Celine.

GERMAN and his name is JACK KEROUAC. Once, I was in Morocco, and I saw a shepherd boy carrying a little LAMB. They told me there shepherd boys are always doing heart-breaking things like that, carrying LAMBS that way. Ah! Ah. When I went to Paris they had no ROOM for me. Queen Elizabeth was there. I hate what France has done to the French language. They've RUINED it. They've fancied it up. No one in France knows how to speak French except a couple of Normans. Where they really speak French is in Quebec.

Of Truman Capote, with whom he once served on a writers' panel, and who said that "Kerouac doesn't write, he TYPEwrites," Kerouac said, "Well I don't like HIM," giving a brief, deadly imitation of Capote, "but I liked his *Other Voices, Other Rooms*. And anyway I don't always TYPEwrite, either. Sometimes I write like this, with a pencil" (scribbling furiously on the table cloth), "until the candle goes out." Why the candle? Why NOT the candle? Kerouac found all this candle-questioning very odd, as though he would consider it amusing, even exotic, NOT to write by candlelight. "When the candle dies, it's my signal to stop. I write the way it comes to me from God. I never revise. To revise is TO SIN."

He said it took five nights to write *Big Sur*. Figured on that, his $10,000 advance on it pays him at the rate of $2000 a night, which is sensational writing money even if he never gets another dollar for it. His favorite Kerouac book is *Tristessa* (about "the girl I loved in Mexico") although most of his fans, he said, prefer his *On the Road*. He's not too happy about having written *The Town and the City* (his first book, about Lowell and New York) which caused the *New York Times'* eminent reviewer, Charles Poore, to compare Kerouac to Thomas Wolfe.

"Now Poore wants me to write like Fitz-ger-RRRALD! Sure I can write like Fitzgerald, listen, 'The room was glittering with diamonds–' That's like Fitzgerald and ah, ah, ah, isn't that bee-YOU-tiful?"

The King of the Beatniks (is it in character for him to carry a comb?) paused to comb his hair before embarking on a long story about how an enthusiastic fan–a photographer–could never greet Kerouac without pulling at him so athletically that he would always tear Kerouac's shirt. At the height of this tale, *Sun* photog Len Irvin arrived, and let it here be recorded to his everlasting credit for poise under extreme fire that he didn't even bat an eyelash when Kerouac jumped at him and asked crooningly, "YOU won't tear my shirt, will you?"

It remains this column's opinion that, whatever he may have done here subsequently, on Sunday evening Kerouac was PLAYING Kerouac as one sees him through his books, darkly. One could imagine him standing aside mentally, coolly calculating the action, APPROVING the way the scene would write. If he hadn't been there, at that Highlands home, but in a movie based on a Kerouac story, he'd be winning the Oscar for it next spring. That's how GOOD his characterization of Kerouac, King of the Beatniks was.

Kerouac Leaves Lowell

"Pertinax," *Lowell Sun* (September 25, 1962)

O n a flower day (to put it in his own Jack Kerouac–*Big Sur* words) he was going to say good-bye to San Francisco and go back home across autumn America and it was going to be the way it was in the beginning–simple golden eternity blessing all.

Only, CAN it ever really be the way it was in the beginning? Lowell could hardly look at Kerouac as just another boy come home again, for which other of her sons had been so widely hailed as the writer generating this decade's most excitement . . . or had his name flashed across the wide screen as author of a Technicolored movie . . . or had read his gleaming prose like poetry to Steve Allen's TV coast-to-coast piano accompaniment . . . or had become a byword even unto the youth of Russia?

And if Lowell could never again look at him without recognizing the international worth in him, then neither could he be entirely unselfconscious here. His defense was attack, so the shyness and sensitivity of him were hidden in the riotous toot, in the big blast, in the nonstop party . . . and the question that remains is not how HE behaved but how did YOU when with him, for after all, HE writes the books.

Look no more for him where the jazz-music floats and the brandy flows, for the go-go-goingest guy is gone. "Pert," he said Saturday night, all sober on the telephone, though he was to turn from it and be again the King of the Beatniks' own sozzled court jester, "Pert, I bought this silver cross in New York before I came here and I didn't know WHY I was buying it, but now I know it's for Marty Gouveia who's going to drive me to New York, to keep him safe when he drives back alone. I'm going back to Orlando, to WORK. I can't take much more here . . ."

(And how sinfully flattering to Lowell, this picture of her suddenly as one of those femme fatale cities, a kind of Massachusetts Macao, with her faster music and stronger wine luring men to inevitable doom. But then, no one has loved Lowell as wildly well as he, who has celebrated a field, a stretch of street, a building profile in such ecstatic terms that Riverside Street and Lowell High and the river are familiarly known to Kerouac-aficionados from Paris all the way to Perth.)

All week long people beseeched this column for the whereabouts of the elusive Kerouac . . . and Saturday he delayed his already six-hour-delayed departure (Mr. Gouveia all this time standing faithfully at-the-ready) till I could take two excited teenage girls to meet him. Did they expect the beatnik-king to be the stereotyped goatee with the "shades" and the studied ennui? What they met was a tanned, clean-shaven, good-looking, hand-kissing courtier who (language immaculately laundered) gave them oblique teenage ADVICE . . . as when expressing dismay that he found some young girls here to be too forward, and not as "nice" as they, as "nice" as he remembered the girls of his Lowell youth to have been . . . . And under his autograph he wrote for one of them a composed-on-the-spot poem:* "All

* Not really "composed-on-the-spot." Kerouac had composed this haiku (he called "Pops") in 1959 as part of his "American Haiku," a series of fifteen separate haiku.

day long wearing . . . a hat . . . that . . . wasn't on my head." ("That means sometimes I, too, lose my head . . .")

And Dr. Joseph Sweeney's son Tom saw another Kerouac, the craftsman. Tom's Boston College assignment was a thousand words on what he thought Kerouac was thinking when he wrote the *Dharma Bums* chapter that is in their English textbook. And now Tom didn't have to imagine, but was getting it straight from The Man Himself.

But then everyone saw a different Kerouac-facet . . . and even those who looked like hangers-on were "friendly friends, the most hospitable people," so that it was always "Jack, have a drink with ME now," and the time came when the beatnik king was "drunkenly" spilling the drinks, for spilled drinks are drinks one is spared from drinking. . . . And there were those who saw him at his yoga, standing on his head daily for many minutes . . . and those who saw him bearhug old buddies, like former-sports-writing pal Frank Moran, in Kearney Square . . . and those who shared his own recordings of Kerouac poetry and Kerouac imitations of comedians like W. C. Fields . . . and those who surrounded him in the jazz-and-folk-song quiet hours with nightclub performers after the clubs had closed.

And now the frantic week was ended. The crowd parted, and the man wearing a gas station attendant's suit ("A friend gave it to me because I like workingmen's clothes") waved a last good-bye, and the crowd followed, looking up the street till the car was gone. And left behind him was the sense of his immense HAPPY-ness, the great LOVING of everything that you meet foremost in his writings, as though he serenades the whole universe with "Embraceable You." Kerouac finds even LIFE larger than life.

On the Road with Marty and Jack

"Pertinax," *Lowell Sun* (October 2, 1962)

I f you've been thinking that the very recent Jack Kerouac visit here might result in another book on his hometown, you've been thinking right: You may take Marty Gouveia's word on Jack Kerouac's word that the King of the Beatniks plans to do that very thing, and soon.

Marty Gouveia, in case you hadn't been paying strict attention lately, is the local fella (lives in Dracut, on Haverhill Street) who chauffeured the Beat King to New York just over a week ago. And don't go assuming Marty just casually jumped into the driver's seat and zoomed away, the way guys are always doing in Kerouac books, for he came by his assignment more sedately. It took Fate four years this wonder to perform.

Marty, an aircraft maintenance man, was working in Manhattan's Idlewild Airport four years ago, when he and some buddies went down to Greenwich Village for some fun. At one spot, excitement suddenly smote Marty's group: "Look," said one of them, dazzled, "there's Jack Kerouac, right THERE!" (Kerouac's *On the Road* had been published, the Beat Generation was booming in the news, and there, in their special milieu, Kerouac was just the LARGEST.) Sharing hometowns the way they did, Marty went over to say Hello. He said Kerouac was very cordial to him.

Skip over four years and several other Gouveia-read Kerouac books, and you can picture Marty's much-multiplied excitement to run into Kerouac right here in town two weeks ago. "He SAID he remembered me, but I don't think he did," Marty said modestly. "Anyhow, I was in the bunch with him just about every night, and it was great. You know, MC's introducing him, and people coming up for autographs. I'd never seen anything like that in Lowell before."

One night, Kerouac gave Marty a silver cross and said luck would henceforth improve for them both. This is not the sort of thing that happens to one every day in the week—having world-famous authors press silver crosses on one—and Marty is keenly aware of this. "Every time I'd see him, he'd ask if I still had the cross. He said he'd ask me next year, too, when he comes back to Lowell."

Since Marty had been planning a trip to see his Idlewild friends, he offered to drive Kerouac whenever he wanted to leave . . . which was a week ago last Saturday:

Mostly, on the ride back, he talked about Lowell, about how nice it was to see all his friends, and how much he enjoyed himself, and how he loves Lowell, and that he's going to write a book on that week here, and he'll change everybody's name, but not too much. He said he didn't care what anybody said, that you could have as good a time in Lowell as in New York, but on a smaller scale. He was silent for a while, listening to an opera on the radio, really FEELING it, you know? And then some hillbilly music came on, and he acted the same way about that, too. Everything gives him pleasure.

They got to Greenwich Village about 2:30 A.M., and Jack stopped
to call a friend who'd moved:

Fellow named Lucien, he's a United Press International editor,
just in from Paris, and he told us his house was on Horatio
Street. We drove around but couldn't find it, then we stopped
on one street and asked people and no one knew and then
someone came by and said we were ON Horatio Street.
Lucien was all excited, seeing Jack, and there was another UPI
man named Bob, and we went to his apartment on Fifth
Avenue to drink to Jack's return, and it was beautiful driving
through the park just before dawn.

Lucien kept us laughing with some stories about his last
days in Paris, and then he said we had to go to the pier right
away to see this boat he was thinking of buying. It sleeps
eighty-six people, he said. Jack's crazy about the sea . . . and
he's planning a big trip soon . . . out to Japan, maybe . . . but
he said Marty's tired, Marty needs to sleep. So he said we'd go
around 11 o'clock in the morning.

But I slept way past that time, and no one was in the house
when I got up. Then I had to go to Idlewild to see my buddies,
and then I had to come home. Ever since I've been back,
everybody's been asking me about the ride, kidding me about
On the Road. Funny thing, too–Jack said my driving style
reminded him of Dean Moriarty in that book. He's going to
send me copies of all of his books from Orlando–he was due
to fly there last Tuesday–and he said not to forget to take care
of that cross. I felt I was right inside a Kerouac book.

And don't bet that he WON'T be.

Kerouac, Joyce, Proust

"Pertinax," *Lowell Sun* (October 24, 1962)

J ack Kerouac, who—besides the thirteen books already published —has written articles for some of the leading magazines here and abroad, has written directly for this column, commenting on the King of the Beatnik's recent visit to his hometown and amplifying on some of our column comments on him:

> Cher Pert—I came to Lowell by taxi not from New York but from Old Saybrook, Conn. From N.Y. it would have been more than $60—I was just so anxious to see my old buddies and to see Lowell, etc., the river, etc., Pawtucketville, Centralville, none of which I saw really because I got hung up with a thousand new interesting guys . . .
>
> The reason why I'm always the "hero" of my novels is the same reason that Joyce and Proust are always the heroes of their novels, i.e. first hand truth reporting of what you see and hear and then feel about it, like, as I say, to look at the world through the key-hole of an author's eye, actually what happened, with just name changes, instead of "fiction"—Yes, my

"crack-up" was fun in Lowell, etc., later N.Y., but in Big Sur I almost choked on my own heart—Okay—(Pretty eerie there anyway—I'm not plugging my book, I don't give a damn about it, I have three more already written and two more to write about Lowell now as soon as I can get my Dexedrine and get rolling by candlelight).

I never write when drinking but I'm also mindful of the fact Rembrandt was a drinker and it didn't stop him from picking up bums on the Amsterdam waterfront and taking them to his studio and dressing them as Biblical Kings and painting them as Biblical Kings and reciting St. Matthew to them as he painted away and the bums sat there bottle at side of Throne weeping to hear him—So I know drinking is not the nemesis of the Artist, it's Gray Hate.

My favorite French writer who's dead now is Louis-Ferdinand Céline, author of *Journey to the End of the Night*—among others—died the same day as Hemingway, or same week—Was not noted much in obituaries in America tho infinitely greater writer than Hemingway.

Yes, the stylyakins of Russia know all about me and also Evtuchenko the poet knows about me—The great poets of Russia in the 20th Century were Mayakovsky and Sergei Esenin—AND Pasternak, verse poet too—That silver cross I gave to Marty was given to me by my mother to take to New York with me to remind me to be a good boy, it is 40 years old and was blessed 40 years ago in Quebec—I gave it to Martino Gouveia because I knew right away he was a blessed man—In fact, you know, such a weird straight kid that I spent a whole hour talking to other people at table and over to the bar, yelling, leaning on poor Marty almost forgetting he was there a whole hour, then when I turned and realized I was LEANING on a guy I gave him my cross—Nein—I who have celebrated the rivers of Lowell wish not to celebrate the men and women thereof.

Young Sweeney, his text question was "What was your attitude when you wrote that chapter about meditating under the trees in North Carolina in the winter with the hound dogs?"—I said "Attitude toward WHAT? What kind of abstract questions are they cooking up these days?"—Then I later explained to him that I'm actually a lay Jesuit, as *Jubilee Catholic Magazine* well knows—And Father Shoyer in New York, not to mention Bishop Sheen.

(Concludes tomorrow.)

Kerouac Remembers Them All

"Pertinax," *Lowell Sun* (October 25, 1962)

C oncluding the letter (somewhat condensed) from Jack Kerouac to this column:

Your item about *Embraceable You* couldn't be truer because when I was alone on a mountain for two months in the northwest Washington State woods, mountains, in 1956, I sang Embraceable You You Silk and Laceable You to all the stars of mountaintop night, scaring the bears, altho my real first favorite song is *I Love You* by Irving Berlin. No. 2 is *Embraceable You* and No. 3 at the time was *Last Night* as sung by Sinatra but now I stick to *Moon River* as No. 3–Of course, I'm not forgetting No. 4 *Lady of the Evening* by Duke Ellington.

When I write a book about Lowell I will see to it that all the names are changed properly and that there will be no calumny whatever, only kicks and pleasure of a good story about real guys and gals.

And also I love Lowell for the golden-domed Greek Orthodox church of the Holy Trinity on the canal only a stone's throw from the dives of the tortured sad hearts of Life and Death.

And I love Lowell for St. Jean Baptiste rising above the rooftops of Moody Street in a dream, when on winter nights in the wash courts the stiff clothes crack and try to flap.

Those who insist that *Hiroshima Mon Amour* is such a sad picture in New York wearing horn rimmed glasses should remember Pearl Harbor.

And Bataan.

And Anzio.

And New Guinea.

And Iwo Jima.

Because on the night of Pearl Harbor, after I had seen *Citizen Kane* I walked home from the movies watching the wash stiffly waving in the cold moonlight snow wash lines of Moody and Cheever and cried.

And how many of my buddies were lost in that war? Billy Chandler, Jimmy Scondras, John Koumantzelis, Sebastian Sampas, Chick Lozeau . . . Joe Voyer finally got back, Red Cronin too . . . Harper O'Dea was wounded bad . . . Descheneaux never came back . . . a lot of guys from Lowell.

I ALSO love Lowell for St. Louis de France in Centralville where I was Baptized and where my brother was buried in a coffin as a hundred little boys sang on a rainy day and we carted him off in a procession to Nashua N.H. and when he was lowered in the ground everybody cried except me. I was 4 years old and I thought he was in Heaven and what was there to cry about.

I love Lowell and it's all old hat but if I ever retire from this life my face will be bent over You-all.

Don't worry, this life IS the stream of the Holy Spirit so why worry it'll all come out in the Holy Wash—And so, Pertinax, please give my regards to:

Then follows a long list of names with designations in parentheses after each one, as though they've already assumed the stance of characters in a book. Among these are:

Huck Finneral (The Cat), George Logos (The Word), Charles E. Jarvis (The Interviewer), George Spence (The Englishman), Fleming (The Painter), Sweeney (The Student), Demosthenes Samaras (The Ball Player), Menelaeus Chiungos (The End), Paul Bourgeois (The Terror), Gerard Gauthier (The Sweet One), Mr. Slattery (The Printer)

Book News from Farrar, Straus & Cudahy, Inc.

Press Release for *Visions of Gerard* (1963)

Visions of Gerard's 1963 publication garnered negative reviews and quickly disappeared from bookshelves. It remains today, however, a favorite of scholars and fans alike, a seminal novel covering the years of 1922 to 1926, beginning with the year of Ti Jean Lebris de Kerouac's birth and ending with his brother Gerard's death at the age of nine on June 2, 1926.

INTERVIEWER: At first glance, the Catholicism in your new novel, *Visions of Gerard* (Farrar, Straus, September 6) seems to be something new for you. Is it?

JK: Catholicism in my books is not a new tack for me. Actually, there was some Catholicism in *The Dharma Bums* which the publishers saw fit to delete. There's a lot of Catholicism in *Big Sur*, in *Lonesome Traveler*, and even more in *Tristessa*, and a running brief on the subject in *Maggie Cassidy*. My first novel, *The Town and the City*, was essentially a Catholic story. The "beat" theme in the hepcat books like *On the Road* and *The*

Subterraneans is not opposed to Catholicism. I'm born a Catholic and it's nothing new with me.

At home or abroad, I always carry my rosary more or less for good luck. Most of the amateur painting I've done is of pietas, crucifixions, saints, and I have a nice collection of sacred music. I always give my stories and poems free to *Jubilee Magazine* as a contribution to the Church. I was baptized, received First Communion and feel quite calm about the whole thing.

INTERVIEWER: How was *Visions of Gerard* written?

JK: *Visions of Gerard* was written at the kitchen table of my sister's home in Big Easonburg Woods, North Carolina, over a ten-night stretch, midnight to dawn, ending with refreshing visits to the piney barrens out behind the cotton field at sunrise. I did no rewriting or revising whatever, except for name changes and one important comma finally inserted somewhere, where I'd made a spontaneous mistake about it being needed, although I did reject a whole night's writing and started all over again on the section the next night.[46]

It was all written by hand, in pencil, in little notebooks. Certain kinds of stories seem to deny the rackety typewriter.

INTERVIEWER: *Visions of Gerard* is part of the series you call the "Duluoz Legend." What are your future plans for that?

JK: Future plans for the "Duluoz Legend" are to fill in the gaps left open in the chronological past. The sequel to *The Dharma Bums* is already written (called *Desolation Angels*) and the sequel to that (already written) is called *Passing Through*. The sequel to *Visions of Gerard* (not yet written) will be called *Vanity of Duluoz*, and then come the post–*Big Sur* adventures of my future life, whatever it will be, if any.

The final scope of the legend will be simply a completely

written lifetime with all its hundreds of characters and events and levels interswirling and reappearing and becoming complete, somewhat à la Balzac and Proust. But each section, that is, each novel, has to stand by itself as an individual story with a flavor of its own and a pivot of its own. Nevertheless, they must all fit together on one shelf as a continuous tale.

INTERVIEWER: The setting for *Visions of Gerard* is your home town of Lowell. When were you last there?

JK: In October '62, and I got a big "celebrity" reception and had to run away back to New York. I'm sort of a hero there. Much fun. The people there, old football cronies, cousins, friends, new acquaintances, old newspaper confreres, the teaching fraternity, gossips, characters, all realize I just go there to bask and drink, but we really have great rapports and I'm going back there soon because there are more books in that little Christian city than you could have packed in Carthage.

A golden Byzantine dome rises from the roofs along the canal; a Gothic copy of Chartres rises from the slums of Moody Street; little children speak French, Greek, Polish, and even Portuguese on their way to school. And I have a recurrent dream of simply walking around the deserted twilight streets of Lowell in the mist, eager to turn every known and fabled corner. A very eerie, recurrent dream, but it always makes me happy when I wake up.

INTERVIEWER: In a recent *Esquire*, Alice Glaser says the Beats are no longer on the road, "that even Kerouac—their god—had settled down on Long Island with his mother?" Do you accept that?

JK: I've always been "settled with my mother" who supported me by working in shoe factories while I wrote most of my books years ago. She's my friend as well as my mother. When I go on the road, I always have a quiet, clean home to come back to and to work in, which probably accounts for the fact that I've published twelve books in the last six years.

Jack Kerouac Reads, etc., at Lowell

Harvard Crimson (March 25, 1964)

On April 22, 1964, Kerouac wrote to Stella Sampas describing his appearance at the Lowell House at Harvard University: "I told everybody anything that came to my mind and it doesn't matter what I said." It was to Kerouac's regret, however, that he was not respected as an American writer but instead considered a fallen clown resting on his literary laurels. Louisa Solano remembers Kerouac after the event:

Jack Kerouac read at Harvard toward the end of his life. Irish poet Desmond O'Grady shoehorned me into a meeting with him. We went to see him read. The audience was packed with students, waiting for Kerouac to behave like Kerouac. He was inebriated. Afterwards Desmond took Kerouac, myself, and a number of students, to visit (it seemed) every single after-hours bar in Cambridge. We eventually walked Kerouac back to the place he was staying. I remember that same weekend Sylvia Plath died. We were at Cronin's in Harvard

Square, and Desmond came in waving a newspaper and said: "She's dead, she's dead; we are now the only remaining poets." He grabbed Kerouac, and Kerouac backhanded Desmond and said "Don't touch me!" Later, two young men came in and told Kerouac they had "gold," and he staggered down the street with them. That's the last we saw of him." (from an interview with Doug Holder)

Louisa Solano was the owner of the famed Grolier Poetry Bookshop in Cambridge, Massachusetts.

Jack Kerouac presided over an evening of chaos in the Lowell House Junior Common Room last night. As members of the House's tutorial staff flitted about worriedly, the author of *On the Road*, *The Subterraneans*, and a dozen other books read poems, offered observations, and sometimes just snorted.

"I'm not afraid of Mao Tse-Tung or Arthur Schlesinger, 'cause I'm straight Catholic!" shouted Kerouac, who was fresh from a hearty Ford dinner.

Kerouac said he thinks Emily Dickinson, James Joyce, and T. S. Eliot were the greatest poets of the twentieth century and Marcel Proust, Jean Genet, and William Faulkner the greatest prose writers. But "Hemingway was nowhere. He wrote childish sentences, like Beckett does."

Kerouac was drunk but quite coherent. As students pulled the screens off the windows to get in, he traded gibes with Desmond O'Grady, the Irish poet of Adams House, and suggested that O'Grady should give the reading himself.

Cackling and smiling, Kerouac read poems from his *Mexico City*

Blues and repeatedly asked for a glass of cognac. When his host, Albert J. Gelpi, Jr., instructor in English, suggested that they just forget the whole thing and go out for a drink, Kerouac gestured at the packed crowd and said, "But these people are here; they can't all go to the bar."

Finally, someone sneaked Kerouac a drink through the open window. Having won his point (and the sympathies of his audience), he read several more poems in a clear, loud voice.

Excerpts from Interview with Miklos Zsedely

Miklos Zsedely, Northport Public Library
Oral History Project (April 14, 1964)

All of the following excerpts are from the April 14, 1964 inter-
view, the first of two interviews with Kerouac that were con-
ducted by the Northport Public Library for its oral history project.
Zsedely, the library's assistant director, was the interviewer. The
interview took place in the studio of Kerouac's friend, artist
Stanley Twardowicz. Twardowicz was present, as were Ker-
ouac's friends, David and Joan Roberts and James Schwaner.

Kerouac's Genealogy

JK: I am an Iroquois Indian, you know that? . . . You ready? In ancient times, in a land which was known as Brittany by the Gauls, but even before the Gauls discovered it—I wonder how they got there, though—there were in Ireland, in Ireland, the Kerouacs. One of them was known as Tristan. No, one of them was known as Isolde the fair, and she was kidnapped by the Cornishmen and taken into Cornwall where Tristan fell in love with her. But to prove his love he had to kill the Modoch, who was the great monster of Ireland. He killed the Modoch—but in any case, in some way or another, the Kernouaks went to Cornwall a thousand years before Christ. And today the name Cornwall is the name of a Cornish. You know Cornwall?

MZ: I know where.

JK: The southwest country of England inhabited by the Celts, not by the Anglo-Saxons. And the name of the language is Kernouak. And we had a castle there—moats!—and I was a young knight and on early mornings in spring when the robins sing in the mist, I had the strap on my hair, and my headdress, and meet the great monsters of Brittany. [Makes the sound of a galloping horse] Clunk! clunk clunk clunk clunk—probably killed five or six times. And then they said, I think something happened with the Cornish rebellion or something, they said, "Let's get the hell out of here and cross the channel into Brittany, France." They went there and their name was no longer Kernouak, it was Kerouac, and they added on "Lebris de" Kerouac—Lebris L-e-b-r-i-s and then comes the French Revolution, and they say, "We don't want our priests destroyed by these republican idiots." He's not listening. Dave never listens! "We don't want our priests in Brittany destroyed by republican agitators and provocateurs." So they started a big war against the French Revolution in Brittany. Did you know that? Called "La Vendée." "La Vendée." You never heard of that? It was a bitter war. They all sent their troops— Napoleon sent his troops up there. They said, "There they are, the Breton troops, Breton troops, Breton peasants." They had trapdoors; they went down under the ground. The French Republican army said, "Where the hell did they go?" They disappeared. They thought they were in a misty land. But the trapdoors opened at night, and they come out and destroy the whole army. And then

one of my forefathers, François Louis Alexander Lebris de Kerouac, says, "I think I'll go to Canada with Montcalme and defeat
Wolfe for the valley of the St. Lawrence." Pshoooo! Come out of
there, you know. But Wolfe defeated the goddamn French. All
defeated French officers, and he was a baron from Brittany . . .
got a hundred miles along Rivière de Loup, Wolfe River, which is
now known as Rivière de Loup, you know, Rivière de Loup, that
belongs to us, and then some Englishman named Frazer came up
and stole it from him, so now it's known as Frazerville. But lately
it's again called Rivière de Loup. Not because I threw bombs in
post office boxes. Just by itself. Belongs to us, you know. Meanwhile this guy François, the Breton baron, meets a beautiful
young Iroquois squaw, says, "Oh brother, what a nice little squaw
princess." Goes north with her, hunting and trapping. Has six or
seven sons. Some of them go hunting and trapping north, some
of them go down. Finally, their grandsons settle, filter down into
New England, start little businesses, see? Working in the mills or
opening little candy stores. Some of them were called the tough
ones, go way up north, trapping, so that today in the North Pole
in Prince of Wales Land—you know where that is?

ST: Way up?

JK: Wait a minute.

ST: Way up.

JK: There are three thousand Iroquois, four nations, four nations of
    the Iroquois—they're all up there, living in log cabins, just trappin'
    and huntin'. And the other parts of the family are down here, being
    big writers in New York and all that business, heh! heh! and see
    I'm mostly eighty percent French and twenty percent Iroquois.
    And way back, like I told you, Cornish and Irish, see? And before

Ireland, where'd they come from? Huh? Four thousand years ago? Were they Picts, do you think? From Scotland?

DR: All I know is that my great-great-grandfather's name was "Oshity" of all things.

ST: Oshity?

JK: Well that's Japanese. Oh, Irish. Thought you were saying "oshi." Oshity, Oshity, that's an old Irish name. [laughs]

ST: Jack, what do they call you where you came from? French-Canadian? There was a word you used.

JK: Canuck?

ST: Canuck, yes.

MZ: Yes. Well now that we've heard the story of the Kerouac family, there's only one thing–

JK: That's the story of my father's family. My mother's family is Norman.

MZ: But there is one thing that I have to bring up. There is a plot in this story.

ST: Oh, it's beautiful.

MZ: This is why you don't write this into the book?

JK: Well, I don't know. I had to go see all these people. Go into the British Museum, look it up, go into Brittany, look it up.

MZ: Is it the trouble that there is a plot in this story?

JK: To verify all this, and I know it's generally true, well, you'd have to write nonfiction, that is, with footnotes, with footnotes.

MZ: And if you should write in fiction there couldn't be a plot in it.

JK: Oh in fiction. I see.

MZ: Here we are back again–plot or no plot.

JK: What I have written so far, Mr. Hungary, has been what I saw with my own eyes. This is what they tell me about my family, not only told to me by distant fool cousins, but by old close uncles. And it's true, old. But to really say it you have to have footnotes, you have to verify it. Do I want to write a romance, you mean?

MZ: No, but what I want to bring out, but you said before, the thing is, there is no plot because the same thing starts—it's still the same, no change.

JK: Sure, what about this story then?

MZ: All right, then, in this story can you say there is, there was, you didn't realize there are no real changes, because it's still the same again?

JK: I don't know. How could I know?

MZ: Yes, but their life changed, didn't it? It wasn't the same the next day.

JK: They were Celts.

MZ: Yes, but in their life, as the family went on. There were always changes and changes. There was plot; the plot was moving.

JK: You know that I was a Celt, by the way? It's an old Irish name, Kerouac.

ST: A Celt?

JK: It's the oldest Irish name on earth.

ST: Kerouac.

JK: Aye.

ST: Irish?

JK: Well, it's Cornish too, but they told me it first came from Irish.

ST: It's corny, all right.

DR: Is that why they call you the black Irishman sometimes?

JK: Right, because I am an Irishman, you know. But I'm really a Cornishman, you know, because it's so far back the Irish part. But Cornwall—don't you know where Cornwall is? The Pirates of

Penzance, Pentagal. The southwest coast of England sticks out into the Atlantic and has moorings. You know what "Kerouac" means? In Celtic? "House in the moor."

ST: "House in the moor"?

JK: Ker—house, ouac—in the moor. Or in the heath.

ST: Heath? Heath or moor?

JK: No, heath.

ST: Not the heat I'm talking about.

JK: The heath is a moor.

ST: Yeah, but not heat; I'm talking about something hot.

JK: Heath! You know, like Heathcliff.

ST: Not hot.

JK: No, no, Heathcliff.

ST: Oh, come on.

JK: Merle Oberon!*

ST: I know Merle Oberon—the moors, yes.

JK: [English accent] I will go walking across the heath, bring me an—

ST: *Wuthering Heights*, right.

JK: Aye, I spit and you spit that time.

ST: Well, you didn't catch it, though.

JK: No, I didn't. [laughter] Next time. Yep, in other words you're a Scotsman, huh?

DR: No, I'm Irish.

JK: "Roberts," I always thought—

DR: A little, they're Welsh.

JK: Yeah, Welsh.

---

* Merle Oberon (February 19, 1911 – November 23, 1979): a sultry film actress who starred as Cathy in the 1939 film version of *Wuthering Heights*.

ST: Well, you have no problem with Twardowicz [tvardowvitch].

JK: The Welshmen in the woods were the most horrible enemies of the kings of England. [whistles] Those black bastards crawled over the walls again . . .

Kerouac on Cancer

JK: Now I will tell you about cancer. In Kenya, Africa, there is a mosquito, very much like the anopheles, that gives malaria, that gives cancer. And Negro people who live there, who come here mingle among the whites, they don't have cancer themselves, but carry it. Like Typhoid Marys.

MZ: How about cancer in those countries where there are no Negroes?

JK: Which ones?

MZ: Austria, Hungary, Czechoslovakia?

JK: There must be. That's my mother's theory. I think there must be a few mosquitoes. I think it comes from a mosquito.

MZ: It's possible, but–

JK: Like the anopheles. Don't laugh.

MZ: I'm not laughing.

JK: How about malaria? I'll be back, turn that [recorder] off. Do you know that theory of Wilhelm Reich?

MZ: Yeah.

JK: About cancer. Well, you know, it is improper orgasm. Now, what do you think of that? You dam up and all that stuff, see, that's Wilhelm Reich. I'm not talking about Theodore Reich, Wilhelm Reich. But my mother says this, but my mother is, did you say there was cancer in Austria and there are no Negroes in Austria? . . . And there is cancer in Mongolia?

MZ: I don't know—I've never been there.

JK: Afghanistan, there are Negroes there.

MZ: Probably there are. No, there are no Negroes there, but what I meant is, in countries where there are no Negroes who come from—

JK: Oh, there are no Negroes in Austria. Oh, I'm not saying the Negroes are the cause of it; I said they carry the bite of the mosquito.

MZ: Well, it's possible, but I must confess I have my doubts.

JK: Well, my mother says that because she doesn't like Negroes but it may be that there are several species of mosquitoes that give it as a virus.

MZ: Again, it's possible, but again on the other hand, the mosquitoes are not the same kind in different places. There are different kinds of mosquitoes, but it's possible, although I don't know what proof there is for it.

JK: Now Wilhelm Reich says that cancer is caused by repression, ill will, malice, spleen. Like for instance my father died of cancer of the spleen. Well, the last five years of his life, he was yelling his head off. "Them fuckin' goddamn Jews! Them fuckin' niggers!" He was yelling all day long, my father, everybody. "Them fuckin' Polacks! Goddamn Scotsmen!"

ST: That's what you told me.

JK: He was yellin' at everything. He died of cancer of the spleen, which is the seat of anger, the spleen.

ST: Yeah, but at the same time, for instance—

JK: That's what I think was the cause of cancer. He was mad as hell, I'll tell you that much. But I think the cause was, I know what it was.

ST: But the prejudice had to be there.

JK: That was an abrasion which was rubbed again and again becomes an ulcer and becomes a cancer.

MZ: Probably for some cancers, yeah, yes.

JK: You better know that.

MZ: But not for all of them.

JK: Let's go cross our legs in front of fireplaces in London and discuss it with Dr. Sherlock Holmes. Burroughs thinks that cancer is a virus.

ST: Jack, the prejudice would have to be there in the first place before it comes out. I mean, sickness brings it out, you know that. You should know that . . .

Kerouac on Balzac, Proust, and Shakespeare

JK: Who said, "On a lonely afternoon, a Sunday afternoon"? I believe it was Balzac: "I had to take a nap before I went out with my new exciting cousin, a guy cousin, who had just met some girls called seaside girls by the trees of the seaside." He lays down on his bed to take a nap, but he can't sleep, and the sun's setting over the North Channel of Normandy and shines from the West, yes from Brittany, on his bookcase, so that he could see various landscapes, seascapes, on his bookcase. The top layer of glass had a seascape, the middle layer, and the books were inside and all these different seascapes. He said, "And in contrast with these pink and varied hued seascapes," which were blue, orange, and yellow, "I could think of nothing but the glittering lights of the promise of the [restless] tonight when I would be with my favorite cousin, listening to the lilting waltzes of the Viennese waltz and dancing to the music." Oh man, that guy really stunk. Well, what do you want me to say about Proust?

MZ: Well, it was that he tried to write, all of his books were about, after all, the same characters.

JK: He said, "In one tragic night—"

ST: No.

JK: "—I found Baron de Charlus, completely bereft of all his defenses, with tears running down through his makeup." He's crying—Baron de Charlus. All his makeup was all smeared up.

ST: —remember earlier when you were talking about Proust, in a sense, like almost like your books?

JK: You mean the mixing of different characters?

ST: From one novel to the other, remember?

JK: From one volume to another, you bring the characters back. Like you won't see Baron de Charlus for two volumes, but all of a sudden that old queer reappears, with his valet, and then the other girls come back, Odette, what was her name?

ST: How come you do it to your books?

JK: The one I really like is the first one.

ST: How come you do it to your books?

JK: Because what I do is take all the people I really knew, and give them different names, and then when they reappear in my life they reappear in the next chapter.

ST: But you don't mention the fact in any of your books, for instance, in your own introductions to your books, that this is what you're really doing anyway, sort of a continuation.

JK: I understand that Proust, all the girls that Proust is writing about were boys. Is that true?

MZ: I don't know. I wasn't there.

JK: Well, that's what they say. That's what Maurois says, but I think Maurois was a crétin.

ST: That means what?

JK: Crétin?

ST: Credit?

JK: Crétin?

ST: A what, button?

JK: Crétin. Crétin!

ST: Means what?

JK: Imbecile.

ST: A critic, exactly.

JK: Not a critic, an imbecile.

ST: Well, that's the same thing, that's the same thing—

JK: According to Neal Cassady, the hero of *On the Road*, Dean Moriarty, these were girls. According to all the big, like I met—the Buck Mulligan of James Joyce's *Ulysses*, I didn't meet Maurois, I didn't meet Mauriac, I didn't meet Cocteau, Gide, those idiots. They all say they were boys, but Neal says, "No!" He says they were girls because nobody could write about girls like that. . . .

ST: You're right, Jack.

JK: Well, I suppose. I don't know.

ST: What are you, Jack?

JK: Huh?

ST: What are you?

JK: An aphrodite. No man, when it comes to gizmo, I know what I'm doing.

ST: You do? What are you doing?

JK: Well, first I have to take the pants off.

ST: That helps, it helps, yeah. Otherwise you're straining it.

JK: I've had many invitations in Turkish baths.

ST: That helps, that helps.

JK: Get away from me, for God's sakes, you hairy fool! I don't like hairy people. I don't like hair. I don't like hair.

ST: I've never been to one, Turkish baths.

JK: God!

MZ: But you were talking about Shakespeare.

ST: You claim he was the greatest poet.

JK: The greatest poet that shall ever live, ever did, does, and ever shall.

MZ: And he was charming, too. But you didn't say that about Shakespeare. You said that about Balzac and, and that's what you said about Proust, but you didn't say that about Shakespeare.

JK: About Shakespeare?

ST: That's right, you didn't.

JK: When he was a teenager, he was raped under an apple tree.

ST: By whom?

JK: He used to go down and get drunk under an apple tree on Stratford-upon-Avon River, Stratford town upon Avon River in England. In comes a woman called Ann Hathaway, and she does hath a way, you know.

ST: Hathaway? I was going to ask you a question. Who was he raped by, a man or a woman?

JK: By a woman called Ann Hathaway! And she doth have, she doth, Ann did have, no, how do you say that? Ann hath a way! She raped him, then she screwed his brother Edmund Shakespeare.

ST: Is that when—

JK: She got him a child from Edmund called Hamnet.

ST: Jack, is that when he turned to writing?

JK: Yes.

ST: After he got raped?

JK: Then he hitchhiked to London.

ST: Then he had nothing left after that?

JK: Then Hamnet died; Hamlet comes from Hamnet.

ST: Is that why Shakespeare wrote after that?

JK: See, I know all the secret scholars of England. I went around. I didn't go to Oxford yet; I'm gonna go lecture at Oxford.

ST: Jack.

JK: Have shoes thrown at me.

ST: Jack, is that—

JK: I'll bring back a whole boatload of shoes, sell 'em wholesale.

ST: Your shoes don't fit? No. To ask you another question, is that why Shakespeare wrote, because he got bored after this rape, in a sense? Is that why you write, because you're bored?

JK: Any guy's a teenager who gets drunk under an apple tree and is lying in the grass under an apple tree, beside the lambs and the river . . .

ST: Well you said originally you write because you're bored.

JK: Then he gets raped by Ann Hathaway, and then his brother lays his wife, and gives her a son called Hamnet, who's supposed to be his son, so he hitchhikes to London, and he holds horses outside the theater. They say, "Willie! Hold those horses tight, here comes Lord Gray." Lord Gray comes in, "Ha! Ha! What play do we have tonight?" You know, maybe a play by Ben Jonson. Finally, they say, "Willie, can you come in here and help us write, rewrite, the second act? Can you write?" He says, "Yes!" Comes in and rewrites the second act. "Willie, will you come and write the whole damn play?" He writes the whole damn play. He says, "Willie, will you go home and write another play?" He goes home and writes *King Lear*, *Macbeth*, and *Hamlet* in one year. One year. *King Lear*, *Macbeth*, and *Hamlet* he wrote in one year . . .

Kerouac on Carl Sandburg

JK: Carl Sandburg. When I was twenty-eight years old, my book was first published in New York, they made me put on a tuxedo with a white tie, white shirt, you know, black tuxedo, rented. I go to a big party with all beautiful models, and there's Carl Sandburg wearing a tuxedo with big white hair going like this, puts his arm around me, says, "Ahhhhhhhhh! Jack! You're just like me." I say, "Why?" He says, "I used to hitchhike through Illinois, Indiana. I was a hobo." See, I was a hobo too, you know. And I said you know that I'm writing a new poem called [sings] "Hop a freight train out of Montana / My father was dyin' of misery." He said, "Change the word 'misery' to 'pleurisy'!" [Sings] "My father was dyin' of pleurisy." Anyway, he lives in Flatrock, North Carolina, with his old wife and has goats, and he eats goat milk, goat cheese, and that's why he's supposed to be so healthy, you know, ninety years old and everything. Goat milk. . . .

Kerouac on His European Travels

JK: I tried to hitchhike in France. I tried to hitchhike out of Marseilles toward Avignon, no rides. So I walked into an old church and stood inside of a sixth-century *baptiserie* while the boys and girls were singing the most beautiful medieval carols, and I cried. Then I bought a long bread, about this long, and put it under my arm with the rucksack, and went out hitchhiking. All the little French bastards went by so I hailed down a bus outside of Avignon outside of Marseilles outside of Aix-en-Provence I got a ride to Avignon. Bought a railroad ticket from Avignon to Paris. Had a whole Sunday afternoon to spend up and down the boulevards of Avignon, and I saw the horror of Flaubert's horror, and the horror of *des musées*, and the horror of *des provinces, la morte de les provinces de France, de l'après midi dimanche*. Sunday afternoon in the French provinces could drive anybody crazy, except then when I bought an ice cream cone and I started to lick my ice cream cone, three teenage girls come up and said, in French, thinking I couldn't understand French, *"Mais, il y est trop bel."* What did I do? Nothin'! *Je n'ai fais rien.* I didn't do nothin'. There were these three girls sayin', "He's too beautiful." 'Cause I was beautiful, then, see, I was thin. So I said, "Ah!" I said, "Think I'll go have a vermouth at the café in Avignon." Picked up the local newspaper. The local newspaper had a big story about a big clown who had left Avignon twenty-five years ago, a circus clown, and was now back. So I read the whole story about the life story of this clown. Then I walked through the back streets of Avignon, and I saw some red shoes floating in water in a gutter. And the wind was blowing, the mistral, mistral wind that annoyed Van Gogh.

MZ: Comes down from the Alps, no?

JK: Is that where it comes from? I thought it came from the ocean— the Mediterranean.

MZ: Now wait a minute. I may, excuse me, I mix it up.

JK: I don't know where it comes from.

MZ: The mistral is southern; that comes from the Mediterranean.

JK: Anyway, blows dust, the Pont d'Avignon and all that shit, the Rhône River. I got on a train from Avignon to Paris, arriving at Paris at dawn. Got off the train at Gare de Lyon, you know Paris, huh? First thing I saw in Paris was an elegant Negro gentleman walking by with a homburg hat, cane, and a briefcase. That's the first thing I saw. Then I got out on the street, I looked in every direction. There were these magnificent, what would you call those things? I used to know what Balzac used to call those. Anyway, apartment houses, not the new apartment houses, the old ones, ornate, Venetian tenements, in every direction in miles and miles, and the statue of Danton pointing nowhere, another statue of Robespierre, pointing nowhere! A statue of Marat, pointing nowhere! A statue of Cordet, pointing nowhere! [Laughter] I'm crazy. So I went down to a little bar, on the Boulevard St. Germain I suppose, and I was waiting for all these beautiful young girls with berets, who come from Sorbonne Law School. Come around reading their law books say, "Hey, would you *parlez avec moi*?" Talk to me? One of them did talk to me; made a date to meet later. I said, *"Je t'aime."* Oh boy, yeah, when I go to Paris. I was about old enough to be her grandfather.

ST: Oh, you're not that old. You're not even that old.

JK: She was ugly as sin anyway.

ST: Well, that makes a difference, then.

JK: So then I went to the Café Bonaparte, Place St. Germain, and I sat in the sun with the well-to-do teenage American painters saying, "Look what I did here!" I said, "Great! Let me do one." Millions of girls started to sit around me. I was in my element, my glory, all the girls were coming. Ha! Here comes Gregory Corso. "Kerouac, every time I see you you're surrounded by girls, surrounded by girls, blah, blah, blah, blah." And he ruined the whole thing.

ST: Is he jealous or what?

JK: Of course he is. Sure he's jealous. He broke up the whole thing.

ST: Ah, that's a shame. All those girls.

JK: Yeah.

ST: Well, you can only take one at a time anyway.

JK: He had a girl called Mimi with him. Her real name was Mimi. Mimi couldn't speak English except, *"Dit à Gregory,"* tell Gregory, *"que je l'aime."* I said, "Gregory, this Parisian girl of yours says that she loves you." He says, "Tell her that I only want to screw the stars." Say, *"Mimi, Gregory dit qu'il veut seulement faire l'amour avec des étoiles."*

ST: Only want to screw the stars?

JK: Yeah, he said, I had to translate these weird poems back and forth.

ST: You should have told him his pecker's not that big.

MZ: They sound like two G.I.s in the room.

ST: I know, that's the whole point.

DR: How come you don't have an act like that?

JK: I'll tell you why, because after I left Gregory and Mimi I was walking down the road . . . boulevard Beaumarchais, walking down the boulevard beaumarchais, and a woman comes up to me in a mink coat perfume all over, she says, *"Voulez-vous un petit moment?" "Mademoiselle, je pense que je n'ai assez d'argent." La raison que j'ai dit ça*, the reason that I said that is before that happened I was walking through Rue Clignacourt in Montmartre. Nobody can pronounce that word except a Frenchman. That famous street in Montmartre–Clignacourt, Clignacourt.

MZ: Clignacourt?

JK: Clignacourt! The main street in Montmartre–Clignacourt, la rue Clignacourt. *Il y a une peine grosse Italienne* in the doorway. A beautiful Italian broad in the doorway with slacks, you know. I said, "Pia–ta ta ta boom!" And I'm out. Two minutes. Two minutes.

ST: You did?

JK: Yeah.

ST: What she do to you?

JK: She took me to the house.

ST: Two minutes? Pretty good.

JK: So then this other woman comes up, "Would you like a pretty little [moment] in a fur coat?" and I had nothing else.

ST: If you had nothing else, you should have told her, "Give me the fur coat and I'll screw that."

JK: No, I didn't want a woman just then, but I think that was the best woman in Montmartre. So I go to all the motel rooms again *une chambre*, "*Complet! Complet! Complet!*" Everything was *complet*, closed. This is for them fifty years from now; they're going to learn how to go to France. So I go turn on the faucet, start to wash my face, finally get a room in a couple of Turkish pimps' hotel. Turkish pimps—two pimps from Turkey. The faucet is talking Cockney talk.

ST: What did they do to you?

JK: The water from the faucet is going, "Oi say there, you're talking Cockney." From there I go to London. Next day I was in London. I go into London there's the most darling blonde on earth going like this with her finger. "Come here, Ducks," coming from the doorway of Soho. "I don't have any money." I didn't have any money. Didn't have any money.

ST: Didn't you have money in your belt?

JK: No, I didn't have any more money.

ST: How come? You have money in your belt all the time. I know about you.

JK: I didn't have no more money then.

ST: He had money.

JK: That was ninety-five string beans.

ST: Yeah. You had money; you know that.

JK: No I didn't.

ST: He hides his money in his belt.

JK: I only had enough money to get a room in Picadilly Circus on the top floor of the hotel, above the top floor, in the attic. Up in the attic on Saturday night I go to bed. When I wake up Sunday morning open up my windows the maid comes in brings me a stack of toast this high with marmalade and the carillons in all the churches in London are going Dee da da da da dee da dong! Dee da da da da dee da dong! [laughs]

ST: Orange marmalade, beautiful. Orange marmalade.

JK: Orange marmalade, certainly. And the carillons of the churches going Dee da dee dee dee dee dee dong! So it was Sunday and on Good Friday afternoon I went to St. Paul's Cathedral to see a performance of Johann Sebastian Bach's St. Matthew's Passion, as sung by a special choir, a boys' choir, a women's choir, the full orchestra, and the organ of St. Paul's Cathedral in London, which was not hit by Hitler's bombs. But all around the cathedral—rubble....

Kerouac Aboard the New Amsterdam*

JK: Anyway, I walked into the dining room and the waiter set me down with a beautiful German girl and two laughing German boys and there's me and they're all well dressed and Hee! Hee! having a big time. And the waiter brings the menu and says, "What will you have?" So I said, "Jesus, God, I could eat the very menu." The menu was good enough to eat, you know. Salmon, avec la sauce, boy what a menu. [whistles] Filet mignon, salmon steak, [whistles] whatever they call it, what do they say? Anyway, the Italian waiter looks at me, says, "Make up your mind." The

---

* Kerouac departed Europe on April 20, 1957 for New York City aboard the *S.S. New Amsterdam*, which cost him a dear $120.

German boy turns to me and says, [German accent] "I would not take that from a waiter if I were you." God. He says, "We take too much from these people." Hoo! Hoo! Hoo! I said, "Wait a minute, wait a minute. I'm an American beatnik! I don't care." He said, "American never take that," he says, "don't take that." I says, "All right." Then they moved me to another table. But the German boy was my friend all the way across the ocean. When we left in New York, it was in New York harbor, he says, "Where is the Statue of Liberty?! We want to take a picture of it." I said, "Boy, it's right there." "Where?" And he takes a picture. "Listen, where are you going?" He says, "I'm going to Minnesota to be a mining engineer." I liked that guy too. The Germans always liked me, by the way. Every time, every time. . . .

Kerouac and the Ghosts of Northport

JK: There is a poltergeist in the dining room cupboard, which was left there by a previous witch. You see, Northport is full of witches. On Halloween night, when I get high, I go out in the yard with my cat, his tail goes up, arched back rises up, pshoooo! He runs away. I look around, I see ghosts everywhere—at the sign of the cross.

ST: So you mean you're the son of a witch?

JK: I told all the ghosts, "Go back to your graves! It's only on Halloween night, for God's sakes." All Soul's Night—there are also Indian ghosts with great red, I mean blue headdresses and long brown hawk noses. . . . This is a real village, by the way, ain't it? He came from Levittown.

MZ: Earlier you mentioned it looks like New England where you came from?

JK: It looks a lot like New England, yeah. Looks like New England, yeah. . . .

Kerouac and W. C. Fields

JK: When I was a little child in my crib this great big ugly bastard looked over me into my crib saying, "Coochee, coochee, coochee, coochee."

ST: Who was it?

JK: W. C. Fields. "Coochee, coochee, coochee, coochee, coochee." [laughs] Oh I would love that any day now. [laughter] . . .

Kerouac and His Father

ST: No kidding. Yeah, but your mother and you told me once the one thing you had against your father was that he was too much of a gambler and lost all your money.

JK: He lost the money on the horses.

ST: On the horses?

JK: On the racehorses, at the racetrack.

ST: Not cards?!

JK: Not cards, no. He was tops as a card player.

ST: You told me a very good story, I remember, about him on his deathbed.

JK: The horses—nobody can beat the horses.

ST: Remember? What was the message he gave you?

JK: Life is too long?

ST: Yeah.

JK: Life is too long.

ST: Yeah.

JK: And take care of my wife.

ST: Yeah.

JK: He told me to take care of his wife, my mother.

ST: Yeah, also didn't he take you to Boston to see some of the early stage players when you were a teenager?

JK: Yeah. George Arliss. Yes sir, all doozies. What do you mean?

ST: I'm going to put some jazz on.

JK: Are you playing that now?

ST: No. What?

JK: That recording.

ST: Sure, why not?

JK: Well now, you interview him about painting.

MZ: Oh, I will interview him.

ST: That's later.

JK: Oh, you're not doing that till later. You're interviewing me now. . . .

Kerouac on Norman Mailer

JK: And then [Mailer] has a picture taken of him in *Esquire* magazine, standing in a corner ready to take on any American novelist. I'm telling you, if he ever wants to have a fight with me, I'd get mad.

ST: Well, you know what would happen between the two of you, don't you? Like nobody would win and nobody would lose.

JK: I would win and I would go to prison.

ST: I told you the story—I clipped him once accidentally.

JK: He's full of shit. Excuse me.

ST: Yeah, that's beside the point.

MZ: This reminds me of an earlier—

JK: I never never never never fought anybody yet, unless they were hurting a friend of mine, and then when they're hurting a friend of mine I lose my mind and their fathers have to drag me off their backs. But if they're hitting me I don't care. . . .

Kerouac on Favorite Novelists

JK: Sinclair Lewis.

MZ: Dreiser.

JK: I like Sinclair Lewis.

ST: You do?

JK: Oh boy. You ever read him?

ST: Yeah!

JK: *Mainstreet, Babbitt, Dodsworth, Arrowsmith.*

ST: I think he was kind of in front of his time, that's true. But you were talking about Melville before.

JK: Well, Melville. Now the nineteenth-century American writers were much greater. There's only one twentieth-century American writer who could compare to Melville, Whitman–Wolfe.

ST: Who?

JK: Thomas Wolfe.

MZ: Yes, he could.

ST: But why don't you tell them about Thomas Wolfe?

JK: Talk about him? He's anti-Semitic!

ST: So are you, so are you. So what's the difference.

JK: Well, he said so.

ST: He didn't say it in print.

JK: Yes he did.

ST: Well, you didn't say it in print.

JK: No, I didn't. Doesn't bother me.

ST: It shouldn't.

JK: Why?

ST: Because you love jazz too much.

JK: Well he wasn't really anti-Semitic. Actually the Jews think he's anti-Semitic. He said, "the lovely long-necked Jewish ladies coming into the theater with their short-necked Jewish millionaire." Everybody's not a millionaire Jew, you know.

ST: He was describing a situation.

JK: They're not all rich, you know.

ST: That's true.

JK: No, but actually Wolfe has been put down by the Jewish critics of America.

ST: He was.

MZ: Yes.

JK: Has been and is being put down now. He's the only spirit of any dimension like real talkin' in the whole country since Melville. Lewis was writing about a little bit of this, and Fitzgerald a little bit of that. Hemingway a little bit of that. But Wolfe, he said, "Put your ear to the ground at night in America and listen to thunderous hooves of the Blackfoot, the Indian. Hear the great railroad train." Ooh, he could hear everything when he put his ear to the ground. . . .

Kerouac on the Holy Ghost

JK: You close your eyes, look that way, that way, and you're gonna see you're gonna see like let's say you're lookin' that way and you think you'll see you are seeing God, but you're only seeing the Holy Ghost.

ST: You know what I could do? For instance, I could close my eyes.

JK: The Holy Ghost!

ST: No!

JK: Because all of this is ghostly.

DR: Symbolic.

JK: Symbolic in the eye. It's not symbolic, no. It's all measurable down to unmeasurable protons, neutrons, atoms, and all that stuff, and electromagnetic gravitational field glazing white shrouds everywhere—it is the Holy Ghost!

ST: Jack, you don't believe in that, Jack.

JK: That's the trouble with you, you're afraid of the Holy Ghost. The Holy Ghost is here! Not me, not you, not him, not her, not him, not me, not you, all of us, and everything all around in ten million directions up, down, that way, that way, and all directions of space forever is the Holy Ghost! It's a completely ghostly existence. For what reason? That I don't know.

ST: This I disagree with.

JK: Although I do know. God wanted to amuse himself with a movie. You know, to watch a movie. God's watchin' us. A funny movie.

MZ: That sounds absurd.

ST: Jack, in answer to that—

JK: You don't believe that? I'll go into a Protestant church tomorrow in North Carolina and tell 'em! . . .

Kerouac Revisited

Val Duncan, *Long Island Newsday* (July 18, 1964)

He sits in the rocking chair, a can of beer in his hand. His eyes
are startlingly blue and they seem to be staring through the
walls. Behind the shag of a black, four-day beard, there's a friendly,
honest face with a ready smile.

"Look," he says, pointing to his sockless feet, encased in a pair of
ragged red slippers. He points to calluses on each ankle. "That's
from doing so much rocking. Hours of it. How about a shot of
Scotch?" Here is Jack Kerouac, so-called bard of the Beat Generation, the spokesman for the cool cats and their chicks, the guru of
the pad dwellers from Greenwich Village to the Coast. His books,
hard and soft covers, have sold in the millions and have been translated into twelve languages. He spots the photographer and fingers
the heavy stubble on his face. "If you're going to take pictures, I'd
better get rid of this. He goes off to shave, nicking his cheek in the
process. He comes back. You ask him how he's doing these days.

"Come with me," he says, and beer can and shot glass in either
hand, leads the way down the corridor of the $24,000 house he
owns at 7 Judy Ann Court, Northport. The room has a thousand

books on many shelves, and everybody's there, from Aristophanes to Allen Ginsberg. Two of the walls blaze with abstract paintings and bright postcards from many lands. Classics, primitives, El Greco, Rouault, Picasso, Van Gogh, Rousseau, Gauguin–and many more, contrasting with oriental plaques and soft Japanese mezzotints. Special spotlights stab down at his typewriter. He spins a dial, and an expensive hi-fi blasts into action. It is far-out jazz. "Now," he says, carefully placing his drinks on coasters so that no stains will mar his books or papers. Then he takes off one of his slippers, centers it precisely in the center of the floor, puts his head down on it and, with the grace of a champion gymnast, elevates his feet until he is standing on his head. Then, with continuously perfect form, he raises and lowers his feet ten times. The rippling stomach muscles show the strain and the strength. But when it's over, he's not even breathing hard. "See," he says, draining his shot glass. "That's how I'm doing these days." He flexes bulging biceps and slaps his belly, hard as a butcher block. Kerouac, at forty-two, stands five feet, eight inches, weighs 190 pounds without an ounce of fat. It's the kind of body you need to do the things he's done–played varsity football for Columbia; sailed the Arctic run during the war; thumbed his way from coast to coast; rode the rods to the Northwest.

It was the telling of his travels across the country and Europe that won him the idolization of 5 million youngsters, hipsters, poets, jazzmen, and rich girls in convertibles. In his books, they lived vicariously as free souls, roaming the earth, shunning civilization–and its responsibilities–reading books on Zen Buddhism, trying to find their Inner Self.

And in him, too, despite his physical strength, they perceived an essential gentleness about him. He is not a hard man. Though he has been drinking heavily, his eyes remain clear, with a purity about them, and his great fist is firm in the handshake.

"Never hit anybody in my life," he says. "Had to slap a guy when he started bothering another smaller guy. Just slapped him with both palms—not hard, just enough to shake him back to sense."

On impulse, he suddenly snaps off the blasting hi-fi. The ensuing silence is deafening. He calls out to his mother in a foreign tongue that sounds vaguely like French. And a few seconds later, a dimple-faced little old lady appears, studying him worriedly through her glasses. "It's your one fault, Jack," she says. "Too much you drink." She sighs but hands him another can of beer.

"Now for the Russian," he says, and he changes tapes. He does this fast because although he has dozens of tapes, he can find any one instantly by an index system of cards, coded with stars, moons, crosses, crescents, and other symbols. He invented the system, and here is another facet of the mercurial Kerouac—a passion for order-liness. He can lay his hand on any book immediately. His thousands of letters and papers are neatly filed and indexed in a metal cabinet.

Again the machine blasts forth. It is Shostakovich's Fifth. Ker-ouac taps his feet, smashes his hands on the skinhead of a conga drum. Then he whirls into a dance, and it is almost classical ballet—the arabesque, entrechat, pirouette. He's good at it. He makes a lot of funny faces. He stops and cocks an ear to the music. "Listen to the pain and the sweetness of it," he says. He gulps beer.

"My mother," he says. "I take good care of her. She speaks to me in English, but I talk medieval French to her. It is the language of François Villon," and knowing its exact position on the shelf, he whips down a copy of the French poet's works. "Great stuff, but Shakespeare was the best of them all, and after him James Joyce." He flourishes five-pound volumes of *Ulysses* and *Finnegan's Wake*.

His reference to Villon and old French brings him close to a topic that is almost a fetish with him—the study of national origins, names, pronunciations, and a mystical belief that he has lived other lives before this.

"My family is five thousand years old," he says. "People bug me. They say what the hell kind of a name is Kerouac, anyway? It's easy. Just a real old Irish name—Keltic. *'Ker'* means house in Celtic. *'Ouac'* means 'on the moor.' But my family traveled far. They started in Ireland, traveled to Wales, then Cornwall, then Brittany, where they learned the old French, then four hundred years ago to Canada. Did you know that one of the Iroquois nations is named Kerouac?"

He strikes a dramatic pose, and you're not sure if he's kidding. "Once I was Tristan looking for Isolde and once I rode the plains of Tartary on a shaggy pony." He tells of a friend he bummed around with on the Coast who said that everyone has lived twenty or thirty lives before. "He's a funny guy, but he might be right."

His mention of friends brings up the question of what is happening in the world of Beatism. Nobody has heard much about it lately. But he doesn't like the question, evades it, says: "It's time to sing a song." But you insist, repeat the question.

He shrugs. "They're still reading poetry, but I never get to the Village any more." (Where once he could command $200 for a single poetry reading.) "They don't like me. All the old-timers are turning politicians, getting up petitions for civil rights and all that kind of stuff. It's politics, not art any more."

Though Kerouac may not have changed, in his eyes the old world of bumming the country with pot-smoking hipsters and pickup chicks, learning how to make tequila from cactus and practicing oriental love rites, seems to be taking a new direction. "There's more money around." He won't say how much his books have brought but he said he's guessed he paid out "about $15,000" in agency fees since 1957, when his classic *On the Road* vaulted him to fame. Agents normally receive a 10 percent commission. Though none of his later books equaled *On the Road*, all sold well, particularly *The Dharma Bums*. His last two books, *Big Sur* and *Visions of Gerard*, both published by Farrar, Straus Inc., are big sellers and in constant demand at libraries. Most of his books tell pretty much the same story—booze-filled wanderings of young people amid the beauty and misery of life. Many of the characters are the same, but for legal reasons he has not been allowed to repeat their names. However, the thread is there: young love, sex, drugs, an endless odyssey in search of self ("call it Dharma, enlightenment—God, if you will").

In his studies of Zen, search for Self, and other unconventionalities, Kerouac sees no conflict with being a Roman Catholic. Over his bed hangs a rosary.

"Know what I do every night?" Reverently he tiptoes over to the beads, gently picks up the crucifix, and presses it to his lips. "The silent kiss," he says. "Every night."

But every night is not the same. Some nights he drinks. Some nights he works. He has two books in the making, with commissions for articles for several slick magazines. His essay on Shakespeare that appeared in a top show business magazine earlier this year received critical acclaim, not because it was written in the usual razzmatazz, semi-gibberish of beat writing, but because it was a highly polished treatise, richly phrased and displaying a profundity of scholarship. He also writes prefaces for art books and has completed a narration for a movie short.

"I need quiet to work," he says, gazing out on a lawn that he has had made into a small grotto, the whole area surrounded by a stout, six-foot fence of Alaska cedar planking. "Self-protection. People always bugging me. Once a guy rushed in at five in the morning and screamed: 'Are you busy?'" When Kerouac types, he does it fast. Truman Capote once said: "He's not a writer, he's a typewriter." Once started, he doesn't stop, using long rolls of paper instead of individual sheets. "Just blast away. Waste no time fooling with paper. Write a book without stopping." He covers all of his paper–single-spaced with margins of only one eighth of an inch. At present, he's working on the draft of a story called *Memory Babe*, set near the Canadian border, an area of nostalgia for Massachusetts-born Kerouac. "My grandfather, Jean-Baptiste, lived up there. He taught me the importance of the rocking chair." His other work will probably be titled *An American Passed Here*,[47] recollections of adventures in Europe and North Africa.

Despite the fence and the quiet of his little side street, it's still "too noisy." He's selling his house here and moving to Florida. After that he's off to Europe–"maybe Russia, too. I hate communism but I'd like to see the country."

Out of it all he believes will come another book–or, as he is beginning to see it, another long chapter to be used in a future masterwork. This would be known as the Duluoz Legend that he intends to write "in my old age and then die happy."

He explains this by quoting from his preface in *Big Sur*, in which he compares this future compilation with the works of Proust, "except that my remembrances are written on the run instead of a sick bed . . . the whole thing forms an enormous comedy, seen through the eyes of poor Ti Jean (me), otherwise known as Jack Duluoz, the world of raging action and folly and also gentle sweetness seen through the keyhole of his eye." Kerouac squints out the window at the setting sun. It is the time when most people are thinking of dinner. "Drop me off downtown," he says, "I'm out of Scotch and I need a shot."

You let him off at a local bar. He shuffles inside, shirttail flapping, still in his tattered slippers. He doesn't know what will happen next and doesn't seem to care. At the bar he may find a quiet oblivion— or a new character to write about.

Beat Is Rhythm, Not an Act

Robert E. Boles, *Yarmouth Port Register* (Undated)

*In 1966, Jack Kerouac and his mother, Gabrielle, sold their St.
Petersburg home and bought a house on Massachusetts's Cape
Cod at 20 Bristol Avenue in Hyannis. There Kerouac remained
lonely and isolated from his friends and acquaintances. He had
married his lifelong friend, Stella Sampas, on September 18,
1966. A little over two months earlier, Gabrielle Kerouac had
suffered a stroke and became dependent on her son physically
and financially. Jack's writing sputtered under the constant care
and worry for his ailing mother. His drinking remained a constant. In December 1966, Kerouac was arrested twice for public
drunkenness. Novelist and Cape Cod resident Kurt Vonnegut
recalled a game of cards with Kerouac in attendance:*

I knew Kerouac only at the end of his life, which is to
say there was no way for me to know him at all, since
he had become a pinwheel. He had settled briefly on
Cape Cod, and a mutual friend, the writer Robert Boles,
brought him over to my house one night. I doubt that

Kerouac knew anything about me or my work, or even where he was. He was crazy. He called Boles, who is black, "a blue-gummed nigger." He said that Jews were the real Nazis, and that Allen Ginsberg had been told by the Communists to befriend Kerouac in order that they might gain control of American young people, whose leader he was. This was pathetic. There were clearly thunderstorms in the head of this once charming and just and intelligent man. He wished to play poker, so I dealt some cards. There were four hands, I think—one for Boles, one for Kerouac, one for Stella, one for me. Kerouac picked up the remainder of the deck, and he threw it across the kitchen.

When Jack was at the Big Sur in California, he sat on rocks washed through and fragile and wrote poetry, modeling it on the sounds of waves. When Jack briefly searched France for the history of his name and descendance, while he was in Brest, he wanted to sit by the sea and write poetry, his hands with pencil and paper inside a plastic bag, writing the words the sea gave him, in the rain—but he did not. There was the irksome business of hotels and thugs to frighten him off.

He got a book out of France. *Satori in Paris*. And he got much more. When he visited Gallimard,* admittedly a little drunk, he was treated coolly. He had made money for the publishing house. There were letters of apology afterwards. He made a friend of a cab driver, another man in a conversation across the floor of a restaurant. And he learned a great deal more: that he was older, that he wasn't as

---

* Kerouac's publisher in France.

handsome as he had been when he was younger, and that it was very easy to be deterred by thugs and hotels from sitting by the Brest sea in the rain with pencil and paper and hands in a plastic bag recording a rhythmic dialogue between a man and the sea.

Jack was in Hyannis when *Satori in Paris* was published.

He had come in the fall and had walked through Barnstable, Yarmouth, Dennis, Harwich, talking with people, his bread and butter and reason; and then bought a rather common ranch house in Hyannis. His mother, an invalid, came to live with him, and he wanted to be close to the hospital.

And then, after the interim of moving, the life, the reputation, all began again. Unknown admirers visited him and walked off with books and clothing and money. The police discovered a sinister aspect of him. Coming out of a Hyannis bar and seeing a girl, quite lovely, he said, "I protest such beauty!" and he was nearly arrested.

The fabric of his Hyannis life is difficult to reconstruct. He is a tremendous drinker and does not trust himself with an automobile so when shopping, pulled a wagon behind him. In the evenings he went to bars. In the afternoons he found that the neighborhood children were instructed to stay away from him.

And then there was another incident with the police. According to (this writer apologizes for the editorialization) Jack, he had complained of a ham or CB operator across the street because the TV was affected, and one night she complained to the police about noise at his house. The police entered his house and arrested him for being drunk. As they were taking him away they nicely crashed him into a tree. The incident was glossed over by the higher-ups, his attorney being a special justice.

Nevertheless he stayed and got married—to a girl from Lowell, the town he had grown up in. He had fallen in love with her when he was in his teens and when he walked with her over the canal bridges in Lowell listening to her recite poetry in Greek.

His marriage to Stella Sampas was duly recorded in *Time* magazine and by various newspapers, this one not included.

He had been married twice before. But this was different. Stella, older than Jack, a virgin, came from managing a cleaning plant in Lowell to be the wife of a man, famous, who had lived well and more lives than most, and found that his life was an entanglement of relationships, friends, ideas, and words.

She guarded the doors.

She cooked and laundered.

She found his manly needs repulsive.

Jack claimed a room in his house.

It was where he kept his library, his Wolensack [a tape recorder], his bed, his brakeman's lantern, his cards (of a baseball game he had invented when much younger), a manuscript, enormous, of poetry, thought, words, and sounds, and all else he claimed.

In there he would listen to his tapes of Billie Holiday or a Mozart Mass.

You should know something about Jack.

You should know that he offends, in a friendly way, to break down reserves. He has no private life. He has published his privacy in seventeen novels and he has written as enthusiastically about his defeats as he has his victories.

You should know that in conversation, when the other is speaking, he closes his eyes in order to do nothing but listen.

You should know that when he talks he lets his voice become theatrical. He will shout a word to make it heard and whisper a phrase that is a whisper of what he means.

You should know that he drinks Scotch (Johnny Walker Red

Label and Schlitz Malt Liquor) and that he often carries Scotch in an Anacin bottle.

You should know that he stands on his head every day and lowers his feet to the floor nine times.

You should know that he cries when someone or something dies.

You should know that he considers Truman Capote a sadist and nothing else.

You should know much about him.

Radio-Canada Interview

Fernand Seguin, *Sel de la Semaine* (March 7, 1967)

Kerouac was charmed to be interviewed by French-Canadian television, and he obliged by agreeing to do so by traveling to Montreal and conversing in their and his native language. Despite his evident pleasure in the interview, his private life mired him in miseries. He became resentful of Stella waiting on him hand and foot, "which makes me feel even more useless as I used to do everything for myself." Springtime brought a new anger at all the "idiots" who came out of the "woodwork." His cat Timmy died of cancer, and in May Gabrielle was admitted to the Holy Ghost Hospital in Cambridge, Massachusetts, for rehabilitation.

[Song by the Alexandrins about Kerouac; final piano notes, the audience applauds.]

FS: Jack Kerouac, you are famous throughout the United States because of the sixteen books you have published, translated into . . . you are translated in forty-seven countries, is that right?

JK: Yes, sixteen languages.

FS: Sixteen languages.

JK: Yes [gestures made by Kerouac giving the impression he is counting or thinking about something].

FS: For the French-Canadians who know you, you are, after all, uh . . . even though you may not admit to it, a Franco-American, you are the one who was born in Lowell, Massachusetts, of French-Canadian parents. And . . . before we begin discussing your career as a writer and how you came to it, we would like you to tell us about the childhood of a Franco-American in Lowell . . . how was it, what kind of family did you have, your father, mother, your brothers, your sisters?

JK: Hm-hm. In Lowell we had some small Canadian neighbor-hoods.

FS: Yes . . . they are know as [inaudible intervention by JK in French] "Little Canadas"?

JK: No, that was . . . the . . . the tenements.

FS: Hm-hm . . . But . . . uh . . . Little Canada was one, yes?

JK: We didn't live there. The other side of the river. The same as living in Canada. We ate potted mince . . .

FS: Ah!

JK: . . . and meat pies. And we went to . . . to . . . uh . . . little parish . . . *parochial* schools . . .

FS: Parochial, yes.

JK: Yes.

FS: Hm-hm. What did your . . . what did your father do?

JK: Printer.

FS: What did he print?

JK: Ah . . . cards, and little . . . and little papers . . . weekly, politics.

FS: Hm.

JK: Little political papers, about the . . . the town. A nice big shop.

FS: Hmm. He lost it in . . . in the . . . flood? In the flood, inundated, hm?

JK: Inundation!

FS: Inundation, Yeah! [Laughter by JK, FS, and the audience]

JK: By the river!

FS: Where was your father born . . . Léo-Alcide Kérouac. Eh? He
. . . he was born as Léo-Alcide Kérouac. Where's . . . He was born
in the Province of Québec?

JK: He was born . . . No, he was born in Saint-Hubert outside of
Rivière-du-Loup . . . at . . .

FS: Yes, in the province of Québec.

JK: Témiscouata?

FS: Témiscouata, yes, in Témiscouata County . . . and your mother?

JK: Kamouraska . . .

FS: She was a . . .

JK: . . . at Saint-Pãcome.

FS: She was a . . . Lévesque, I believe, hm?

JK: Lévesque.

FS: Do you have any brothers and sisters?

JK: I had a sister, Carolyn, and a brother, Gerard [looks into space,
a few laughs in the audience]. They are both dead now [more
laughter in the audience]. Eh, what are they laughing at? [Ker-
ouac joins in the laughter] He's the one asking questions! Excuse
me, Mr. Something. And . . .

FS: Ah . . . You went to a . . . French school?

JK: [Kerouac laughs but quickly regains his composure] Yes, yes,
Saint Louis-de-France. And also, eh . . . I didn't speak English
until . . . until I was six years old.

FS: You didn't learn to speak English until . . . you were six years
old?

JK: Yes.

FS: That means that in your family, one didn't speak English?

JK: We spoke French in the shack . . . in the house. Also, it was a neighborhood, all French, Beaulieu Street and Boisvert Street, and . . . and the club, it was all old Frenchmen who played cards, who played pool, and . . . Christmas, New Year, they made meat pies and they screamed their heads off . . . And, ah . . . once a year, Canadians would come down . . . from . . . Québec . . . in dog sleighs in the snow, to celebrate. Did you know that? To Lowell!

FS: To Lowell?

JK: Ah, yes! With stocking caps on!

FS: In your first book . . .

JK: It's all changed now, eh?

FS: It's all changed?

JK: Yeah, they have machines, Pontiacs now.

FS: Ah, yes.

JK: It's quicker than sleighs.

FS: In your first book, *The Town and the City*, you write about a family in a village that you called "Galloway."

JK: Yes, that's Lowell, a fictional arrangement. I didn't have a big family like that, I had only two siblings, my sister and my brother.

FS: And your brother. And also, ah . . . [Kerouac sighs and drops his head]

FS: But the story you tell in that book, ah . . . the kind of solidarity that there was in the family . . . the . . . the protecting role of . . . of the mother . . . is all that truth or fiction?

JK: Truth.

FS: It's the truth, that?

JK: Yes, my father was my protector! My mother too.

FS: Your . . . your father . . . is dead now. How old were you when he died?

JK: Twenty-four.

FS: And your . . . your mother is still alive however, huh?

JK: Yes. Gabrielle Lévesque [Kerouac laughs]. She's a funny one!

FS: Oh yes?! [FS laughs with the audience] How old is she now?

JK: She sends you *"pataraffes"* and *"chalivaris."* [laughter from the audience and FS]

FS: What's the matter?

JK: She sings our old songs [points to the microphone].

FS: Oh, yes?

JK: [singing] "It's such . . . sitting . . . sitting with my little dog, it's such a shame" I forgot it! [JK laughs] "My darling, its such a shame . . ." You know that . . .

FS: Well . . . [in a cordial tone] you are living once again, in Lowell. There, I'm overlooking your whole . . .

JK: [intervenes] I returned after . . .

FS: . . . whole career. We'll get to that shortly. I would also like to bring the discussion back to Lowell again. You . . . you are now living in Lowell, huh?

JK: Yes, I've returned.

FS: What attracts you to Lowell as opposed to New York or to San Francisco or . . .

JK: Well, I know all the police there! [prolonged laughter by FS and the audience] And . . . and . . .

FS: You know everybody, not only the police, because everyone there knows you.

JK: Yes. And my wife is Greek, and she wanted to return to . . . her family comes from Lowell.

FS: Oh, her family is from Lowell also?

JK: A big family, three hundred Greeks! [everybody laughs]

FS: That . . . that makes for a lot of meat pies and potted mince on New Year's Day . . . If all of them . . . all those people still eat meat pies?

JK: Not the Greeks.

FS: No?

JK: The French!

FS: What do they eat?

JK: The Greeks?

FS: Yes?

JK: Spinach pie . . .

FS: Ah yes!

JK: . . . and all sorts of Greek stuff.

FS: Well, since you're speaking of Lowell, where you now live, our team went down there, and here are the shots they made of Lowell, your birthplace, as well as the commentaries of the Franco-Americans who are still trying to survive there.

JK: Oh, I missed all that. Say that again? I missed all that, I was thinking . . . [pointing with the index finger and nodding the head as if he was trying to follow a line of thought]

FS: [in English] The film we're going to show is . . . on Lowell.

JK: [in English] Oh, the film!

[Another Alexandrins' song, this time about Franco-Americans, accompanies the images of Lowell; then, in a social club, some Franco-Americans speak of their origins, of Kerouac, and of his origins; we see Kerouac playing pool.]

FS: That, that's the Jack Kerouac of Lowell, with those who know him, those who knew him when he was young! The one who traveled all over the United States, from one coast to the other. To Mexico, Africa, Kerouac the voyager, who finished by writing this book, which was the beginning of your consecration, which was called *On the Road*. Where did your taste for travel come from?

JK: Ahh . . . I'm an old . . . Breton adventurer . . . hm! No adventurer . . . Americans are adventurous.

FS: Yes.

JK: Adventurous and independent.

FS: But you were a little more so than the others?

JK: With my Irish friend there, yes . . . ah . . . you know, the story of *On the Road* is not the story of two beatniks, it's the story of an ex-football player.

FS: Hm-hm.

JK: "Ex," that means "I was" in college, Columbia.

FS: Columbia College, yes.

JK: I left Lowell to go to Columbia . . .

FS: Hm-hm. You broke your leg playing football there?

JK: Yes, I broke a leg. And the guy who ran the outfit, he was a cowboy, a real cowboy. *Joual!* And we went all over America in search of girls ["girls" said with both amusement and embarrassment] and work and friends.

FS: But for you to write through on that . . .

JK: Huh?

FS: Because . . . to write too? Because *On the Road* . . .

JK: When I came home, I wrote.

FS: Yes . . . your . . . your first novel, *The Town and the City* . . . you took three years to write it.

JK: Yes.

FS: *On the Road* took three weeks to write.

JK: Well I discovered . . . I discovered the spontaneous way . . .

FS: Yes, spontaneous. The . . .

JK: Spontaneous!

FS: . . . spontaneous prose of Jack Kerouac, that's his . . . that's his trademark.

JK: When you start a story, and when you go to a bar, and you start to tell a story to the men, you don't stop to erase your mistakes, huh? You continue, and you continue, and you continue! [Kerouac's arm gestures to indicate going forward]

FS: But, I've been told that you purchased . . . not sheets of paper you don't have to change, but rather, rolls . . . rolls . . .

JK: Ah, but the rolls, that's . . . that's to . . . obvier . . . How do you say that in French?

FS: To avoid . . . ?

JK: Avoid changing the page! You use a large roll, and you continue, you continue . . . [easy typing gestures] You can do it with your eyes closed [laughter in the auditorium]. You recall everything like that. And the pages, and the crossings out, and the . . . uh . . .

FS: With *On the Road*, you became, as I said at the beginning of the show . . .

JK: Jean-Jacques Rousseau, he wrote like that!

FS: But not with a typewriter . . .

JK: No, but he wrote fast, fast, fast, and he changed nothing. Also Rabelais. I think . . . François Rabelais . . .

FS: Possible!

JK: . . . and Shakespeare, we know that.

FS: Hm-hm, yes. With . . . with that book, *On the Road*, I'm coming back, the one that was . . . written on rolls of paper, without stopping in three weeks . . .

JK: *Big Sur* also . . .

FS: . . . you used . . . the same technique? And *Dharma Bums* too.

FS: But the first one that . . . that assured your success, *On the Road* . . .

JK: Yes.

FS: . . . with that you became the founder of the Beat Generation. What was the Beat Generation for you? Because earlier . . . ah . . . you were saying . . .

JK: Well, there was the Lost Generation of 1920.

FS: Yes.

JK: Then it was 1949, then '50 and we were asking: What are we going to call this? What are going to call this?

FS: It's you that invented the term Beat Generation?

JK: Yes, I'd . . . heard two old, old men say that in the South, old Negroes, "beat."

FS: In the sense of "crushed" . . .

JK: . . . in the American South.

FS: . . . "beaten."

JK: Yes! Poor! After that, I was in the little church of Sainte-Jeanne-d'Arc, and all of a sudden, I said: "Ah, ah! Beat . . . beatitude."

FS: Beatitude.

JK: Hm-hm [indicating approval], that changed the meaning. *"Beato"* in Italian. *"Be . . . beato." "Béatifique"* in French.

FS: Yes, but didn't it also have the sense of the "beat" of a jazz band?

JK: Yes, and the sense of that [pretends to row a boat], and of that [pretends to paddle a canoe]. How do we do that? Fsst! Fsst! The canoes . . .

FS: The canoes.

JK: And the drums [pointing to the orchestra to his right], toom-tchoop-poom . . . and all, all . . . It's not important! The name is not important . . .

FS: But, let's say that . . .

JK: Children are important.

FS: Yes, you say the name is not important, but you refuse to be called a beatnik. You are not a beatnik.

JK: "Beatnik" is a term . . . ah . . . ooo!, I had nice word for that one [taps his forehead as if to remember; audience laughs] *degrinateur* . . . denigrating? [closes his eyes, searches for the exact word]

FS: Pejorative.

JK: Pejorative?

FS: It's a nice word!

JK: Invented after "sputnik," you know, in order to make us look like little American idealists who are independent, make us look like Russian spies . . . nik, beatnik, sputnik [laughter in the audience], vietnik, vietnik, peacenik.

FS: In short, what you mean to say, is that . . . starting with the Beat Generation, which was a literary movement, and even a . . . ah . . . a poetic . . .

JK: Politic?

FS: Poetic.

JK: Poetic?

FS: Yes . . .

JK: But literature, that's poetic.

FS: But I mean prose and also verse, things which . . .

JK: Oh yes, oh yes.

FS: Good . . .

JK: [in French] "Verses" . . . Doesn't one say "verse"?!

FS: Verse.

JK: Oh, yes . . .

FS: Starting with . . .

JK: Why doesn't one say "verse"?

FS: Why not?!

JK: We'll say "verse." There was prose and also "verse" [FS laughs].

JK: [laughing and shaking his head, lifts his eyes and sighs] Aaah boy!

FS: Starting with this core movement, which was literary, lets say . . .

JK: Yes!

FS: . . . there were parasites who came along, people who wanted to appear to belong to this movement and who were . . .

JK: Yes, the Bohemians . . . the Bohemians came along with their beards and their sandals and they sat around all night, and they observed me and this and that; and they did nothing, they didn't work, and . . . We all worked, the . . . the writers. All kinds of jobs . . . I was a journalist once. I still am a journalist, huh? And, that gave a . . . No, its more important than that. That made me angry. It's been ten years since the Bohemians come on the scene . . . But, after that, the young people entered the picture and called themselves Now Generation, Action Generation . . . or didn't have a name . . . Love Generation . . . LSD Generation [laughs]. But they're children, the new ones today, eighteen, nineteen, you don't know what they will do, but . . . I'm old enough to be their father [FS laughs] . . . forty-five!

FS: Yes, that's it . . . the . . . the devil that turns hermit!

JK: Huh? The . . . what?! [audience laughs]

FS: [in English] The devil that turns hermit!

JK: What does that mean?

FS: It's . . . now that . . . you start!

JK: "The devil becomes hermit?"

FS: Yes!

JK: I've never been a bloody hermit! [FS, the audience, and JK laugh]

FS: . . . But when . . . now that you're forty-five, you look at the . . . the young people, and you say "Well, I could be their father . . ."

JK: No, I'm saying that the . . .

FS: [intervenes] Yes!

JK: The new youth are alright, and they're searching for something.

FS: If you were twenty years old today, would you do the same as you have already done?

JK: Well I've already done it, and I'm fed up [FS and audience laugh].

FS: And the last question in thirty seconds: what does Jack Kerouac think of Jean Kerouac?

JK: Huh . . . what does that mean? Wait . . . [looks toward FS and knits his brow as if trying to understand; audience laughs]

FS: [in English] What do you think of yourself?

JK: Oh, what do you think . . . me what do I think of myself?

FS: Yes! Yes!

JK: I'm fed up with myself! [FS and audience laugh] Well, I know I'm a good writer, a great writer. I'm not . . . I am not a brave man . . . and also . . . but there is one thing I know how to do—write stories, and that's all.

FS: Well, I hope you continue to write, for the pleasure of all of us! Thank you very much for coming for the interview, Mister Kerouac.

JK: Okay!

Excerpt from an Interview with Allen Ginsberg, Part 2

Yves Le Pellec, *Composed on the Tongue* (Grey Fox, 1980)

YLP: . . . later on you move toward a more "political" consciousness, in "Wichita Vortex Sutra," for instance.

AG: yes, that's in the mid-sixties.

YLP: Whereas Jack sort of went away from it.

AG: . . . By that time Kerouac had suffered so much attack and abuse from all sides, left and right, particularly left in terms of the venomousness of it, and had become so entangled in personal problems with his mother, and most of all had become so ill physically with alcoholism that he was not in a position to go out in the world very much. From 1960 on, every move he made outside his home was dangerous for him because he would always drink himself ill and get in trouble, people beating him up actually, left-wing literary critics beating him up [laughs]. Once he came drunk into a bar saying "I'm Jack Kerouac," and some radical goon, from the longshoreman's union, I think, beat his head on the pavement. It wasn't political quite, it was just some sort of macho ego thing. And Kerouac was very open, totally helpless. Then there was the tendency to vulgarize the renaissant spirituality of what he had proposed. One built-in stereotype which still exists and is poisoning the left here insists on "hatred" as a "revolutionary weapon," an old-fashioned prepsychedelic nineteenth-century hatred, father and mother hatred actually, which was contrary to his nature as it is contrary to mine. This hatred is at the root of most radical consciousness in America [. . .] when the entire left went into a completely masturbatory period of social violence, calling everybody pigs, with self-righteousness and self-isolation which finally led to the election of Nixon. That gross element in the left repelled Kerouac, who felt that it was a betrayal of what he had prophesied. He prophesied a spiritual, angelic generation that would ultimately take over with long hair and exquisite manners, you know, "wise as serpents and harmless as doves." Instead they were, like, greedy as pigs and harmful as dogs. It's still a problem, the left being poisoned by its own anger. Also his thing was very wise in that he was basically himself a populist redneck and his mother was like a French-Canadian peasant, narrow-minded, selfish, naïve, hard-hearted, family-oriented lady. She wanted to keep Jack to herself and needed Jack, and he was tied up with her in the sense that he said he didn't want to throw her to the "Dogs of Eternity," as he thought I had done, putting my mother in a mental hospital. So he felt bound to take care of her and, having to live with her, he had to put up with her opinions. In that sense Jack was always an "Americanist," always interested in American archetypes, and his mother was like a George Wallace archetype, so to speak. Like Céline, like Dostoyevsky in old age, like Pound in some respect, like any Tolstoy anywhere, he had an odd cranky appreciation for right-wing archetypes that most left-wing writers are not subtle enough to appreciate. And so in a sense he fulfilled an interesting role there in poetizing that type. Harmless I would say, because it served to curb violent left excesses in myself and in other people. I mean, I always had Kerouac in mind when I got on a peace march and I always made sure it was, like really, straight, pure, surrealist, lamblike, nonviolent, magical, mantric, spiritual politics rather than just marching up and down the street screaming hatred at the president. In a funny way he didn't have a position, he was just himself, his own character, reacting. He was against the war, actually, in a redneck way. On a TV program with prowar scholar William F. Buckley, Jr., in 1968, he said of the South Vietnamese politicians, "All those guys, all they're trying to do is steal our jeeps." That's a very archetypal proposition and it's really true. He put the whole thing in a very intelligent way that could be universally understood, unlike New York dialectical double-talk.

YLP: Well, you could hear that sort of thing in any Café du Commerce in Bretagne.

AG: Yeah. If you read his essays like *Lonesome Traveler*, they were really attacks on the police state. Always. The whole thrust of his work was toward individualism and freedom, the only thing is he very definitely took a stand on communist brainwashing. He designated it with the name of "Arapatienz." I don't know what his source was, in the encyclopedia I think, from the name of the Russian who invented mind conditioning. That he felt was the great evil, which he ascribed to Russian Communism as well as to the American *Time–Life* network. So his preoccupation was with individualism. Later he never got into a communal effort, possibly that was because there was no commune sufficiently mature and sweet to be able to take care of him and his mother. And above all there was the problem of his physical illness. When he died, his body was in a terrible condition: he had a broken arm, a hernia in his belly-button area that he refused to have fixed, and apparently his liver was gone. I believe it was the night he finished the last chapter of *Pic*, his last novel, that he had the hemorrhage.

YLP: He had started *Pic* in '51, '52, hadn't he?

AG: I don't remember. It's just a little thing that he did long ago. This is just the last chapter. Actually there is another last chapter that he didn't add, when Pic meets Dean Moriarty on his hitchhiking north. He wrote that chapter, but I think his mother or his wife didn't like it. When that suppressed chapter is published ultimately, you'll see it's all tied back to the *On the Road* themes.

YLP: Yeah, and the episode of the Ghost of the Susquehanna recurs in *Pic*. Speaking of that period, I found a letter from you to Neal saying that you didn't like Jack's new style when he started writing *On the Road*.* And John Clellon Holmes also says in a letter of that time that he thought Jack was on the wrong way.

AG: I changed my mind very soon after that. It was sort of superficial egotism on my part not to understand what he was doing. I was just a stupid kid. What did the letter say—I don't remember—that his new writing was all crazy or something?

YLP: Yes and that it could be interesting only for somebody that had been blowing Jack for years [laughs].

AG: Oh what a stupid thing to say! You know, I was very naïve, he taught me everything I knew about writing. It took a long time, a couple of years, I think, for me to appreciate his ability there and even a longer time for me to begin practicing in spontaneous

* Ginsberg was actually referring to Kerouac's *Visions of Neal* (published as *Visions of Cody*) manuscript in his July 3, 1952 letter to Neal Cassady: "Jack's book arrived and it is a holy mess—it's great all right but he did everything to fuck it up with a lot of meaningless bullshit I think, page after page of surrealist free association that don't make sense to nobody except to someone who had blown Jack."

composition, but my stupidity about his prose couldn't have lasted too long, because pretty soon after I was running around New York with his manuscript trying to get people to publish it. At that time I was still writing very laborious square rhymed verse and revising, revising and revising. He was on my neck to improvise more and not to get hung up, but I resisted that for a long, long time. All my conceptions of literature, everything I was taught at Columbia, would fall down if I followed him on that scary road! So it took me a long time to realize the enormous amount of freedom and intuition that he was opening up in composition.

YLP: Was it with "The Green Automobile"?

AG: No, that was revised but I was getting close. Actually it wasn't till I went out to his house, when he was living in Northport I believe, so this was '53, '54 really . . . I sat down at his typewriter and just typed what was in my head and came up with a funny poem about the Statue of Liberty that was about three pages, a very sloppy poem, and I never published it because it was inferior. But he looked at it and pointed out all the interesting images and he said, "See, you can do it too." It was just that I was afraid to try, afraid too throw myself out into the sea of language, afraid to swim.

YLP: In a June '53 letter to Neal, you said that you are "trying to build a modern contemporary metaphorical yak poem using the kind of weaving original rhythm that Jack does in his prose." And it comes out with "Howl."

AG: Yes about two years later. "Howl" is very definitely influenced by Jack's spontaneous method of composition. So I always found Jack extremely right, like a Zen master, and completely alone in his originality, and because of that I always hesitated to question his judgment thereafter. He always had a depth of character and appreciation that I found later on to be prophetic and useful.

Interview with Jack Kerouac

Ted Berrigan, *Paris Review* No. 43 (Summer 1968)

*After his short-lived stay in Hyannis, Massachusetts, Kerouac,
his wife Stella, and Gabrielle moved back to Lowell in January 1967. Soon afterward, he was approached by some young
poets, one of them Aram Saroyan, the son of Kerouac's childhood favorite, the author William Saroyan. The interview was
finally agreed upon by a hesitant Kerouac and conducted in
the spring of 1967 in his hometown.*

J ack Kerouac is now forty-five years old. His thirteenth novel,
Vanity of Duluoz was published earlier this year. He lives with
his wife of one year, Stella, and his invalid mother in a brick ranch-
style house in a residential district of Lowell, Massachusetts, the city
in which he spent all of his childhood. The Kerouacs have no telephone. Ted Berrigan had contacted Kerouac some months earlier
and persuaded him to do the interview. When he felt the time had
come for their meeting to take place, he simply showed up at the
Kerouacs' house. Two friends, poets Aram Saroyan and Duncan
McNaughton, accompanied him. Kerouac answered his ring;

Berrigan quickly told him his name and the visit's purpose. Kerouac welcomed the poets, but before he could show them in, his wife, a very determined woman, seized him from behind and told the group to leave at once.

"Jack and I began talking simultaneously, saying '*Paris Review!*' 'Interview!' et cetera," Berrigan recalls:

while Duncan and Aram began to slink back toward the car. All seemed lost, but I kept talking in what I hoped was a civilized, reasonable, calming, and friendly tone of voice, and soon Mrs. Kerouac agreed to let us in for twenty minutes, on the condition that there be no drinking.

Once inside, as it became evident that we actually were in pursuit of a serious purpose, Mrs. Kerouac became more friendly, and we were able to commence the interview. It seems that people still show up constantly at the Kerouacs' looking for the author of *On the Road* and stay for days, drinking all the liquor and diverting Jack from his serious occupations.

As the evening progressed, the atmosphere changed considerably, and Mrs. Kerouac—Stella—proved a gracious and charming hostess. The most amazing thing about Jack Kerouac is his magic voice, which sounds exactly like his works and is capable of the most astounding and disconcerting changes in no time flat. It dictates everything, including this interview.

After the interview, Kerouac, who had been sitting throughout the interview in a President Kennedy–type rocker, moved over to a big poppa chair and said, "So you boys are poets, hey? Well, let's hear some of your poetry." We stayed for about an hour longer, and Aram and I read some of our things. Finally, he gave each of us a signed broadside of a recent poem of his, and we left.

Some portions of this interview have been filled out with Kerouac's written replies to questions put to him subsequent to the interview. It was felt these additions would add substance to the portrait of the author and his métier.

TB: Could we put the footstool over here to put this on?

SK: Yes.

JK: God, you're so inadequate there, Berrigan.

TB: Well, I'm no tape-recorder man, Jack. I'm just a big talker, like you. Okay, we're off.

JK: Okay? [whistles] Okay?

TB: Actually I'd like to start . . . the first book I ever read by you, oddly enough, since most people first read *On the Road* . . . the first one I read was *The Town and the City* . . .

JK: Gee!

TB: I checked it out of the library . . .

JK: Gee! . . . Did you read *Dr. Sax*? . . . *Tristessa*? . . .

TB: You better believe it. I even read Rimbaud. I have a copy of *Visions of Cody* that Ron Padgett bought in Tulsa, Oklahoma.

JK: Screw Ron Padgett! You know why? He started a little magazine called *White Dove Review* in Kansas City, was it? Tulsa? Oklahoma . . . yes. He wrote, "Start our magazine off by sending us a great big poem." So I sent him the "Thrashing Doves." And then I sent him another one, and he rejected the second one because his magazine was already started. That's to show you how punks try to make their way by scratching down on a man's back. Aw, he's no poet. You know who's a great poet? I know who the great poets are.

TB: Who?

JK: Let's see, is it . . . William Bissette of Vancouver. An Indian boy. Bill Bissette, or Bissonnette.

SAROYAN: Let's talk about Jack Kerouac.

JK: He's not better than Bill Bissette, but he's very original.

TB: Why don't we begin with editors. How do you . . .

JK: O.K. All my editors since Malcolm Cowley have had instructions to leave my prose exactly as I wrote it. In the days of Malcolm Cowley, with *On the Road* and *The Dharma Bums*, I had no power to stand by my style for better or for worse. When Malcolm Cowley made endless revisions and inserted thousands of needless commas like, say, Cheyenne, Wyoming (why not just say Cheyenne Wyoming and let it go at that, for instance), why, I spent five hundred dollars making the complete restitution of the *Bums* manuscript and got a bill from Viking Press called "Revisions." Ha ho ho. And so you asked about how do I work with an editor . . . well, nowadays I am just grateful to him for his assistance in proofreading the manuscript and in discovering logical errors, such as dates, names of places. For instance, in my last book I wrote "Firth of Forth" then looked it up, on the suggestion of my editor, and found that I'd really sailed off the Firth of Clyde. Things like that. Or I spelled Aleister Crowley "Alisteir," or he discovered little mistakes about the yardage in football games . . . and so forth. By not revising what you've already written, you simply give the reader the actual workings of your mind during the writing itself; you confess your thoughts about events in your own unchangeable way . . . well, look, did you ever hear a guy telling a long wild tale to a bunch of men in a bar and all are listening and smiling, did you ever hear that guy stop to revise himself, go back to a previous sentence to improve it, to defray its rhythmic thought impact . . . if he pauses to blow his nose, isn't he planning his next sentence? and when he lets that next sentence loose, isn't it once and for all the way he wanted to say it?

Doesn't he depart the thought of that sentence and, as Shakespeare says, "forever holds his tongue on the subject, since he's
passed over it like a part of the river flows over a rock once and
for all and never returns and can never flow any other way in
time? Incidentally, as for my bug against periods, that was for the
prose in "October in the Railroad Earth," very experimental,
intended to clack along all the way like a steam engine pulling a
hundred-car freight with a talky caboose at the end, that was my
way at the time and it still can be done if the thinking during the
swift writing is confessional and pure and all excited with the life
of it. And be sure of this, I spent my entire youth writing slowly
with revisions and endless rehashing speculation and deleting
and got so I was writing one sentence a day and the sentence had
no FEELING. Goddamn it, FEELING is what I like in art, not
CRAFTINESS and the hiding of feelings.

TB: What encouraged you to use the "spontaneous" style of *On the
Road*?

JK: I got the idea for the spontaneous style of *On the Road* from
seeing how good old Neal Cassady wrote his letters to me, all
first-person, fast, mad, confessional, completely serious, all
detailed, with real names in his case, however (being letters). I
remembered also Goethe's admonition, well, Goethe's prophecy
that the future literature of the West would be confessional in
nature; also Dostoyevsky prophesied as much and might have
started in on that if he'd lived long enough to do his projected
masterwork, *The Great Sinner*. Cassady also began his early
youthful writing with attempts at slow, painstaking, and-all-that-
crap craft business, but got sick of it like I did, seeing it wasn't
getting out his guts and heart the way it felt coming out. But I got
the flash from his style. It's a cruel lie for those West Coast punks

to say that I got the idea of *On the Road* from him. All his letters to me were about his younger days before I met him, a child with his father, et cetera, and about his later teenage experiences. The letter he sent me is erroneously reported to be a thirteen-thousand-word letter . . . no, the 13,000 word piece was his novel, *The First Third*, which he kept in his possession. The letter, the main letter I mean, was forty thousand words long, mind you, a whole short novel. It was the greatest piece of writing I ever saw, better'n anybody in America, or at least enough to make Melville, Twain, Dreiser, Wolfe, I dunno who, spin in their graves. Allen Ginsberg asked me to lend him this vast letter so he could read it. He read it, then loaned it to a guy called Gerd Stern who lived on a houseboat in Sausalito, California, in 1955, and this fellow lost the letter: overboard I presume. Neal and I called it, for convenience, the "Joan Anderson Letter" . . . all about a Christmas weekend in the pool halls, hotel rooms, and jails of Denver, with hilarious events throughout and tragic too, even a drawing of a window, with measurements to make the reader understand, all that. Now listen: this letter would have been printed under Neal's copyright, if we could find it, but as you know, it was my property as a letter to me, so Allen shouldn't have been so careless with it, nor the guy on the houseboat. If we can unearth this entire forty thousand-word letter, Neal shall be justified. We also did so much fast talking between the two of us, on tape recorders, way back in 1952, and listened to them so much, we both got the secret of LINGO in telling a tale and figured that was the only way to express the speed and tension and ecstatic tomfoolery of the age . . . is that enough?

TB: How do you think this style has changed since *On the Road*?

JK: What style? Oh, the style of *On the Road*. Well, as I say, Cowley riddled the original style of the manuscript there, without my power to complain, and since then my books are all published as written, as I say, and the style has varied from the highly experimental speedwriting of "Railroad Earth" to the ingrown-toenail-packed mystical style of *Tristessa*, the *Notes from the Underground* (by Dostoyevsky) confessional madness of *The Subterraneans*, the perfection of the three as one in *Big Sur*, I'd say, which tells a plain tale in a smooth butter literate run, to *Satori in Paris* which is really the first book I wrote with drink at my side (cognac and malt liquor) . . . and not to overlook *Book of Dreams*, the style of a person half awake from sleep and ripping it out in pencil by the bed . . . yes, pencil . . . what a job! Bleary eyes, insane mind bemused and mystified by sleep, details that pop out—even as you write them, you don't know what they mean—till you wake up, have coffee, look at it, and see the logic of dreams in dream language itself, see? . . . and finally I decided in my tired middle age to slow down and did *Vanity of Duluoz* in a more moderate style so that, having been so esoteric all these years, some earlier readers would come back and see what ten years had done to my life and thinking . . . which is after all the only thing I've got to offer, the true story of what I saw and how I saw it.

TB: You dictated sections of *Visions of Cody*. Have you used this method since?

JK: I didn't dictate sections of *Visions of Cody*. I typed up a segment of taped conversation with Neal Cassady, or Cody, talking about his early adventures in L.A. It's four chapters. I haven't used this method since; it really doesn't come out right, well, with Neal and with myself, when all written down and with all the *Ahs* and the *Ohs* and the *Ahums* and the fearful fact that the damn thing is turning and you're forced not to waste electricity or tape . . . then again, I don't know, I might have to resort to that eventually; I'm getting tired and going blind. This question stumps me. At any rate, everybody's doing it, I hear, but I'm still scribbling . . . McLuhan says we're getting more oral, so I guess we'll all learn to talk into the machine better and better.

TB: What is that state of "Yeatsian semi-trance" which provides the ideal atmosphere for spontaneous writing?

JK: Well, there it is, how can you be in a trance with your mouth yapping away . . . writing at least is a silent meditation, even though you're going a hundred miles an hour. Remember that scene in *La Dolce Vita* where the old priest is mad because a mob of maniacs have shown up to see the tree where the kids saw the Virgin Mary? He says, "Visions are not available in all this frenetic foolishness and yelling and pushing; visions are only obtainable in silence and meditation." Thar. Yup.

TB: You have said that haiku is not written spontaneously but is reworked and revised. Is this true of all your poetry? Why must the method for writing poetry differ from that of prose?

JK: No, first; haiku is best reworked and revised. I know, I tried. It has to be completely economical, no foliage and flowers and language rhythm, it has to be a simple little picture in three little lines. At least that's the way the old masters did it, spending months on three little lines and coming up, say, with:

In the abandoned boat,
The hail
Bounces about.

That's Shiki.

But as for my regular English verse, I knocked it off fast like the prose, using, get this, the size of the notebook page for the form and length of the poem, just as a musician has to get out, a jazz musician, his statement within a certain number of bars, within one chorus, which spills over into the next, but he has to stop where the chorus page stops. And finally, too, in poetry you can be completely free to say anything you want. You don't have to tell a story, you can use secret puns. That's why I always say, when writing prose: No time for poetry now, get your plain tale. [Drinks are served]

TB: How do you write haiku?

JK: Haiku? You want to hear haiku? You see, you got to compress into three short lines a great big story. First you start with a haiku situation—so you see a leaf, as I told her the other night, falling on the back of a sparrow during a great big October wind storm. A big leaf falls on the back of a little sparrow. How you going to compress that into three lines? Now in Japanese you got to compress it into seventeen syllables. We don't have to do that in American—or English—because we don't have the same syllabic bullshit that your Japanese language has. So you say: Little sparrow—you don't have to say little—everybody knows a sparrow is little . . . because they fall . . . so you say:

Sparrow
with big leaf on its back—
Windstorm.

No good, don't work, I reject it.

A little sparrow
When an Autumn leaf suddenly sticks to its back
From the wind.

Hah, that does it. No, it's a little bit too long. See? It's already a little bit too long, Berrigan, you know what I mean?

TB: Seems like there's an extra word or something, like "when." How about leaving out "when?" Say:

A sparrow
an autumn leaf suddenly sticks to its back–
From the wind!

JK: Hey, that's all right. I think "when" was the extra word. You got the right idea there, O'Hara! A sparrow, an autumn leaf suddenly—we don't have to say "suddenly" do we?

A sparrow
An autumn leaf sticks to its back–
From the wind!

[Kerouac writes final version into spiral notebook]

TB: "Suddenly" is absolutely the kind of word we don't need there. When you publish that, will you give me a footnote saying you asked me a couple of questions?

JK: [writes] Berrigan noticed. Right?

TB: Do you write poetry very much? Do you write other poetry besides haiku?

JK: It's hard to write haiku. I write long, silly, Indian poems. You want to hear my long, silly, Indian poem?

TB: What kind of Indian?

JK: Iroquois. As you know from looking at me [reads from notebook]:

> *On the lawn on the way to the store*
> *44 years old for the neighbors to hear*
> *hey, looka, Ma I hurt myself. Especially*
> *with that squirt.*

What's that mean?

TB: Say it again.

JK: Hey, looka, Ma, I hurt myself, while on the way to the store I hurt myself I fell on the lawn I yell to my mother hey looka, Ma, I hurt myself. I add, especially with that squirt.

TB: You fell over a sprinkler?

JK: No, my father's squirt into my Ma.

TB: From that distance?

JK: Oh, I quit. No, I know you wouldn't get that one. I had to explain it [opens notebook again and reads]: "Goy means Joy."

TB: Send that one to Ginsberg.

JK: [reads] "Happy people so called are hypocrites—it means the happiness wavelength can't work without necessary deceit, without certain scheming and lies and hiding. Hypocrisy and deceit, no Indians. No smiling."

TB: No Indians?

JK: The reason you really have a hidden hostility toward me, Berrigan, is because of the French and Indian War.

TB: That could be.

AS: I saw a football picture of you in the cellar of Horace Mann. You were pretty fat in those days.

SK: Tuffy! Here, Tuffy! Come on kitty . . .

JK: Stella, let's have another bottle or two. Yeah, I'm going to murder everybody if they let me go. I did. Hot fudge sundaes! Boom! I used to have two or three hot fudge sundaes before every game. Lou Little . . .

TB: He was your coach at Columbia?

JK: Lou Little was my coach at Columbia. My father went up to him and said, "You sneaky long-nosed finagler," he says, "why don't you let my son, Ti Jean, Jack, start in the Army game so he can get back at his great enemy from Lowell?" And Lou Little says, "Because he's not ready." "Who says he's not ready?" "I say he's not ready." My father says why you long-nose banana-nose big crook, get out of my sight!" And he comes stomping out of the office smoking a big cigar. "Come out of here Jack, let's get out of here." So we left Columbia together. And also when I was in the United States Navy during the war—1942—right in front of the admirals, he walked in and says, "Jack, you are right! The Germans should not be our enemies. They should be our allies, as it will be proven in time." And the admirals were all there with their mouths open, and my father would take no shit from nobody—my father didn't have nothing but a big belly about this big [gestures with arms out in front of him] and he would go POOM! [Kerouac gets up and demonstrates by puffing his belly out in front of him with explosive force and saying POOM!] One time he was walking down the street with my mother, arm in arm, down the Lower East Side. In the old days, you know, the 1940s. And here comes a whole bunch of rabbis walking arm in arm–teedah teedah teedah–and they wouldn't part for this Christian and his wife. So my father went POOM! and he knocked a rabbi right in the gutter. Then he took my mother and walked on through. Now, if you don't like that, Berrigan, that's the history of my family. They don't take no shit from nobody. In due time I ain't going to take no shit from nobody. You can record that. Is this my wine?

TB: Was *The Town and the City* written under spontaneous composition principles?

JK: Some of it, sire. I also wrote another version that's hidden under the floorboards, with Burroughs.

TB: Yes, I've heard rumors of that book. Everybody wants to get at that book.

JK: It's called *And the Hippos Were Boiled in Their Tanks*. The hippos. Because Burroughs and I were sitting in a bar one night and we heard a newscaster saying: "and so the Egyptians attacked," blah blah, "and meanwhile there was a great fire in the zoo in London and the fire raced across the fields and the hippos were boiled in their tanks! Goodnight everyone!" That's Bill, he noticed that. Because he notices them kind of things.

TB: You really did type up his *Naked Lunch* manuscript for him in Tangiers?

JK: No . . . the first part. The first two chapters. I went to bed, and I had nightmares . . . of great long balonies coming out of my mouth. I had nightmares typing up that manuscript . . . I said, "Bill!" He said, "Keep typing it." He said, "I bought you a goddamn kerosene stove here in North Africa, you know." Among the Arabs . . . it's hard to get a kerosene stove. I'd light up the kerosene stove, and take some bedding and a little pot, or kif, as we called it there . . . or maybe sometimes hasheesh . . . there, by the way, it's legal . . . and I'd go toktoktoktoktoktok and when I went to bed at night, these things kept coming out of my mouth. So finally these other guys showed up like Alan Ansen and Allen Ginsberg, and they spoiled the whole manuscript because they didn't type it up the way he wrote it.

TB: Grove Press has been issuing his Olympia Press books with lots of changes and things added.

JK: Well, in my opinion, Burroughs hasn't given us anything that would interest our breaking hearts since he wrote like he did in *Naked Lunch*. Now all he does is that breakup stuff, it's called . . . where you write a page of prose, you write another page of prose . . . then you fold it over and you cut it up and you put it together . . . and shit like that . . .

TB: What about *Junkie*, though?

JK: It's a classic. It's better than Hemingway—it's just like Hemingway but even a little better too. It says: "Danny comes into my pad one night and says, 'Hey, Bill, can I borrow your sap.'" Your sap—do you know what a sap is?

AS: A blackjack?

JK: It's a blackjack. Bill says, "I pulled out my underneath drawer, and underneath some nice shirts I pulled out my blackjack. I gave it to Danny and said, 'Now don't lose it, Danny.' Danny says, 'Don't worry, I won't lose it.' He goes off and loses it." Sap . . . blackjack . . . that's me. Sap . . . blackjack.

TB: That's a haiku: sap, blackjack, that's me. You better write that down.

JK: No.

TB: Maybe I'll write that down. Do you mind if I use that one?

JK: Up your ass with Mobil gas!

TB: You don't believe in collaborations? Have you ever done any collaborations, other than with publishers?

JK: I did a couple of collaborations in bed with Bill Cannastra in lofts. With blondes.

TB: Was he the guy that tried to climb off the subway train at Astor Place, in Holmes's *Go*?

JK: Yes. Yeah, well he says, "let's take all our clothes off and run around the block" . . . it was raining you know. Sixteenth Street off Seventh Avenue. I said, "well, I'll keep my shorts on." He says, "no, no shorts." I said, "I'm going to keep my shorts on." He said, "All right, but I'm not going to wear mine." And we trot trot trot trot down the block. Sixteenth to Seventeenth . . . and we come back and run up the stairs—nobody saw us.

TB: What time of day?

JK: But he was absolutely naked . . . about 3 or 4 A.M. It rained. And everybody was there. He was dancing on broken glass and playing Bach. Bill was the guy who used to teeter off his roof—six flights up, you know? He'd go, "You want me to fall?" We'd say, "No, Bill, no." He was an Italian. Italians are wild you know.

TB: Did he write? What did he do?

JK: He says, "Jack, come with me and look down through this peep-hole." We looked down through the peephole, we saw a lot of things . . . into his toilet. I said, "I'm not interested in that, Bill." He said, "You're not interested in anything." Auden would come the next day, the next afternoon, for cocktails. Maybe with Chester Kallman, Tennessee Williams.

TB: Was Neal Cassady around in those days? Did you already know Neal Cassady when you were involved with Bill Cannastra?

JK: Oh yes, yes, ahem . . . he had a great big pack of pot. He always was a pot-happy man.

TB: Why do you think Neal doesn't write?

JK: He has written . . . beautifully! He has written better than I have.

Neal's a very funny guy. He's a real Californian. We had more fun than five thousand Socony Gasoline Station attendants can have. In my opinion, he's the most intelligent man I've ever met in my life, Neal Cassady. He's a Jesuit, by the way. He used to sing in the choir. He was a choirboy in the Catholic churches of Denver. And he taught me everything that I now do believe about anything that there may be to be believed about divinity.

TB: About Edgar Cayce?

JK: No, before he found out about Edgar Cayce he told me all these things in the section of the life he led when he was on the road with me—he said, "We know God, don't we Jack?" I said, "Yessir boy." He said, "Don't we know that nothing's going to happen wrong?" "Yessir." "And we're going to go on and on . . . and hmmmmm ja-bmmmmmmm . . . ." He was perfect. And he's always perfect. Every time he comes to see me, I can't get a word in edgewise.

TB: You wrote about Neal playing football, in *Visions of Cody*.

JK: Yes, he was a very good football player. He picked up two beatniks that time in blue jeans in North Beach Frisco. He said, "I got to go, bang bang, do I got to go?" He's working on the railroad . . . had his watch out . . . "2:15, boy I got to be there by 2:20. I tell you boys, drive me over down there so I be on time with my train . . . so I can get my train on down to"—what's the name of that place—San Jose? They say, "sure, Kid," and Neal says, "Here's the pot." So—"We maybe look like great beatniks with great beards . . . but we are cops. And we are arresting you." So a guy went to the jailhouse and interviewed him from the *New York Post* and he said, "Tell that Kerouac if he still believes in me to send me a typewriter." So I sent Allen Ginsberg one hundred dollars to get a typewriter for Neal. And Neal got the typewriter. And he wrote notes on it, but they wouldn't let him take the notes out. I don't know where the typewriter is. Genet wrote all of *Our Lady of the Flowers* in the shithouse . . . the jailhouse. There's a great writer, Jean Genet. He kept writing and kept writing until he got to a point where he was going to come by writing about it . . . until he came into his bed—in the can. The French can. The French jail. Prison. And that was the end of the chapter. Every chapter is Genet coming off. Which I must admit Sartre noticed.

TB: You think that's a different kind of spontaneous writing?

JK: Well, I could go to jail and I could write every night a chapter about Magee, Magoo, and Molly. It's beautiful. Genet is really the most honest writer we've had since Kerouac and Burroughs. But he came before us. He's older. Well, he's the same age as Burroughs. But I don't think I've been dishonest. Man, I've had a good time! God, man, I rode around this country free as a bee. But Genet is a very tragic and beautiful writer. And I give them the crown. And the laurel wreath. I don't give the laurel wreath to Richard Wilbur! Or Robert Lowell. Give it to Jean Genet and William Seward Burroughs. And to Allen Ginsberg and to Gregory Corso especially.

TB: Jack, how about Peter Orlovsky's writings. Do you like Peter's things?

JK: Peter Orlovsky is an idiot!! He's a Russian idiot. Not even Russian, he's Polish.

TB: He's written some fine poems.

JK: Oh yeah. My . . . what poems?

TB: He has a beautiful poem called "Second Poem."

JK: "My brother pisses in the bed . . . and I go in the subway and I see two people kissing . . ."

TB: No, the poem that says "it's more creative to paint the floor than to sweep it."

JK: That's a lot of shit! That is the kind of poetry that was written by another Polish idiot who was a Polish nut called Apollinaire. Apollinaire is not his real name, you know. There are some fellows in San Francisco that told me that Peter was an idiot. But I like idiots, and I enjoy his poetry. Think about that, Berrigan. But for my taste, it's Gregory. Give me one of those.

TB: One of these pills?

JK: Yeah. What are they? Forked clarinets?

TB: They recalled Obetrol. Neal is the one that told me about them.

JK: Overtones?

TB: Overtones? No, overcoats.

AS: What was that you said . . . at the back of the Grove anthology . . . that you let the line go a little longer to fill it up with secret images that come at the end of the sentence.

JK: He's a real Armenian! Sediment. Delta. Mud. It's where you start a poem . . .

"As I was walking down the street one day I saw a lake where people were cutting off my rear, 17,000 priests singing like George Burns"

and then you go on . . .

"And I'm making jokes about me and breaking my bones in the earth and here I am the great John Armenian coming back to earth"

now you remember where you were in the beginning and you say . . .

"Ahaha! Tatatatadooda . . . Screw Turkey!"

See? You remembered the line at the end . . . you lose your mind in the middle.

AS: Right.

JK: That applies to prose as well as poetry.

TB: But in prose you are telling a story . . .

JK: In prose you make the paragraph. Every paragraph is a poem.

TB: Is that how you write a paragraph?

JK: When I was running downtown there, and I was going to do this, and I was laying there, with that girl there, and a guy took out his scissors, and I took him inside there, he showed me some dirty pictures. And I went out and fell downstairs with the potato bags.

TB: Did you ever like Gertrude Stein's work?

JK: Never interested me too much. I liked *Melanctha* a little bit. I should really go to school and teach these kids. I could make two thousand bucks a week. You can't learn these things. You know why? Because you have to be born with tragic fathers.

TB: You can only do that if you are born in New England.

JK: Incidentally, my father said your father wasn't tragic.

AS: I don't think my father is tragic.

JK: My father said that Saroyan . . . William Saroyan ain't tragic at all . . . he's fulla shit. And I had a big argument with him. *The Daring Young Man on the Flying Trapeze* is pretty tragic, I would say.

AS: He was just a young man then, you know.

JK: Yeah, but he was hungry, and he was on Times Square. Flying. A young man on the flying trapeze. That was a beautiful story. It killed me when I was a kid.

TB: Do you remember a story by William Saroyan about the Indian who came to town and bought a car and got the little kid to drive it for him?

SK: A Cadillac.

JK: What town was that?

AS: Fresno. That was Fresno.

JK: Well, you remember the night I was taking a big nap and you came up outside my window on a white horse . . .

AS: "The Summer of the Beautiful White Horse."

JK: And I looked out the window and said, "What is this?" You said, "My name is Aram. And I'm on a white horse."

AS: Moorad.

JK: My name is Moorad, excuse me. No, my name is . . . I was Aram, you were Moorad. You said, "Wake up!" I didn't want to wake up. I wanted to sleep. *My Name is Aram* is the name of the book. You stole a white horse from a farmer and you woke up me, Aram, to go riding with you.

AS: Moorad was the crazy one who stole the horse.

JK: Hey, what's that you gave me there?

TB: Obetrol.

JK: Oh, obies.

TB: What about jazz and bop as influences, rather than . . . Saroyan, Hemingway, and Wolfe?

JK: Yes, jazz and bop, in the sense of a, say, a tenor man drawing a breath and blowing a phrase on his saxophone, till he runs out of breath, and when he does, his sentence, his statement's been made . . . that's how I therefore separate my sentences, as breath separations of the mind . . . I formulated the theory of breath as measure, in prose and verse, never mind what Olson, Charles Olson says, I formulated that theory in 1953 at the request of Burroughs and Ginsberg. Then there's the raciness and freedom and humor of jazz instead of all that dreary analysis and things like "James entered the room, and lit a cigarette. He thought Jane might have thought this too vague a gesture." You know the stuff. As for Saroyan, yes I loved him as a teenager, he really got me out of the nineteenth-century rut I was trying to study, not only his funny tone but his neat Armenian poetic I don't know what . . . he just got me . . . Hemingway was fascinating, the pearls of words on a white page giving you an exact picture . . . but Wolfe was a torrent of American heaven and hell that opened my eyes to America as a subject in itself.

TB: How about the movies?

JK: Yes, we've all been influenced by movies. Malcolm Cowley, incidentally, mentioned this many times. He's very perceptive sometimes: he mentioned that *Doctor Sax* continually mentions urine, and quite naturally it does, because I had no other place to write it but on a closed toilet seat in a little tiled toilet in Mexico City so as to get away from the guests inside the apartment. There, incidentally, is a style truly hallucinated, as I wrote it all on pot. No pun intended. Ho ho.

TB: How has Zen influenced your work?

JK: What's really influenced my work is the Mahayana Buddhism, the original Buddhism of Gotama Sakyamuni, the Buddha himself, of the India of old . . . Zen is what's left of his Buddhism, or Bodhi, after its passing into China and then into Japan. The part of Zen that's influenced my writing is the Zen contained in the haiku, like I said, the three-line, seventeen-syllable poems written hundreds of years ago by guys like Basho, Issa, Shiki, and there've been recent masters. A sentence that's short and sweet with a sudden jump of thought in it is a kind of haiku, and there's a lot of freedom and fun in surprising yourself with that, let the mind willy-nilly jump from the branch to the bird. But my serious Buddhism, that of ancient India, has influenced that part in my writing that you might call religious, or fervent, or pious almost as much as Catholicism has. Original Buddhism referred to continual conscious compassion, brotherhood, the *dana paramita*, meaning the perfection of charity, don't step on the bug, all that, humility, mendicancy, the sweet, sorrowful face of the Buddha (who was of Aryan origin, by the way, I mean of Persian warrior caste, and not Oriental as pictured) . . . in original Buddhism no young kid coming to a monastery was warned that ment to meditate and be kind. The beginning of Zen was when Buddha, however, assembled all the monks together to announce a sermon and choose the first patriarch of the Mahayana Church: instead of speaking, he simply held up a flower. Everybody was flabbergasted except Kasyapa, who smiled. Kasyapa was appointed the first patriarch. This idea appealed to the Chinese, like the Sixth Patriarch, Hui-Neng, who said, "From the beginning nothing ever was" and wanted to tear up the records of Buddha's sayings as kept in the sutras; sutras are "threads of discourse." In a way, then, Zen is a gentle but goofy form of heresy, though there must be some real kindly old monks somewhere, and we've heard about the nutty ones. I haven't been to Japan. Your Maha Roshi Yoshi is simply a disciple of all this and not the founder of anything new at all, of course. On the Johnny Carson show he didn't even mention Buddha's name. Maybe his Buddha is Mia.

TB: How come you've never written about Jesus? You've written about Buddha. Wasn't Jesus a great guy too?

JK: I've never written about Jesus? In other words, you re an insane phony who comes to my house . . . and . . . all I write about is Jesus. I am Everhard Mercurian, general of the Jesuit Army.

AS: What's the difference between Jesus and Buddha?

JK: That's a very good question. There is no difference.

AS: No difference?

JK: But there is a difference between the original Buddha of India and the Buddha of Vietnam, who just shaves his hair and puts on a yellow robe and is a communist agitating agent. The original

Buddha wouldn't even walk on young grass so that he wouldn't destroy it. He was born in Gorakpur, the son of the consul of the invading Persian hordes. And he was called Sage of the Warriors, and he had seventeen thousand broads dancing for him all night, holding out flowers, saying "You want to smell it, my Lord?" He says "Git outta here, you whore." He laid a lot of them you know. But by the time he was thirty-one years old, he got sick and tired . . . his father was protecting him from what was going on outside the town. And so he went out on a horse against his father's orders and he saw a woman dying—a man being burnt on a ghat. And he said, "What is all this death and decay?" The servant said "That is the way things go on. Your father was hiding you from the way things go on." He says, "What? My father!!—Get my horse, saddle my horse! Ride me into the forest!" They ride into the forest; he says, "Now take the saddle off the horse. Put it on your horse, hang it on . . . take my horse by the rein and ride back to the castle and tell my father I'll never see him again!" And the servant, Kandaka, cried, he said, "I'll never see you again." "I don't care! Go on! Shoosh! get away!!" He spent seven years in the forest. Biting his teeth together. Nothing happened. Tormenting himself with starvation. He said, "I will keep my teeth bit together until I find the cause of death." Then one day he was stumbling across the Rapti River, and he fainted in the river. And a young girl came by with a bowl of milk and said, "My lord, a bowl of milk" [slurpppp]. He said, "That gives me great energy, thank you my dear." Then he went and sat under the Bo tree. Figuerosa. The fig tree. He said, "Now . . . [demonstrates posture] . . . I will cross my legs . . . and grit my teeth until I find the cause of death." Two o'clock in the morning, a hundred thousand phantoms assailed him. He didn't move. Three o'clock in the morning, the great blue ghosts!!

Arrghhh!!! All accosted him [you see I am really Scottish]. Four o'clock in the morning, the mad maniacs of hell . . . came out of manhole covers . . . in New York City. You know Wall Street, where the steam comes out? You know Wall Street, where the manhole covers . . . steam comes up? You take off them covers— yaaaaaahhh!!!!! Six o'clock, everything was peaceful—the birds started to trill, and he said, "Aha! . . . the cause of death . . . the cause of death is birth." Simple? So he started walking down the road to Benares in India . . . with long hair, like you, see. So, three guys. One says "Hey, here comes Buddha there, who, uh, starved with us in the forest. When he sits down here on that bucket, don't wash his feet." So Buddha sits down on the bucket . . . the guy rushes up and washes his feet. "Why dost thou wash his feet?" Buddha says, "Because I go to Benares to beat the drum of life." And what is that? "That the cause of death is birth." "What do you mean?" "I'll show you." A woman comes up with a dead baby in her arms, says, "Bring my child back to life if you are the Lord." He says, "Sure I'll do that anytime. Just go and find one family in Sravasti that ain't had a death in the last five years. Get a mustard seed from them and bring it to me. And I'll bring your child back to life." She went all over town, man, two million people, Sravasti the town was, a bigger town than Benares, by the way, and she came back and said, "I can't find no such family. They've all had deaths within five years." He said, "Then, bury your baby." Then, his jealous cousin, Devadatta (that's Ginsberg you see . . . I am Buddha and Ginsberg is Devadatta), gets this elephant drunk . . . great big bull elephant drunk on whiskey. The elephant goes up!!!! [trumpets like elephant going up]—with a big trunk, and Buddha comes up in the road and gets the elephant and goes like this [kneels]. And the elephant kneels down. "You are buried in sorrow's mud! Quiet your trunk! Stay there!" . . . He's an elephant trainer. Then Devadatta rolled a big boulder over a cliff. And it almost hit Buddha's head. Just missed. Boooom! He says, "That's Devadatta again." Then Buddha went like this [paces back and forth] in front of his boys, you see. Behind him was his cousin that loved him . . . Ananda . . . which means love in Sanskrit [keeps pacing]. This is what you do in jail to keep in shape. I know a lot of stories about Buddha, but I don't know exactly what he said every time. But I know what he said about the guy who spit at him. He said, "Since I can't use your abuse, you may have it back." He was great. [Kerouac plays piano. Drinks are served.]

AS: There's something there.

TB: My mother used to play that. I'm not sure how we can transcribe those notes onto a page. We may have to include a record of you playing the piano. Will you play that piece again for the record, Mr. Paderewski? Can you play "Alouette?"

JK: No. Only Afro-Germanic music. After all, I'm a square-head. I wonder what whiskey will do to those obies?

TB: What about ritual and superstition? Do you have any about yourself when you get down to work?

JK: I had a ritual once of lighting a candle and writing by its light and blowing it out when I was done for the night . . . also kneeling and praying before starting (I got that from a French movie about George Frideric Handel) . . . but now I simply hate to write. My superstition? I'm beginning to suspect that full moon. Also I'm hung up on the number nine, though I'm told a Piscean like myself should stick to number seven; but I try to do nine touchdowns a day, that is, I stand on my head in the bathroom, on a slipper, and touch the floor nine times with my toe tips, while balanced. This is incidentally more than Yoga, it's an athletic feat, I mean imagine calling me "unbalanced" after that. Frankly I do feel that my mind is going. So another "ritual," as you call it, is to pray to Jesus to preserve my sanity and my energy so I can help my family: that being my paralyzed mother, and my wife, and the ever-present kitties. Okay?

TB: You typed out *On the Road* in three weeks, *The Subterraneans* in three days and nights. Do you still produce at this fantastic rate? Can you say something of the genesis of a work before you sit down and begin that terrific typing—how much of it is set in your mind, for example?

JK: You think out what actually happened, you tell friends long stories about it, you mull it over in your mind, you connect it together at leisure, then when the time comes to pay the rent again, you force yourself to sit at the typewriter, or at the writing notebook, and get it over with as fast as you can . . . and there's no harm in that, because you've got the whole story lined up. Now how that's done depends on what kind of steel trap you've got up in that little old head. This sounds boastful, but a girl once told me I had a steel-trap brain, meaning I'd catch her with a statement she'd made an hour ago even though our talk had rambled a million light-years away from that point . . . you know what I mean, like a lawyer's mind, say. All of it is in my mind, naturally, except that language that is used at the time that it is used . . . . And as for *On the Road* and *The Subterraneans*, no, I can't write that fast any more . . . Writing the *Subs* in three nights was really a fantastic athletic feat as well as mental, you shoulda seen me after I was done . . . I was pale as a sheet and had lost fifteen pounds and looked strange in the mirror. What I do now is write something like an average of eight thousand words a sitting in the middle of the night, and another about a week later, resting and sighing in between. I really hate to write. I get no fun out of it because I can't get up and say "I'm working," close my door, have coffee brought to me, and sit there camping like a "man of letters doing his eight hour day of work" and thereby incidentally filling the printing world with a lot of dreary self-imposed cant and bombast . . . bombast is Scottish word for stuffing for a pillow. Haven't you heard a politician use fifteen hundred words to say something he could have said in exactly three words? So I get it out of the way so as not to bore myself either.

AS: Do you usually try to see everything clearly and not think of any words—just to see everything as clear as possible and then write out of the feeling. With *Tristessa*, for example.

JK: You sound like a writing seminar at Indiana University.

AS: I know but . . .

JK: All I did was suffer with that poor girl and then when she fell on her head and almost killed herself . . . remember when she fell on her head? . . . and she was all busted up and everything. She was the most gorgeous little Indian chick you ever saw. I say Indian, pure Indian. Esperanza Villanueva. Villanueva is a Spanish name from I don't know where—Castile. But she's Indian. So she's half Indian, half Spanish . . . beauty. Absolute beauty. She had bones, man, just bones, skin and bones. And I didn't write in the book how I finally nailed her. You know? I did. I finally nailed her. She said, "Shhhhhhhhhh! Don't let the landlord hear." She said, "Remember, I'm very weak and sick." I said, "I know, I've been writing a book about how you're weak and sick."

TB: How come you didn't put that part in the book?

JK: Because Claude's wife told me not to put it in. She said it would spoil the book. But it was not a conquest. She was out like a light. On M–M, that's morphine. And in fact I made a big run for her from way uptown to downtown to the slum district . . . and I said, here's your stuff. She said, "Shhhhhh!" She gave herself a shot . . . and I said, Ah . . . now's the time. And I got my little nogood piece. But . . . it was certainly justification of Mexico!

SK: Here kitty! He's gone out again.

JK: She was nice, you would have liked her. Her real name was Esperanza. You know what that means?

TB: No.

JK: In Spanish, *hope*. Tristessa means in Spanish, *sadness*, but her real name was Hope. And she's now married to the police chief of Mexico City.

SK: Not quite.

JK: Well, you're not Esperanza—I'll tell you that.

SK: No, I know that, dear.

JK: She was the skinniest . . . and shy . . . as a rail.

SK: She's married to one of the lieutenants, you told me, not to the chief.

JK: She's all right. One of these days I'm going to go see her again.

SK: Over my dead body.

TB: Were you really writing *Tristessa* while you were there in Mexico? You didn't write it later?

JK: First part written in Mexico, second part written in . . . Mexico. That's right—'55 first part, '56 second part. What's the importance about that? I'm not Charles Olson, the great artist!

TB: We're just getting the facts.

JK: Charles Olson gives you all the dates. You know. Everything about how he found the hound dog on the beach in Gloucester. Found somebody jacking off on the beach at . . . what do they call it? Vancouver Beach? Dig Dog River? . . . Dogtown. That's what they call it, "Dogtown." Well this is Shit Town on the Merrimack. Lowell is called Shit Town on the Merrimack. I'm not going to write a poem called Shit Town and insult my town. But if I was six-foot-six, I could write anything, couldn't I?

TB: How do you get along now with other writers? Do you correspond with them?

JK: I correspond with John Clellon Holmes but less and less each year, I'm getting lazy. I can't answer my fan mail because I haven't got a secretary to take dictation, do the typing, get the stamps, envelopes, all that . . . and I have nothing to answer. I ain't gonna spend the rest of my life smiling and shaking hands and sending and receiving platitudes, like a candidate for political office, because I'm a writer—I've got to let my mind alone, like Greta Garbo. Yet when I go out or receive sudden guests, we all have more fun than a barrel of monkeys.

TB: What are the work-destroyers?

JK: Work-destroyers . . . work-destroyers. Time-killers? I'd say mainly the attentions which are tendered to a writer of "notoriety" (notice I don't say "fame") by secretly ambitious would-be writers who come around, or write, or call, for the sake of the services which are properly the services of a bloody literary agent. When I was an unknown struggling young writer, as saying goes, I did my own footwork, I hotfooted up and down Madison Avenue for years, publisher to publisher, agent to agent, and never once in my life wrote a letter to a published famous author asking for advice or help or, in Heaven above, have the nerve to actually mail my manuscripts to some poor author who then has to hustle to mail it back before he's accused of stealing my ideas. My advice to young writers is to get themselves an agent on their

own, maybe through their college professors (as I got my first
publishers through my prof, Mark Van Doren) and do their own
footwork, or "thing" as the slang goes . . . So the work-destroyers
are nothing but certain people. The work-preservers are the soli-
tudes of night, "when the whole wide world is fast asleep."

TB: What do you find the best time and place for writing?

JK: The desk in the room, near the bed, with a good light, midnight till
dawn, a drink when you get tired, preferably at home, but if you
have no home, make a home out of your hotel room or motel room
or pad: peace [picks up harmonica and plays]. Boy, can I play!

TB: What about writing under the influence of drugs?

JK: Poem 230 from *Mexico City Blues* is a poem written purely on
morphine. Every line in this poem was written within an hour of
one another . . . high on a big dose of M [finds volume and
reads]:

Love's multitudinous boneyard of decay,
An hour later: The spilled milk of heroes,
An hour later: Destruction of silk kerchiefs by dust storm,
An hour later: Caress of heroes blindfolded to posts,
An hour later: Murder victims admitted to this life,
An hour later: Skeletons bartering fingers and joints,
An hour later: The quivering meat of the elephants of kind-
ness being torn apart by vultures

[see where Ginsberg stole that from me?]

An hour later: Conceptions of delicate kneecaps.

Say that, Saroyan.

AS: Conceptions of delicate kneecaps.

JK: Very good.

Fear of rats dripping with bacteria.
An hour later: Golgotha Cold Hope for Gold Hope.

Say that.

AS: Golgotha Cold Hope for Cold Hope.

JK: That's pretty cold.

An hour later: Damp leaves of Autumn against the wood of
boats,
An hour later: Sea horse's delicate imagery of glue . . .

Ever see a little sea horse in the ocean? They're built of glue
. . . did you ever sniff a sea horse? No, say that.

AS: Sea horse's delicate imagery of glue.

JK: You'll do, Saroyan.

Death by long exposure to defilement.

AS: Death by long exposure to defilement.

JK: *Frightening ravishing mysterious beings concealing their sex.*

AS: Frightening ravishing mysterious beings concealing their sex.

JK: *Pieces of the Buddha—material frozen and sliced microscopically*
In Morgues of the North

AS: Hey, I can't say that. Pieces of the Buddha-material frozen and
sliced microscopically in Morgues of the North.

JK: *Penis apples going to seed.*

AS: Penis apples going to seed.

JK: *The severed gullets more numerous than sands.*

AS: The severed gullets more numerous than sands.

JK: *Like kissing my kitten in the belly.*

AS: Like kissing my kitten in the belly.

JK: *The softness of our reward.*

AS: The softness of our reward.

JK: Is he really William Saroyan's son? That's wonderful! Would you mind repeating that?

TB: We should be asking you a lot of very straight serious questions. When did you meet Allen Ginsberg?

JK: First I met Claude.* And then I met Allen and then I met Burroughs. Claude came in through the fire escape . . . there were gunshots down in the alley—Pow! Pow! and it was raining, and my wife says, "Here comes Claude." And here comes this blond guy through the fire escape, all wet. I said, "What's this all about, what the hell is this?" He says, "They're chasing me." Next day, in walks Allen Ginsberg carrying books. Sixteen years old with his ears sticking out. He says, "Well, discretion is the better part of valor!" I said, "Aw shutup. You little twitch." Then the next day, here comes Burroughs wearing a seersucker suit, followed by the other guy.

TB: What other guy?

JK: It was the guy who wound up in the river. This was this guy from New Orleans that Claude killed and threw in the river. Stabbed him twelve times in the heart with a Boy Scout knife. When Claude was fourteen, he was the most beautiful blond boy in New Orleans. And he joined the Boy Scout troop . . . and the Boy

---

* "Claude," a pseudonym, is also used in *Vanity of Duluoz.*

Scout Master was a big redheaded fairy who went to school at St. Louis University, I think it was. And he had already been in love with a guy who looked just like Claude in Paris. And this guy chased Claude all over the country; this guy had him thrown out of Baldwin, Tulane, and Andover Prep . . . . It's a queer tale, but Claude isn't a queer.

TB: What about the influence of Ginsberg and Burroughs? Did you ever have any sense then of the mark the three of you would have on American writing?

JK: I was determined to be a "great writer," in quotes, like Thomas Wolfe, see . . . Allen was always reading and writing poetry . . . Burroughs read a lot and walked around looking at things . . . . The influence we exerted on one another has been written about over and over again . . . We were just three interested characters in the interesting big city of New York, around campuses, libraries, cafeterias. A lot of the details you'll find in *Vanity* . . . in *On the Road*, where Burroughs is Bull Lee and Ginsberg is Carlo Marx . . . in *Subterraneans*, where they're Frank Carmody and Adam Moorad, respectively . . . elsewhere. In other words, though I don't want to be rude to you for this honor, I am so busy interviewing myself in my novels, and have been so busy writing down these self-interviews, that I don't see why I should draw breath in pain every year of the last ten years to repeat and repeat to everybody who interviews me what I've already explained in the books themselves . . . hundreds of journalists, thousands of students. It beggars sense. And it's not that important. It's our work that counts, if anything at all, and I'm not proud of mine or theirs or anybody's since Thoreau and others like that, maybe because it's still too close to home for comfort. Notoriety and public confession in literary form is a frazzler of the heart you were born with, believe me.

TB: Allen said once that he learned how to read Shakespeare, that he never did understand Shakespeare until he heard you read Shakespeare to him.

JK: Because in a previous lifetime that's who I was.

> *How like a Winter hath my absence been from thee?*
> *The pleasure of the fleeting year . . . what freezings*
> *have I felt? What dark days seen? Yet Summer with his*
> *lord surcease hath laid a big turd in my orchard*
> *And one hog after another comes to eat*
> *and break my broken mountain trap, and my mousetrap*
> *too! And here to end the sonnet, you must make sure*
> *to say, tara-tara-tara!!!!!!*

TB: Is that spontaneous composition?

JK: Well, the first part was Shakespeare . . . and the second part was . . .

TB: Have you ever written any sonnets?

JK: I'll give you a spontaneous sonnet. It has to be what, now?

TB: Fourteen lines.

JK: That's twelve lines with two dragging lines. That's where you bring up your heavy artillery.

> *Here the fish of Scotland seen your eye*
> *and all my nets did creak . . .*

> Does it have to rhyme?

TB: No.

JK: *My poor chapped hands fall awry*
　　and seen the Pope, his devilled eye.

And maniacs with wild hair hanging about my room
and listening to my tomb
which does not rhyme.

Seven lines?

TB: That was eight lines.
JK: *And all the orgones of the earth will crawl*
like dogs across the graves of Peru
and Scotland too.

That's ten.

Yet do not worry, sweet angel of mine
That hast thine inheritance
imbedded in mine.

TB: That's pretty good, Jack. How did you do that?
JK: Without studying dactyls . . . like Ginsberg . . . I met Ginsberg
. . . I'd hitchhiked all the way back from Mexico City to Berkeley,
and that's a long way baby, a long way. Mexico City across
Durango . . . Chihuahua . . . Texas. I go back to Ginsberg, I go to
his cottage, I say, "Hah, we're gonna play the music" . . . he says,
"You know what I'm going to do tomorrow? I'm going to throw
on Mark Schorer's desk a new theory of prosody! About the
dactylic arrangements of Ovid!" [laughter] I said, "Quit, man. Sit
under a tree and forget it and drink wine with me . . . and Phil
Whalen and Gary Snyder and all the bums of San Francisco.
Don't you try to be a big Berkeley teacher. Just be a poet under
the trees . . . and we'll wrestle and we'll break holds." And he did
take my advice. He remembered that. He said, "What are you

going to teach . . . you have parched lips!" I said, "Naturally, I just came from Chihuahua. It's very hot down there, phew! you go out and little pigs rub against your legs. Phew!" So here comes Snyder with a bottle of wine . . . and here comes Whalen, and here comes what's his name . . . Rexroth . . . and everybody . . . and we had the poetry renaissance of San Francisco.

TB: What about Allen getting kicked out of Columbia? Didn't you have something to do with that?

JK: Oh, no . . . he let me sleep in his room. He was not kicked out of Columbia for that. The first time he let me sleep in his room, and the guy that slept in our room with us was Lancaster who was descended from the White Roses or Red Roses of England. But a guy came in . . . the guy that ran the floor . . . and he thought that I was trying to make Allen, and Allen had already written in the paper that I wasn't sleeping there because I was trying to make him, but he was trying to make me. But we were just actually sleeping. Then after that he got a pad . . . he got some stolen goods in there . . . and he got some thieves up there, Vicky and Huncke. And they were all busted for stolen goods, and a car turned over, and Allen's glasses broke, it's all in John Holmes's *Go*. Allen Ginsberg asked me when he was nineteen years old, "Should I change my name to Allen Renard?" "You change your name to Allen Renard I'll kick you right in the balls! Stick to Ginsberg" . . . and he did. That's one thing I like about Allen. Allen Renard!!!

TB: What was it that brought all of you together in the '50s? What was it that seemed to unify the Beat Generation?

JK: Oh the Beat Generation was just a phrase I used in the 1951 written manuscript of *On the Road* to describe guys like Moriarty who run around the country in cars looking for odd jobs, girlfriends, kicks. It was thereafter picked up by West Coast leftist groups and turned into a meaning like "Beat mutiny" and "Beat insurrection" and all that nonsense; they just wanted some youth movement to grab onto for their own political and social purposes. I had nothing to do with any of that. I was a football player, a scholarship college student, a merchant seaman, a railroad brakeman on road freights, a script synopsizer, a secretary . . . And Moriarty-Cassady was an actual cowboy on Dave Uhl's ranch in New Raymer, Colorado . . . What kind of beatnik is that?

TB: Was there any sense of "community" among the Beat crowd?

JK: That community feeling was largely inspired by the same characters I mentioned, like Ferlinghetti, Ginsberg; they are very socialistically minded and want everybody to live in some kind of frenetic kibbutz, solidarity and all that. I was a loner. Snyder is not like Whalen, Whalen is not like McClure, I am not like McClure, McClure is not like Ferlinghetti, Ginsberg is not like Ferlinghetti, but we all had fun over wine anyway. We knew thousands of poets and painters and jazz musicians. There's no "Beat crowd" like you say . . . what about Scott Fitzgerald and his "lost crowd," does that sound right? Or Goethe and his "Wilhelm Meister crowd?" The subject is such a bore. Pass me that glass.

TB: Well, why did they split in the early sixties?

JK: Ginsberg got interested in left-wing politics . . . like Joyce I say, as Joyce said to Ezra Pound in the 1920s, "Don't bother me with politics, the only thing that interests me is style." Besides, I'm bored with the new avant-garde and the skyrocketing sensationalism. I'm reading Blaise Pascal and taking notes on religion. I like to hang around now with nonintellectuals, as you might call them, and not have my mind proselytized, ad infinitum. They've even started crucifying chickens in happenings, what's the next step? An actual crucifixion of a man . . . The Beat group dispersed, as you say, in the early sixties, all went their own way, and this is my way: home life, as in the beginning, with a little toot once in a while in local bars.

TB: What do you think of what they're up to now? Allen's radical political involvement? Burroughs' cutup methods?

JK: I'm pro-American, and the radical political involvements seem to tend elsewhere . . . The country gave my Canadian family a good break, more or less, and we see no reason to demean said country. As for Burroughs' cutup method, I wish he'd get back to those awfully funny stories of his he used to write and those marvelously dry vignettes in *Naked Lunch*. Cutup is nothing new, in fact that steel-trap brain of mine does a lot of cutting up as it goes along . . . as does everyone's brain while talking or thinking or writing . . . It's just an old Dada trick, and a kind of literary collage. He comes out with some great effects though. I like him to be elegant and logical and that's why I don't like the cutup, which is supposed to teach us that the mind is cracked. Sure the mind's cracked, as anybody can see in a hallucinated high, but how about an explanation of the crackedness that can be understood in a workaday moment?

TB: What do you think about the hippies and the LSD scene?

JK: They're already changing, I shouldn't be able to make a judgment. And they're not all of the same mind. The Diggers are different . . . I don't know one hippie anyhow . . . I think they think I'm a truck driver. And I am. As for LSD, it's bad for people with incidence of heart disease in the family [knocks microphone off foot stool . . . recovers it]. Is there any reason why you can see anything good in this here mortality?

TB: Excuse me, would you mind repeating that?

JK: You said you had a little white beard in your belly. Why is there a little white beard in your mortality belly?

TB: Let me think about it. Actually it's a little white pill.

JK: A little white pill?

TB: It's good.

JK: Give me.

TB: We should wait till the scene cools a little.

JK: Right. This little white pill is a little white beard in your mortality which advises you and advertises to you that you will be growing long fingernails in the graves of Peru.

AS: Do you feel middle-aged?

JK: No. Listen, we're coming to the end of the tape. I want to add something on. Ask me what Kerouac means.

TB: Jack, tell me again what Kerouac means.

JK: Now, *Kairn*. K (or C) A-I-R-N. What is a kairn? It's a heap of stones. Now Cornwall, kairn-wall. Now, right, *kern*, also K-E-R-N, means the same thing as *kairn, kern, kairn. Ouac* means "language of," so Kernuac means "the language of Cornwall." *Kerr*—which is like Deborah Kerr—*ouack* means "language of the water," because *kerr, carr*, et cetera, means "water." And *kairn* means "heap of stones." There is no language in a heap of stones. Kerouac. *Ker*, "water," *ouac*, "language of." And it's related to the old Irish name, Kerwick, which is a corruption. And it's a Cornish name, which in itself means Kairnish. And according to Sherlock Holmes, it's all Persian. Of course you know he's not Persian. Don't you remember in Sherlock Holmes when he went down with Dr. Watson and solved the case down in old Cornwall and he solved the case and then he said, "Watson, the needle! Watson, the needle . . ." He said, "I've solved this case here in Cornwall. Now I have the liberty to sit around here and decide and read books, which will prove to me . . . why the Cornish people, otherwise known as the Kernuaks, or Kerouacs, are of Persian origin. The enterprise which I am about to embark upon," he then said, after he got his shot, "is fraught with eminent peril, and not fit for a lady of your tender years." Remember that?

DM: I remember that.

JK: McNaughton remembers that. McNaughton. You think I would forget the name of a Scotsman?

Interview with Ted Berrigan

From *Talking in Tranquility: Interviews with Ted Berrigan* (Avenue B, 1991)

INTERVIEWER: What are your memories of the Kerouac interview in the *Paris Review*?

TB: That was a complicated situation in that Tom Clark was poetry editor of the *Paris Review* at that time. And he conceived the notion that it would be nice for the *Paris Review* to interview Kerouac, and maybe I would like to do it since I really liked Jack's work. And so George Plimpton asked me if I wanted to do it, and I said, "Yeah, I would."

I didn't really know Jack. I did know Allen Ginsberg and a couple other of Jack's friends. I knew his work very thoroughly. So after I agreed that I would do it, I kind of put off getting in touch with Jack. I didn't have a phone. He was kind of in seclusion at Lowell. But accidentally, I happened to get in contact with him. I was staying at the house of a friend of his, and Jack called, and the friend wasn't home, and I was. Meanwhile, Allen Ginsberg had mentioned to Jack that I wanted to do it. So when Jack called me, he knew what I wanted to do, so when he talked to me he said, "Yeah, I could do it." But we didn't really set a date, and I still couldn't reach him on the phone, of course. I'm not very good at business-like transactions. So I decided that at some point I'd just go up there and hope that I could get it done, and at some point I *did* have to go to Massachusetts. I went with Ron Padgett and Tom Clark to visit Aram Saroyan. We published this little book about it, in fact, called *Back in Boston Again*. After we went to visit Aram, Ron and Tom went back to New York, and I convinced Aram to come on up to Lowell with me to try and see if I could interview Jack. And it was a nice thing to have Aram there, because I knew that Jack liked his father's work. I thought that maybe that would make the situation warmer.

So we went to Lowell, and we went there early in the evening, and we found the house and rang the doorbell, and Jack came to the door, and I told him who I was. And he said, "C'mon in." At that point, his wife seized him from behind and attempted to remove him from the doorway, and told us to go away, thinking we were these terrible beatniks who wanted to get him drunk and tell him to go on the road again. I started saying things like, and simultaneously Jack started saying things like, "*Paris Review* interview. Very serious literary business." Finally, Stella, who was a very nice lady, decided it was all right if she let us in, and it was on the condition that there would be no drinking, which turned out to be a condition that was only for us. She couldn't really make Jack do anything he didn't . . . within certain limits Jack would do anything he wanted. So he had a few drinks.

Jack turned out to be a terrific person to interview. You didn't have to say too much to him; you could just feed him a little bit, and he would perform; he performed wonderfully. And we said very little, actually. Often when we say anything, either Aram or

I, Jack kind of gives us a little bit of the business, as if that's really not a very interesting idea to talk about. And he did a really terrific job. And also he realized, though, from the little we did say, that we really *were* admirers, that we really *did* know his work, that we were serious artists ourselves.

Once that interview ended, I took it back to New York and I transcribed it. It's a difficult job transcribing a tape, as you'll find out. I finally got it finished, leaving just about everything in, and it was just a beautiful piece of work. I thought it was like a play by Chekhov, a one-act play, in which there were these characters, and one of them did most of the talking, but that's what happened—there was a real environment. And inside that environment, you could find out almost everything about Jack Kerouac, what he was like, because he totally exposed himself, and made himself vulnerable. There was enough, I thought, historical reference, literary conversation, and so on. And I presented it to the *Paris Review*, and I shortly discovered that that wasn't what they wanted. I mean, they had a tradition of how they did their interviews. They wanted certain things asked and answered. They wanted to know whether or not he wrote on a typewriter, and they wanted to know other historical things. They wanted the whole story of his life: When did he first meet Allen Ginsberg? When he was at Columbia, and things like that. All stuff that's in his books, and all stuff that is touched on a little bit in the interview. That kind of thing didn't have to be gone into in detail.

And so George Plimpton asked me if I would mind if they would send Jack some questions to answer, and he would insert them in the interview. On the one hand, I didn't mind. It was *their* interview. They asked me to do it, and I felt like I was working as their employee, and I thought they could do anything they wanted to. It wasn't as if I had conceived this work all by myself. But on the other hand, I really thought it was a beautiful work by itself. It had gotten made accidentally, in a way that rarely happens. So I had a big talk with George, and I tried to convince him that Aram Saroyan, and myself, and Ron Padgett, and Tom Clark and so on, that we were the next generation, and that he should play it *our* way just for that reason. There's a gorgeous interview, back in an early issue of the *Paris Review*, with Harry Green, who is a novelist, by Terry Southern, who himself was a very young novelist at the time. It's very much like the interview that Jack and I did. It's an incredible happening. And he had run it, George had run it. George thought that what I said was amusing, but he said no. So I said, "Well, you can send the questions to Jack. If he's willing to do it, I'm willing to do it." So they made up some questions and sent them and Jack answered them. And they inserted them here and there, four or five places. You can find them quite easily if you want to. They inserted them quite professionally.

Unfortunately, the other thing they did was, they took out a few things that were in there already. They thought they were a little . . . squalid, I think. Jack was telling his personal history, and he described to some small extent what it was like on the literary-poetry scene when he was a young man trying to be a writer. And he got into this whole business of what it was like with everybody else being queer. And he was very specific about it, and he gave a lot of very personal character revelations. I mean like what he would do, and how far he would go because he didn't mind. But then there were some things he did mind. And George took all that out. He didn't seem very colorful-minded; he just dropped all that out. Which was a shame, because it was all hilarious, truly hilarious.

George did this very funny thing. He inserted here and there in parenthesis a little . . . he asked me if he could do this . . . and when he asked me, I was so *stupefied* by what he was saying that I didn't say anything, and so he just did it. He inserted these parenthetical interludes here and there that said things like, "Drinks are served." Well, none of that happened at all. There were no drinks served. I mean until the very end when the interview was over, and we shut off the tape, then Stella, having been listening in all the time, and satisfied with what was going on, asked us if we would like a beer. Jack was drinking whiskey all the time. I slipped Jack a little speed, because he asked me if I had any "tea," which to my ear at the time was an outdated expression. I wasn't quite sure what he was saying, but I thought he meant did I have *any*thing. And I did have something. And it was something conducive to talk. That's why I had the pills. All that's in the interview in a very funny way. And so he said, "Well, give me some. And then I started to give him a couple, and then Stella came in. And then there's this mysterious section where he says, "Better cool it now." And I said, "Ahhh, yeah, right." And then she went back out, and I gave him and he took the pills. But he would have been the same without them anyway.

You know, one thing I remember that was really startling: I interviewed Jack maybe three or four years before he died, no more than three, I believe; he wasn't really in very good shape in certain ways. He was no longer that terrific-looking guy you see on the back of his books. But he was a middle-aged guy, and he had always lived a hard life and drank a lot. And he looked like he had tired. He was plenty robust, and had a lot of energy, and there was certainly a great wildness to him, a streak of wildness to him, mixed with a very gentle and sweet streak.

Jack asked me, after the interview was over, if there was anything else I needed to know, and I said, "I'd like to see the room where you work." And so he said, "Stella will show you." She took me up to his study. Well, this study was impeccable. There were his file cabinets, bookshelves, his desk, with everything in incredible order. And I said, "This is really remarkable. Did you do this for Jack?" And she said, "No, he wouldn't let me touch a thing of his. That's the way he does it." You see, a large part of his mind was *phenomenally* organized onto what he was and what did. He was a professional artist, and that was beautifully clear. That's why the interview was so good, I thought. He was a professional artist, he knew what he was doing. And a lot of things that we didn't know how to do, he did for us.

Firing Line with
William F. Buckley

William F. Buckley, *Firing Line* (September 3, 1968)

Panel participants:

Kerouac, Jack–American novelist and poet (JK)

Yablonsky, Lewis–Chairman of the Sociology Department at San Fernando State College in California, author of *The Hippie Trip* (LY)

Sanders, Ed–poet; musician with the group the Fugs (ES)

WB: [introducing guests] The topic tonight is the hippies, an understanding of whom we must, I guess, acquire or die painfully. We certainly should make considerable progress in the next hour, because we have with us a professional student of hippies, and also someone who has said to have started the whole Beat Generation business and, finally, a hippie type who can correct us, ever so gently, please, if we are wrong. Mr. Lewis Yablonsky is the sociologist, who studied at Rutgers and took his doctorate at New York University and teaches at San Fernando State College in California, where he is chairman of his department. His first book, which focused on teenage gang life and drug addiction, prepared him for his magnum opus, which is called *The Hippie Trip*, a firsthand account of the beliefs and behavior of hippies in America. Mr. Jack Kerouac over here became famous when his book *On the Road* was published. It seemed to be preaching a life of disengagement, making a virtue out of restlessness. The irony is that when the book was belatedly published in 1958, seven years after it was written, Mr. Kerouac had fought his way out of the Beat Generation and is now thought of as orthodox, or at least a regular, practicing novelist who's thirteenth book, *Vanity of Duluoz*, is widely regarded as his best. Mr. Ed Sanders is a musician, poet, and a polemicist. He is one of The Fugs, a widely patronized combo. He has published four books of poetry and has vigorously preached pacifism for a number of years. I should like to begin by asking Mr. Sanders whether we have serious terminological problems. For instance, are you a hippie, Mr. Sanders, and if not, wherein not?

ES: Well, I'm not exactly a hippie, I mean, I have certain sentiments for that "hippie movement." I would say that I'm different from the hippies in that I would have a more radical political solution to the problems of this part of the century. And I have my roots more strongly in, say, the classical tradition and in poetry and literature rather than in dope and street sex.

WB: This, you think?

JK: And you wrote, you publish that magazine called what?

ES: *Gutter Expletive–A Magazine of the Arts*.[48] [audience laughter]

WB: Well, now, do I understand from this that we are supposed to make the inference that the hippies don't have a highly developed political schedule, a highly developed political ideology?

ES: The problem with terms like "hippie" is that they have a definition forced on them by the media, and that the word "hippie" has been limited by the necessities of the type of journalism that promote it. And you know, you can't rely on the name "hippie" to include a human being, you know, everything about a particular human being. You know? So it's a bad term, I think, because it has no meaning. I mean, you might think of "hippopotamus," I mean, it's like it has no other connections, spiritual or emotional, like say the Beat Generation title had, you know, it had other implications. By the word "hippie," you immediately think you don't have any good connections.

LY: I kind of disagree with that. I spent last year traveling around the country, various communes, and various Haight-Ashbury, Lower East Side, various city scenes, and there was an identifiable . . . uh . . . define a "hippie" rather as a generally young person in several categories as kind of a priestly type, that includes Allen Ginsberg and Tim Leary, and individuals like that in that category. People trying, searching for some loving solutions to society's ills, trying to tune in to the cosmos, whatever that means, and we can explore that. Generally, using psychedelic drugs, and then there's a whole cadre of individuals who . . .

JK: "Cadre."

LY: . . . Uh, whom I've termed novices, who are attempting to achieve a certain transcendental state, and a lot of teenybopper kids who are sort of hanging on, and then there are some ancient folks like Kerouac here. Why couldn't you keep quiet while I was talking? I'll keep quiet when you talk.

WB: Yeah, that's fair, isn't it? I think that's fair enough.

JK: [correcting Yablonsky's pronunciation] You said *cadrees*—it's *cadré*.

LY: Oh, I'm sorry, I apologize, my semantics are . . .

JK: And I show my thumbs-down to Ginsberg over there in the back. He's a nice fellow, yeah. We'll throw him to the lions.

WB: Well, that's it, Mr. Kerouac, you're exercised *about* something here, or *by* something.

JK: Restless is true, you had the right word, "restless," that's right.

WB: Well, what is it that in your judgment distinguishes the hippie movement from, for instance, simply a routine . . .

JK: Get your question over with.

WB: . . . political movement.

JK: I interrupted your sentence. Sent . . . en . . . sentence. ULP. ULP.

WB: Yeaaah . . . I say what distinguishes the hippie movement from simply an orthodox radical . . . say . . .

JK: Nothing.

WB: . . . an Adamite movement.

JK: Adamite? You mean *Adam* and Eve or *atom*?

WB: Aadduummm [laughter], as in Adam and Eve.

JK: Why not say Adam and Eve? What's Adamite? Where they all wear their hair long, lairs, and caves?

WB: Yeah, and sort of back to nature, and . . .

JK: Well, that's all right.

WB: . . . and exclusive concern for their own pleasure.

JK: They might have to, in due time, due to the ATOM—ite bomb, HA-HA!

WB: Hey, that was good, wasn't it?

JK: I'm good all the time, boy.

WB: Give that man a drink. Now Jack, Mr. Kerouac, what I want to ask is this: to what extent do you believe that the Beat Generation is related to the hippies? What do they have in common? Was this an evolution from one to the other?

JK: This is the older ones, you see . . . I'm forty-six years old, these kids are eighteen, but it's the same movement, which is apparently some kind of Dionysian movement in late civilization, and which I did not intend anymore than, I suppose, Dionysius did, or whatever his name was. Although I'm not Dionysius to your Euripides. I should have been.

WB: Yeah, that's a point, yeah.

JK: No, it's just a movement which is supposed to be licentious. But, it isn't really.

WB: Well, now, licentious—in what respect?

JK: The hippies are good kids, they're better than the Beats. The Beats, you see, Ginsberg and I, well . . . Ginsberg [is] boring. We're forty, we're all in our forties, and we started this and the kids took it up, and everything, but a lot of hoods, hoodlums, and communists, jumped on our backs, well my back, not his [gestures toward Allen Ginsberg sitting in audience]. Ferlinghetti jumped on my back and turned the idea that I had that the Beat Generation was a generation of Beatitude and pleasure in life and tenderness, but they called it in the papers the "Beat Mutiny," the "Beat Insurrection," words I never used, being a Catholic. I believe in order, tenderness, and piety.

WB: Well, then your point was that a movement which you conceived as relatively pure has become ideologized, misanthropic, and generally objectionable.

JK: A movement that was . . . a movement that was considered what?

WB: Pure.

JK: Yes, it *was* pure, in my heart.

WB: What about that Mr. Yablonsky? Do you see that as happened somewhere between the Beats and the hippies?

LY: Well, I think there in early '67, going back to around, oh I suppose '64 or '65, there were a lot of people trying to return to sort of an Indian style of life, or relate to the land differently, trying to love each other and communicate, to be more open with each other, and I think recently it's taken a turn in a violent direction, a lot of responsibility, I think, is due to drugs like methedrine, the amphetamines, and perhaps the overuse, because it's been around for quite a while now, of drugs like LSD.

JK: How about Heering [pronouncing it as *"herring"*]?

WB: What is Heering? Is that a kind of drug?

ES: It's Cherry Heering [laughter].

LY: Kerouac is out of style. He' s still on alcohol, which is . . . uh, there are a number of drugs now.

WB: How about Mr. Sanders, is that out of style?

ES: Well you mentioned misanthropic, uh, an objectionable . . .

JK: Misanthropic.

ES: I think that any of the so-called misanthropic elements of this generation are due to the war, in that you have a surly generation of draft-eligible but literate and articulate people who are confronted with the hideous probability of having to go to an Asian land war, and that and that, so that they have to go to war and they're faced with this looming, gloomy future, and rather than die in Vietnam, they'd rather prepare themselves to articulate a lifestyle in the streets and in the open that really reflects something they really want to do, rather than this other thing they'll have to do later on that they don't really believe in and that they will do because push comes to shove, most kids go to war, you know?

WB: Of course, the trouble with that is it doesn't account, for instance, for the restlessness in, say, Paris, where they don't have that particular problem, do they?

ES: Well, that's the "up against the wall" sort of thing.

JK: Who's Daniel Cohn?*

BREAK

WB: Mr. Sanders, I'm interested in trying to pin this point down because a lot of us have heard that the restlessness of so much of American youth which has contributed to the growth of the hippie movement has to do with the trauma of Vietnam, but then, all of a sudden, a while ago in France the entire or what seemed like the entire student population exploded, even though that particular provocation was singularly, in fact conspicuously absent, France having been officially very pro-Vietnam, very anti-America, now, how do you account for that, and has it caused you to perhaps look in for more generic sources . . .

ES: I think it's the nefarious occurrences in French civilization of Madame DeGaulle.

WB: Madame DeGaulle?

ES: Because she has exercised obnoxious influence on French television sitting up and personally censoring it, and, I think [laughter], no, I think, it's absolutely true, and I think that when you have a type of obnoxious matriarchy as [laughter] that's evident in France plus an encrusted, boring, boorish university structure, uh, this and, you know, and the old man himself, and who wouldn't? I mean, it's a whole thing, God, there's a huge structure there to revolt against.

---

* Kerouac's reference is to Daniel Cohn-Bendit. Bendit, as a young boy, spent his childhood in Paris, France after his Jewish parents fled Berlin, Germany in 1933 after the National Socialists assumed power by force. In 1958, Bendit returned to Germany. He later co-founded the "Revolutionary Struggle," which was a student group attempting to work alongside laborers.

WB: So, Madame DeGaulle is roughly equal to Vietnam?

Professor Yablonsky, what would you say if a student of yours told you that?

LY: Well, I think in the United States, uh, the hippie, with all the tantamount difficulties of defining them, come from the middle, upper classes, upper socioeconomic situation, and these are generally people who have tasted the best that American society seems to have to offer, they have access to all the goodies, and they're turned off by it. They feel that it's kind of a plastic society, there's no room for political change. I'm talking about the pure hippie. The pure hippie isn't particularly involved in politics. He sort of retreats from that, he's withdrawn from it, and he's involved in, I mentioned the term "cosmic consciousness" before, there is an experience one seems to get under LSD that, uh, a lot of people talk about as putting them in touch with all things, with all people, and there's an effort, a kind of an extremist effort, at love that seems to dominate the hippie scene, and, uh, a retreat from, uh, politics.

WB: Well, is there a causal relation between their going, their adopting these attitudes, and the Vietnam War? Or do you reject the Vietnam War as the proximate of this movement?

LY: I think the Vietnam War is part of it.

WB: But if there had been no Vietnam War, we might have had these identical things? Is that your point?

LY: Well, I think part, a lot of, there's no single cause for a particular movement. I think part of it may have been the assassination of JFK. I think people on the left felt that through the Establishment, through political devices, the society could move in other directions . . .

WB: In what direction was it moving in 1963 that was pleasing to them?

LY: Uh, there was a movement toward greater welfare programs, toward resolving in some way the civil rights, there seemed to be some hope, and then that seemed to be snapped off, and a lot of kids who went to Mississippi . . .

WB: If I may say so, precisely the movements that didn't get passed in 1961, '62, and '63, and '66, so there would seem to be almost a negative correlation between the civil rights legislation and welfare passages and the growth of the movement.

LY: Well, I can only cross-compare the limited JFK administration and the rather lengthy LBJ administration. I think the LBJ situation is kind of been going through the motions of doing something, and there was a certain, I feel, and a lot of people have told me, the spirit afoot in the country, and there seemed to be a bit of a revival with Bobby Kennedy, and there again, and to some extent, the McCarthy involvement, and I think a lot of people are turned off from the political establishment because they don't see any hope for changing it, that is, in the terms like "plastic," and more severe words about it. And they've disengaged, they're uncommitted to it.

WB: How about that, Mr. Kerouac? Does that make sense to you, in terms of your own . . .

JK: I lost the entire train of thought.

WB: Well, the train of thought has to do with whether in the last few years people have ceased to look at the political processes as profitable in terms of bringing on the kind of world they want to live in and maybe that has nothing to do with the assassination of Kennedy—that kind of thing.

JK: No, that was an accident. I refer back to Count Leo Tolstoy, who wrote *War and Peace*, you know, who said that at one time the hourglass, the sand is coming down from one top of the hourglass down to the other, and that will be the end of war. I think that war will be over very soon. Although, I don't know for sure. That's what Tolstoy said.

WB: Well . . .

JK: And he was the guy Mahatma Gandhi and Thoreau, Henry David Thoreau . . .

WB: Yeah. he said a lot of foolish things.

JK: No, but I didn't get the full context of your question.

WB: Well, the full context of the question is: Are a significant number of Americans precisely at an age when we enunciated the Great Society . . .

JK: There's no Great Society![49]

WB: . . . i.e., the society that was actually going to introduce politics as . . .

JK: As far as I'm concerned . . .

WB: . . . as relevant in everything, are they disillusioned, and does this have to do with the growth of the hippie movement?

JK: Well, in the first place, I think that the Vietnamese War is nothing but a plot between the North Vietnamese and the South Vietnamese, who are cousins, to get jeeps in the country [laughter].

WB: Well, they're not very good plotters, are they?

JK: But they got a lot of jeeps [laughter]. I think they're good at pulling the wool over our eyes, and we're American lambs.

WB: They turned out to be more expensive than Sears, Roebuck jeeps. Didn't they?

JK: Yes. But that's what I really think there. As for the Russian takeover of Czechoslovakia, that showed the world what they're like, what the Communists are really like. They're really fascists.

WB: Well, yeah, when it gets down to that, excepting Mr. Sanders, right?

ES: No, I think it was a terrible thing. And if I were in Czechoslovakia and a Czechoslovakian student, I'd be putting out an underground newspaper and doing my best.

JK: Called what?

ES: Called *Gutter Expletive* [laughter].

WB: Well, since you aren't in Czechoslovakia, Mr. Sanders, what do you consider it appropriate to do in the United States?

ES: During the presidential campaign?

WB: Yeah, by way of protest against the Czechoslovakian situation?

ES: Well, I recommend sit-ins in front of the Russian missions.

JK: What for?

ES: To vigorously and more forcefully, yet nonviolently, to witness against it. And I would advocate writing articles and I would advocate, you know, maybe going to Czechoslovakia, I mean, The Fugs are going to Europe in a couple of weeks, and we may just . . .

JK: You going to bring your carbines?

ES: We're going to the Essen Song Festival in Germany, and we may just try to freak across Czechoslovakia to visit Kafka's birthplace, I guess, was he born in Prague?

JK: Yeah.

ES: So, we may go play, have a homage to Kafka with our band.

WB: Well, do you draw any, do you drawn any generalities on the basis of the behavior of the Soviet Union which instruct you in assessing other political situations?

ES: Yeah, like Mayor Daley in Chicago.

WB: Uh-hm. What are those?

ES: Well, those are that when you attempt to essentially peacefully gather together to press a point about a war, or about a freedom, or about freedom of journalism, that when you're confronted with people like the Soviet leaders and like the leaders in Chicago, namely, Mayor Daley, and Mr. Stahl, and Mr. Barter of the Chicago Municipal Office, that you're confronted with essentially the same position. You're not allowed; you're clubbed, you're gassed, you're freaked, zapped, pushed over, if you're an old lady, you're thrown through a plate glass [window], and if you're a cripple, you're thrown against a streetlight, if you're a peaceful, long-haired, loving protester, you're smashed and knocked down, if you're a cameraman, you're bricked and your camera is destroyed, and your blood is splattered all over you, I mean it's a nefarious scene and there's all kinds of correlations, and the only lesson you would draw would be to prepare yourself in the sense that, if you're a nonviolent [person], like I am, and if you believe in pacifism, you attempt to create a body of love and life so that that thing can't happen, that there'll be so many loving people there that you will have a festival of life and all its attributes, and you can do that by praying together, by loving together, by singing OM in the streets, which is a benevolent word, and by doing, by getting together and creating love, I think it's a great force, and at least in allowing you to demonstrate in the United States against a Daley, who is Al Capone, you know, it's . . .

WB: Yeah, sure.

JK: Beware of false prophets who come unto you dressed in sheep's clothing and underneath are ravening wolves.[50]

ES: Well, who's that?

BREAK

WB: Uh, now, Mr. Yablonsky, I'd like to ask you this, because you have studied very carefully the whole hippie mentality. I was in

Chicago and so were a lot of people who would not really have recognized what had happened on the basis of Mr. Sanders's description, but I do think that Mr. Sanders means it, I think that he really thinks the cops were looking for old ladies to maim, and gentle people to savage, and I think that the fact that he thinks it is interesting. Now . . .

ES: It happened.

WB: Yeah, I know, sure, sure, sure. Yes, yes. I think [laugher] I would like to hear your analysis of why it is that they seem so compulsive to believe that a Daley, who is after all a hero of John F. Kennedy and Bobby Kennedy . . .

JK: What hero?

WB: . . . Whom you associate with the best of the aspirations of the youth—How come they feel this way? What is it in their creed that requires . . .

LY: Well, first of all, I wouldn't hook Daley in with JFK and that he's a big-city boss. I think that, I just observed you and others on television in Chicago . . .

WB: Nothing bellicose about me, was there?

LY: Oh boy! [laughter] You slugged someone there. I think that if the people who were involved with the hippies or the Yippies had been permitted to sort of do their thing and to chant and to have a peaceful march . . .

WB: Their thing involved the assassination of a few Democrats, didn't it?

JK: No.

LY: Oh, no, not at all. I think there were around maybe ten thousand young people there who would have sang a few songs in the park and done things like that. But I do believe . . .

WB: But in fact they threw bricks, and in fact some of them wanted to assassinate a few people.

LY: No, I don't there was . . . there was apparently a lot frustration . . .

WB: Yeah.

LY: . . . of their effort to do something . . .

WB: Now then, wait a minute.

LY: . . . in that direction.

WB: Look, you know Tom Hayden, you know Rennie Davis, you know these characters, everybody here knows them . . .[51]

ES: Yeah, I do.

WB: . . . and we know that these are not sweet little old flower children.

ES: But they didn't have anything to do with . . .

WB: They are here intending to make a scientific, ideologic point, which is to engage the police in violence in order to try to produce ideology, in order to produce a wave of sympathy, which they succeeded, and they are absolutely elated, it would have been impossible for the police to withdraw in such a way as to satisfy them, because the only way they could have been satisfied is by forcible encounter.

LY: You asked me about the hippies and the Yippies . . .

WB: Yeah.

LY: . . . and I was talking about what they would have done. Now, I tend to agree with you that there were other segments of the population, possibly including the Blackstone Rangers[52] and other groups, who were prepared to stir something up if it didn't happen. But I think there was such an overreaction, such a trigger-finger kind of situation, that these kids began to open the thing up, and before anything could get going, there was a lot of smashing, and then the others moved in, and I think there would

have been kind of a love-in type of scene in Chicago, by a large
segment of the young people . . .

WB: If you could have separated the two . . .

ES: Well, because they were very clearly separated until they were
mixed together, there were two movements operating in
Chicago: the Yippies, who wanted Lincoln Park, which is
many, many miles from the amphitheater and is many, many
miles from the Hilton, they wanted to have a festival of life with
rock music in the park, with theater classes, with guerrilla theater, with, like, various poets and people coming together for a
festival of life.

WB: What is guerrilla theater?

ES: Guerrilla theater is a bunch of people who engage in, who don't
need props and who don't need regular stage . . .

JK: Do they crucify chickens?

ES: Well, no, that's not guerrilla theater, but, anyway, the guerrilla
theater people just need themselves and their own body makeup,
and you know props like that. Well, anyway, we wanted Lincoln
Park, and to use the beach to swim and sleep at, and the Chicago
authorities continually thwarted us throughout our whole six
months of negotiations, refusing at any point to allow any
demonstrations, so that we were forced, they drove, literally,
Allen, Jean Genet, William Burroughs, even Clive Barnes of the
New York Times, were driven out of the park at night . . .

JK: Good.

ES: . . . by tear gas. That's true, by tear gas, by these, by cops who
refused to let peaceful people . . . so all of these people were
forced into the streets, and with no place to go except for the
benevolence of a couple of churches, to sleep, so they were . . .
and there was a bus strike in Chicago, there was a cab strike, and

there was no live TV coverage of anything, so they were forced into the street, the police attacked, pushed, mauled, maimed, and that's really what happened. Now, the other movement was the mobilization movement, which . . . they wanted to march on the amphitheater, and that's Rennie Davis, and that's Tom Hayden, but also Dave Dillinger, who is an avowed pacifist, [and a] benevolent leader of some standing. And they wanted to have a peaceful march on the amphitheater and split up into groups, those who wanted to march on, would march on, those who wanted to sit down, would sit down, but there was never any violent confrontation planned. And then the Chicago people thwarted and frustrated constantly anybody's attempts to have a peaceful demonstration—naturally frustration mounted, but the amount of brick-throwing was for no negligible purpose, namely to protest with their loving bodies what was going down at the alcoholic amphitheater.

WB: What were you saying, Mr. Kerouac?

JK: I said there are people who make a rule of creating chaos so that once that chaos is underway they can then be elected as the people who take care of the chaos.

WB: And you think this applies to the Chicago situation?

JK: No, I'm not talking about Daley, I don't know anything about him, I wasn't there, but I'm talking about his idea of protesting and running around and making noise all over the place. If you create chaos you can become the commissar of the controlled chaos.

WB: Uh-hm.

LY: I think there's . . .

JK: That's my idea, that's how I see it.

WB: Yeah.

LY: . . . a situation that was operative there. To go back to Prague, maybe to the thirties, a guy named Kapek wrote a book called RUR.* Right. A great writer. Uh' related to the universal robot. Well, what he was doing was making a statement about the fact that man is turning into kind of a machine. That there's no, well, there's no communication humanity, and in Chicago, we had a political machine, which was airtight, plastic, solid as a rock, and here were some antagonists. But not really antagonists, they were people who were trying to be spontaneous to do something else, to loosen the situation up, and we had these forces at kind of at opposite ends of the continuum, and a clash took place. I think this was part of the problem there.

WB: Well, I think that that's an interesting theory, but I'm not sure how convincing it is in the light of the fact that the Democratic Party was by no means airtight. It may have been airtight up against people who wanted to storm the amphitheater and burn it down, but it was certainly not airtight in terms of the tussles going on within it. There was very spirited debate, and there was a very high permeability there for ideas that were fired in from about every Democratic philosopher in America. Now, in other words, this was not a totally neat little nominating possession—it looked for a while as though Teddy Kennedy would be nominated if he . . .

LY: But, I feel that there was left . . . I think there was lip service given to an open convention, but I think . . .

WB: Well, that's so . . . [both talking simultaneously]

LY: . . . at the heart of the matter it was all set . . .

WB: Now, wait a minute . . .

LY: . . right down to the . . .

---

* *Rossum's Universal Robots* by Carel Kapek.

WB: Look. When it's all set, it can mean nothing more than that people have made up their minds. Now, if the . . . if we decide in this room that it's our duties toward free speech that requires us to listen to the nostrums of, let's say, the Labor Progressive Party,[53] but, having listened to them, we then proceed to reject them, I don't think they have a right to say that our views were airtight.

LY: Well, there was evidence that the . . .

WB: The point is that a lot of people had decided that they wanted Humphrey, and a lot of people weren't shaken in their particular resolution, which doesn't necessarily make it a static convention.

ES: Yeah, but you don't have to stack the galleries with "WE LOVE DALEY" signs, you don't have to shake down Mrs. McCarthy just because she's . . . and search her purse when she's surrounded by four Secret Service guards. You don't have to run people up the wall and smack 'em down.

WB: Well, a lot of people can say you don't have to publish the kind of stuff you publish in order to love people.

ES: Yeah, but how can you . . . yeah, but, you know, why don't we just unite with the Russians and dance around, I mean . . .

WB: Yes, go ahead.

ES: You want a particular?

JK: You want to know what my mother called Humphrey?

WB: I don't know.

JK: "Flat-faced floogie with the floy-floy" [laughter and applause].

WB: I gather . . . I'm surprised she wasn't nominated as vice president.

JK: And you know what Agnew's real name is? Anagnostopoulos, which means "the son of the reader." And in Messina, in ancient Greece, the Turks had taken over ancient Greece, Messina, and they said, "Don't read, you're censored." And his father read all the books, and the *Bible*, it's a . . .

WB: . . . and said, "Someday you'll become vice president."

JK: It's a very *proud* name. Huh?

WB: I said, someday you'll become vice president.

JK: I?

WB: Not. No, the reason that I find this interesting . . .

JK: My father and my mother and my sister and I have always voted Republican. Always. We voted for Hoover.

WB: Have you no ambition?

JK: Those people were all votin' for Hoover. Kickin' water meters [laughter].

ES: Well, you see the only thing that type of police state oppression forces on us is that at the next convention we're gonna have to take ten thousand of us and run naked through the streets smeared with strawberry preserves or something [laughter].

JK: Maybe I could lick you [laughter].

ES: My wife, maybe. No, but yet, I say, you know, I mean, they force you into an incredible position in the world when you want to protest, when you want to make your voice known in a benevolent way, and yet at the same time you're pushed and clubbed, and you know . . .

JK: You make yourself famous by protest.

ES: That's not . . . who does? Not me.

JK: You.

ES: No, I make myself famous by singing smut.

JK: I made myself famous by writing songs and lyrics about the beauty of the things that I did, and the ugliness, too.

ES: You're a great poet, I'll admit.

JK: But you made yourself famous by saying "Down with this, down with that. Throw eggs at this, throw eggs at that."

ES: I hope not. That's not what I want.

JK: Take it with you. I cannot use your abuse, you may have it back.*

ES: Okay, you're a great poet, and we admire you, in fact, it's your fault that we . . .

BREAK

WB: Now, Mr. Yablonsky, in your book you list what you call the "psychedelic creed." I take it that these are articles of faith to which most hippies would adhere. I think it would be interesting to check them out with Mr. Sanders and Mr. Kerouac. For instance, you say that the hippie is a "spontaneous evolution," it is not a heavy, worked-out plan, right?

LY: Most people believe that . . . I would say that those creeds are kind of summarizations of . . . based on several hundred interviews with people on the scene and what *they* say. It's not especially what *I* say.

WB: Right. I know, I know. Right. It wasn't handed down on some tablet, but you infer it. Yeah, okay. Now and then you say drugs are the key to the god in men, drugs are sacraments for a greater knowledge of the universe, drugs are a vehicle to a cosmic consciousness. Is there a considerable consensus on this point?

LY: Well, a lot of people in the movement do take the position that that's the way, that every man is a god, and it's a very individualistic

---

* Kerouac paraphrases from the *Akkosa Sutta*, a Buddhist text: "Well, good Brahmin, you have invited me to alms and entertained me with abuse which I decline to accept. So now it belongs to you."

kind of a movement. Each individual should be free "to do his own thing," whatever that may be. It's rather anarchistic, actually, and I think here are the seeds of its failure.

WB: Well, how are standards arrived at in hippie culture on the basis of which one decides whether somebody's thing is insufferable. Hm?

LY: Well, I just want to finish this and then . . . I saw someone assaulting someone at a commune up in northern California, and I started to intervene, and several people rather gently said, well, he's just going through his violence bag. Let him do his own thing. I said, well what if he kills him, you know, and . . .

WB: Good point.

LY: . . . their position was everyone should be free to do their own number, I don't share this view, and, uh, but this is part of the philosophy.

WB: Do you endorse that particular impulse, Mr. Sanders?

ES: Well, I've seen a lot of communes, and I've never seen a commune that really tolerated violence. I think that's one of the chief characteristics of a community of free people, that they're there to get away from violence, and when there's drug-induced violence or other types of violence, it's generally, in my view, in my experience, it's generally quelled.

JK: You mean kibbutzes?

ES: Well, that's one part of it [talking simultaneously]

LY: Every commune I went to, people were . . . I saw some degree of violence and anarchy and chaos, and they would tell me that, about another one [another commune]. I went to around four, and the last one was . . . I, I . . . it was way back in the hills, and I was rather frightened because there was a rather high degree of violence. There were a lot of people freaked out on drugs, uh, it was a rather chaotic scene.

WB: And how do the victims of this violence characteristically react?

ES: Ouch.

WB: It hurt?

LY: Like, like most people do.

WB: But they had, but they have no mechanism in which to appeal, correct?

LY: Right. This was one of the few times in my life I wished there were police around.

JK: There goes the black flag of anarchy.[54]

WB: Well, would you say that their leaders are quote, "spontaneous," they're not pushy leaders who are self-appointed, they're selected by hippie constituents because they are "spiritual centers"? How are they selected, and what authority, once selected, do they have?

LY: Well, the theme . . . the philosophical theme would be that certain individuals are purer, more loving, more tuned in to nature, and toward other people than others [seem to be], and that people seek them out as the leaders.

WB: But what authority do they have?

LY: They . . . they deny having any and claim to have no power.

WB: So that a victim in one of these situations would get nowhere by addressing his complaints to the "leader," because the leader would have no authority to redress those grievances.

LY: Well, there's no *paid* organizations.

ES: Are we talking about reality, or not? I mean, you know, I've never seen a situation where he's talking about "communes."

WB: Well, he's been in four communes, he's written a book about it, he observed it with his own eyes.

ES: Indeed, but he's talking about a commune, let's say, a desert commune, or a commune that's isolated from the fabric, the police fabric, Now, I'm familiar with the communes in New York City, for instance, where you are constantly reacting, relating to the so-called *other* world, you know, with it, and so that you're really never without police protection, you know you usually have a phone, or something.

LY: Well, up in Big Sur, places like that, you're, you know, people are kind of wiped out.

ES: But the point is there's nothing . . . I think we're emphasizing violence, and it doesn't have to be . . .

WB: Well, is it all right?

JK: I was at Big Sur.

WB: You've written a book?

LY: When were you there, Jack?

JK: Oh, get off it. I lived alone.

LY: Were you there lately?

JK: I lived with a mule, up there.

WB: Well, is it okay for a hippie to call the police when he needs help, or is that considered a . . .

ES: Of course.

WB: . . . uh, anti-something?

ES: Sure, you see someone trying to get you, you call the police, why not? I mean, you can't, you're attaching all these theoretical tags. That's the problem with using the word *hippies*, in that it's a tag, you know? You can't say they're anarchistic to the degree, they're all . . . they all have middle-class equipment, a lot of them, and they can plug right back in, you know—it's easy. Gee, let's see, police, you know, yeah, you dial, you know, 911.

LY: Well, isn't one of the goals of a lot of people on the scene to turn off all middle-class values and to tune in to some other sense of reality?

JK: Nixon is a middle man. A man for the middle man, and Agnew.

ES: What we're really involved in is the definition of the word *drop out*, you know, and I think that what the thinking hippies are involved in is a new type of a new interpretation of what dropping out means, you know, like, you naturally retain some connections with say the police, and the hospital, and the fire department, and the legal aid, the medical . . .

LY: But isn't this a negative retention? Uh, you know, it's like . . .

JK: Hey Ed? You hear me, Ed? I was arrested two weeks ago, and the arresting policeman said "I'm arresting you for decay"[55] [laughter].

WB: I assume he was able to prove it [laughter].

LY: This may be the start of a new movement.

ES: Decayists?

BREAK

WB: All right, we have a question here on the floor.

Q: Mr. Yablonsky, I'm interested in what kind of a future you see for the hippie movement?

LY: Well, I think a lot depends on American society. If it becomes more open and less plastic, more loving, and a lot of the rigid institutions that have developed . . . like many, a lot of our families, whatever, if things begin to change, there won't be any need for people to react in a rather extreme form looking for love, it will be found in the regular social system, and in that case, it will disappear, or it may grow, if things become more rigid, or Nixon gets elected, or . . .

WB: I'd like to comment on that, and that it may very well grow to the extent that we all encourage (A) intellectual irresponsibility and (B) personal irresponsibility. It may very well be that the psychologists are correct who say that precisely what has encouraged the hippie movement to become irresponsible is a complete lack of leadership. It may be that when we start writing books about them, we ought even to muster up the courage to say that certain things they do, they ought to be permitted to do. Ah yes, a question over there.

Q: Would any of you regard the hippie movement not only as a reflection of the inadequacies of society as a whole but also a manifestation of the psychological inadequacies of the individual hippies themselves?

LY: Well, I think that there's such freedom within the framework of the movement that people that society would classify as "psychotic" are allowed to do their thing and they live and eat and they're taken care of by others and appreciated. In fact, to a great extent, I think, this is one of the interesting facets of the hippie movement—that there is a humane approach to people who society would label in some extreme fashion, and so there a lot of young people who are . . . who don't make it through the usual channels, who find a life for themselves on the hippie scene.

WB: But the question itself poses a methodological challenge, doesn't it? Because it's hard to establish by mutually agreed-on means what normalcy consists of, right?

LY: Right.

WB: I mean, maybe Mr. Sanders is normal, for all we know.

JK: Maybe I am, too.

LY: Well, if people get nude, as Ed described, and put "strawberry jam" on, I think you said "strawberry," and run through the streets, as . . .

JK: . . . scatological there, Sanders.

LY: . . . you know, if hundreds do this, it's kind of a movement. If one guy does it, he'll get arrested in a moment. Well, he'll have to get some followers, you know?

WB: Yeah. Of course, it's all very well [talking simultaneously] to imitate St. Francis, all one has to do is be like him, which is another talent. Did you want to comment on that, Mr. Kerouac?

JK: Well, I was asking why he wants followers?

WB: Who? Mr. Sanders?

JK: Abramowitz, or whatever his name is [laughter].

LY: Don't be anti-Semitic with me. I happen to be Jewish. My name is "Yablonsky."

JK: That's the classic answer, isn't it?

WB: What is the classic answer?

JK: To call you by your name.

LY: Well, why did you call me Abramowitz?

JK: Well, uh, what is it?

LY: Yablonsky.

JK: Oh, Yablonsky, he's Polish.

WB: Hey, you didn't mean to be rude, did you Mr. Kerouac? Come on, now.

JK: No, no. I forgot his name.

WB: Now, did you want an answer to that question?

JK: Which question?

WB: Obviously not.

JK: Yes, yes, I'll answer that question over there about the methodological . . .

ES: It was about emotional paraplegics [laughter].

JK: No, what was the question?

ES: Let's get another one.

WB: Okay. This lady's been waiting.

JK: I can answer that one too, you know.

WB: Yeah. Here's one for you, now . . . wait a minute.

Q: As far as the hippies, and people who live in the communes, and those who work in the bands, do they plan on making it a lifetime occupation? I mean, are they just gonna' sit down and watch the world go by? Because they're not really doing anything.

ES: Well, that's not what they're doing, well, everybody sits down part of the time and watches the world go by.

Q: What are they doing? Are they adding anything to . . . .

ES: Well, they're living, it's called, like, there are certain religious movements, like the Brethren, or the Quakers, who don't believe in proselytizing but live by example. And you'll never get any queries from the Church of the Brethren to join their belief, but at the same time, they try to live an exemplary life, and that's probably the main motivation behind a commune life, rather than say, come here and join us, they would show an example and hopefully accrue.

Q: Do you plan to be a Fug when you're fifty?

ES: When I'm fifty? I'm fifty, uh, I plan to be an emotional para-plegic, smoking peace herbs.

JK: Neurosthenic psychotic.

ES: No, you know.

WB: Do you think that would be an improvement, Mr. Kerouac?

JK: No, no, I'm just kidding.

WB: You said psychotic, didn't you?

JK: I did say that.

WB: I think that's an interesting point. How about this youth busi-ness? Why should, uh, why should this particular impulse evanesce? Why, when you get to be around thirty or thirty-five, do you think, "Oh, I'm gonna put my youth behind me and go to work for the First National Bank?"

LY: Well, a lot of the young people who are in the movement, they look up and they see their fifty-year-old father, who did everything, has all the goodies, two-point-eight cars and three houses and whatever, and he's kind of miserable, and he's not communicating with his wife and whatever, and they say, well, if I go to the right schools, and do all these things, this is what's going to happen to me. Well, I'm going to try something else. And, I think this is part, the hippie movement is partly this, a kind of a social experiment.

WB: Partly a social experiment that understands the likelihood of its own futility? Put it this way: Will anybody be thinking about the hippies ten years from now? Other than in a sort of a hula skirt sense? As just something that happened?

ES: Well, no. By then, the Yippies will be in the command generation, and their pot-smoking law students and all the young legislatures who are introducing legalization of pot bills, and all the young professionals who are "turned on" and articulate and who are aware of Mr. Kerouac and Mr. Ginsberg's great contribution to American society.

JK: You hope. I'm not connected to Ginsberg, and don't you put my name next to his!

ES: Okay, Mr. Kerouac's contribution to American civilization. Those people will be "command generation," and will hopefully retain some of the humane.

JK: Command generation! *Heil Hitler!*

ES: Well, that's what they're gonna be, that's what *Time* magazine calls them, I don't call them that.

Off the Road: The Celtic Twilight of Jack Kerouac

Gregory MacDonald, *Boston Globe* (August 1968)

"You have to be crazy to be a writer in this country!"

—Jack Kerouac

T he house in Hyannis had already been let and there was a For Sale sign plastered on the development house in Lowell.

In what was designed to be the dining room of that house lay his mother, the skin of her face as smooth as a baby's, her left side paralyzed by a stroke two years before. All she wanted was to move to St. Petersburg, Florida, where a house was waiting for them.

"I know Jackie's trying very hard to get some money, but I don't know."

A few feet away, in the living room, just the other side of a thin, plastic, folding accordion door, facing the other way, sat Jack Kerouac in a rocking chair, red slippers, white socks, pajama pants, open plaid flannel shirt, T-shirt over a big belly, still-bigger chest, not having shaved or eaten for four days, not since we had arranged to do this thing, "Completely surrounded by booze," in his own words, averaging twelve to fifteen shots of whiskey and gulps of beer an hour, seven feet from his own television, staring at the midday pap, his mind as sensitive as a frog's open heart, talking.

"If I didn't have my Scotch and beer I wouldn't speak to anybody."

Over the mantelpiece, to the right of his television, was a fine pencil drawing of his brother, who died at the age of nine of rheumatic fever, done by a German. The drawing was on the cover of a Kerouac book, *Visions of Gerard*, "which nobody reads anymore. It's too sad."

On the wall behind Kerouac was a painting called *Night Wash*, done by a friend, which was exactly that, a literal pun. Directly over his head was a painting of Pope Paul as a cardinal (copied from *Life* magazine eight years previously) by Kerouac himself.

"Painting's my hobby. I don't like to do it. It makes my hands dirty."

In the background, the present Mrs. Kerouac, Stella, looking old enough to be everybody's mother (Jack's first marriage was annulled; his second ended in divorce; he was married for the third time in Hyannis, November 1966), moved from the dining room to the kitchen to the living room, nursing them both, getting coffee for me, helping things to be understood, arranging for the lawn to be fertilized, giving Greek cookies to a young man who came to the door, for his mother, collecting what photographs they had for me to use with this story.

"I absolutely will not be photographed," Kerouac said.

"It's all right, Jackie," Stella said. "There will be no photographers. He promised."

She had told me that the previous winter a reporter and photographer from *Newsweek* magazine had worked with Kerouac for hours. He had even splashed around, fully dressed, in a stream in which the ice was just breaking, snow still on the banks, for the camera.

As a result he was ill for months.

And *Newsweek* never used the story, or photographs.

"I guess I wouldn't have made a soldier. My theory is to give all the soldiers belts with bottles of whiskey hanging from them. That way they'd win the battle. Makes you sentimental. Everybody would look out for his buddy."

Two months before, his brother-in-law, who had been a World War II army sergeant, went on a sentimental trip back to Europe.

He took the great novelist Kerouac with him, thinking that way he would get red-carpet treatment everywhere he went.

They were thrown out of several places.

Among other things, Jack paid a prostitute in Portugal named Linda ten dollars to stare into his eyes for a solid hour by the clock. Then he gave her another ten.

In Germany, Kerouac became fascinated by the way the "Aryan types" walked along the street.

He got up to strut, march, goose-step with himself up and down the living room sixteen times in hilarious imitation. The narrow, modern living room was full of the movement of this one-hundred-and-ninety-pound bear of a man.

"I came back to America saying, 'the poor Jews.'"

In his chair again, staring at the continuous daytime pap, taking constant Scotch and beer: "I want to be commissioned to do my next book, which will be called *Beat Spotlight*. I want five thousand dollars' advance on that and five thousand dollars' advance on *Visions of Cody* so I can get the hell out of here and get to Florida. The people here are nice. The water's no good."

His last book, published only a few months previously by

Coward-McCann, *Vanity of Duluoz* (three syllables: Du-lu-oz: the louse; Kerouac: the cockroach), is autobiography, from his Lowell boyhood to prep school in New York, Columbia University, the Navy, the merchant marine, to the point where he went on the road. It's a good book.

About 10 percent of *Cody* had been published in a limited edition in 1960.

"The Complete Visions of Cody. Not published yet. I wrote it sixteen years ago, in 1952. Ginsberg told me it's the masterpiece of all ages. It's a fantastic poem. A five-hundred-and-twelve-page paean to a cowboy I once knew, Cody, whose real name is Neal Cassady, who was the Moriarty in *On the Road*. I've changed his name now four or five times.

"You know, a little magazine on the West Coast is saying that he died trying to live up to the image I created for him. A crock of shit. The fact is, he's not even dead. It's a trick."

"Jack, you don't know he's not dead," Stella said. "His wife said so."

"I think he's in Spain. Mexico's a big place, too. It's just a trick to get out from under his wife."

"You'll see him, Jack."

"I don't mean transcendental things. I think he might be dead. Last time I saw him he was ranting. Do you want to hear how he talked?"

Jack then did an imitation of how Cassady had talked four years before: irrationally.

"I said, 'Why haven't you changed, Cassady? You're still stupid!' He was losing control. They got him a bus, flowers painted all over it that said *Nowhere* on it. And he drove the bus from California to New Orleans to New York. With fifty couples playing guitars and throwing flowers out the windows. They had a microphone in front of his face and he talked all the way, onto tape, from California to New York. No wonder he went mad.

"We met Ginsberg in the East Village and he said, 'Let's go to a party,' and I said, 'Who's going to be there?' and Ginsberg said, 'Ken Kesey, there are movies and lights and dancing on the flag.' Ginsberg put the flag around my shoulders and I took it off and folded it up and put it over the sofa. I was disgusted and I still am.

"America was an idea that was proposed and began to deteriorate at the turn of the century when people came in waving flags. And now their grandchildren dance on the flag. Damn them."

Reading Kerouac's great books of the Beat Generation, *On the Road*, *The Dharma Bums*, *Big Sur*, you had to wonder what would happen to the characters therein, to the leaders of any exuberant, youth-freedom movement once youth was gone, fifteen years later.

"Neal Cassady's wife, Carolyn, called Jack February fourth, a few months ago, and told him they had found Neal dead beside a railroad track in Mexico," Stella said to me. "Coincidentally enough, February fourth is his mother's, Memere's, birthday."

In 1971, the very unfinished writings of Neal Cassady were to be published by City Lights, called *The First Third*, a partial autobiography.

And the first third of that book is wonderful.

According to Kerouac's own account, he himself had written eighteen books, which had been translated into eighteen languages and published in forty-three countries.

His income that year, the year he was forty-six, averaged $60 a week.

The most he ever made from a book was $40,000, off *On the Road*, which was taxed as straight income. Much of the rest was used paying for his mother's interminable north-south-north moves. Only *The Subterraneans* was bought for a movie, from which he profited little.

"Why should they buy *On the Road* when they can steal it?" Stella asked. "Did you ever see that television program, *Route 66*?"

Jack said, "In New York it is quite common to make light of someone who is honest and not demanding."

In that morning's mail had been a letter from his agent saying Kerouac owed him $157.

There had also been a letter from some creeps in Oregon saying they were going to have a seance to contact the spirit of Neal Cassady, and it might be easier for them if Kerouac were there.

When his wife read this letter to him, Kerouac shrieked: "On my magic carpet I will fly!"

He jumped up. "I want you to note that besides being a great painter and a great writer, I'm a great pianist and composer."

He then sat at the upright piano.

"You'll only wake up Memere, Jack."

And played notes and chords. "'God Rest Ye Merry, Gentlemen' is a Cornish folk tune," he said. "I'm Cornish."

"He saw a Cornish movie on television last night," Stella said. "With Rex Harrison."

He sat in his rocker again.

I asked why he had never spent much time in Europe.

He put his head in his hands.

He said slowly, "I'd like to have a little farm in southern France, like Picasso."

I should have told you before this that every time Kerouac spoke, with self-consciousness, he used a different accent, high British, Cockney, Southern, Irish, Southwestern.

"Why don't you tell him the truth, Jack, why you've never lived in Europe?"

He stood up, heavily.

"Because I'm an American pioneer."

He went upstairs. She said, "He can't get enough of it, that's all."

He came back down the stairs with two slim boxes in his hand. "You want to know why I like America. I'll tell you why."

Sitting in his rocker, hunched over, eyes closed, he played "Across the Wide Missouri" on one of the two harmonicas so sweetly in the midday shade of the room, it would have made Mao love America.

He played a sort of flamenco on the other harmonica: "That covers Mexico," he said.

And "O Canada" on the first harmonica, sort of wetly.

"And that covers Canada."

"He just can't get enough of it," Stella said. "This country."

"The American Civil Liberties Union is communist. The police are afraid to arrest genuine malefactors," he shouted.

He opened the window behind my head and gently waved a bug through it.

"My brother taught me that," he said, indicating the drawing of the nine-year-old boy over the fireplace.

"All they arrest is harmless drunks like me!

"I came to Lowell because I thought I was coming home again. America used to be a pretty good country. Kids used to hang themselves at Camp Lee in 1942 to '43, rather than be sent overseas."

Much of Kerouac's short time in the service was spent in a naval mental hospital. Any real action he saw was in the merchant marine.

From his rocker, he pointed to my car through the window.

"Is that your car? I can drive, but I've never had a license. I can drive on the highway, but not downtown. All my friends are the best drivers. Neal driving me three thousand miles across the country, all the time looking me in the eyes.

"I'm afraid of cars. I'm not afraid of horses. Horses can fight back. Cars might hit somebody."

He then did an imitation, complete with mouth noises of horses' hoof beats, of a lancer on a horse.

"I'm afraid of all machines. I have machinophobia. My mother can only sleep in the backseat when I'm at the wheel."

The family car was a thirteen-year-old black Ford coupe, in the driveway.

"How do you write?" I asked. "Is it much trouble for you to get yourself up for it?"

"As Saint Matthew says, 'Do not store up in your mind what you will say, for it is the Holy Ghost who speaks through you.' I don't write. The Holy Ghost writes through me. You're surprised, aren't you? This is the first time you've ever met the Holy Ghost in person. I do a certain mechanical thing. But I am the Holy Ghost speaking."

"What purpose are you serving through the Holy Ghost?"

"I'm taking orders from Heaven. In Heaven sits God. On his left, Mary. On his right, Jesus. In front of them, the golden baby of paradise: Jackie Kerouac. I have a high opinion of myself, right? I'm serious. I was sent here to do something."

"What are you doing?"

"I'm a messenger. I didn't want to come here. May I remind you that you have never seen my Father's face? I have seen his face. I am the brother of Jesus. We're a very holy family.

"Incidentally, my mother is a descendant of Napoleon."

"You're the messenger. What's the message?"

"The message from Heaven? That after we die we're all raised to the highest part of Heaven, no matter what we do, as a fitting reward to answer Lucifer's plea to fall from Heaven. Lucifer comes to us in Heaven, you see, and says, 'You like it up here, Jackie?

Couldn't things be better?' You say, 'Yeah, maybe,' and Tha-wong! you're born. But it couldn't be better. Beds of roses. Clouds making refreshing faces all day long."

He looked at me most seriously, as if to scold me.

He said, "Religion, *señor*, is your own broken heart. You think I'm insane, don't you? I am insane. All American authors are insane. You have to be crazy to be a writer in this country!"

While Kerouac tried to get his agent on the phone (his agent was "out of the country" that day), I talked with Jack's mother about Florida and looked at some paintings Stella brought up from the basement, one by Gregory Corso, six or seven by Jack Kerouac, one of which was bright and happy. Stella said he had done it while on mescaline.

Jack then called his publisher: "Give me five thousand dollars on complete *Visions of Cody* and five thousand dollars on *Beat Spotlight* so I can get my mother to Florida and get to work on *Beat Spotlight*. Listen. Give me no money. Just publish complete *Visions of Cody*. Ginsberg says it's an important book."

Jack then allowed me to understand the publishers are not too keen on the complete *Visions of Cody*.

"It's always been too dirty," he said.

Stella tried to induce him to stay home by reminding him that *The Merv Griffin Show* started at four-thirty. While I had been upstairs for a minute, Jack had sort of dressed in trousers, shoes, a windbreaker, and a porkpie hat.

On the sidewalk he screamed at kids playing basketball in the next driveway to shut up, and when they looked terrified at him, he gave them the raspberry.

In the car, I said, "How come you've never been able to finish anything, a year of school, a football season, yet you have been able to finish so many books?"

"I don't finish. I just write it continuously. Sooner or later you reach the point in a book where you feel everybody's bored, and you bring it around somehow and end it. That's deep form."

He entered every bar shouting ferociously: "I'm Kerouac!"

In every bar in Lowell, following his nose sideways across every street, Kerouac is known.

"When you first thought of writing, when you were a kid, what kind of a writer did you think you were going to be?"

"I thought I was going to be Mark Twain."

"In your own mind, what kind of a writer are you?"

"A naturalistic. Like Dreiser. A German Romanticist. Write 'em both down. A Celtic twilight."

"Anybody writing today better than you are?"

"No. Not since Shakespeare. When he went out for a beer in the afternoon, people called him Sweet Will. They should call me Sweet Jack. Except maybe Laurence Sterne." Beside his chair at the house was a book by Laurence Sterne.[56] "Maybe George Herbert."

He had taken $5 from his wife before he left the house. Second bar we were in, he gave a kid named Morris $1 for shining his shoes.

"What do you think of Norman Mailer?"

"He's an ugly and ridiculous man."

To everybody's amusement and disdain, watering the corner of nearly every redbrick building we passed, Kerouac pursued sleep through every bar in Lowell.

At some point in our progress, a kindly cop named Pasquale, "Pat," cigar held in a toothless gap in the front of his mouth, told me about the time Jack had seen three pedigreed dogs through a pet shop window—a malamute, a collie, and something else—and had bought all three at once, to have them drag him through the bars.

"What were you so vain about, Duluoz?"

"Beating everybody athletically and by scholarship." He recited Emily Dickinson in the green bars, most of which looked like stage sets for a play by William Alfred, shamrocks everywhere, tall and short men called Councilor, Commissioner, in shiny suits standing up at the bar, talking about ward politics, who is in, who is out, and of jail, who is in, who is out, scowling at the half-staffed trousers of this man they grew up with who carries a bit of the world (he knows where Oregon is, and Oregon knows where he is) and a lot of books on the weight of his breath.

"What would have happened to you, Jack, if you had never left Lowell?"

"I would have worked in a mill all my life."

He shouted nonsense tone poems of his own (Beejeebee-jeebee), the personal meanings of which brought tears to his own eyes, wide set, gray-blue, as different from each other as the tragicomic masks, and pleadingly expressive.

He took literary advice from everybody we met—every cop, fly, and broad—that he should write, and when, and about what, saying only each time, his wide and handsome grin beneath four days' stubble: "You know what? It's weird, but what he says is true."

What he wanted to fight about was whether Al Mello was the best boxer ever to come out of Lowell.

The first time he punched me, he had the preppy's grace to grab his workman's square, intellectual's soft hand and say, "Ouch!" as if he meant it, and the second time he hit me more softly.

I think he wanted to say that he had been the best boxer, the best anything, to have come out of Lowell.

Then he sprayed me with wet laughter.

"Have you ever felt one-to-one with anyone, Jack?"

"Yes. Neal Cassady. He can't be dead. Oh, God. He can't be dead."

At the house he had said, "I don't speak with an accent all the time. I've got to get out of here."

"Have you ever been yourself with anyone, Jack?"

"I know another bar."

I was to leave him, asleep, sitting at a bar owned by his brother-in-law.

"'Religion, *señor*, is your own broken heart.'"

"What about it?"

"That's a beautiful line, Sweet Jack."

Fourteen months later, Jack Kerouac died of a hemorrhage in Florida.

Jack Kerouac–End of the Road

Larry Vickers, from *Kerouac at the "Wild Boar" and Other Skirmishes,*
edited by John Montgomery (Beat Books, 1986)

Well maybe he did come to Florida to die. He came to Florida and talked about his mother and his/her cats in the house in St. Pete, and among the deeds he probably set free a couple of people otherwise lined up for newspaper sports-writing careers; set them free maybe to go back to school, or to tend bar, or to go crashing through the cool Florida night-sweet countryside guzzling Moselle and hollering at one another, with the driver taking part as well as the revelers, with nobody ever staying sober to get the rest home and often not getting there anyway. Then, blip–he disappeared back to Lowell, where he married Stella and then his scene got to be what they call "heavy," when a group went sashing up there to visit in Clifford Anderson's 1950 Chevy, drinking wine and playing guitars and Patty Mitchell in the back blowing hell for breakfast on his harmonica, while Mike Baldwin sang blues.

They visited some name poets, former Beats, now in the respectable publishing business, and came back trying to hang onto as always the sentimental shout-me-down, good time, rock-hard get-it that had slipped off and starved to death somewhere during the night. I never saw Kerouac after that. When he came to Florida the last time, it was in a station wagon with his mother and Stella on mattresses in the back and Joe Chaput of Lowell–rated by Kerouac as the best driver in the world next to Neal Cassady–driving the car while Jack drank and talked.

But Jack Kerouac had been there when we were going to the new University of South Florida and that made it something else for us– though I was never really that close, just on the fringes in a way, seeing what I saw. The first time a real *literary* man had come to live among us, it was something to celebrate. It was the time of Montgomery, on the near edge of the Kennedy era, between then and now.

There was a lecture series called "Meet the Author" or something of the sort at USF, and Gerry Wagner, great of belly, warm of heart, disenchanted speech professor who ran a bar called the Wild Boar, pulled strings to get Kerouac and some of the English faculty together. The result, after careful handling, was an invitation for Gerry to read Jack's poems.

The subsequent withdrawal of that invitation, for whatever reason, caused the first demonstration on the young campus, an orderly affair in which Pete Gladue, a thick-haired, earnest talker and writer, read Jack's *Mexico City Blues* loudly while the rest of us marched around in a circle carrying signs of indignation–a little timid even to enter the administration building, the occupation of which would have scared the boldest of us.

Kerouac sitting in the Wild Boar, a rustic little tavern, often harassed by officers checking for underage drinking and marijuana, he was

King there, before the Boar burned one night after a raid, before the novelist and the dream dissolved.

"Ti Jean," Gerry Wagner would bellow at the obviously scrappy little Kerouac, who would be sitting at the bar arguing baseball with a don't-give-a-damn-who-you-are redneck. "I love you, you little Canuck!"

And Gerry, six-three, about 230, curly-headed and wearing a big handlebar moustache, who grew up a Mississippi stud, then got a master's degree from Southern Mississippi on beer and Bess, his incredibly great wife. Old Gerry would bound around the end of the bar and square off with his eyes glowing and double chin taut, and he and Jack, who had meanwhile leapt from the barstool to the floor, would bust bellies. They'd run slap into each other two or three times; then they'd roar and hug tight, and Gerry would give short Jack a loud kiss right on the forehead, to which Jack would grin that "astonishing, sheepish, little-boy grin."

That's the way Kerouac was when we were mostly in school, as much out of defiance as anything else, before I went with Methodist Reverend Allen Burry and Mike Baldwin to Martin Luther King's march on Montgomery—Jack was indisputably among us, the King.

The night I met him was at the Boar. Kerouac was obviously a drunk lord that evening when Baldwin said to come over and be introduced, and I, wearing my only suit, which was a gray wash-and-wear from Sears, had just come from a terrible local opera with Renee, who later married me, and she was dressed out-of-place for the tavern as well, since standard uniform was a chambray work shirt and denim jeans. I went over to meet the author, nervous in the face of much bowing and bootlicking, and afraid Kerouac would deal me out with a single flip of the tongue. Cleverer devils than I had been crucified with a single comment and left bleeding there, and the object of the game was not to let that happen. Baldwin introduced us—said my name—and Kerouac made immediate note of my clothes: "Well isn't he a pretty one?"

What I said was simple, cut a calculated gamble considering the surroundings:

"Fuck you, Kerouac." He looked again and buked his eyes and asked what I had said. I repeated it in a louder shout to overcome the din.

After closing that night, we were all going to a party at Gerry's, his barn of a house on a lake, and Kerouac rode out in my Falcon with Renee and me and two bottles of chilled wine. On the ride she asked him, "I read your 'Got up, dressed up, went out, got laid; died, got buried, ina coffin in the grave,' and now, what about that?"

"That was long ago," he said. "I was very much younger then; it embarrasses me now and I do not wish to discuss it," So, of course, we didn't.

He would come from St. Petersburg to Tampa when Clifford would go to get him, and then he'd drink wine, beer, any kind of whisky, two or three days until somebody would make him eat a meal; then he'd sleep six or seven hours and want to be taken back to St. Pete. We'd usually try to handle Kerouac in shifts, one or two people sleeping while one or two stayed awake to drink and talk with him, or simply listen to him go into long monologues, which could last over an hour. Once I took him to a party and we were thrown out when Jack became abrasively anti-Semitic.

Kerouac loved Russian writers. He was critical of our education— "What are you doing, reading Camus, when you haven't even read the elemental greats yet, like Dostoyevsky?" he would shout, in a bar, not realizing most of us were reading very little outside of required writers and some of his books. In his last year he talked about Nabokov, according to McClintock, who interviewed him last. For some reason he despised Norman Mailer, I suspect because Mailer was obviously more supple. He had a favorite story he used to tell about finding Mailer in a men's room once and pissing on the other author. He told the story a number of times, but I don't remember the details now.

Kerouac was a scrapper; he called to mind a rough kid, maybe wearing wool knickers and a creejawed cap, with either a bat or a chunk of coal in his hand. He would argue about the Irish (and there was a cry he introduced, "Screw the Irish!") with any salty redneck who sat beside him in the bar, and after some attempts at intimidation, if things looked unpromising, he'd shout, "Do you know who I am? I am the world-famous author, Jack Kerouac!" which would make almost no impression on the person he was confronting.

In Florida, he considered his presence a privilege, and during the time before his mother became paralyzed, when he went back to Lowell, the news that Kerouac was around was a command to drop other plans and go with him. Most of the time we did, though retaining one's own personality was sometimes difficult. Some were accused of playing roles to get into Jack's books, and perhaps that was part of his magic; he could grant immortality.

But after that crisis in Lowell, he seemed, from reports, to be waiting for death—his mother's more than his own, but with a dread that couldn't have been more ominous. The people who had called him out weren't with him and he wasn't in the bars near the campus any longer.

"It's too heavy," said Buddy Klein of the scene in St. Petersburg less than two weeks before Jack died. "It's just depressing as hell to go over there."

Most people who knew him well tried to treat Jack right. They knew the "I hope" was always behind that boast that he could "beat you up" and that qualifier was what made you love him. We didn't call him King or write articles about his demise, his lonesomeness, his mother, or his wife Stella. At one time he held the key to a heaven in which none of us really believed–and that, too, was part of his magic. We knew sometimes that if we couldn't help him then we ought to just let him be. His life was built on honest words and we knew he could appreciate honest actions.

But Jack made his boast once too often–in a black man's bar in St. Petersburg, among people who didn't know or care that he was the "world-famous author." He had thought barroom brawls a great sport, and he was badly beaten.

Yes, violence killed Jack Kerouac. The romance of America had made him, and her reality wiped him out.

Jack Kerouac Is
on the Road No More

Jack McClintock, *St. Petersburg Times* (October 12, 1969)

What happens to a Beatnik in the age of Aquarius?

Some, like Allen Ginsberg, accommodate to the times and become gurus, OM-ing their way from campus to campus, demonstration to demonstration.

But what of those other cult heroes of the fifities, those picturesque, picaresque, poetic wanderers of the open road, the Beats? The Corsos, the Cassadys, the Ferlinghettis?

And what of Jack Kerouac, the king of them all, the king of On the Road?

He is forty-six. He lives in St. Petersburg with his third wife Stella and his paralyzed mother. The house, neat concrete and brick, is his mother's.

"I don't go out much anymore," he says. "I don't really go out at all." Nor does he particularly seek publicity.

When a photographer was assigned to get a picture of Kerouac recently, Stella answered the door and said, "he's sick. He'll call you when he feels better."

He never called.

A week or so later a reporter walked between the palms by the sidewalk and knocked on the same door. Stella, a gray-haired woman with a wide, sad smile, said: "He's not home."

And then a face came peering over Stella's shoulder. A face with grizzled jowls and red-rimmed eyes under spikey, dark tousled hair. Kerouac? The face said, "Yeah," and then: "You want to come in?"

Although the sun was two hours from taking its evening dip in the Gulf ten miles to the west, the house was dim inside. A television set in the corner was on, soundless. The sound you heard was Handel's *Messiah* blaring from speakers in the next room.

"I like to watch television like that," Kerouac said.

"You ain't going to take my photo, are you? You better not try to take my photo or I'll kick your ass."A threatening leer, then a laugh.

"Stella, *Hey!* Turn the music up!" Stella went and turned the music up. Her feet were silent on the floor.

Kerouac dragged up a rocking chair for the reporter, then slumped into another one in the corner.

He was wearing unpressed brown pants, a yellow-and-brown striped sport shirt, with the sleeves rolled to the elbow.

This Is How the Ride Ends

Jack McClintock, *Esquire* (March 1970)

Like a little boy, an eternal innocent, he had no defenses. He seemed neither to need them nor to care for them, although he was sensitive enough to understand that many people do, and in beery conversation Jack Kerouac was like a one-man group. He always, in the phrase of Ken Kesey (whom he didn't like), brought it all up front.

The innocence in his last months made him do things that appeared simply foolhardy. A few weeks before he died in St. Petersburg, Florida, he and a friend went out (as he rarely did), drank too much, and were beaten up by several angry blacks in a ghetto bar. I think it never occurred to Kerouac that he was not wanted there, not in these times. It hadn't been like that on the road.

But he had not been on the road in a long time. "You can't do what I did anymore," he said one evening about two weeks before he died. "I tried, in 1960, and I couldn't get a ride. Cars going by, kids eating ice cream, people with hats with long visors driving, and, in the backseat, suits and dresses hanging. No room for a bum with a rucksack."

For that reason and others, he had lived in obscurity for at least the last eight years, many of them in St. Petersburg, perhaps the last place in the world one would expect to find Sal Paradise. It is an appallingly typical Florida city, with palm trees by the roadside, pastel concrete-block houses with plaster-of-paris marlins pasted on their facades, sprinklers whirling silver pellets onto green lawns, polluted bays to cross when you go for a drive. Kerouac, ironically enough, never learned to drive, but somehow as he grew older he wound up here, in a town trying valiantly, if vainly, to throw off its old-fogy image. His paralyzed mother lived here (and I will indulge a maudlin impulse and say that I'll never forget her wailing over his gray face in its casket: "Oh my little boy . . . . . Isn't he pretty? . . . What will I do now?" as Jack's wife Stella stood in a black dress and gripped the handles of her wheelchair). It was Stella, mostly, who cared for Mrs. Kerouac, getting up and gliding toward the back of the house whenever the little bell rang.

A few months before his death, Kerouac had written a magazine article, "After Me, the Deluge," in which he castigated no less than the 1960s, and tried to assess his own feelings on being credited in large part with the development of the hippie "movement."

"It's about the Communist Conspiracy," he said of the article—in deadly seriousness, it must be added.

The article was selling well to newspaper Sunday magazines, and the *Miami Herald* asked me to visit Kerouac and dispatch a short profile to publish along with it. I had been thinking of approaching him anyway, and was glad to have an excuse for overcoming my reluctance to bother a man who I knew valued his privacy.

He lived in a suburb. The house was concrete-block with a partial fake-brick façade and palm trees flanking the sidewalk. You had to shove the fronds aside to get on the front porch. I knocked on the door and met Stella.

She is a gray-haired woman in her early fifties with a wide, bitter-sad smile and a deferent manner. She said, "He's not here," when I asked for Jack Kerouac.

He was, though. A shadow moved in the dim room behind her and then a face peered over her shoulder. The only photographs I had seen of Kerouac were old Associated Press biog shots in the files of the *St. Petersburg Times*. They show a young man, lean and handsome with chiseled features, dark eyes, and rakishly tousled hair. Such pictures were still appearing on the dust jackets of his books, and Jack told me once, later on, "I'm always getting letters from girls who think I'm still twenty-six."

This was a different face. It had red-rimmed eyes and a day's growth of salt-and-pepper whiskers. But the hair was tousled and he wore a brightly colored sport shirt, and the only time I saw him with his hair combed was in his casket.

"Jack Kerouac?"

"Yeah," said the face, "You want to come in?"

Although the sun was two hours away from setting in the Gulf of Mexico, ten miles to the west, the house was dim inside. The drapes were all drawn tightly shut. Early American furniture, cherry wood and print cushions tied on with little bows. An oil painting of Pope Paul, almost cartoon-like with big blue eyes. Gray images dancing on the screen of a television set in the corner across from an early American rocker, but no sound coming from the speakers. The sound was Handel's *Messiah* lifting mightily from stereo speakers in another room.

Kerouac planted his feet into the carpet, tilted his head in a characteristic, little-boy way, offered a bellicose glower, and said, "Are you gonna take my photo? If you try to take my photo, I'll kick your ass."

No, I assured him, I just wanted to talk. I told him why, and,

when he learned that a magazine had bought the article, he became
more friendly. He was pleased.

He dragged up another rocker, found an ashtray to go with it, and
then slumped into the dim corner in front of the television set.

"I like to watch television like that," he said, then turned his head
to call out: "Stella. *Hey!* Turn the music up!" Stella went and turned
the music up.

He was wearing unpressed brown trousers, a yellow-and-brown-
striped sport shirt with the sleeves rolled to the elbow. The shirt was
unbuttoned, and beneath it the T-shirt was inside out. His belly was
large and round, oddly too large for the stocky body. He pointed to it.

"I got a goddamn hernia, you know that? My goddamn belly
button is popping out. That's why I'm dressed like this . . . Well, I
got no place to go anyway. You want a beer? Hah?"

He picked up a pack of Camels in a green plastic case. "Some
whiskey? I'm glad to see you 'cause I'm so lonesome here."

We sat there and drank and talked for the rest of the evening. It
was the first of perhaps a dozen such visits, and there was never a
time until the last one or two visits when he didn't mention his loneliness. When I left that night about midnight, he said, "Are you
coming back to see me?"

I said yes, and would phone before dropping in if he would give
me the number.

"I don't have a phone," he said. "I don't have anybody to call.
Nobody ever calls me. Just come. I'm always here."

The visits seldom varied. Sometimes I brought a friend. We would
pick up a dozen half-quart cans of Falstaff, his favorite beer, and shove
aside the palm fronds and knock on the door. Stella would greet us
with obvious and touching gratitude. "Jackie needs company," she
would say in her quiet way.

We would push and pull the chairs around, find ashtrays, crack open the beer. There would always be a couple of books on the table next to what we came to think of as Jack's chair, usually classics. Once there was Boswell's *Life of Johnson*, another time a volume of Balzac, on whom he doted. There was always a stack of *National Review* magazines somewhere, for if Kerouac had a hero, it was William F. Buckley, Jr.

In addition to this paraphernalia, there was invariably a half-quart can of Falstaff, a pack of Camels, and a little two-ounce medicine vial with one of those white plastic caps that snap on and off. The medicine vial mystified us at first until we learned that it contained nothing more exotic than Johnny Walker Red.

"Call me Mister Boilermaker," Jack said, and when I ventured to ask why he drank the Scotch from that tiny container, he looked at me as though I were an idiot, as though I had disappointed him, and said, "So I won't spill it."

And then we would talk for hours. I think he could have been an actor. He loved to read aloud and was exceptionally good at it. Boisterously he'd say, "Wheer the divil are me glawsses?" and pick up something with type on it and read with broad, wild gestures of self-parody, grinning and mugging and dipping into a cornucopia of foreign accents for just the right one. The voice would go along, swoop up high, drop confidentially low. It sped, it dragged portentously. It understood the words and brought them alive. These times were altogether astonishing performances from this man with bare feet, whiskers, and a Kennedy half-dollar taped over his navel hernia.

Kerouac was forty-seven when he died. He had been out of the house very few times since he came to St. Petersburg the last time eleven months before, blaming his seclusion variously on illness, laziness, fear of "the niggers," lack of transportation, or merely joking it off as meaningless.

Once a professor asked me to invite Jack to speak to his class, and Kerouac answered, "Naw. I'd just get drunk." Then he illuminated the diminishing room with one of his astonishing little-boy grins. Now and then in the silver television light, he seemed to become very young again, until you remembered his ravaged face looked in the harsh light of the refrigerator. The way it looked sometimes gave me a chill I couldn't attribute to the draft from the icebox. It was almost as if Kerouac, in the last years, had burrowed farther and farther back into his own personality, back into the dense-packed delights and detritus of a life, and then turned around, and was peering out at the thronged world through the tunnel he made going in. Perhaps being back there clarified his sight in some ways, focused it more clearly on the things he could see. Perhaps it just gave him tunnel vision. I don't know.

You go the impression that, unlike his occasional friend Allen Ginsberg, who adapted slickly to the Aquarian Age by becoming one of its gurus and OM-ing his way from coast to coast, Kerouac was determined to remain out of fashion, or at least to appear that way.

He would rant for hours about the Jewish literary mafia that he believed had placed a moratorium on publication of his work. Once, when the real mafia came up, he said: "The Mafia? The real enemy is the Communist, the Jew."

The notion that he started out a freethinking leftist and moved to the right later on was one he resisted. "I'm not a Beatnik," he said once, "I'm a Catholic. The Communists jumped on my movement and turned it onto a Beat insurrection. They wanted a youth movement to exploit."

His rancor toward the left and his ultra-patriotism had come close to splitting him away from Ginsberg, whom he hadn't seen for years. Kerouac told us once of a party of Ken Kesey's in New York, at which Ginsberg came up and wrapped Jack's shoulders with an American flag—with obvious satiric intent.

"So I took it [he showed how he took it, and the movements were tender] and I folded it up the way you're supposed to, and I put it on the back of the sofa. The flag is not a rag."

The names and faces of his youth had grown away from him, Kerouac said, and it made him frankly sad. He didn't whine, he merely allowed himself to feel that way and never tried to hide it.

The death of Neal Cassady bothered him the most. Sometimes he denied that Neal had died. "They say he's dead," he would mutter, "But I don't believe it. I don't want to believe it." But other times he would tell how he had heard how Cassady met his end, walking down a Mexican railroad track in a T-shirt, in the middle of the night, stoned on grass and drunk on beer, and finally freezing to death.

It was Cassady, in fact, who was the pivot on whom Kerouac's opinion of Ken Kesey rotated: "I don't like Kesey," he said, "because he ruined Neal."

Four or five of us had been visiting Kerouac regularly for a couple of months when, one night, I showed up with the beer and another friend, the writer Richard Hill. We stowed the beer in the refrigerator, dragged the chairs around, and were hardly seated when Kerouac burst out: "Hey! I finished a book! *Pic*. I finished it yesterday and sent it to Sterling [Sterling Lord, his agent]. I started it in 1951 and finished it yesterday, what do you think about that? Only took me nineteen years!"

And he laughed and laughed, and we laughed, too. He had a copy of the manuscript, and I glanced at the first page. The protagonist was a ten-year-old black boy in the South, Pictorial Review Jackson, writing his own story in Negro dialect.

"Is it a story of prejudice?" Hill asked, mostly for something to say.

"Shit," said Kerouac, "It's a story of life. Of people living."

That was a week and a half before he died. A few evenings later, after we had opened beers, Stella said, "Look, Jackie's lost weight."

"About twenty pounds," Kerouac said, and leaned back in his rocking chair and sang: "I'm romantic, / And strictly frantic, I love those old-fashioned times."

That evening, the last time I saw him alive, we just drank and talked as usual. He was the perfect drinking buddy: uninhibited, creative in conversation, inventive in mimicry, erudite in the range of his knowledge. Some of what he said was trash, but some was the fruit of his erratic genius. I remember only a little of what we talked about that particular night. It was, as usual, mostly about his boyhood, and about writers and writing.

"Who was the greatest American writer?" he asked, leaning forward and adding his bellicose challenge: "Hah?"

I was about to toss out Melville for lack of anything better to say, but he couldn't wait. "Wolfe! Thomas Wolfe. After me, of course."

Somehow that led to autograph-seekers, whom he detested. "What do they want my damn name for?" He once wrote a fan and said he charged five dollars apiece for signatures. I jokingly said I wanted his autograph and would be glad to amortize it at a dollar down and a dollar a week, but the subject was boring, and conversation skipped to razzle-dazzle onto other things.

Cassady again: "I really loved that guy. He looked like Kirk Douglas, you know that? A little. He didn't have the dimple. He said 'Douglas may have dimples, but I've got pimples.'"

Football, and music (he played piano a little), and women

(Stella's presence did nothing to impede talk on that topic). And painting (it was Kerouac himself who had painted the picture of the Pope on his wall, and he loved the way the blue eyes seemed to follow you). All that evening, a week before he died, he seemed extra cheerful.

The subject of the autograph never came up again, but a few days later the mail turned up a small envelope addressed in block letters. Inside it were a three-by-five card with Kerouac's name signed on it and a piece of notebook paper on which was scrawled: "Jack Mac–Sorry I forgot–Would you like a piece of my toenail too, with Scotch tape?–Come on over–St. George." There was a cross drawn on the paper next to the signature.

"I just sneak into church now," he had said, "at dusk, at vespers. But yeah, as you get older you get more . . . genealogical."

There is one more thing to tell. Jack Kerouac had died on a Tuesday. On the Sunday before that, Al Ellis, a law student, had dropped by to return a book he had borrowed from Jack. Jack had something to show him. He led Al to the kitchen and pointed. On the wall was a telephone. And on the table beside it was a telephone book, with four or five names and phone numbers carefully circled in ink.

Jack Kerouac: Off the Road for Good

Carl Adkins, *Story: The Yearbook of Discovery* (1971)

J ack Kerouac is off the road for good now: he died Tuesday, October 21, 1969, in a St. Petersburg, Florida, hospital. He was forty-seven.

To some of us who knew him, the wonder is not that he died so young but that he lasted as long as he did. I think that at some time during the last years of his life, he must have weighed the consequence of living at the frenzied pace that he loved against the prospect of longevity—and longevity lost the argument. It was as if he had some mad jazzman, like Ornette Coleman, beating out the tempo of his life. Not many people can get with Ornette Coleman; his rhythms don't lend themselves to the pace of a long-distance run. Not many people could keep up with Jack Kerouac.

I first met Kerouac on New Year's Eve, in 1965, in St. Petersburg, through a mutual friend named Cliff Anderson, whom Kerouac referred to later that year, in a book called *Satori in Paris*, as his "Southern pool-shooting partner."

I think I should tell how Cliff met Jack. Cliff was sitting in the Tic-Toc, a favorite St. Petersburg hangout of ours. He had been watching a couple of guys shooting a stick of pool. He figured from the way they were dressed, they might be construction workers. One of the men came over to Cliff and bummed him for a quarter. Cliff knew, as we all did at the time, how it felt to be traveling without any coins of the realm jangling in his pockets, so he flipped the guy for a quarter.

After spending the quarter for another game of pool, the man came back to Cliff's table to tank him. "I'm Jack Kerouac," he said. Of course, Cliff didn't believe him; in fact he laughed out loud. "Not Jack Kerouac, the writer," Cliff said. "Yeah, yeah, that's me, I'm the guy." "I've read everything Jack Kerouac ever wrote. If you're Jack Kerouac, tell me who Doctor Sax was." The man said Doctor Sax was the phantom who had haunted him when he was a boy in Lowell. "Who was Dean Moriarty? What was his real name, I mean?" Dean Moriarty was a fast-talking con artist and good friend named Neal Cassady who was then living on the West Coast. Cliff still was not satisfied; he put question after question to the man. He answered them all. There could be no doubt.

"You really are Jack Kerouac," Cliff said now that he was a believer. "I know," Kerouac said in the tone of one who had always been a believer.

A friendship began that night that was to last until Jack's death. Cliff was the closest friend Kerouac had through those last years that someone had called "the melancholy years." It was Cliff who got Jack through the very rough time when his only sister died and he was so sad he could hardly look anyone in the eye without bursting into tears. It was Cliff who kept him out of trouble when he would pull one of his outrageous stunts in public. It was Cliff who introduced him to the Tampa hippie crowd and Jerry Wagner's Wild Boar Tavern (which has since mysteriously burned down). Cliff and Jack were inseparable after that first night they met in the Tic-Toc.

I had just come to town this trip and as always went immediately to Cliff's house, because that was the easiest way to find everybody. Cliffie is a sort of human cataloguer who can tell you where everybody he has ever known is in the world at any given time.

He told me the story of how he had met Kerouac.

"Do you want to meet him?" Cliff asked.

"Is Sophie Tucker the last of the red hot mamas?" I said.

Later that day we went to Kerouac's house and spent the rest of the afternoon in his room, talking and drinking beer. The best description I have ever seen of Jack Kerouac is the one he wrote about himself in *On the Road*: "I took a straight picture that made me look like a thirty-year-old Italian who'd kill anybody who said anything against his mother." Except that by now he was thirteen years older, and thicker through the middle; he had a rugged, bearish look like a hockey player. And, of course, he was French-Canadian, not Italian.

He seemed extremely shy at first, and Cliff, who is outgoing enough for the three of us, did most of the talking, while Kerouac and I just sat and blinked at each other.

That night we piled into Cliff's beat-up old Chevrolet and headed for a party someone was having in a rented hall on the beach. All the elements for disaster were Jack Kerouac and a crowd, any crowd. The party was peaceable enough at first. Jack wandered around taking to people, and it was not long before the word was out that Kerouac, the famous writer, was on the premises.

A man came up to him and said, "Mr. Kerouac, I'd like you to meet my wife. She's from Paris. I understand you speak French." This man had unwittingly put the party on the road to its raucously premature ending. Jack strolled away with the young lady from Paris. I have never fully understood the chemistry involved in what happened next, but it seemed that Jack, at will, could instigate a commotion which bordered on riot.

The next sound I heard was the shrill cry of an enraged woman. In the midst of the ensuing confusion, I could see Jack and the young lady from Paris gesticulating wildly. They were screaming at each other in French. And it was obvious from the way they glared at each other, they were not talking about the pen being on the table.

"What happened?" somebody in the crowd asked.

"He called me an Algerian!" sputtered the young lady from Paris, vehemently. It must have been roughly at this point that someone, believing that murder and mayhem were imminent, called the police. Fortunately, enough innocent bystanders had become involved by now so that Cliff and I were able to extract Jack from the mêlée, and by the time the police actually arrived, we were downtown having a coffee in a cheap burger joint.

"Did you, by the way, call the young lady from Paris an Algerian?" I asked Jack, trying to remember what it was the previous afternoon that had led me to believe he was shy.

He let me have one of his best innocent expressions which eloquently conveyed his belief that I had turned coat and joined the opposition. "What I said was, she spoke French like an Algerian," he said.

The moral to this story is best known to young ladies from Paris, to Algerians, and to certain literati among French-Canadians. I offer it here merely as an illustration of what it was like to be around Jack Kerouac when he was in top form.

It would not be possible to talk about Jack Kerouac without mentioning his marathon drinking. Allen Ginsberg called him "the last of the great Christian drinkers." He was a phenomenal drinker. He drank long and he drank hard. However, the truly phenomenal thing to me, the thing not often mentioned about Kerouac, was his capacity for abstinence. I learned some time ago not to confuse the public clown who would stand up in a bar and yell, "I'm the little golden baby of heaven!" with the private man who possessed tremendous discipline and could lock himself in his room for days and weeks in an attempt to contain some of the world's madness between the covers of a book so that the rest of us might understand it a little.

One of his favorite sports was something he called "belly-busting." The belly-busting bouts usually took place in Tampa at the Wild Boar, and his opponent was a maniac who reputedly had bitten a man's nose off in a fight. Each contestant would back up to opposite ends of the Boar and run full-speed, hands behind his back, and try to crash into the other belly first. Kerouac's opponent had about a fifty-pound weight advantage and usually sent Jack careening off the nearest wall.

Sometimes at parties, when the music was right, Jack would jump up and dance bop; he was a wildly comic dancer and yet somehow, through it all, graceful. And when I was first trying to learn the flamenco guitar, he would improvise the singing. His Spanish seemed as suspect as my playing, but he sang with such mourning and pathos that he managed to sound authentic.

After we had made a night of it, if we decided to get something to eat we would go to an all-night joint in St. Petersburg where the attraction was not the food so much as it was John, the short-order man. Jack liked to watch John work. In a time when people don't seem much to give a damn for themselves or what they have to do to make a living, John certainly was to be considered an illuminating anomaly in the natural haze of mediocrity. He worked the grill and counter as if his movements had been choreographed by Bojangles. Here was John flipping griddle cakes; now running to the other end of the counter to draw the big heavy mugs of steaming coffee; now the masterful building of three or four gorgeous sandwiches; now ringing up a customer's bill and back to the grill to start some bacon and eggs while jiggling plates with his free hand. And Jack sitting at the counter, enthralled by this beanery madman, laughing and clapping his hands, yelling, "Go, John, go!" And John, as always, appreciative of such a receptive audience, performing ever more daring maneuvers with an order of eggs over easy.

Before long the whole joint would be frantic. When Jack felt good, he could generate happiness as effortlessly as a Cadillac battery could fire up the bulb in a flashlight. I remember reading somewhere in one of his books, "The mad ones are the only ones for me." It was true.

His antimaterialistic reputation was well earned. He was never a rich man, even at the height of fame. "This house is too fancy for me," he said once, when we were in his room talking. "I bought it for my mother. She supported me when I started to write. I'd rather have a cabin out in the woods." He did not own a car, and there was no telephone in the Kerouac house.

But occasionally Kerouac would worry about money. The sales of his books were up and down, and he was never sure what his income would be. "All the rich kids buy J. D. Salinger in hardback, and what do I get? Bums like you buy one paperback for half a buck and then let ten of your friends read it." I felt guilty hearing this, because I had done the very thing he said. In fact, one of the friends who read my paperback of *On the Road* was Cliff Anderson.

In the summer of 1965, Cliff and I went to Mexico while Jack packed up a bundle of money—enough to last him six months or so, he thought—and went to Paris, where he wrote *Satori [in Paris]*. Before we all left town, I saw Jack at the bus stop near our house. He was on his way downtown (something about his passport) and was wearing his traveling outfit: a new $2 shirt which looked suspiciously as if it would glow in the dark; a pair of woven straw shoes with crepe soles and "plenty of ventilation—good for walking," khaki pants, and an old belt which could easily have circled his waist twice.

About a month or so after we got back from Mexico, Cliff called me to say Jack was back in town too.

"What happened?" I asked Cliff. "I thought he was going to stay for a while and work on the book."

"Oh, he's got the book finished already. He would have stayed in Paris a lot longer but he ran out of money."

"What happened to the money he had when he left? It would have lasted an ordinary man six months or more."

"He says he either lost it or spent it; he doesn't know which. You know how Jack is."

"That crazy Canuck," we both agreed.

I think that associated with Jack Kerouac's antimaterialism was a religious conviction, strong in its intensity if often seemingly absurd to others. It was certainly his own brand of mysticism which combined an affinity for the life and work of Jesus with certain tenets of Buddhism. He used to say, any time he heard a critical remark about Jesus, "Ah, he died for bums like you." On the other hand, he believed that standing on your head was a universal cure for the physical ills of man.

After I had known him awhile, he started burlesquing my West Virginia drawl. But his interpretation sounded more like a movie cowboy than a hillbilly. When the joke finally wore thin, I asked him if it were true that Canucks were built close to the ground to make it easier for them to pick potatoes. That, he said, was getting personal.

Ordinarily he did not advertise the fact that he was *the* Jack Kerouac, the fellow who had written those twenty or so books which had been translated into all those foreign languages. But I remember one occasion particularly, when a girl he had just met said she had never heard of him or his work. He went into a rage and gave her a very heated lecture on the life and times of Jack Kerouac.

Another thing which seemed to bother him, though in a different way—his reaction was more that of a disappointed child—was for a new acquaintance to be familiar with his work but refuse to believe that he was actually Jack Kerouac. "You're not Jack Kerouac." "I am. I really am Jack Kerouac." He stoutly maintained that there were several impostors passing themselves off as Jack Kerouac and they were responsible for his receiving that kind of harassment.

He seldom discussed the mechanics of writing. Writing was a personal matter, a battle he had thrashed out for himself long before. He had a very sincere conviction that he was then the greatest living American writer. His name for his own writing was "time-action prose." A few times he showed me letters, mostly from kids, asking his advice about writing and exhibiting their admiration for him by imitating the freewheeling Kerouac prose style. "These people will never write," he said. "Writers write; they don't ask people how."

His best advice to aspiring writers was to go into another line of work. He would read a piece by a young writer and say, "Writing teachers today don't know how to teach writing. Look. 'He closed the door.' What is that? In a hundred years everybody will write like me."

At that time Jack lived with his mother, who was in her seventies. Mrs. Kerouac still called him "Jackie" and liked to tell stories about him as a little boy, her Ti Jean (little John), in Lowell, Massachusetts, or about her playing piano in the old nickelodeons, which she had done as a young girl.

Sometimes she talked of Gerard, Jack's brother who had died

when only eight or nine. There was a large pencil drawing of Gerard on one wall; he was feeding some birds on the windowsill while a large cat sat beside him, looking on benignly. Mrs. Kerouac said that the cat disappeared the day of Gerard's funeral, and they never saw it again.

There was another rather odd painting hanging in the living room. It had been painted by an artist friend of theirs in New York, and the subject, according to Jack, was his "mother's underwear hanging on a line."

Mrs. Kerouac had no love for the "Beat" crowd that Jack had written so much about. Of one very famous Beat poet,* Mrs. Kerouac said: "If you see him, you are looking at the devil himself. If he takes a drink of water in my house, I break the glass, so no one else will have to use it."

And while Jack was not as overtly hostile toward them as his mother was, he seemed to have no desire to see any of them. He showed me a newspaper clipping, a picture of Allen Ginsberg and Peter Orlovsky picketing to promote the cause of legalized marijuana. "That's all this guy ever does now," Jack said. "He doesn't work any more." The only one he still seemed to have any genuine affection for was Neal Cassady, on whom he had based the character Dean Moriarty in *On the Road*.

The last thing Jack's mother would say as we were going out the door was, "Don't leave him alone anywhere." We used to laugh about his mother's concern. After all, Jack was forty-three. Unfortunately, her point was driven home the hard way. One night when Jack couldn't find any of the usual crowd, he went alone into one of the roughest, meanest bars in St. Petersburg. To my knowledge,

* Allen Ginsberg

nobody ever got the story straight as to what he said or did, but he came away from the excursion with a broken nose and a number of cracked ribs. He recovered from the physical injuries soon enough, but it was several months before he would risk coming out of his house to expose his battered ego again.

One Sunday morning, I was sitting in my room typing a philosophy paper that I had to hand in. My scholastic career had degenerated to the point where it was: Write this paper or else. The "or else" was the prospect of facing the fact I might be forced to seek honest employment. About five minutes after I started to work, Kerouac walked in with two other friends of ours who owned a sailboat. They wanted me to go sailing with them.

This posed not a *di*-but a tri-lemma. Nobody likes to sail better than I do, but I had my orders; my wife had even left me alone and gone to see some friends so that I wouldn't be distracted from writing my idiotic paper. I rejected the first alternative immediately; I obviously would not be able to do any mental work with these three sitting under my nose drinking beer and raising the rafters. That was out—definitely. Secondly, I realized that although my wife is very small, she is also half German, and if she came home and caught me with Kerouac and company, having no paper written, she would in all probability strike me down on the spot, if not killing me, at least maiming me for life. The third alternative was to say *qué será?* And go sailing.

We decided to go sailing. Not, I might add, without my wrestling with my conscience for a good twelve to fifteen seconds.

"Cheer up, Carl," Jack said. I think I must have resembled a condemned man who was having a great deal of difficulty keeping his last meal down. I informed him of the problem.

"You gotta get a job? You want me to write you a recommendation?" Jack said gravely. Before I could even answer, he went over to my typewriter and wound in a clean sheet of paper and tapped out the following:

MEMO

To: Whom it may concern

From: Jack Kerouac the novelist

Carl Adkins is a wonderful human being worthy of anyone's time or money.

"There," he said. So far as he was concerned, there was no longer a problem. "That'll get you a job anywhere in the world." It never occurred to him that there may have been some people in the world who had never heard of him.

Anyway, it was settled. We were off for our day of sailing. But first we had to stop by Kerouac's house to get his brakeman's lantern—for what contingency I could not imagine. Also we received a half-hour's lecture from Jack's mother, which I think she must have delivered in my wife's behalf. We left the house feeling that at best we were in dire peril of being swallowed by a sea monster.

The boat, which was an eighteen-foot corsair, was moored in a slip directly across the street from where they moor the ship that was used in the filming of the Marlon Brando version of *Mutiny on the Bounty*. It is a tourist attraction. We got on board the little sailboat. Kerouac immediately assigned us all seafaring titles. If I remembered correctly, he made himself the "chief boatswain's mate," which I assumed in his mariner's lexicography meant "beer-tender," because that's mainly what he did. We decided to sail around the million-dollar pier (a joke of a kind, if you've ever seen it) and come up on the far side and take a closer look at the *Bounty*, since we were all too cheap to pay admission to see it. In effect, we were sailing a mile and a half to get across the street and save a dollar. But being a quartet of romantic and derring-do fellows, we never gave it a thought.

We had no more than pulled out of the marina, the sails filled with wind, than Kerouac came up to the captain and saluted and said, "Request permission to go ashore, sir." The captain replied quickly in unprintably lucid sailor's language that we had only been under way for five minutes and why didn't he get below and keep his mouth shut!

Consequently, Jack sat in the cabin and sulked for fifteen minutes. The captain relented and apologized. After all, nobody had intended to hurt Jack's feelings. Then he came up top again.

This time he started yelling at the fishermen who were flickering their lines off the side of the pier. Then we ran over an old man's line, and the fisherman started yelling back. Jack started yelling for them to turn the fish loose. "Murderers!" he yelled.

"Crazy people!" Among the fishermen this sentiment seemed unanimous.

"They think we're pirates," Jack said when we got away from them. "They're jealous."

It took a while, but at last we rounded the pier and came in sight of the *Bounty*. Jack was ecstatic. He was on top of the cabin now, yelling at the people on board the *Bounty*.

"Avast there, me hearties! Batten down the mizzen! Belay the bilge, or I'll keelhaul the scurvy lot o' you!" and then to our very able skipper: "Fire a shot across her bow and heave 'er to!"

When we came up beside the *Bounty*, Jack, in the midst of shouting and jumping around, lost his footing and fell into the bay. The corsair we were sailing that day had been raced in the English Channel and was an extremely fast little boat, so we had to make a circle back to pick him up. Jack thought at first we were deserting him and was gurgling through mouthfuls of saltwater that he would have *us* keelhauled along with the scurvy crew of the *Bounty*.

We came by him again and again, and this time, not without great difficulty, pulled him into the boat. Meanwhile, everybody on board the *Bounty* who owned a movie camera had run over to the side and filmed our dramatic sea rescue.

Jack, for his part, drank another can of beer, went down into the cabin where he stretched out in two inches of bilge, and promptly fell asleep.

The excitement seemed to be over, so we sailed back to the slip and tied up. It had taken us approximately an one hour and a half to sail across the street and back. And we had lost one man over-board in the process. Enough sailing for one day.

Somehow it gives me great satisfaction to know that somewhere in this country today somebody is showing his home movies of a boatload of maniacs trying to fish a great French-Canadian man of letters out of the drink, where he is floundering and sputtering like a hopelessly ruptured duck. And I know if Jack were alive, it would give him satisfaction too.

To be with Jack Kerouac for any length of time was a taxing expe-rience, both physically and emotionally. He was himself an extremely emotional man who laughed easily and was almost as easily moved to tears. His behavior, I suppose, would be best com-pared to that of a small child. A reviewer said of *The Vanity of Duluoz*, the last book Jack brought out before his death: "It is the story of a man who has regained his innocence." If I had to define the unique aspect of his personality, the thing that made him Jack Kerouac, the quality which contributed both to his public success and his private agony, I could do it in one word. The word is inno-cence—as far as I'm concerned, he never lost it.

The day we learned of Jack's death, my wife planted some flowers for him on the hillside facing our house. We don't believe in plastic flowers or perpetual care. One morning not long ago, she came to me and said, "Jack's flowers came out today."

With that in mind, when I think of Jack Kerouac, I see him:

Trooping down Ninth Avenue North in St. Petersburg with a rucksack on his back, heading for the library to exchange another load of books.

Sneaking in the back door of the burlesque, as I suppose he had done all his life.

Shooting pool at the Dew Drop. He is yelling, "Gimme a beah!" to celebrate the fact that he has just slopped one in, something he refers to as a "Jesus Christ shot."

Performing his beautifully obscene impression of Bela Lugosi.

Sitting on the floor of the Wild Boar beside the jukebox, listening to Leontyne Price sing operatic arias.

Coming into my house for the first time, looking and sounding more like the double-talking Professor Irwin Corey than the great American novelist; beguiling my children; growling at my door.

And finally this—

He was standing there on the beach with a group of people, talking. There were some kids there who were immersed to their middle-class eyebrows in the Tampa drug scene. One of them asked Jack if he ever turned on with LSD. "What for?" Jack wanted to know. "To expand your consciousness," the kid said.

"If my consciousness were any more expanded, I'd be out there," Jack said. He pointed out across the Gulf of Mexico to the place where the sea touches the sky.

Jack Kerouac: Beat Even in Northport

Mike McGrady, *Long Island Newsday*
(October 25, 1969 and April 19, 1973)

The books about Jack Kerouac are just starting to appear. The first one–*Kerouac* by Ann Charters–has just come out to nice reviews, and I am thinking about reading it.

But I am resisting it. All that holds me back is the fact that I knew Jack Kerouac when he lived in Northport and I am concerned what will happen to him between the covers of a book. The people who knew Jack best–the artist, the architect, the postman, the plumber, a bartender or two–have all been interviewed recently by biographers who are trying to piece together Jack's life, a feat he was never quite able to manage while alive.

The biographers have all been exposed to Jack's dark side. We all saw him drinking beer and playing the coin-operated pool tables at the bars along Main Street. We saw him there late at night, night after night, as dapper as an unmade bed, the sweat rolling from his uncombed hair, and still, no matter the hour, never missing the intent of what you were saying, never ignoring a shade of your meaning.

When Jack Kerouac lived in Northport, I was not one of his

closest friends, possibly because I felt the kind of awe for him that any starling writer should feel for a man able to write *On the Road*. Yet I came to know something of his life, of his way of life, enough to know that with Jack it was often four o'clock in the morning, and a party that should have ended hours or days earlier was kept alive only by his presence, his insistence.

In 1958, Kerouac moved with his mother into a small, not-untypical suburban house on a quiet street. During his first week in Northport, Kerouac came to the conclusion that his house needed a second bathroom. He came to this conclusion after a long night of beer and Scotch; he came to this conclusion at three-thirty in the morning and immediately dialed the telephone number of a local plumber.

"How much would it cost to install a bathroom?" asked Kerouac.

"Who is this anyhow?" the plumber said.

"Jack Kerouac," he said. "How much?"

"I have done it for fifteen hundred dollars," the plumber said. "Do you know what time it is?"

"Time to install a bathroom," Kerouac said. "Fifteen hundred sounds right; come on over."

"All right," the plumber said. "Tuesday."

"Now."

"Now I'm sleeping."

Before the conversation ended, the plumber had been persuaded. He arrived at the Kerouac home before dawn and by late afternoon of the following day had completed his work. I introduce this incident not by way of revealing anything about Kerouac's personality, just by way of noting that Jack Kerouac and I had the same plumber, and that the plumber asked me the following week whether I would like to stop over with him and meet Jack Kerouac some night.

Would I? You have to picture the relationship. At that time I was a freelance writer surviving by the grave of the *Saturday Evening Post* and a local finance firm. Jack Kerouac was then *the* writer of America.

And so one night, in the company of a mutual friend, a plumber, we stopped and paid a call on Jack Kerouac. At first one did not know what to make of the setting. The house was archetypally suburban; the furnishings were early Montgomery Ward; television sets were going on two floors; the kitchen appliances—oven, refrigerator, even sink—were pink; there was an electric fire in the fireplace.

The first picture of Kerouac offered contrast to the environment. There was the four-day-old beard, a sweatshirt that seemed to come down to his knees, paint-splattered black trousers, sandals. The initial impression was one of toughness—the fighter's nose, the thick strand of unbrushed hair, the jewel-cold blue eyes.

But Kerouac then and always was a gentleman. With the wife—with all women—he was courtly in what can almost be described as an old-world manner.

Kerouac seemed most taken by the presence of our six-month-old baby. I can remember him leading us up to his attic study and turning on his elaborate hi-fi equipment, tapes of Chet Baker and Miles Davis, tapes made at private recording sessions. That first night, Kerouac started dancing—first alone in the middle of the room, then holding the baby in his arms. In retrospect, perhaps we should have been concerned about the safety of the baby—but there was no cause for concern; he was as gentle as a woman.

The talk that evening was general, exploratory. I can recall Kerouac often referring to a pocket-sized loose-leaf notebook filled with his notes—quotations from Buddhist literature, the Bible, Walt Whitman. At one point I introduced the thought from *The Book of*

Tao—"Human life in this world is but the form of a white pony flashing across a rock crevice. In a moment it is gone"—and he liked it enough to add it to the book.

Kerouac was asked the standard questions a beginning writer might ask an established writer, *the* established writer.

His method was simplicity itself: he sat down and wrote. The words came out nonstop onto a roll of teletype paper, and when he was through, he didn't rewrite.

But Kerouac was a man of little polish—in his dress, in his speech, in his writing. What he seemed to distrust most were those who were too polished. His friends in Northport were a group of weekend softball players—Larry Smith, an architect; Stan Twardowicz, an artist; Bob Walters, a psychologist; others.

Kerouac was a clown on the softball field—missing a long fly ball, he would suddenly decide to give up the chase and began doing a series of somersaults or backflips. He secretly longed for the end of the contest when everyone would collapse on the infield grass and dig into the six-packs. The conversation never became literary—just a bunch of friends talking about the football Giants, about aching muscles, about women.

The author seemed at his happiest then. Being one of the guys. Taking pains not to interject opinions that would be at variance with the established norms, only occasionally quoting passages from Eastern religions.

In a sense, the Northport years passed and the books continued to come out, but fewer and fewer people took notice of them. Although Kerouac was in the process of creating a substantial body of purely autobiographical literature, he became a favorite target of the critics.

And there were constant interruptions. The kids tracked him

down, of course. College girls would knock on his door and, seeing Jack, older than his sleek book-jacket pictures, they would ask if they might talk to Mr. Kerouac. This happened often and never failed to disappoint him.

"And those crazy boys," his mother would complain, "coming here at all hours of the night."

A steady procession of local youths came to Kerouac's house at night, tossed pebbles against his study window, asked him to come out with them. And always Kerouac would go, out to Teddy's bar and to Gunther's tavern, where he spent long evenings mastering the coin-operated pool table. And always, later, he would complain that it was becoming impossible to work. At one time, in desperation, he put up a cedar fence to keep the uninvited away.

"Jack couldn't cope," Larry Smith was saying the other day.

When he wanted to go downtown, his mother would give him a roll of nickels—two-dollars-worth—and he would try to make it last. He never learned to drive a car, and sometimes his mother would call a taxi to go shopping. If he was going to go somewhere, he would have a neighbor call to make the arrangements.

That weakness enabled you to sympathize with him. Sometimes you resented it, but you felt that you had to help him. He was utterly dependent on people. I remember one night he didn't go home from the bars; the next day we found out he was walking home through the woods and had just decided to stop there and sleep. He did.

Fame began to desert Kerouac. He still gave interviews to reporters. He still told them his philosophy. Still talked about his goals in life: "I would say fun and pity. That's a very good combination. So often the people who have fun have no pity—no compassion. And those who have compassion have no fun. There should be both."

During his last week in Northport, Kerouac suddenly disappeared. One evening he showed up at our house—T-shirt ripped, beard flourishing, a lacework of red. The wife prepared an omelette for him; as always, he was extravagant in his praise. He had come in just short of midnight.

He had decided on a whim to go to Fire Island; he had been wandering from ocean beach to ocean beach trying to persuade the young people that he was Jack Kerouac, the Jack Kerouac. They disbelieved him, and finally someone called the cops, and he was taken in.

"They brought me in," Jack said:

and they thought I was going to start protesting and putting up playing cards and being a big civil rights worker or something. So this one guy says to me, "You're intoxicated apparently." I said, "How can I get intoxicated on beer?" He said, "Well, let's call the lieutenant." That was very interesting. I was quiet. When they walked in, I moved my ass aside and said, "Excuse me," you know, and this guy showed me his badge and said he was the lieutenant. I said, "yeah, I had heard about that." I said I couldn't appear on Saturday morning, and could I send the ten dollar? He said, "Well, you did break the village ordinance against drinking on the street." Then he said, "Okay, send me the ten dollars." And I walked out.

The night before he was scheduled to leave Northport, Kerouac seemed apprehensive. For the first time since his boyhood, in

Lowell, Massachusetts, he had been dug in, rooted, off the road. There were softball games on Sunday, bars with coin-operated pool tables, a select few who would be willing to drink through the dawn with him. The prospect of the morrow—a move to St. Petersburg— was not altogether pleasing. It was a move he was making at the request of his ailing mother.

"There's no throwing beer cans out the window in St. Petersburg," he said that last night. "They've got old ladies walking down the streets at midnight talking to themselves."

But the arrangement had been made. One neighbor had called and made the ticket reservations. Another had completed arrangements with the moving company. The only furniture that Kerouac valued was the cabinet containing his tape recordings.

"Nothing to it," he said. "The movers come in at six o'clock tomorrow morning and I say, 'Hey, mover, take out my goddam million-dollar cabinet there.' Then I just pack up my suitcase. Nothing to worry about."

He was sitting in his bedroom, his hand curled around a can of Bud. That last night in Northport, he was with his few closest friends—Larry Smith and Stan Twardowicz and their wives. The tape recording was Mel Tormé singing "Welcome to the Club." It was suggested in jest that Jack Kerouac consider joining the Navy and seeing the world again; he considered that prospect but couldn't think of an assignment he would enjoy.

"I could be a . . . typist," he decided. "I wouldn't want to stay sober though."

"They've got a journalist's rating," it was suggested.

"Nah, I'm too good to be a journalist."

"But if you're in the service, you've got to be something."

"Yeah, a *general*!" he decided. "Hey, ma, bring me some ice cream."

Anyone intent on charting Kerouac's actual military career might encounter some small difficulties. He attempted to join the Navy—a career that ended abruptly during his boot training at Newport, Rhode Island.

"See, I was marching on the drill field with these guys," he was saying:

and I threw my gun down and went to the library. They said, "What's the matter with you?" I knew what to tell them: perpetual headaches. Then I finally had to tell them down in Bethesda—the naval hospital in Maryland—I had to tell them, it's not that I will not accept discipline; I *cannot*. I didn't like that stuff about I couldn't smoke before breakfast. Every morning the captain comes around, and you have to have everything clean. Field day, my ass!

His stay at Bethesda hospital was not uneventful.

I remember sitting with a schizophrenic by the window. We were singing, harmonizing "Shine on, Harvest Moon." There's another guy sitting in a wheelchair. He has a bandage around his head. He takes a gun and—bam!—the bullet went in one side of his head and out the other. So they came and put another bandage around his head and he kept saying, "Oh dammit!" Just went right through him without killing him. He didn't do it right. I was trying to talk to him: "Hey buddy, how do you feel?"

Following his stay at Bethesda, the Navy presented Kerouac with that he called an Honorable Indifferent Discharge.

"Indifferent, yeah," he said:

I was indifferent. I am indifferent to war. I am not a pacifist.
Just indifferent. They were trying to make me into a Ranger;
they wanted me to swim ashore at night with a dagger between
my teeth and demolish the enemy commandos . . . Actually, I
just don't like that stuff about dressing up and having discipline and stuff.

As it turns out, however, this was not to be the end of Kerouac's
military career. "I joined the Marines, too, you know," he said:

I joined the Marines. They examined me. They looked at my
eyes, my body and all that. Then they said, "You are now a
member of the United States Marines." That night I got drunk.
I met this seaman and we sailed off to Greenland. It's not that
I didn't want to join the Marines; it's just that I found a ship.
For all I know, I'm still a member of the Marines.

The talk went on. Talk about politics, about an unforgettable
black girl in Oakland, about being arrested, about dying.

"You know, there's admiration for your art after you're dead,"
Kerouac said.

"Sympathy anyway."

"Yeah," he said, "they all start crying then."

The next morning at six o'clock, the movers came and crated up
the furniture. Later that day, Larry Smith went by to see that all was
well. He found Jack Kerouac's mother sitting on a bare floor in an
empty room beside a bottle of Scotch, sobbing, Jack had disappeared again. He was found the next day playing pool at Gunther's.

What will the biographers make of this? Well, at least they are coming around to a new respect for his work, something that didn't happen when he was alive. It was what he always missed.

I hope the biographers find the other side of Jack. They are doubtless going to isolate more important events; they will focus on more meaningful moments. His friends in Northport will always remember a less important Kerouac. We are concerned what will happen to Jack between hard covers, and it will take some effort to read the biographies.

Strange Gray Myth of the West

Richard Hill, *L.A. Free Press* (August 7, 1970)

J ack Kerouac loved the West and hated it. He ran to it—and away from it in his mad flights of discovery. He regarded it with Eastern snobbishness and saw it at other times as his only source of spiritual refreshment. He studied it under the tutelage of westerners like Neal Cassady and Gary Snyder and shared many of the secrets he learned with a worldwide audience. The West was part of his work and life.

But when he died, it was in the East—more accurately, in St. Petersburg, Florida, the elephant's graveyard of the East. Clearly he was dying when we met. He sat in an early American rocker with stack of *National Reviews* by his side, sipping Scotch from a pill bottle and chasing it with beer. "Don't go West, Hilly," he said. "Especially to L.A. It'll ruin you."

Ironic advice, since it had been Kerouac, years before I'd meet him, who'd given me the westering itch. I'd grown up in that city of funeral homes and plaster flamingos, hating it most of the time and yearning for THERE, or really for anything else. I'd read Jack in high school, coming home nights drunk on beer to read about his THERE in *On the Road, The Dharma Bums, The Subterraneans*, and the others. For years I'd planned the big move, and now that I was going, really going, here was Sal Paradise, Ray Smith, Jack Duluoz, all names of roman candle Jack Kerouac, telling me *not to go*.

"Jesus, Jack, why?" I asked.

"I told you it would ruin you," he said, and implied himself with a gesture as example.

"But it might also save me, or might do nothing."

Jack looked then like an exasperated father. Obviously I was not going to take his word for it, just as he had never taken anybody's word for anything but had to experience it. I was going right ahead with my plans, fatherly advice notwithstanding, and it made him sad to see it. Why couldn't they listen?

As I said, ironic. But this is not a story of Jack's conservatism, or his rejection of earlier values and friends, or even of his last days. That's been written about elsewhere. It's enough to say that Jack had returned, physically and spiritually and philosophically, to the East. He was living quietly with his third wife, Stella, and his crippled mother. He had accepted conservative political and social attitudes. He had embraced the Catholic Church of his childhood. He was spinning genealogical cobwebs about the Kerouac family.

But he was still Jack Kerouac, which meant he still loved to talk. He was bellicose at times, jumping to his feet to shout and pace the room when it seemed we were refusing to understand him. He had been isolated for a long time before we began visiting, and he was venting frustrations built over that period. But he was also willing to listen, sometimes even to change his opinions. And once the shouting was over, you knew you were having one of the best conversations of your life.

Stella was glad to see it. "He hasn't had many visitors lately, and it's good for him to be with friends again. He says he doesn't want to be bothered, but he's lonely." And once the three or four of us became regular visitors, Jack was angry when we didn't come often enough to suit him. "Boswell was with Johnson all the goddamn time," he said. "How do you guys expect to write about me if you never come over?" Two of us were writers, and that had been the original idea of the visits–to write about Jack. Jack McClintock and I eventually did write about him, when his death seemed to make that painful and ghoulish job necessary. But that was usually far from our minds. After the first visit, we were there as friends. We knew and Jack knew that he was dying, and there was a great deal to say. Much of it concerned the West, where I was determined to go.

"Of all the goddamn places to go, Hilly, you gotta go to L.A. Hasn't anybody told you about that place?"

Of course everybody had, including Jack. I remembered his lines from *On the Road*:

L.A. is the loneliest and most brutal of American cities. New York gets godawful cold in the winter but there's a feeling of wacky comradeship somewhere in some streets. L.A. is a jungle . . . the beatest characters in the country swarmed on the sidewalks–all of it under those soft Southern California stars that are lost in the brown halo of the huge desert encampment L.A. really is.

L.A. was cruel and plastic, and how ironic to find such coldness in such a warm, lovely setting, and all the other clichés. "L.A. break down and let me in." "Do you know the way to San Jose?" I knew all those numbers. Practically everybody had written about it and practically everybody agreed. Scott Fitzgerald, Nathaniel West, Evelyn

Waugh, Tom Wolfe. Jack was only repeating the cliché when he wrote of "handsome queer boys who had come to Hollywood to be cowboys" and of the L.A. cops who "looked like handsome gigolos."

I didn't doubt the cliché. Nor did I doubt the honesty of Jack's reactions to it. I remembered that sad passage in *The Dharma Bums* in which he wrote, "The smog was heavy, my eyes were weeping from it, the sun was hot, the air stank, a regular hell is L.A."

But his and other reactions were those of Easterners, whose opinions had been formed before television had spread its plastic culture—largely from L.A.—across the land. I had grown up in that culture and was much less ashamed of it. I had seen the old booze-Bohemian sensibility of the East and of San Francisco dying while people of my generation picked up on new lifestyles made chiefly in Southern California. A writer friend told me "We can spot Easterners right away. They're always bunched up around the bar, drinking and talking. Californians are more likely to do things." I found myself in the middle, yet I wanted to see more before I made any choice.

How to explain that to Jack? How to say I would dig seeing Hollywood because its phoniness was part of my reality? They were making reality out there and I wanted to be in on it. I tried.

"The hell with the bright lights of Hollywood," Jack roared. Then he smiled and looked boyish again.

"I remember being on the *Steve Allen Show* in Burbank. Beautiful Downtown Burbank," he said, contemptuously. He told of Allen's efforts to get him to rehearse his reading. "I told him I couldn't do it, and went across the street to get drunk. But I showed up in time for the show and did my reading all right. It was terrible, though, to have to do. I wrote about that in *Big Sur*."

But hadn't Allen done a good thing in having him on? I

remembered how many jazz musicians I'd seen on his show as a lad. I could never have seen them otherwise.

"Sure, he's great," said Jack. "But I couldn't stand it. I didn't like being on Buckley's show either, and he's my hero. I got so drunk before that he postponed the show and took me into his office for coffee. He told me if I didn't straighten up he'd cancel it. I went out and gave Ginsberg the raspberry. He was in the audience."

Jack had to be drunk to face an audience. Unlike Ginsberg, he had never become a good mass-media performer—a fact which surely contributed to his resentment of his old friend. Unlike Ken Kesey, he had never tried to play his pranks on a national scale. He was Eastern, reserved, surprisingly faceless in his novels. Jack never really wanted the leadership and reputation assigned him by the media, sensing early that it would hurt him.

Jack met Kesey in New York, after running from coast to coast all those years. Kesey was on his own trip by then. Tom Wolfe describes the encounter in his *Electric Kool-Aid Acid Test:*

> Kesey and Kerouac didn't say much to each other. Here was Kerouac and here was Kesey, and here was Cassady in between them, once the mercury for Kerouac and the whole Beat Generation and now the mercury for Kesey and the whole—what?— something wilder and weirder out on the road. It was hail and farewell. Kerouac was the old star. Kesey was the wild new comet from the west heading Christ knew where.

The East, says Wolfe, had rejected the American trip, while the West had picked it up. The Eastern intellectuals still looked across the Atlantic and to the Far East for a simpler, more "tasteful" lifestyle, while Kesey, Cassady, and other Westerners embraced

American gadgetry and made it part of their lives. Kesey had been Captain America long before Peter Fonda was.

Jack had obviously rejected all that, losing at the same time his Western friend Cassady, who had gotten Jack onto the road in the first place.

"Kesey ruined Cassady," Jack told me. "Ruined him with acid and all that artificial, goofy, electronic stuff. But Neal's not dead. He'll show up some day and we'll go someplace."

Cassady had gone on Kesey's "Western" trip and had died in Mexico, leaving Jack with a ravaged liver in the graveyard of the East.

So he was bitter. But he could also speak of the West with love. And you find passages like this, from *On the Road*, in which he seemed to recognize even the lure of Los Angeles. "I love the way everybody says L.A. on the coast; it's their one and only golden town, when all is said and done."

But Jack was especially drawn to northern California. It was there he met and joined the San Francisco poets—Allen Ginsberg, Lawrence Ferlinghetti, Gregory Corso, Michael McClure, and Gary Snyder. He went mountain climbing with Snyder, discussed Buddhism with him and Ginsberg, assumed a kind of wacky leadership of what newspapers were to call the Beat Generation. He went to the Northwest for a summer as a Forest Service lookout, spent the time meditating alone atop a mountain. For a while that peaceful Buddhist knowledge had sustained him. He wrote tenderly of those days in *The Dharma Bums*.

"Those were good times," he told me:

That was before I got famous. I wasn't drinking much then, though most of them thought I was drinking too much. I didn't see why booze and Buddhism couldn't mix. But it didn't last.

On the Road made me famous, and then everybody started
coming around waiting for me to do something. Ginsberg
became a performer for the goddamn hippies, but I got drunk.

Fame shattered the serenity he'd found on that Western trip. He
went back to Long Island to live with his mother. "Kids used to
jump fences to try to see me, expecting a twenty-six-year-old hipster
who'd just quit what he was doing and take a trip with them. Some
guys came one night with jackets that had "Dharma Bums" painted
on them. Jesus, I couldn't take it."

So he went West, as he usually did when "the weird dark myth of
the East" became oppressive. He headed for "the strange gray myth
of the West," and, as usual, found there a reflection of his own state
of mind.

"The idea," Jack said, "was to find some of the peace I had in that earlier summer. I thought if I could live incognito in Ferlinghetti's cabin in
Big Sur, I could be all right again. But you read that, I guess, in *Big Sur.*"
I had, but I said I hadn't so he'd talk about it. Jack never minded if you
said you hadn't read his books. That gave him a chance to talk about
what was in them, and what was in them were the important things of
his life. "I don't write fiction," he told me. "I write only the truth."
Because he wrote only what happened to him, he pushed his hero, Jack
Kerouac, too hard. "If you don't think I did all that stuff, look at me," he
said, looking gray and old, then smiling and rubbing his feet on the
carpet so that he looked twenty-five again.

When he got like that, we forgot that he was going to die. "Let's
get up a party," he would say. But Stella would look at us mean-
ingfully, and we'd try to think of some excuse. He'd been beaten
up in a Negro bar a few weeks earlier and still had symptoms of
a concussion. He had a hernia he'd gotten from exercising—the

hernia that would burst soon and kill him, because the doctors couldn't stop the bleeding, and the liver was so weak from drinking. So we'd resist the temptation and listen.

"Anyway, it didn't work out," he said:

In the first place I didn't keep it a secret and got drunk all around San Francisco. When I did get out to Big Sur, it was more scary than peaceful. Christ, how come people don't talk about how scary that place is? At least it was for me, but maybe I'd have been scared anywhere just then.

Big Sur was the crucial book in Jack's chronicle. It was the book in which his drinking, his hangover paranoia that his friends were using him, destroyed the old ties with the West. The seeds of reaction were already sown; they blossomed one morning at Big Sur when, after a night of alcoholic terror, Jack saw his vision of the True Cross.

For a moment I see blue Heaven and the Virgin's white veil, but suddenly a great evil blur like an ink spot spread over it. "The devil!–the devil's coming after me tonight! That's that!"– But the angels are laughing and having a big barn dance in the rocks of the sea, nobody cares any more–Suddenly as clear as anything I ever saw in my life, I see the Cross.

Ironically, it was on the raw edge of the West that Jack saw his final Eastern vision. In the last lines of *Big Sur* he says:

I'll get my ticket and say goodbye on a flower day and leave all San Francisco behind and go back home across autumn America and it'll all be like it was in the beginning . . . And it will be golden and eternal just like that—There's no need to say another word.

Most of what Jack wrote and said about the West after that was nostalgia. Although he never completely abandoned his friends of those Western years, he wasn't sure he understood them any more. "I don't know what Ginsberg is doing," he told me. "He's hurting the kids who listen to him. Sometimes I think the movement we started has been taken over by the Communists. All this stuff with acid scares me. Turn on your mind, they say. I've been trying to turn mine off."

Jack was trying to turn off whole areas of his past, trying to order his life around family and faith. That part of it was sad, except when he forgot and was the old Jack for a while. In the weeks before he died, he seemed more tolerant of other opinions and told Al Ellis, a law student friend, that he was going to put aside political bickering. After his long isolation, he had a phone installed. The week before he died, he chased away some young fascists who had read an article of his called "After Me, the Deluge," in the *Chicago Tribune* and had come by to compliment him on his anticommunism. "I told 'em I was a pacifist," Jack said. "And that I had a gun in the other room. I defended this country against people like them."

Then he died, and those who had known or admired him wondered how to assess his life. Did it matter about his crankiness toward the end? Did it make any difference that Jack was only human and could deal with less experience as he grew older—that he had narrowed his scope after trying to embrace all of America? Not when you considered what he had done.

And what could we do to recognize his life? Thousands attended the funeral in Lowell, Massachusetts. People who had never met him attended the smaller ceremony in St. Petersburg. Writers who had and who hadn't known him tried to say what he had meant to them. Ginsberg carved his name in a tree. And I made my first trip West—because of, despite, and for Jack.

I didn't stay long—only two months. I was excited and disappointed. I wondered, like Jack, why nobody seemed to drink much, and drunk too much myself. Much of what he said I found true, some of it I liked anyway, as I thought I would.

It won't be my last trip. Somehow it's still a valid thing to do, to travel like that back and forth and try to understand how both origin and destination are reconcilable, part of the same whole.

Coming back into Florida, I remembered a line from an article Jack had done called "The Great Western Bus Ride."

"Old Eastern sadness returned to me," he wrote. "But I had seen the West."

David Amram Remembers

David Amram, *Evergreen Review* (October 24, 1969)

I used to see Jack often at the old Five Spot in the beginning of 1957, when I was working there. I knew he was a writer, and all musicians knew that he loved music. You could tell by the way he sat and listened. He never tried to seem hip. He was too interested in life around him to ever think of how he appeared. Musicians understood this and were always glad to see him, because we knew that meant at least one person would be I listening. Jack was on the same wavelength as we were, so it was never neccssary to talk.

A few months later, poets Howard Hart and Philip Lamantia came by my place with Jack. They had decided to read their poetry with music, and Jack said he would join in, reading, improvising, rapping with the audience and singing along. Our first performance was in December of 1957 at the Brata Art Gallery on East 10th Street. It was the first jazz-poetry reading in New York. There was no advertising and it was raining, but the place was packed. Jack had become the most important figure of the time. His name was magic. In spite of the carping, whining put-downs by the furious critics and the jealousy of some of his contemporaries for his overnight success (he had written ten books in addition to *On the Road* with almost no recognition), Jack hadn't changed. But people's reaction to him was sometimes frightening.

He was suddenly being billed as the "King of the Beatniks," and manufactured against his will as some kind of public guru for a movement that never existed. Jack was a private person, extremely shy, and dedicated to writing. When he drank, he became much more expansive, and this was the only part of his personality that became publicized. The people who came to the Brata Gallery weren't tastemakers; they were friends.

A few months later, we began some readings at the Circle in the Square. Everyone improvised, including the light man, who had his first chance to wail on the lighting board. The audience joined in, heckling, requesting Jack to read parts of *On the Road*, and asking him to expound on anything that came into his head. He also would sing while I was playing the horn, sometimes making up verses. He had a phenomenal ear. It was like playing duets with a great musician.

Jack was proud of his knowledge of music and of the musicians of his time. He used to come by and play the piano by ear for hours. He had some wonderful ideas for combining the spoken word with music. A few weeks later, jazz-poetry became "Official Entertainment" and a few months later was discarded as another bit of refuse, added to the huge mound of our junk culture. It was harder to dispose of Jack. The same journalist and radio and TV personalities who had heralded him were now ripping him to shreds. Fortunately, they couldn't rip up his manuscripts. His work was being published, more widely read, and translated.

In early 1958, all of us went to Brooklyn College, where Jack, Philip, and Howard read. Jack spent most of the time answering the student's questions with questions of his own. He was the down-home Zen master, and the students finally realized he wasn't putting them on. He was showing them himself. If they wanted to meet the author Jack Kerouac, they would have to read his books.

His public appearances were never to promote his books. They were to share a state of mind and a way of being. The only journalist who picked up on this was Al Aronowitz. He saw Jack as an artist.

In the spring of 1959, the film *Pull My Daisy* was made. Allen Ginsberg, Gregory Corso, Peter Orlovsky, Larry Rivers, and myself–the Third Avenue All-Stars, as one wit described us–appeared in it. Alfred Leslie directed it, and Robert Frank filmed it. Jack had written the scenario, and after the film had been edited, Jack saw it. Because it was a silent movie, Jack was to narrate it, and I was to write the music afterwards. He, Allen, and Neal Cassady also wrote the lyrics for the title song, "Pull My Daisy," for which I wrote the music and which was sung in the film by Anita Ellis. Jack put on earphones and asked me to play so that he could improvise the narration to music, the way we had done at our readings. He watched the film and made up the narration on the spot. He did it two times through spontaneously, and that was it. He refused to do it again. He believed in spontaneity, and the narration turned out to be the very best thing about the film. We recorded it at Jerry Newman's studio. Jerry was an old friend of Jack's from the early forties, and afterwards we had a party-jam session that lasted all night. Jack played the piano, sang, and improvised for hours.

In the early sixties, I used to see Jack when he would come in from Northport to visit town. Once, he called up at one in the morning and told me I had to come over so that he could tell me a story. I brought over some music to copy, and Jack spoke nonstop until 8:30 A.M., describing a trip he had made through North Africa and Europe. It was like hearing a whole book of his being read aloud, and Jack was the best reader of his own work, with the exception of Dylan Thomas, that I ever heard.

"That's a fantastic story." I told him. "It sounds just like your books."

"I try to make my writing sound just the way I talk." he said. His ideal was not to display his literary skill but to have a conversation with the reader.

I told Jack about an idea I had for a cantata about the four seasons in America, using the works of American authors. He launched into a travelogue of his voyages around the country, and referred to writers I might look into. I took notes and ended up reading nearly fifty books to find the texts. I included a passage from his book *Lonesome Traveller*. The concert was at Town Hall [in New York City], and Jack wrote that he couldn't come. It was the spring of 1965, and he didn't like being in New York.

Sometimes he would call from different parts of the country just to talk, and we continued to write to each other. In one letter he said, "Ug-g-h. Fame is such a drag." He wanted time to work but found that success robbed him of his freedom. At the same time, he felt that he was forgotten. I told him that all the young people I met when I toured colleges loved his books. To many, he was their favorite writer. But "writer" meant something different now. It was what was being said, not how it was said. It was content that counted, not style. Jack's message was a whole way of being, and he was becoming more an influence than ever.

Truman Capote dismissed Jack's work as "typing." I never heard Jack put down another writer. He went out of his way to encourage young writers. His work reflects this spirit of generosity, kindness, and love. This is why his "typing" is so meaningful to young people today. Jack was ahead of his time spiritually. Like Charlie Parker, Lenny Bruce, and Lord Buckley, his work is constantly being rediscovered.

Through knowing Jack, I wrote some of my best music. Without knowing him, I never would have written my book. More important, young people all over the world are reading and rereading his work. His death only means the beginning of a new life for everyone who shares in the joy of knowing him through his books.

Gone in October

John Clellon Holmes, from *Gone in October:*
Last Reflections on Jack Kerouac (Limberlost Press, 1985)

Journal–Oct. 21, 1969–12:45 P.M.–Old Saybrook Jack is dead in St. Pete. I was reading about him in an old journal when Shirley called out from downstairs, having heard it on the radio. There were the bad moments waiting for a repeat of the newscast; there were the waves of awareness coming up and receding . . . I have always addressed my sentences to him, to his canny eye, and it will be different to write from now on . . . Allen G. called. By happenstance, he will be in New Haven tomorrow, and we will go down. "He didn't live much beyond Neal," Allen said as a matter of interest. "Only a year and a half." . . . I spoke to Gregory and Peter too–they were all at the Cherry Valley farm . . . We wired Memere and Stella–useless words. Portents of his death somewhere, sometime, have plagued me for 8–10 years–as recently as last Thursday I thought of him dying in St. Louis or Chicago on some Kerouac-crazy trip . . . I haven't dared think of his mind in his last hours. What can one say? He's gone. It's over for him.

One

Shirley and I drive down to New Haven for Ginsberg's reading at Yale under clear, high skies of blue. The trees had turned in the last days to full autumn, and the afternoon before (walking the fact into consciousness), I'd thought that it was apt that Jack had gone away in October, which was his favorite month, and that now it was one of those red-and-gold New England afternoons through which footballs used to loft in such brave arcs when we were young.

No more Jack, I repeated to myself as I drove, his death a fact too inexplicable, too final to go down. I'd known him for half my life. Whatever sort of man and writer I'd become was due in no small measure to our friendship. As young men, we had shared those important, exuberant years that sometimes shape the rest of life. Damn him! I caught myself thinking. Why does he do things like this? I'd talked to him for an hour on the phone not ten days ago, and we had bickered as we often did when he was drunk, and he had challenged me to call him back in an hour, and I hadn't done it, exasperated by his boozy monologues. And now the phone was permanently dead.

We parked near the Yale Co-Op and walked through chilly streets to the Political Union Library, where the students were holding a reception for Allen. In a paneled upstairs room, twenty or thirty young people, drinking port and sherry, sat on the floor around the ringleted, Karl Marx beard spread out benignly on Allen's chest, and his dome of balding forehead gave him the look of a worldly Talmud scholar who had retired to the Negev. Gregory squatted on his heels in an enormous George Raft overcoat, working on a tumbler of sherry, and Peter, now become a grizzled wrangler of bitter winters in upstate New York, stared silently out from under the three-inch brim of a hat of Day-Glo red. It was the first time that we had all been in the same room in over five years.

In the middle of a long answer about ecology, Allen waved, and Gregory came over, whispering, "What a time to get together, huh?" Allen finished, and he and Peter worked their way through the crowd of students, and we embraced. "I hardly recognized you in your tweedy-professor disguise," Allen said, though actually I had on a red flannel shirt and a corduroy suit. "Well, old Jack's dead, I guess," he added, and we looked at one another, wordless with the fact.

"Yup."

We straggled through the evening streets toward dinner with some of the students, arranging that the three of them would drive home with us that night, and we'd all go up to Lowell the next day for the funeral. Then on to the reading, which was held in a large, dingy, high-ceilinged hall, already filled with young people in their army jackets, beards, ragged blue jeans, maidenly falls of hair, love beads, and peace amulets—the army of the war against death-drive in the modern world, which, for some of us, had already been going on for two decades. We were taken down front to wait, and there on the stage was a paper banner, twelve by four feet in size, on which was written: "IN MEMORIAM: Jack Kerouac, 1922–1969," and below that: "Neal Cassady, 1927–1968."

Allen and Peter came down the side aisle and up onto the stage with their harmonium, where they removed their jackets to get down to work. Gregory, who was down in the audience with us, filmed all this with an expensive, zoom-lensed movie camera and glistening tripod (he was into film now; he filmed bits and pieces of everything; he was making a record of his existence). Allen introduced us all from the stage, and the reading started. "We'll begin with a prayer," he said, and he and Peter began chanting a sutra, Jack's sutra, the Diamond, standing together in their shirts, Peter palming the bellows of the harmonium with the metronomic motion of a weaver with his beater, and both wailing the clear, high-pitched chant, which was followed by a scatter of applause from the perplexed, politicized students, who expected something more inflammatory or more "relevant." Allen was quietly remonstrative. "You don't have to applaud a prayer," he said.

Then he read three or four choruses from Jack's *Mexico City Blues*, repeating the 211th Chorus, "The wheel of the quivering meat conception," because of the lines:

Poor! I wish I was free
of that slaving meat wheel
and safe in heaven dead

He repeated this three times for emphasis, as if to say: "See, there's your politics, that's your art, that's your reality, that was life to him." Then he read the last Chorus with some deliberation:

Vanish.
Which will be your best reward,
T'were better to get rid o
John O'Twill, then sit-a-mortying
In this Half Eternity with nobody
To save the old man being hanged
In my closet for nothing
And everybody watches
When the act is done—
Stop the murder & the suicide!
All's well!
I am the Guard

Perhaps no one on the outside of Jack's life ever really understood these lines, but years ago they had made me realize he didn't want to stay in such a world, and even say as much in *Nothing More to Declare*, and have him chide me about putting him in his grave.

After this, Allen read for almost an hour out of his own poems, mostly from *Planet News*, the ones addressed to Jack, those couched as questions, particularly one entitled, "Why Is God Love, Jack?" with its stubborn celebratory end:

Seeking still seeking the
thrill–delicious
bliss in the
heart abdomen loins
& thighs
Not refusing this
38 yr. 145 lb. head
arms & feet of meat
Nor one single Whitmanic
toenail condemn
nor hair prophetic banish
to remorseless Hell,
Because wrapped with machinery
I confess my ashamed desire.

The kids were now a little less confused, they had been absorbed into the poetry by Allen's quiet austerity and were having a political experience after all, and Allen went on, losing some, making no comment, but working on the remnant, knowing what he was about.

Then he said: "I've been setting some of Blake's poems to music, and Peter and I will sing a few after we take ten minutes off, so John

Holmes can hear them," and after the break they both turned to look down at me, Allen smiling with the healing euphoria of song, having been able to add something at last to our old master, Blake— if it was only these incantatory, Hebraic, singsong melodies that piped so wild.

When they were done, Allen opened it up to questions from the audience, and the questions weren't too silly, just a little solemn, with the "nonnegotiable" Puritanism of kids that year, who seemed so hungry for confrontation that it suggested a psychic rather than a political need, and who often didn't seem to realize that all radical politics are a response to a spiritual crisis—or, as Ginsberg believes, it's all your own Being. You're not separate from the process you wish to change, much less from the older processes of Nature. It's all of us—aphids, Nixon, buffaloes, Dylan—all together in the eco-logical twilight.

Then a blond kid got up, somewhat shy, bespectacled, grave, and confused, and stumbled out that he thought they'd like to know what Allen thought about Kerouac's death, and where Jack fit into the scene today, and why he seemed to have drifted off into curious cranky ideas in recent years, and should they care about him. Was he—well, *important*? They couldn't say. Would Allen?

Allen sighed and leaned on the lectern toward the microphone on his elbows, and didn't say anything for fifty seconds. I knew what he was thinking: How did you sum it up in a few glib words? How could you bring back the eager Jack, Jack of the tender eyes, the rau-cous Jack of midnights, Jack's earnest sweatmaddening Jack of the end of the nights, maudlin Jack of all the songs, the Jack who knew for sure, canny Jack who trusted to his whims, Jack simple as a corn-flower, fist-proud Jack, the bongo-Jack of saucepans, Jack of the Chi-nese restaurants, Jack mooning under streetlamps about guilt, the

Jack of Jacks?—when all they probably knew anything about was drunken, contentious Jack, bigoted, mind-stormed Jack, the Jack of sneers, the boozy bum of Buckley, the imitator of Stepin Fetchit who wrote all those unreadable books and somehow now appeared to have drunk a hole in his Balzac-belly. How could you? No way.

But Allen gathered his thoughts and leaned closer to the mike, and simply said: "Well, he was the first one to make a new crack in the consciousness," and everything else—pot, rock, doin' your thing, make a new Jerusalem, et cetera, had come out of that crack. "Years ago, he rolled around on my floor, laughing his head off at something I'd said, and said, 'Allen, you're a hairy loss,' and I concluded he was only drunk again, but then, of course, I am, that's what I am. I admitted it a few years ago. And you see, he knew that—like he knew that he was only a lonesome, self-absorbed Canuck, a big dumb Dharma bum," and what he had done was to try to follow the implications of this said-comic view of things down to the bottom of his own nature, and transcribe it in its own onrushing spontaneous flow, and leave it there for later, for others.

"So he drank himself to death," Allen said bluntly, "which is only another way of living, of handling the pain and foolishness of knowing that its all a dream, a great, baffling, silly emptiness, after all." And then abruptly he said nothing more.

There were a few more questions, and then he read "Wales Visitation" (his ecology revelation of 1967, in which the simple oneness of all organic life had come home to him on acid), after which he and Peter did Hare Krishna for an end, and, lo and behold, most of these politicized kids joined in—the girls swaying to the chant and staring pensively inward, the young, solemn faces of the boys washed of schismatic bad trips for that moment, everyone chanting softly, abashedly in that large, echoing auditorium, everyone standing up toward the finish, and then drifting away when it was over. We milled around, waiting for Allen to get free of those special few who always pass you notes after an appearance, notes that read: "The Age of Aquarius is here, I am into the realms of light, come and use me for anything." Or: "If you are ever near Santa Fe, look up So-and-so, she's So-and-so's cousin, and she's one of us." Or: "Could I send you my poem that I wrote coming off Speed on Saturday, Oct. 10, 1968, when I discovered that I am a flea in God's whisker?"

Allen had to go tape an interview for the university radio station, so Gregory and Shirley and I went to clean out the dormitory room they had been assigned but wouldn't need now. As we hurried through the bitter-cold New Haven streets, struggling with the heavy camera and tripod, Gregory said: "They always keep you talking that way, like they never had anyone they could really talk to, but I say to them, 'Listen, I was born when people smoked straights and drank booze. Let me have a drink and I'll noodle your doodle, or save your soul—whatever you're after—,'" laughing in a breathless, delighted little cackle, which, the next day, driving to Lowell, I would hear from the backseat—heh-heh-heh-heh-heh-heh—and realize, "By God, it's Jack's laugh, Gregory laughs like Jack now, modestly, as at some private thought, *happy*." I'd forgotten Jack's old laugh, he hadn't laughed that way much in recent years, not that soft *heh-heh-heh* of pleasure, and I remembered it without a pang.

We went through shadowy quads as icy as your winter nose-tip, shrouded students hurrying home under old elms, and up into the dorm to collect their stuff: Gregory's camera case, a suitcase of what Jack used to call "needments," a green sports shirt and a pair of jockey shorts drying on the venetian blind. Shirley made us a bourbon in the single tooth glass, and we sipped it while Gregory told us about how they had gone out into the upstate woods after they heard the news about Jack, just the day before, all of them up in Cherry Valley, and carved Jack's initial into a tree—"You know, in the name of American poetry."

We struggled all the baggage down into my car and then walked down the block to the radio station, where Allen sat in a smoke-bleared recording booth with seven or eight student-activists, patiently going into his sixth straight hour of talk. Gregory and I went in for a minute to be interviewed too, but of course the three of us kept drifting into personal things, having had no real chance till then—such as how the rainwater runs down the stone embankments in Eureka Springs, Arkansas, and how, yes, we'd all been there, though never together, and it was where Carry Nation conducted her last campaign against drink. The young men seemed bewildered by this, and one of them finally said: "Why do you guys always talk about where people are from and what happened there? Does all that really matter?" How to explain.

It was too hot in the booth, and Shirley and Gregory and I went into another room and waited, and finally Allen got free, and we piled into the car, and circled the large, deserted green with its row of ghostly churches, and got onto the Connecticut Turnpike, and talked about Jack at last: "Isn't it weird?" Allen kept saying, "What are we all doing here? Do you know why he drank like that, John? I don't understand *that* kind of drinking . . . But what did we do wrong? Do you think we should have made a greater effort to get down to Florida? Could we have *done* anything?"

I didn't think so. There was nothing one friend could do for another but accept his nature wholeheartedly, and in the last few months, during those endless phone calls at unlikely hours that had become a habit with Jack, I had heard the booze speaking out of him like the voice of one of those baleful spirits that take possession of the soul in Gothic novels. But we had been far too close for the admonishments that are possible in shallower relationships. I knew he was serious, even about his dissipations, and the basic seriousness of a man's struggle with his destiny is beyond "help."

We drove the thirty-five miles home to Saybrook in the dark and cold, stars pin-bright like so many stars on so many driving nights when we had all gone somewhere for forgotten reasons, full of expectations when we climbed into the car, only to become quenched and ruminant as the hours went by in the huge, graphic winter night. Home to a fire, an immense bowl of Shirley's vegetable soup for famished Allen (who'd quit smoking), and whiskey for the rest of us.

Gregory had a bad toothache, and Peter kept scolding him for being chary of the dentist. "You'll have to go through life in your gums," he said—Peter now ran the farm, planted gardens, milked cows, drove tractors, cooked, said they ought to sell that spavined horse "who just stands around"; and Peter who, the next morning, went all over our old house asking questions about how I'd raised "that beam there," was it hard cutting the fireplace opening, laying the hearth, getting it to draw? How much were our heat bills? Did okra come up this year? How did we keep vegetables through the winter? The practical, rural Peter with his repeated, "Uh-*huh*," at everything anyone said, which meant: Yes, yes, okay, I get that, go on, uh-*huh*.

We all went off to bed eventually, all of us dead out, Allen saying as he glanced around my shelves: "Well, you have all of Jack's books, I see. I keep lending mine away and I haven't got them anymore. Now I'll have to sit down and read them again, I guess,"—a funny, private little laugh admitting the ambiguities of the emotions at such a moment. Bone-tired, smoked-out, I had one more booze, but began to think, so didn't finish it, and slept the sleep of a hoarder of resources.

Two

Up to the russets and ochers of an October day through which leaves scattered into bright drifts, a day that was bland in the sun but hinted at winter once you stepped out of it. I went off to get the car's broken heater fixed, which proved impossible on such short notice, but I got extra antifreeze anyway, in case we had a sudden drop of temperature overnight. When I got back, we all sat around, while Shirley made biscuits and fresh coffee, and ranged far afield in our separate intelligences.

At some remark of Gregory's, Allen launched into a description of the Gnostic theory of the universe. The basic idea (he explained) was that the Creation was only the first instant of the Void's awareness of itself, from which original act of consciousness all successive enlayerings of consciousness had come, each covering up the insight of the other, but all seeking to hide the knowledge of the perfect emptiness of origins (the snake-in-the-garden itself sent to tip us off to this truth), and from that, of course, the Western idea of evil had inevitably come.

"And you see, Jack knew all that," Allen said, "That's what he was writing about—the agony of differentiated consciousness. He knew it was all a dream."

"Still, he was stuck in it," Gregory said, "just like all of us."

It didn't seem unusual to be establishing a metaphysical ground from which to think about Jack's death. Simple sorrow for the friend was a private matter, an individual loss, but what he had been trying to say, the world of his unique eye, the still point toward which all the words were aimed, seemed necessary to know with some clarity that crisp October morning, when at last we would all go to Lowell together. At one time or another, each of us had talked with Jack about doing it and made impromptu plans, only to lose them in a fume of booze or distraction, and only Allen had ever made it for a night or two a few years before.

Over the coffee and biscuits, my mother arrived with maps to show me the quick route to Maine that would take us right by Lowell, and Allen put his arm around her in simple creaturely friendliness as she drew it out, though they hadn't seen one another in fourteen years, and then we all sat down for a while and talked—organic gardening, root cellars, Scott Nearing,* the properties of *bancha* tea. Gregory wanted to take movies of us all, and so we went out in front of the house in the cold sun and lined up like members of The Band, Allen saying of my mother, "Behold, the survivor!" at which her eyes moistened, because she had known Jack for a long time and, like most mothers, thought of him as a gifted but unruly man in whom she glimpsed the loyal and affectionate son.

But it was time to go, and we took off up the Connecticut Turnpike through rolling hills, as richly mottled with autumn foliage as the texture of a parti-colored sponge, the car's rear end slewing around with all the added weight, and the wind coming so strong across the highway that my wrists ached holding the car on the road. After a while, Allen and Peter got out the harmonium and sang

---

* Scott Nearing (1883–1983) was a peace activist, conversationist, and writer of the book (co-written with his wife, Helen) *Living the Good Life: How to Live Sanely and Simply in a Troubled World* and an influential pamphlet, *The Great Madness*, that documented the commercial causes and outcome of war.

for an hour, Allen saying, "What would you like to hear next? 'London'? Yes, we've done that," and they performed it. "All right, what's next? Call out your favorites . . . No, I'm leaving 'Tyger, Tyger' to the last because it's the most obvious and hardest to do . . ."

The car rocked with wind and wailing voices as we rolled through little towns like Oxford, the birthplace of Clara Barton. (It makes you remember it, kids. It marks it indelibly in your head. You think of her *there*.) And Webster, full of crazy, every-man-for-himself Massachusetts drivers, imperiling our carload of poets. I thought it might take us three and a quarter hours to get to Lowell, and as we neared the cutoff, roaring up Route 495 among the barreling trucks, the day gloomed over (as I knew it would, as it had to near the "Snake Mountain" of *Doctor Sax*), the harsh, gray sky darkening with that hint of Arctic north that always murmurs the mysterious word "Saskatchewan" to me—with its images of fir forests awesome in winter snow at twilight and prairie immensities north of Dakota over the line, and finally the terrible majesties of the Canadian Rockies that make the mind *ache* with awareness of its own insignificance. In my time, only Jack had found a prose commensurate to the dimensions of the continent as they weighed on human consciousness. Most writers no longer even *tried* for that kind of range anymore.

Lowell, of course, turned out to be an ugly, ratchety mill town in unplanned sprawl along the Merrimack: shuttered factories, rail yards blown with hapless papers, unpainted wooden buildings with their date-plaques blurred by weather over the doors, and the turreted town hall with the library next to it where Jack had read his Balzac when he was a polite, bow-tied, moody youth, when he was Jackie (as he was still Jackie to everyone who'd known him in Lowell)—all in a mad tangle of evening traffic on crazy, unmarked, one-way streets of cobble, all of it plain with that New England mill-town brick-and-siding plainness.

My direction signals weren't working properly, the nerves of driving in the rush of cars hurrying home to supper were wearing me down, but we got parked near where Allen thought Nick Sampas (Jack's brother-in-law) had a bar. We'd go in there and get located. We tumbled out into a bone-cold little square, all but grassless, the air full of those vagrant swirls of snowflakes that always seem to blow so forlornly in squares in the run-down part of any town where the drunks wander with chapped hands in old overcoats and the Ballantine signs in the saloons are the only coziness. We went into a bar that resembled Allen's recollection of Nick's place. Here we came—every honest Greek workingman's idea of what is wrong with the fucking country: long hair, beards, old coats, red hats, cracked shoes. And what was a pretty woman, in her black leather coat and black pumps, doing with a bunch of weirdoes?

But though we were strange to the drinkers there, they didn't freeze us with hostility, and Shirley and I had whiskeys, while the others sipped a glass of wine apiece. It wasn't the right bar after all, but the men in there knew the place we wanted: "Sure, Nicky's place, used to be the old Sixty-Six Club, cross town, you go up here, take your first right at the light, blah, blah, blah—," but they were helpful, and scrawled out the directions on a beer coaster for Allen, who (used to being *everyone*'s "hairy loss") quietly and politely persisted through the blunt stares of men to whom he must have seemed as alien as St. Francis in the Vatican.

Back to the car again. Peter took over the driving, and we went up to the first right, made the correct turn this time, went down further dreary blocks, and yes, there was Nick's—we'd come right by it on our way into the center of town. Beyond its steamy plate glass, it was blissfully overwarm (the way I remembered small-town stores off New Hampshire winter sidewalks in the thirties) and "modernized"—creamy, indirect lights set into the back bar, captain's-backed stools, a shuffleboard game, and a few tables in the eating half of the place where you imagined rows of men dancing slow, arms-on-shoulders bouzouki dances on Saturday nights.

Yes, the bartender said, he had that day's Lowell papers with the funeral plans, and, yes, he recognized Allen from the time Allen had had been in there with Jack some years ago, and, yes, Nick would be back anytime now. He'd gone out to Logan Airport to pick up Stella (Jack's wife) and Tony (another Sampas brother) who was bringing her up from St. Petersburg, but he'd be there shortly, and Jack's body was already in Lowell, having come in on an earlier flight. What did we want to drink?

We read the funeral announcement in the *Lowell Sun*: the body would be on view from seven to ten that night, the funeral was tomorrow morning at eleven at St. Jean-Baptiste Cathedral. Allen seemed strangely sobered as we read this together: "It's such good, succinct prose," he said, "don't you think? . . . Hey, can I keep this?" to the bartender. Then we read, amazingly, an account of last night's Yale reading. "God, and here we sit, reading it, in Lowell," he marveled, "and where's Jack?"

At that moment, in came Nick—big-faced, bluff, blue-suited, with large, somehow heavy eyes, the eyes of a tired, harried man dealing with some bad turning that his life had taken; the talkative, assertive, helpful, bearlike brother who was at home in the loquacities of winter taverns. Stella, he said, was outside in the car. So out we all went. Only Allen had ever met her, because when Jack came to New York or Connecticut, he always came alone.

There in the frigid street, with the wind at our backs and the northern dusk coming down with the implacability of a shroud, she looked up as Nick opened the car door, as startled as a bird but knowing for a certainty who we were, and got out—so much smaller than I had imagined, with a strong-featured, intense face, a wide mouth, and bright black eyes that filled with tears at the sight of us (no, the eyes sprung tears against the mind's instructions), and she choked on a sob as if she'd been struck in the stomach, and got out, "All of you here! *Why* didn't you come to Florida when he needed you?" with a tone of fierce, involuntary recrimination that was followed immediately by a kiss for Shirley, and then for each of us in turn, because we'd been his friends and had come to his funeral, after all.

I leaned over and kissed her hand, and a smile—crooked, brave, and somehow worse than the tears—managed to contort her mouth: "He loved you all," she said. "He never stopped talking about you," the tears welling up again, just coming of themselves, and then she looked at Gregory, and actually laughed: "Oh Gregory, he used to talk—" shaking her head back and forth at funny stories Jack must have told her about this crazy, ex-juvenile-delinquent, Italian Shelley who helped her back into the car and then climbed in beside her.

We were introduced to Tony Sampas—the thin brother, the lawyer, who lived over Nicky's bar with no wife in sight and stayed up with the difficult drunks, like Jack, and perhaps slept in a single bed in a dim room with only a bureau and a chair in it; weary, dependable Tony, who had flown down to Florida immediately and hadn't slept in two or three days. "I'll take her over to the mother's place now," he said to me in an undertone, "and see you later . . . And really, it means a lot to her, and all of us, that you could come."

So we all trailed back into the bar again with Nick, who took over the details of the next hours with the gruff and thoughtful ease of the best of hosts:

Now you'll have dinner right here, I'll make the dinner myself,
a steak, how about steaks, and shrimp, some shrimp to start
. . . No, no, you'll eat here. I set up a kitchen just last month,
just for me to cook in when I feel like it, everything's taken
care of . . . Now you have your drinks, anything you want . . .
Walter, give them anything they want . . .

So there we were: Shirley and I with more whiskey, Gregory
having retsina, Allen and Peter sipping sherry, and all of us going
back into the kitchen now and then, where Nick was hauling out
steaks and shrimp and lobster and talking steadily, the big, heavy,
tough, imploring eyes saying: Just don't worry, everything's taken
care of, the Sampases appreciate your coming all this way, and of
course you'll stay at Mike's (still another brother, a social worker,
the quieter brother who hadn't married Greek and somehow
seemed to lack the easy, central place in the middle of the family's
ambiance, and had a fifteen-room house for his six kids and Protestant wife), you'll stay there, say no more about it—Why are they
protesting? You mean, they should stay in some motel when they've
come all the way up here for Jackie's funeral?

I was amazed at how difficult it was for us simply to accept the
Sampases' generosity—the opening of house, pantry, purse; the
giving of beds and food; the willingness to include us in the rituals
of their bereavement. We were continually trying to find words to
thank them, as if each of us needed to remain poised in a kind of
stoic equilibrium if we were to get through, and so had withdrawn
slightly into ourselves where even kindness was an intrusion. The
Sampases, on the contrary, automatically drew together in the emergency and became a tribe once more, their differences from each
other put aside for the moment, only the likenesses remaining. It

came to me in the hours that followed that, as Jack had known, the primal basis for society is still the family after all, and, uprooted from its supportiveness, our individual attempts at understatement seemed a pathetic psychic orphaning. For if death is one of the great life experiences, it is precisely because it awakens all the hungers that define our mortality—the need to weep, to laugh, to touch, to help—and its consolation is the reminder of human fraternity that it offers to anyone not too armored by fear to receive it. Thankfully, our "notorious" individualities melted, and we joined the group.

Dinner was spread out on a long table in the eating half of the bar—a pile of steaks, a dish of lobster meat, shrimp, breads, a bottle of retsina—eat, eat, eat! While we did, we were occupied with the thought that we hadn't thought of flowers. There should be some from Jack's friends, from "American literature," as Allen said. So Gregory sketched out an elaborate floral symbol—a large red heart resting on a lotus, with spikes of fire shooting out of it, and five thorns with our first names on them. But what to say on the ribbon? "Hold the heart," Allen suggested. Then the end of *Mexico City Blues* came to mind, and I said: "No, *guard* the heart. Or, *he* guarded the heart."

"Maybe it's too military?" Gregory wondered.

Later, the lotus and the spikes of fire and even the thorns proved impossible for the florist to create at that late hour, but a large heart of red roses was made for us, with white roses around it, and ribbons with our names on them, and these names added, because they were close friends of Jack's: Lucien (Carr), Bill (Burroughs), and Robert (Creeley). And in the center, *Guard the Heart.*

After eating, we sat in the bar, waiting to go to the funeral home. A flush-faced, sandy-haired young man with the look of an ex-basketballer starting to lose his muscle tone to the beer, was hunched over a drink a stool away, and Nick insisted that we meet him, because he had gotten drunk with Jack so many times. He shook hands with each of us gravely, and said: "He was something, though, wasn't he? I mean, I'm no slouch with the sauce myself, but Jack—" shaking his head at Jack's prodigious thirst, his red-rimmed eyes sobered with shock.

I thought: How many hundreds of guys there must be who had gone along on historic, days-long binges with Jack and told the stories over and over ever since, not because Jack was Jack Kerouac, but because he was a boozer's boozer, and something always happened, something uproarious or outlandish or mind-boggling, that often ended in the ludicrous jail tank in the ashes of dehydrated dawn. How many there must be who felt they were his good old buddies because they had known the surprising intimacy and candor of his cups and remembered that florid, volatile face yelling or laughing, playing the records on any juke, telling them with feckless exuberance, "Hey, I'm Jack Kerouac," but never giving too much of a damn whether they'd heard of him or not, because it was a great night, it was a good place, let's go somewhere else, let's find us a mad goddamn pasty. And how many fastened on to him just *because* he was Jack Kerouac—"Hey, man, you know who I got stoned with last night? Jack fucking-well *Kerouac!* Yah, you know, the Beatwriter! I'm going to drive him up into New England some place next week." How many had laughed *with* him (or at him) and spent *his* money (or their own) and passed out to his voice still indefatigably trying to keep pace with the reel of his imagination, but never heard the drowning note of the maddened fatalism that had blurred it recently.

There were the people among whom Jack had spent a lot of his last years—barflies, mechanics with a Saturday-night thirst, the jocks around the local saloon, tyro writers talking their books away, the punks-of-the-night looking for a latch to build tomorrow on, the wifeless, overworked, bored, sweat-socked men and boys of bewildered inner America, who could recognize a certified roarer and his roll. These kept him company, and with them he burned up his intelligence in the conflagration of those boozy monologues over a scarred bar top.

Why did he drink like that? I think it was because his was a deeply traditional nature, so sensitive to social and familial cohesions and their breakdown in the modern world that he intuited more about the contemporary human mood in his nerves and mind than anyone I had ever known. And yet most of his close friends were alienated, rootless, urban types, and so he lived simultaneously in both worlds, a tremulous bridge between two realities bent on denying one another, a seismograph trying to register an earthquake in the middle of a tornado—and drink temporarily seemed to stabilize his psychic ground. He drank, as well, because he had no gift for even a saving cynicism and couldn't act out the simplest role (much less the infinitely complex role of "spokesman" or "prophet"), and because, though he was the most insatiably gregarious man when tipsy, he was not easily sociable when sober, and increasingly, as he got older, was occupied with the enigma of his own identity ("I'm descended from an Iroquois chief," he would announce. "I'm a Breton nobleman," he would insist a week later), and finally he drank because I don't think he wanted to live anymore if there were no place to direct his kind of creative drive except inward. But I don't really know. All I know for sure is that it has pained *this* head for years to imagine the waste to him of those thousand barroom nights, and that something must be awry in an America where a man of such human richness and such extraordinary gifts would be

most appropriately mourned in a hundred saloons because he felt
he had no other place to go—the fraternal warmth for which his
whole soul longed having been exiled to the outer edge of life in the
America of his time.

While we waited, Gregory went upstairs to shave, because in the
car Stella said: "Comb your hair, take a shave—do it for Jack," and
as he went off, he said: "I'll shave for Jack, for Jack's woman, but
damn it, when I'm ninety, they're still going to want to cut my hair,
shave me, dress me up—when I'm *ninety*! Oughtn't a man to know
the way he wants to be, and be left to it, when he's ninety?"

Then we were off to Archambault's Funeral Home, with Nick
directing us, rolling down empty streets of small-city American neon
with cracked sidewalks down which one imagined Doctor Sax's
manuscript "riffling" in the winter wind, which was how Jack had
gleefully described it to me once outside the San Remo in the Village on a night as cold, when we were both in our twenties and
bursting with Melville, five years before he wrote the book: "And
then, see, this manuscript comes riffling down the sidewalk out of
nowhere—this terrible, prophetic testament of what lies at the end of
the night!"—a manuscript which (it had always seemed to me) Jack
had spent the rest of his life transcribing out of the original version.

Funeral homes are all alike, of course. Archambeault's was Victorian in decor, with pale-green walls, lofty ceilings, an ornate
balustrade going up from the vestibule to—what? The formaldehyde
rooms. The butcher shops. Wherever it was they stored the coffins
and showed them to customers susceptible in their bereavement.
Two "showings" were going on in opposite rooms, and the neatly
lettered placards (like those in hotel lobbies telling you in which
room your convention is being held) announced "Kerouac" on the
left and "Levesque" on the right.

The Kerouac room was filled with people—middle-class, well-dressed Lowell people, and a few kids (Custer-bearded youths with grave, out-of-place faces, and mini-skirted girls, solemn with they-know-not-what unclear emotions). Most of the local people seemed to be Sampas relatives, and suddenly I realized how few Kerouacs there had ever been. Later, we met a row of young Kerouac second cousins—pretty little girls with that dark, round-faced Breton look, and muscular, abashed boys from Dracut or Nashua. Among the crowd was Charley, the eldest Sampas, news editor of the *Lowell Sun*, a large, suave man with flesh on him, in a well-cut business suit, balding now, the successful head of the clan, his urbane eyes on all the details.

It was Charley who had encouraged Jack to write when Jack was best friends with his younger brother, Sebastian, who had been killed in Europe in 1944. Charley had told Jack that if he wanted to write he ought to get out of Lowell, and perhaps Charley, too, had wanted something more than to be standing there in his expensive suit, with certain private ambitions unachieved despite his position in the community. We met further Sampas relatives, and friends, and friends of friends, most of the Greeks in that French funeral home, and there, too, was Stella on a settee to one side, out of the theatrical lights that bathed the coffin, and the banks of fresh flowers, and—Jack.

Down to it, I didn't want to "view" whatever some mortician had thought to fashion out of what was left of him, but I knew I would. Allen and Peter and Gregory went right up through the crowd to have a look, but whether they had seen the handiwork of funeral homes before, I didn't know. Allen and Peter had observed dozens of corpses on the burning ghats of India, but (as Allen said later) that was natural, you see the husk of the body for what it is—organs, so much simple meat, just the garbage of our chrysalis from which the butterfly has flown, nothing but the residue of transitory life. But in the war, I had seen half a hundred dead sailors being gotten ready for shipping home to inconsolable parents and wives, and later "viewed" my father laid out under the lights like a waxwork figure in Madame Tussaud's that is somehow unlike the person precisely because cold skill has so striven to make it resemble them, feature to feature, and you stand in utter perplexity, wondering why it doesn't, only to become aware that what is missing is not merely movement, animation, but something else, the invisible spark that makes the mask cohere, the soul lighting up the persona from within, the unique and irreplaceable Being that invests the face with human possibilities.

Anyway, I pushed my way through the crowd alone, fearful I might be revulsed and that it would all come down on me if anything of Jack was actually there, and over the dark silhouette of a shoulder, I saw him—laid out in flowers, in the prescribed funerary attitude of tranquil slumber, hands folded with a rosary entwined, in a pale shirt, a natty bow tie, and a sport jacket. No need to say that no one had ever seen him that way since he was Harcourt Brace's soulful young Thomas Wolfe twenty years before. And the face? It had been made to look as peaceful as a babe, the brows slightly knotted but with perplex rather than pain, all the fevers gone, the mouth not his mouth at all, the color of the flesh a rather pale pink in the lights. Jack's sweaty, grinning, changeable expression nowhere to be seen. He looked thin, calm, waxen, almost choirboyish—and Jack had once been choirboyish, all right—but this was a faintly prissy, I'm-alright-Jack Jack, and no Jack I'd ever known. Later, Allen would say: "I stood there, and suddenly I expected him to *wink*. That is, the Jack that was watching all of us watching him would have made that eyelid wink to tell us that everything was all just so much vapor circling upwards in the void."

Gregory was kneeling at one side of the coffin, crying now, and I remembered the easy, public tears of Italy, the bawling men coming back from Venice's burial island in the dignity of a grief that is openly acknowledged, and I looked at Jack again, and felt for just a moment the sheer obscenity of death, the irreparable period that it places at the end of portions of our lives, closing us off forever from the consciousness that has gone, and the first sick feeling of gut-loss came over me. "It will be different to write from now on . . .": the words came back, and I hoped that no one would ever mourn me so self-centeredly. Tears welled up into my eyes, the involuntary tears that we sometimes shed for the mute flesh itself. He wouldn't walk, he wouldn't run, he wouldn't ever come into my house again, yelling like a banshee, or grinning pensively, or moody with his special thoughts. That's what I felt—his body died before my eyes, and I had to accept that I was stuck in my own body, in my own flesh, and that this mannequin was the last I'd see of a friend of twenty-one years of feverish association. I put an arm around Gregory, and we turned away.

I found Shirley, who had taken only the briefest look from a distance, and we went up to Stella, who broke down again as we bent over her, and Shirley knelt down and stayed with her for a while after I'd muttered a futile word or two, hugged her, and cursed under my breath. Cursed what? My own closed throat that wanted to bring up something consoling, something that wouldn't push her over any further—all that grief-role crap which, like joy-role crap, is only crap, after all. Better to stumble out: Jack's *dead!* What am I going to *do!* But instead trying for control, trying not to say a word that would trigger emotions neither of us could afford. And all the while her eyes observed me, something going on behind her tears: "Is *this* John Holmes? Is this Jack's friend? Why isn't he suffering? Is he suffering? What kind of suffering is that?"

Hours, hours—the room too hot—too many people to meet—too many names to remember. After a while, Shirley and I went down to the smoking lounge (oh, the imaginations of morticians, all of whom aspire to the respectability of theater managers), where we sat and smoked and talked about other things and kept each other company. Then, coming down the stairs, I saw a face I recognized but couldn't place for a second. It was Ann Charters, who had compiled Jack's bibliography a few years before. She was wearing a large, knitted tam and a chic suede coat, and her alert, intelligent face, with the observant eyes and quick smile, was pale with cold, and her husband, Sam, whom I'd never met, was with her. He was a big, handsome man in a stylish, box-back overcoat, with the longish hair of someone older "on the scene"; a poet and a producer of rock records, who exuded a sense of physical health and the natural optimism of someone who is usually too busy to mope.

We all started chattering at once (death makes you talk, you talk so as not to think, you chatter as if you'd found a similar soul at the worst cocktail party of all time), and at one point, Sam said: "I reread your Kerouac chapter in *Nothing More to Declare* the other night, and it's the best thing on Jack so far." I felt a curious twinge in my gut but didn't recognize what it was, except that it wasn't just my old reflex of being unable to accept praise. "You should do the book," Sam said. "There's going to be a book, and you're probably the one to do it." *Twinge.* Later, the next afternoon, Sterling Lord, Jack's literary agent and mine, would say to me: "You know, John, you're really the one to do the *book.* You knew him from the inside, you were there when so much of it happened, but you can stand away from it all, too." *Twinge.* "No, really, you're the one to do it," and the twinge became knowledge. The idea of the *book*—that combination of authorized biography and cool critical assessment without which America does not know how to think about its most challenged writers—revolted me. It seemed a coffin no less adequate to contain the Jack I'd known than the one in which he lay.

I didn't want to go through it all again, I didn't want to have to rifle my own memories, much less other people's, and try to be objective, measured, scholarly. I realized that I had loved him because, on an entirely private level, I had understood his point of view with an instant empathy that was the closest thing to clairvoyance in my life, and the goddam book would have to be done by someone other than this survivor of the last, maddening quarter-century, who had his own secrets, bad habits, awful mornings of hangover, resolutions to save himself, arduous days of getting through on nothing but nerve, futile hopes for two months' rest, for a calm life once the fever eased, for mint-fresh mornings of zestful work. For I did know why Jack drank. We talked to each other sometimes late at night, utterly different men with a similar cast of mind, the same wound in the heart, and he talked to me as an alcoholic in the Age of Pot. "How glum is life without the booze," he said to me once, raising his glass mockingly, able to say it right out to me, knowing I would understand just what it was made men like us feel glum—our disappointed expectations and the novelist's necessity to accept into his work the irreconcilables that his own personal hopes struggle to deny.

When we went back upstairs, people were starting to drift out of the "viewing" room, leaving Stella there, kneeling by Jack, caressing his face, kissing him, a hunched, small, abandoned figure in the theatrical lights, her shoulders heaving just a little.

We crowded into the car again to go to the Sampases' mother's house for "the wake." Nick coming along to give directions, Peter navigating through the narrow, rutted streets of residential Lowell and missing turns because Nick was always craning over his shoulder to talk to those of us in back (patient Peter "uh-*huh*-ing" when corrected), to stop on a corner under a few spare trees, on a block of plain, old, commodious houses with an empty lot across the street and a shuttered factory beyond a chain-link fence. We piled out and went into the house across a small veranda.

It was already overcrowded with people. There was a baby grand in the front hall, off of which was a pin-neat parlor with doilies on the chair arms and landscapes on the walls. Beyond was the TV room with a butt-sprung couch and a wall of photographs—Nick in his Army tunic, Mike as a young student, Sebastian in the central spot—a thin, beaming young man in uniform, with curly blondish hair, looking out of the forties at this night. The kitchen was full of dark, heavily attractive women bustling about a large, restaurant-size coffee urn, and shooing everyone out. A sumptuous spread was laid out on the dining-room table—feta in chalk-white wedges, heaping plates of pastries, slices of delicious spinach pie, and cup on cup of coffee.

The house was too small for all the people who milled around the immense, two-hundred-and-fifty-pound Sampas matriarch who spoke little English and wheezed down into sagging armchairs in her bedroom slippers, and was brought food and drink by other, aging Greek ladies. Stella sat among these women, attended by her friends from long-ago high school days, looking at everything as if from a new, strange distance—at the warm, thronged circle of Jack's Lowell (and her own) within which moved his curious friends from the disordered city years—her eyes asking herself: Can all this be true? When will I wake up?

We ate and drank coffee, and Gregory came up to me with that day's copy of the *Harvard Crimson* that had an obituary. "John, you've gotta read this . . . this says it all." What it said was what I had seen on the faces of the Yalies the night before, and in the bewildered young men at the funeral home: We don't know exactly why it's such a shock. We never really read him that much. But today we realize that he meant something to us after all, and we don't know why he's dead. And this curious last line: "We should say a prayer for him: God give us strength to be as alive as Kerouac was. Send us more to help burn away the bullshit."

A word about this matter of the kids—the hippies, the activists, the *children* of the Beats. The next day they were at the church, and again at the cemetery, in their scruffy duds and Franz-Joseph wings of sideburn, each with a camera clicking away, getting "shots" as if they were recording an event the meaning of which only become clear in the developer, and most of them seemed to have been impelled to come for reasons that they only began to comprehend once there. They all looked as if this was their first funeral, and they were uneasy about being that close to the death they talked and sang about so much. They were interviewed continually by newsmen from Boston or New York, who sensed a surefire human-interest story here (Now Generation Talks about Father of Beats), but I don't think most of them had thought very much about Kerouac in the last few years. They had probably read *On the Road*, or one of the easier books, when they were fifteen or sixteen, and had written him off in the light of his recent political statements, tuned out by his unfashionable love of his country and his disinterest in their subculture and its heroes. And yet they came.

At the cemetery, I overheard a young reporter from *Rolling Stone* say to Sterling Lord: "Well it was his politics—I mean, we can't relate to all that America shit," and I heard myself break in, and say: "Don't understand him too easily. His politics began on another level from yours." But how could I say what I meant? The Jack who came out for William Buckley, who occasionally was about as intolerant as Archie Bunker and sometimes skirted perilously close to anti-Semitism—how could I say that he really wasn't that way? "All right, smartass," the young man could have quite reasonably demanded, "What's your evidence?" There was nothing I could say but this: *I know in my heart the man wasn't that way.*

I had argued with him over issues for twenty years, only to realize that politics weren't real to him at all, convinced, as he was, that most "issues" were evasions of our actual human complicity and that truth lay elsewhere—down in what Yeats had called "the foul rag and bone shop of the heart." Also, he had the impatience with logic and the cartwheeling leaps of insight that sometimes characterized the alcoholic mind. But above all, he was a lonely, disappointed man who had been down all the roads—the drugs, the screws, the fantasies, the highs, the hopes—and knew in his own ravaged nerves what was left at "the end of the night." Beyond that, I think he felt emotionally disenfranchised by the polarization of an America that no longer seemed to care about the urge toward harmony that he believed to be its founding truth.

It was too soon to say that he was wrong, and so I said nothing more to the young man from *Rolling Stone*. Still, the presence of those kids at his funeral leads me to conclude that the obit in the *Crimson* accurately reflected a feeling of mysterious kinship which Jack's sudden death aroused in so many of the young.

The evening inched along with exquisite slowness. We were all depleted, our brains numbed by remembering names, and some of us longed for a drink, and others for sleep, and finally Stella got up and padded through the crowds without a word, and went to bed. We stayed on for a while, and then piled into the car again and went on to Mike's house, following the red eye of his taillight.

The house was a large, three-storied, Victorian mansion with a porte-cochere, in a style that might be dubbed Millowner New England. We brought our bags and our weary eyes into a huge, dark-paneled kitchen. Betty, Mike's wife, the Protestant girl from Maritta, Ohio (her direct, hospitable nature shaped by the splendid curve of the river there, as particular rivers shape the natures of those who live beside them)—Betty was chubby, good-looking, a no-nonsense nestler of children, quietly observant, the kind of woman who likes to sink down in an easy chair after the day is over and have a convivial drink with her husband. She had been around most of the evening, pleasant but unobtrusive, keeping in the background the way an "outsider" in a large, tight-knit, boisterous family usually does. But now she was in her own house, and she got out drinks while Mike took us up to the third floor and our rooms.

We went up through the enormous house, with its twelve-foot ceilings and heavily varnished woodwork, its black-and-gold marble mantels and ornate brass fixtures in the bathrooms. Two little boys were sleeping so soundly in one room that even our tramping through didn't cause them to stir, and there were two little girls in another room amid a profusion of dolls and Twiggy posters, and there was Tony, with son of twelve, who had his room up on the third floor near ours. It was a jumble of hi-fi, flower-power, Charlie Brown, and, lo, a huge Allen Ginsberg poster-photo. The boy was giddy with the idea that he was actually in his very own house, and you could feel his impatience for tomorrow, and school, and his buddies. Allen promptly whipped out a pen and wrote his name and a line or two on the poster.

Downstairs, the fifteen-year-old daughter, a self-contained young creature with a fall of fine brown hair on her shoulders and a pretty, coltish face, sat with us in one of the parlors as, exhausted, we finally had a big drink with her parents. Peter had resolutely gone off to bed, and Gregory got himself a drink and went off too. Allen sat with Shirley on a couch, I sank into a large armchair to savor the taste of the bourbon on gums anesthetized by too many cigarettes, and we talked of death, the girl listening gravely, saying little or nothing, but very adult in her attention.

"It's really strange," Allen said. "With all of you, all of this, all Lowell . . . Do you think it mightn't have happened if he'd stayed here instead of moving to Florida?"

"Well, we could have at least protected him a little," Mike said. "I mean, you know, the police all knew him here, and we'd go down and get him out of jail when he went on a binge. We could have looked after him . . . We shouldn't have let his mother insist on the move. I mean, Jack and Stella didn't really want to go down there. He wrote Tony just about two weeks ago that somehow they'd come back in the spring. We didn't do enough, I guess—" this solemn, worried man, resembling none of the other Sampases (none of whom resembled each other, as if the loins of the parents had contained whole tribes), with his dark brows of puzzled concern, his bony nose; a man kept thin with worry as his wife got plump with childbearing; an upright man worried about his responsibility to the death of a crazy brother-in-law.

"Well," Allen said, "I was interested to see his face. Did anyone think to take a picture of him?" This tightened my gut a little, but I understood Allen's long view, and time makes most proprieties seem silly. "I heard from Ann Charters," he went on, "that some of his papers and some photos were burned. Do you know what he

wrote just before the hemorrhage? The papers said he wrote something . . . And by the way, I really think one of his friends should
be a pallbearer."

I, too, was worried about Jack's meticulously preserved record of
his life, his countless notebooks, sketchbooks, journals, and fugitive
jottings-on-the-road. I, too, felt that one of us, one of Jack's friends,
should help bear his pall, but rejected Allen's notion that we draw
lots and insisted that he be the one, being the oldest friend among
us, and he accepted the suggestion. But I was bone-weary too, and
gulped a quick second drink, and Shirley and I went off to bed up
under the eaves of that many-chambered house, opening the shut-
ters of one window to look briefly out at the fierce stars burning
over New Hampshire, under which Jack and I had discovered that
we had both walked (me, along the Pemigewassett River; he, along
the Merrimack into which it flowed) on the same windy night after
the big flood of 1937—only one of the many odd coincidences (like
the fact that we had been born on the same day in March) that had
lent our friendship a special, brotherly quality. I hung my corduroys
from the top bureau drawer so that some semblance of press might
remain for tomorrow, and climbed into the firm Victorian bed under
the warm weight of three cotton blankets, and slept like the dead
until seven the next morning.

Three

Which dawned fair and milder than the day before, with tall, white,
supple birches outside that high window. I shaved as Shirley packed
us up. Probably we wouldn't be coming back here. Allen had to go
to New York that night, and he would be driving into Logan with
the Charterses. Peter and Gregory would go back to the farm with

Robert Creeley, who was coming over from Rochester for the funeral. We would just go on home.

Down in the kitchen, two of Jack's friends from Albany were going into their twentieth hour awake. I'd seen them the night before at the Sampases' house, and afterwards, as it turned out, they'd gone to the bars to mourn and carouse, and now they had turned up here at Mike's for coffee and some of Betty's French toast. One, a massive, tousled-hair man, who knew he looked as poetic and virile as the early Brendan Behan, had a barrel chest like Jack's of recent years. He had run a bar in Florida where Jack drank, and then he had moved back North to go into teaching. With him was a knotty, walnut-faced little psychiatrist, who rambled on continually in a raspy, cigarette-roughened voice, telling stories he had told too many times before. Betty cooked and listened, her copious hair let down over the shoulders of her kimono.

Allen appeared, his face scoured by sleep, not a psychic burr on him, and had a cup of tea. Gregory came down muzzily and sipped a light whiskey for his tooth. We were due at the funeral home at ten, as it turned out, so that the cars could be properly lined up for the procession to the church. I had hoped to go out for a walk on my own, just to get the air, to sniff out Lowell ambiance, to look at trees, but there wasn't going to be time. Suddenly, in fact, it was ten of ten, and Peter was awakened with only time to gulp a quick mug of coffee while Gregory loaded his camera, and we were off.

Morning Lowell reminded me of Fall River or New Bedford—trampled school lots full of children, factories a-smoke, the mild air of autumn amid the yellowing trees. The street in front of Archambeault's was full of funeral directors in gray suede gloves, striped trousers, and the self-satisfied faces of traffic managers in communion with the mysteries of logistics. We were gotten in the line, and went inside.

It was just like the night before, except that a pale-yellow, Chekhovian sun bathed the room where Jack lay in his waxen, musing pose. Gregory took movies, to the silent shock of Sampases, and Shirley and I sat in the vestibule, waiting. Then our names were called, and we went back to the car again, Gregory lingering behind to get "shots" of the coffin coming out, Allen to ride in the pallbearers' car. We waited again, Peter (good Peter, without breakfast, in need of more coffee, still at the wheel of my cold car) watching for Gregory in the rearview mirror. When he came, we pulled out into the line and rolled slowly toward the church.

There were cops and funeral directors in the narrow street, people were thronging up the wide steps to the cathedral, a wan sun gilded the brick-red upper stories of commercial buildings. We double-parked in the line and got out and queued up with the "family and friends"—who, according to the logistics, were to troop in solemnly at the last moment, like actors in a mystery play as it might have been written by Samuel Beckett. Moving along, there was Sterling Lord at the bottom of the steps, natty as ever in his blue shirt with the white collar and a dark necktie, with his encouraging eyes behind the glasses and his reticent half-smile betraying the sensitivity of a decent man to the unknown emotions of others; Sterling who had known Jack in such a different way from most of us—as an agent, but as Jack's agent, which meant no chilly professionalism, for Jack put his head as well as his work into your hands. He came forward, and we shook hands on the occasion, and I wanted to stop a moment, but no, we were urged on—logistics again!—up the steps and through a high portal into the church itself. Inside it was all lofty light, pale marble columns, dark-wood pews, the stained-glass windows over the altar—blue and green and red in the lovely sun—depicting saints in the tall, Grecoesque majesty of their robes.

We were led down to a point just behind the pews reserved for the family, and Shirley (shrouded in a black-lace scarf that had materialized out of her purse) pulled down the knee-rest automatically, ex-Catholic as she was, and all at once I could feel her grief. She was tensing toward the austere words of the Mass that would finalize it all for her. There was no help for her now, she was going to have to endure that celebration of the mystery of Death from which the renegade Catholic can flee, but never far enough, and she couldn't just "get through it" as I could. The fact was going to be nailed down in her consciousness. She and Jack had been lapsed Catholics together, they had had that between them like the stoicism of cigarette smokers who accept the cancer statistics but refuse to quit, and so much else too—a certain bantering camaraderie, a line-perfect memory for the lyrics of all the songs, an unspoken acknowledgment of the frailty behind life's poses, *me*. To Shirley, I knew, Jack's death had been an inevitability, not because of the booze (she was married to a boozer of sorts, she'd nursed my groanings, she'd learned to accept the prodigious thirsts of a secret idealist whose private motto was Break the Black Heart) but because down in herself she believed that the best of life came down to this. She believed that there was a mortality that tracked every one of us out of season. She was a soldier who was revulsed by the war of life but stubbornly wouldn't desert it. She had that toughness that only comes from certain bitter acceptances made when one is too young to recognize the sadder, more ambivalent options, and she had learned to hold onto people who were special to her with open hands—and Jack had been special to her in a way that had little to do with me. And now the ritual of the Mass, which would have been a catharsis for the devout, promised her nothing but the cold clarities and losses of the morgue.

The coffin and the pallbearers came down past us (Allen there, with his beard and duffel coat and shoulder-slung bag) and the Mass began. It was a High Requiem Mass performed in English, with the priest facing us instead of the altar, but I couldn't concentrate on it. I got up and stood, I sat when others sat, I listened to the chants, the responses, and registered none of it. I stared at the coffin and thought of Jack inside it. The priest, an old friend of Jack's of whom I'd heard stories for twenty years, gave the eulogy, a good eulogy too (in my doubter's troubled mind I thought it a good job of work), and I got up and stood dumb in my shoes, and sat down, and couldn't pray, but said the words of the Lord's Prayer when it came, and honestly hoped their hope, thinking that Jack's hunger for continuity, Jack's essential reverence, was being well served. Then communion. Because most of the people there were Greeks, only a few took it– one, a lank-haired Ippolit* hurried up late, as if responding to a sudden impulse. And at last Shirley wept.

Then it was finished, the priest circling the casket with the swaying censer as his "helper" held his robes back from the candles. The funeral directors came up, genuflecting automatically with the wheeze of too many lavish dinners, shepherding the pallbearers to their proper places, and we filed out, down the long aisle behind Stella and the family, out into the sun again, where photographers jumped about, and Allen stood next to the hearse being interviewed, a crisp wind ruffling his beard there in the traffic-jammed street.

Sterling came down the steps with Jimmy Breslin, whom I'd never met, and we stood there in the crowd and talked for a minute. "Jimmy came up with me," Sterling said with his wide smile. "He didn't think I should come up by myself." Breslin had that sober,

* Ippolit Terrentiev is a character from Fyodor Dostoevsky's novel *The Idiot*.

tousled, knotted look of a man who is sharing other people's loss, people who might not know how to get through a ritual that he understands in his very gristle, and I liked him instantly. Then, suddenly, there was Robert Creeley, too—wiry as a guitar string, and graceful, with the meticulous small beard of a bravo or a cavalier, in a proper suit and short overcoat, his one busy eye saying, "Yes. At last. Funny. Well. We all *do* exist, after all," as we were introduced.

We piled into the car in a maze of photographers, among them Gregory, who'd gotten more "perfect shots," and again moved off in the procession, Creeley coming along with us. There was nothing to say, and so we chatted. Peter drove, and I lit cigarettes for him, and Shirley commented on the brevity of the new Mass, and I thought about these streets, every name of which I'd known for two decades, and it seemed to be miles before we reached the cemetery gates where the line of cars paused, then moved on, then came to a stop at last. We got out into the musing, somber air that New England graveyards exude, the leaves drifting amid old stones and meandering walks, and there, beyond some trees, across a strip of macadam, a green canopy had been raised over the fresh-dug grave.

Brief ceremonies, ceremonial words to which I didn't listen. The late October breeze stirred in the elms, the crowds milled, photographers posed, getting poses. But no ceremonies ease the sight of a coffin poised over a grave's raw hole, and Stella stood there before it, shrouded now in widow's veils, her arm held by Charlie, the eldest, as the last stark prayer was said.

Then there was a rush to grab flowers and toss them on the casket. I looked on, a few steps away. Allen and Peter and Gregory were selecting roses from our flower heart, red roses that they laid on the burnished bronze surface of the casket. I went up and took a white rose and put it over the place where Jack's head lay.

Sterling and Allen were being "set up" for a TV interview (great shot: Ginsberg talking about Kerouac, and behind him the coffin going down into the earth—"So, Mr. Ginsberg, I'll ask you to assess his career briefly, the camera's not rolling yet, but in a minute, and then you make your statement and just stand a little farther over to the left so that we can get it all in the picture.") I registered all this, but felt nothing. It seemed as meaningless as the commercials that interrupt the disasters on the TV news. The young man from *Rolling Stone* was at my elbow, asking irrelevant questions. Why did Jack drink? Was he, in my opinion, significant? What had he thought of rock? But I was numb—even to irony.

I saw Allen and Gregory standing near the coffin that was about to be lowered, and I broke away. I didn't have another word in me. I stood with them, and the funeral man pressed some sort of button, and, easy as grease, Jack went down into the ground. "Here, you should throw the first dirt," someone said to Allen, a strange young man in work clothes, and Allen reached down to the pile and clenched up a handful, and tossed it. Then Gregory the same. It was hard to get a real handful because of the stones. Then me. I took up the stones, too, and open-handed them down on Jack's head.

Confusion, milling again. I stood around and didn't know what to do. Shirley stayed on the edges of the crowd, which was dispersing now. Breslin had gone back to the rented Cadillac in which he and Sterling had come from Boston Airport. Creeley looked on with a cold eye, doing it his own way. We all tarried and then turned to leave, but the gravediggers were spading the dirt down onto the casket, joking to each other (which was apt somehow, workmen doing, as they do, the dirty jobs, and not making much of it), so we turned back there under the cold, fluttering trees, and watched the pile of earth fill the hole. I don't know why we all turned back at the same time—some last awareness of what was being sealed off from us by the spades, I suppose. And then we'd all had enough, and drifted back to the car—Gregory and Peter and Shirley and Bob Creeley and me, scuffling through the leaves back to the car in the graphic sunlight of a perfect October day, to finish up.

There was a lighter mood in the little rooms of the Sampases' mother's house now, a mood not unmixed with that familiar upwelling of relief that follows a bad experience. There were paper cups of Scotch, and cans of soda and beer, and another lavish spread—the fish that is traditional on such occasions with the Greeks, plus macaroni dishes, salads, enough for twenty more than there were of us, brought around in the crowd by those large, darkly attractive women.

Drinks were being urged on Breslin by Nick, who was intent on introducing him to everyone: "Jimmy, want you to meet so-and-so" to feel that his name, and his fame too, were intrusions here. I was looking for an opportunity to talk to Stella, so I waited my time and ate some of the good food. Then Sterling was nearby, against a wall in the dining room with his plate, and we talked a little. No, Jack hadn't been "drinking heavily for three days" as most of the papers had it, just drinking along as usual, but he'd been feeling baddish for a month, and all of a sudden he'd started to hemorrhage, and didn't want a doctor, but Stella had called the ambulance anyway, and they'd worked over him for hours, then his liver quit, and the surgery didn't help, and that was that. No, he probably hadn't been conscious much after he'd been taken from the house.

I drifted off to get my single drink, only to be buttonholed by the barrel-chested bar owner from Florida, sleepy-eyed and slow-talking now. "I wonder if I could ask you—" he began, fumbling in his brief-case, and producing a manuscript. "It's only about twelve hundred words . . . I've been moving words around these last months." I was speechless with the inappropriateness of the request, but it seemed easier to read it than to wrangle. I stepped outside onto the little porch, and sat in the crisp breeze, and read another half-cynical, half-sentimental version of the one story everyone tries to tell eventually: the death of a father, or brother, or mother, or wife, or friend. Years of reading snatches of fugitive manuscript under such conditions made it easy enough for me to tell at just what juncture the work failed to come off. Years of talking about writing to younger people made it possible for me to articulate at least some of this to him and to get through the first look of confusion and disappointment and the blunt question, "Is it publishable?" I knew just how little outside comments helped if the author wasn't ready to hear them, if he hadn't reached that point where the work was more important than his own feelings about it, and how much they could help if he truly wanted to know what it was he had, or hadn't, done. When I was the rawest of tyros, Jack used to read my manuscripts that way and sketch in all the levels of experience that hadn't gotten on the page. To me, it had been of inestimable help, and I'd rarely turned a manuscript away without reading since, though one soon became aware that most of the time the young writer would be saying to his friends a half-hour later: "Oh, you know these fat-headed Establishment writers . . . some bullshit about the goddamn structure . . . I mean, he took all of five precious minutes to read it! I never liked his stuff much anyway . . ." Nothing to do. Hundreds of such encounters had helped make Jack an impatient, opinionated man.

Anyway, I noticed that Stella was sitting near the door to the dining room with a friend, and I pulled away from the hurt, angry expression on that big man's face and went up to her. She seemed put together, though again the sight of me brought tears up into her eyes, tears that acknowledged the strange situation between us: we had never met, yet there was no way for us to be reserved, polite, or cautious with one another; we had to stumble through some reference to the occurrence that had brought about our meeting at last; the irony was too bald to be covered by a witticism. So we said the words: what Jack had meant to me, what I had meant to Jack. And that being over, she could brighten a little, and we could get to know one another.

"I've had a few drinks," she said, dry-eyed now, small, a fine toughness of fiber emerging. "You know, I never drank with Jack. He didn't want me to . . ." We laughed about that, because Jack had the boozer's secret disapproval of booze, he thought of it in moral terms; also he tended to idealize women and fall back on what he believed to be their greater resiliency and common sense.

Those last days—I'd never know the fun they'd had together! The Met's last pennant run, the Series. He'd taught her to play chess, she'd taught him to play poker. They'd done a lot of sitting around. He hadn't wanted to leave the house much. And that place, St. Pete—it was no town for younger people. A funeral parlor across the street, one down on the next corner. Jack hadn't known anyone there. It was only because of his mother that they'd moved from Lowell. She shook her head, able not to say some of the things that were stirring up in her, able to suggest them, contained now. "But those vultures!" she said suddenly. "The people who came around to see the famous writer . . . You know Jackie could never say 'No.' And they'd say, even to his face, 'I'm gonna use you, you ol' bastard!' You know—supposedly joking, but they *weren't* joking."

· I'd seen it, particularly in the first days after *On the Road* appeared: the curious mixture of adulation and resentment that a certain kind of celebrity seems to bring out in others; that combination of sycophancy and petulance that demands attention, or they'll conclude you're swell-headed; all the energy and exacerbated ego of the idle and purposeless who see a famous writer having a drink at a bar, and figure that writer has nothing better to do than go to a party, or on a three-day bat, or drive to Cincinnati on a whim. I'd lost Jack often enough in the early stages of an evening because he'd been drawn away into all that swirl of nerves and wastage and anticipated kicks. He had never learned to conserve himself, not if the story was interesting enough, or the person seemed to have anything unique in his spiel, or there was some promise of gaudy forgetfulness for a few hours. And all the time, he was burning up the strengths that enable him to keep upright in the yawning contradictions of his nature.

Stella's friend expressed concern about her finances, and she said: "Well, I can always go into the factories if I have to . . . As long as Memere is taken care of . . ." The friend thought she could probably lecture about Jack if she wanted to, but something hard came up into her face: "I'll never do that," she said harshly. "I'll never use him that way. No, *never*," her voice fiercely jealous of her private memories, as if she could already feel Literary History making its unseemly claims on them.

I crouched at her feet, and we talked some more for a while, not about Jack but about other things, nothings, getting a little acquainted, studying one another, discovering that, yes, we liked each other. It was a moment of that brief, intense comminglement between strangers that death sometimes makes possible.

Then Sterling was there. He had to make his plane, she wasn't to worry about money. Breslin bent down, almost ceremonially, with some embarrassment, and I heard the survivor of a dozen Irish wakes say: "Sorry to meet you on this day." And he turned from Stella, and he and I shook hands without a word.

It was getting late, nearly three o'clock, and there was all that road ahead, and we had to get Allen and the others together to go back to Mike Sampas's to pick up their things. We started circulating through the rooms, saying our good-byes. We had been warmed by them all, we had been welcomed. And perhaps the difficult acceptance of Jack's death had become less difficult for all of us because we had been together. I'd often thought that it was this older, simpler communion, this natural flow of emotions outward from one's self, that Jack had looked for so tirelessly in his contemporaries. Now, of course, like so much in his life, something like it had emerged among the young in America, but emerged, for him, too late. They were forming communes, and the spiritual perspectives, the religious ecstasies of which he had written were the common coinage of these endeavors. Visionary drugs, music as group sacrament, the nonviolent witness to the holiness of all sentient life—all this had surfaced as he knew it would, and, far from being derided in the media or patronized by the Academy (as had happened in this case), it was being heralded as the unique culture of a New Age. And Jack? Jack had dropped out of it, and been ignored by it, and grown querulous with drink and age, embittered by the unrelenting indifference to the scope and intention of his life's work, so that when he died, the *New York Times* had had to call me up, asking if I could direct their obit man to a sober, critical assessment of that work, and I had to say that I didn't know of a single one, and that (aside from his friends) I had never met anyone who had read the entire, vast cycle of the books. He remained an essentially unknown element in our literature.

I felt the parting with Stella keenly now because, perhaps better than anyone, she had known the loneliness and anger and physical horror of his last years, and I wanted her to know. I told her straight out, and embraced her, and we left.

Outside, in the trampled little yard, Gregory was horsing around with the loquacious psychiatrist and the bartender-cum-teacher-cum-writer, and I knew he wanted more, and didn't want it all to end, and was being lured (by the promise of bottles and talk and hijinks) to drive back to Albany with them. Jack would have felt the same. Tony Sampas took my arm. Exhaustion had drained his face like a balloon with a slow leak, his short collar hung around his neck loosely, and once more he thanked us for coming—this perceptive man who took on the dirty jobs stoically.

"My God, Tony," I said, "where *else* would we have been today?"

"I'll see you all later," Gregory said to Allen. "I'm going in . . . John, I'm gonna get down to work from now on, write poems, no more 'green armpits' stuff. We'll all meet among the buffaloes," and he gave me a big, giggling suck of a kiss on the neck, and we drove off.

Back at Mike's, we collected everything. The Charterses were packed in the street, waiting to take Allen to Logan. We said good-bye to good, worried Mike and calm Betty with her arms full of little children, and waved at the Charterses, and had started down the driveway when I realized that I hadn't said good-bye to Allen, and craned out the window with my hand raised, yelling, "Good-bye, man!" There he was, with the pale-gold light of mid-afternoon shining on that high, sallow dome of forehead, waving and calling out, "Good-bye, John. Stay sweet!" This was the way it usually happened with us. We stood side by side, we chattered, we got distracted, and then lost one another in confusions, with too much left unsaid. There was never time.

I drove Bob Creeley and Peter back to the cathedral where Creeley's car was parked, and we said our so-longs. We were all, I think, feeling an unusual warmth toward each other, that warmth that puts a sense of twilight into some moments in life as you inexorably get older and come to accept that now you expect less, and the feelings passed between us. The last thing I saw was Peter's Day-Glo hat disappearing behind a car.

Shirley and I drove home without a break through a crisp, gathering of dusk of reds and golds, the sinking sun drawing the sap up into the last of the day, that apple-tang of late autumn elusive as leaf-smoke in the air. We were quiet and close, and we found a letter from Don Wallis, an ex-student of mine, when we finally opened our door, a letter that said in part:

> I came to see what I had always, I think, sensed: that Kerouac was a true and magnificent ORIGINAL whose vision of America was a true and magnificent one, at least for me; that thing I keep going back to, whenever Nixon & company drive me to it, is something of the open-souled country that lives in Kerouac and is alive fighting to get free throughout the land. For you who knew this long ago, and knew him, and knew all along the stupid & careless neglect or willed misreading he got from most everyone, I am sure his death is that much harder to accept.

And yes, that's true, but accept it I do, because the only alternative is a bitterness that demeans the spirit a man must serve, or a grief that belittles the love he feels. And accept it I can, because I finally had my own private wake once we got back, and decided to write up this account when I felt I could.

Words? Sometimes they nauseate a wordman with their easy

evasions, their slick sentiments, their ultimate futility to catch anything but the barest shadow of events, the fleeting aftertaste of emotions. But Jack, like all serious writers, knew that writing was a vow in the continuity of life, a vow that often had to be fashioned out of all the little deaths that precede the big one.

And now he's gone in October, but it's no less true.

Jack Kerouac: He Wrote the Great Lowell Novel

Charles G. Sampas, *Lowell Sun* (October 26, 1969)

I have written tons of history about the old Lowelltown. I have written about Kirk Boott and Dr. Elisha Bartlett and all the great worthies of the early Lowell life. I have written about the Lowelltown when it was on the make—and about twentieth-century political figures who have swayed the Lowell scene. It has all been printed in newspapers—in newsprint, and after a few years, nay, even decades, it flakes, becomes dust.

I would venture to say I have written at least 25,000,000 words about the Lowelltown, and that is a minimum. Bear in mind, when you write a daily column for thirty-six years, you manage to pour out a lot of stuff.

It won't last. Some of the history stuff will be quoted a hundred years from now when someone rewrites what I rewrote from Lowell history back, say, in 1935. No matter. My point is very simple: The one writer whose writings about Lowelltown will last for decades and centuries and who is forever, now, part of American and world literature, is Jack Kerouac, who was buried in Edson Cemetery two days ago.

And this is not personal: just because he was my sister Stella's husband is not germane. The fact is that he was one of the great writers of this twentieth century. He wrote the Great Lowell Novel. And that was *The Town and the City* and a lot of other novels which had so much of Lowell in it.

Jack Kerouac burned himself out chasing after the Muse. He wrote endlessly and he wrote tirelessly and he wrote because it was in him to write. He simply had to.

And out of his Lowell life, he evoked so much of the Lowell boyhood all of us born here in Lowell have lived. He brought Lowell High School life into focus, and the torment and joy of being young in Lowell in the 1930s.

Rereading some of his Lowell novels, you realize how much excitement there was in being young and in Lowelltown in those days and nights . . . Ah, the terrific fun it was in those days in simply being young . . . A new generation has grown up which never was really young.

His boyhood was in Pawtucketville, in streets like Phoebe Avenue and the Riverside Street complex in those days when to have been young was to have known the magic of Amateur Nights at the old Rialto Theater, of getting a job as an usher in the same theater; the thrill of the Lowell-Lawrence High School football game . . . And no one could write better and more colorfully about football than Jack Kerouac, who started out as a sports reporter for the *Lowell Sun* . . . Who can forget these wonderful sports words in *The Town and the City* and *Maggie Cassidy*? I have in front of me the latest paperback reprint in two years—and here is LHS life captured for always and forever.

Reporters and critics will write of him. They never knew him. I did. I knew him when he was in Lowell High School with his buddy, my brother Sam. I knew him when the fever of Thomas Wolfe was in his blood and he had to write—or perish.

I knew him when life was young and the whole world was young . . . when a whole generation was trying to understand life rather than trying to revolt from it.

It does not matter, some of the harsh criticism. Sure, he drank too much. Sure, he could be pretty rough with some critics. Sure, he was worn out by life. But I can tell you this: he was one of the kindest of men, and one of the most thoughtful. I have seen him take hours to help a young man trying to become a writer. I have seen him take the trouble to be polite to someone he had no use for. He did it, as he told me, "to discipline myself."

He was restless and he was lonesome and he was forever a wanderer in this world. He pondered over the great philosophers and the great thinkers—and he certainly was one of the most completely read men on earth. He read, like Thomas Wolfe, not just books—but entire libraries.

You know, in writing Lowell history, I have often told of the visits here to Lowelltown of Edgar Allan Poe . . . and how he found comfort in his tormented life in the taverns of the Lowelltown. How, here in the taverns of Hometown, he found solace and inspiration and was inspired too, to write some of his greatest poems, including "The Bells."

With the passing of time and the rolling of years, there will be other Lowell historians, other Lowell novelists to do justice to this city, all too often maligned by reporters who would never be writers . . . No matter . . . Jack Kerouac will stand above them—a Lowell boy whose books were read all over the world, a Lowell boy who didn't quite get the Nobel prize in literature, but who managed to put down the Lowell and the American Dream for eternity. And that is the greatness to last for always . . .

Is There Any End to Kerouac Highway?
The Demise of Conformity

Ken Kesey, *Esquire* (December 1983)

It was Kerouac, a shy young man, who foretold the mood of a generation. To millions coming of age in the aftermath of World War II—when America entered the odd merging of the atomic age and the Eisenhower era—society offered little more than a consuming restlessness. Kerouac wouldn't buy it; rather than succumb to the conformity and uniformity of a prosperous and complacent America, he hit the highway, a cultural outlaw. He would set a style later to be adopted by the beats, the hippies, the punks. He would inspire such icons as Brando, Dean, Dylan, and, most currently, Gere and Springsteen.

For better or worse, Ramblin' Jack had more followers than readers

Ahhh, I hate writing about a writer. Especially about Jack Kerouac, what with all these other tepid tomes being cranked out about the poor man year after prying year. But damnitall, it's time somebody spoke up for the man's work and the impact it had on us young book-reading swains a quarter of a century ago (the impact of the work, not the man; all these intimate-insights-about-the-man biographies are primarily pornographic and oughta be taken as such).

On the Road. Good ol' nation-shaking feet-stirring *On the Road.* What can we call to mind that was like unto it, impactwise? I can't recall its equal in politics or art . . . not even in music. Wait. I got one. Here's a fair parallel:

Remember coming up the aisle outta the captured black-and-white murk of the Rialto after your first seeing of *The Wild One* with Marion Brando? and going into the Men's to sideways scope, notice, that all your familiar teenage contemporaries are standing in front of the mirrors or at the urinals in a *totally unfamiliar new stance*? a kind of slouching cool indolence, yet alert, like tomcats might slouch amid the trash-can shadows, indolent on the surface, only with secret danger cocked in their alley-wise eyes. And how none of the boys ever stood quite the same again, after seeing Brando in that historic flick?

Well, for the questing book readers of us, stumbling out of the mid-century murk of Hemingway's sad suicide and Dylan Thomas's sodden demise, *On the Road* was equally stance-changing. We all tried to imitate it. Yet, even then, no one considered it the work of a Truly Great Writer. I recall my initial interpretation of the phenomenon, that, yeah, it was a pretty groovy book, but not because this guy Ker-oh-wak was such hot potatoes; that what it was actually was one of those little serendipitous accidents of fate, that's all— just the lucky catch of a once-a-generation wave by a bush-league surfer who just happened to be paddling in the right waters at the right time when that season's ninth wave came rolling by.

And like most readers, I contented myself with that view of Kerouac and his work through the bulk of the sixties. *Doctor Sax*? Second-rate Ray Bradbury spooky kid fantasy. *The Subterraneans*? Third-rate Aldous Huxley. *The Dharma Bums*? Really nothin' more'n a kinda jazzed-up remake of Kellogg Albran's *The Profit*. In fact, I didn't really begin to appreciate the slouching genius of Jack's great sprawling vision until the seventies, when Allen Ginsberg towed me into a Boulder bookstore, berating:

You haven't read *Tristessa* or *Maggie Cassidyv*. Jack's tenderest love novels? Tsk. And you haven't read *Desolation Angels* or *Lonesome Traveller*?v Or *Satori in Paris*, which is just your cup of Mystical Christian tea? Fie, Kenneth; that's scandalous. Especially for one who thinks he knows the heart and spine of Jack's work. Tsk and fie and shame . . . !

—as he piled on me a collection about seven times the size of my meager work, which happened to be next on the K shelf:

You'll love this one—published, you'll notice, abroad because hard-hearted houses in this country wouldn't touch it—and this, about Jack's little angel brother Gerard who died in his youth, and especially this, the *Vanity of Duluoz*, which happens to not only be Jack's best retrospective of America's Golden Disillusionment but is as well probably some of the best football stuff ever written, it's the final installment in the huge Kerouacian drama, without which none of the rest can be hindsightedly understood. I mean, just look at all these pages, the incredible scope of it all. Faulkner's Yoknapatawpha saga is the only domain remotely close. The sorry difference is Faulkner's territory has been secured. But there haven't been any kindly old critics come forth to rescue poor Jack the way Malcolm Cowley did for Faulkner.

I had to admit it was a considerable heft of work. I started to go for my wallet. Ginsberg put a soft hand on my sleeve:

These are on me. If you'll promise to read them all. I want you to see Jack was a lot more than merely the gold boy bard of one so-called Beat Generation. He was the Sammy Pepys, the Rudy Kipling, the Charlie Dickens of at least three American generations. And on top of that, a saint, I'll be hanged if he ain't. What we've called him here at the Jack Kerouac School of Disembodied Poetics, corny as it sounds, is Saint Jack. Oh, you've an eye-opener in store, callow quester Kenny.

How right he was. At first I was mainly reimpressed with the fluid grace of the prose and the integrity achieved by that famous fastashandscantype method of writing it. There's a sort of promise implied by this method that makes one think of the Fool card in the tarot, the singing jester blithely stepping over the edge of a cliff with rucksack over shoulder and eyes to the sky and no safety net below—the rough yipes and yodels spieled out during the Fool's fall, occurring under conditions too urgent for the convenience of careful composition, too late for the luxury of revision.

Next I noticed the continual current of gentleness running beneath that raw spiel of rough words, the mercy with which he described the vast and varied flock summoned from his memory—the tootsies and floozies, fags and wimps and dope fiends, killers and convicts and bullying sailors, hustlers and losers and phonies of the first water—yet, in all his long considering, he never puts a soul of them down.

Finally, as I wound toward the culmination of his long work, I began to feel surrounding me that rare warm glory that shines out of only the best efforts of the greatest artists. It is the light that uplifts and exhorts, that reveals us to each other as the glorious marvels we are, no matter the plugged crapper and the athlete's foot, and it shines on us at the expense of the artist's personal reserve of lamp oil.

No wonder he burned out—all those years illuminating and glorifying all the dim little scenes of our daily mundanities. No wonder he expired in a cloud of acrid smoke.

So in spite of biographers who want to brand him a boozy right-wing bigot, and ex-wifeys and girlfriends trying to label him a cad or a mama's baby, I have come to realize that, corny as it sounds, I have to go along with Ginsberg: sweet sad Jack has every right to be, in the most traditional Catholic sense, considered a candidate for canonization. He not only manifested Grace, and Mercy, and Glory, he also in some beatific way died for our scenes.

Ain't that what it takes to be a saint?

There'll be a little passage in the history of American literature on his revelation that there was a new underground generation with new standards. He was a precursor, of course, of the revolution of the 1960s. Strangely, that revolution of the sixties has receded, but *On the Road* keeps on being read.

—Malcolm Cowley

NOTES

1. Mark Van Doren, Ph.D. (1894–1972) joined the faculty of Columbia University in 1920. His legendary classroom presence inspired generations of Columbia students—many of them future writers and critics. Van Doren was also a poet, editor, and biographer. Among his writings are *Collected Poems*, which won a Pulitzer Prize in 1939; *American and British Literature since 1890*, with his brother, Carl Van Doren; critical studies of various authors, including John Dryden and Nathaniel Hawthorne; several anthologies; and *The Noble Voice*, a collection of essays. Van Doren retired from full-time teaching in 1959.

2. Louis-Ferdinand Céline (1894–1961), French author, whose real name was Louis-Ferdinand Destouches. Céline wrote grim, scatological, and blackly humorous novels. His first and best-known work, *Journey to the End of the Night*, is based on his service at the front in World War I, his travels through Africa, and his service as a League of Nations doctor. He is now generally regarded as one of the most important and influential—as well as controversial—modern French novelists.

3. Alcibiades was twenty years younger than Socrates. The *Alcibiades* dialogue is set in 432 BC in Alcibiades's eighteenth year and expressed, among other things, the "need for knowledge and goodness."

4. Ginsberg was mistaken as to the recepient of Rimbaud's letter; on May 15, 1871, Rimbaud wrote to his friend, the poet Paul Demeny: "The Poet makes himself into a *seer* by a long, involved, and logical *derangement of all the senses*. Every kind of love, of suffering, of madness; he searches himself; he exhausts every possible poison so that only essence remains."

5. The actual composition of the "scroll" version of *On the Road* took place in April 1951, ending on April 20, 1950.

6. 6 Gallery, on 3119 Fillmore St. in San Francisco, was a former auto repair shop converted to a small art gallery. The advert for this event read as follows: "6 Angels at 6 Gallery—Philip Lamantia reading mss. of late John Hoffman—Mike McClure, Allen Ginsberg, Gary Snyder & Phil Whalen—all sharp new straightforward writing—remarkable collection of angels on one stage reading their poetry. No charge, small collection for wine, and postcards. Charming event. Kenneth Rexroth, MC. 8 PM Friday Night October." Kerouac remained in the audience as a participant and a collector of coins to buy jugs of red wine.

7. Unfortunately, Kerouac's television interview with John Wingate on *Nightbeat* cannot be located in either its video or audio format, nor as a transcript. There are numerous references made to it. One such reference resides in the collection of letters by Hunter S. Thompson edited by Douglas Brinkley, *The Proud Highway: Saga of a Desperate Southern Gentleman 1955-1967*: "I recall one night in the West End Tavern [located near Columbia University in New York City], when hundreds of people gathered to watch Kerouac's first appearance on TV. It was the John Wingate show, and when Kerouac came slinking out of the wings a great cheer went up in the West End. He was, I suppose, the Bob Dylan of his day—and saying that makes me feel damed old."

8. Oswald Spengler (1880–1936), German philospher and historian. His studies also covered other fields, such as mathematics, science, and art. His masterwork, *The Decline of the West* (2 vols., 1918–1922; tranlated 1926–1928), brought him worldwide recognition. Spengler asserted that every culture endures a life cycle from youth through maturity and old age to death. Western culture, he theorized, had passed through this same cycle and consequently entered a period of decline which there was no evading. Spengler upheld the ideal of obedience to the state and endorsed German hegemony in Europe. His refusal to maintain an alliance with Nazi theories of racial superiority led to his ostracism after the Nazis came to power in 1933. *The Decline of the West* was a work of considerable interest and influence for Kerouac and the Beats as it was for Fitzgerald and other writers of the Lost Generation.

9. Apparently publishers weren't ready for it until after the death of Kerouac in 1969; *Visions of Neal* was published as *Visions of Cody* by McGraw-Hill in 1972.

10. Carmine De Sapio (December 10, 1908–July 27, 2004) was an American politician from New York City. Floyd Patterson (January 4, 1935–)was a middle-to-heavyweight boxer who ultimately defeated heavyweight champion Archie Moore on November 30, 1956.

11. Carl Sandburg (January 6, 1878–July 22, 1967) was an American poet and biographer of Abraham Lincoln.

12. Ginsberg's "latest poem" was "Kaddish," written in memory of Ginsberg's mother, Naomi Ginsberg.

13. Richard Wilbur, one of the world's most highly regarded poets, is also considered one of America's finest. Wilbur utilizes traditional meters and forms in his poetry and served as poet laureate of the United States from 1987 to 1988. His numerous books of poetry have earned him two Pulitzer prizes, two Bollingen prizes, and the National Book Award. Besides being an internationally recognized translator of poems and plays from French and other languages, Mr. Wilbur has also published books of nonfiction prose and two books for children, and wrote the lyrics for Leonard Bernstein's score for the musical *Candide*. He has taught on the faculties of Harvard, Wesleyan University, Wellesley College, and Smith College. He has also served as the president and chancellor of the American Academy of Arts and Letters. (biography from the Web site of the English Department of the University of Illinois at Urbana-Champaign)

14. Perhaps a reference to the Congregation of Marians of the Immaculate Conception, a monastic order of Poland founded in 1673 that promotes the teachings of Christ and the personal value of self-sacrifice.

15. Kerouac's allusion to "empty phantoms" is derived from Virgil's *Aeneid*. Virgil describes the account of the descent of Aeneas to the gate of hell under the guidance of the Sibyl: "Full in the midst of this infernal Road, An Elm displays her dusky Arms abroad; The God of Sleep there hides his heavy Head And empty Dreams on ev'ry Leaf are spread. Of various Forms, unnumber'd Specters more; Centaurs, and double Shapes, besiege the Door: Before the Passage horrid Hydra stands, And Briareus with all his hundred Hands: Gorgons, Geryon with his triple Frame; And vain Chimaera vomits empty Flame. The Chief unsheath'd his shining Steel, prepar'd Tho seiz'd with sudden Fear, to force the Guard. Off'ring his brandish'd Weapon at their Face; Had not the Sibyl stop'd his eager Pace, And told him what those empty Phantoms were; Forms without Bodies, and impassive Air."

16. Gnosticism places the salvation of the soul in the possession merely of a believer's quasi-intuitive knowledge of the mysteries of the universe. Therefore, Gnostics were "people who knew," and their intuited knowledge marked them as a superior class of beings whose present and future status was essentially different from that of those who, for whatever reason, did not know.

17. Cassady had mailed the letter to Kerouac on December 23, 1950. It was the best Christmas gift he could have sent him; from this missive Kerouac finally found the solution to writing *On the Road*, which would be fleshed out in its realized form mere months later.

18. Kerouac describes this Tibetan ceremony in his novel, *The Dharma Bums*, p. 25: "The man sits crosslegged on a pillow on the floor naked. The woman comes over and sits down on him naked, facing him with her arms about his neck, and they sit like that, saying nothing, for a while. Don in the temples of Tibet. It's a holy ceremony, it's done just like this in front of chanting priests. People pray and recite Om Meani Pahdme Hum, 'Amen the Thunderbolt in the Dark Void.' And they meditate until they fall to the side and then begin . . . . The man is the thunderbolt and the woman is the dark void. Others join in . . . . Bodhisattva women of Tibet and parts of ancient India, were taken and used as holy concubines in temples and sometimes in ritual caves and would get to lay up a stock of merit and they meditated too. Meditation, fasting, then thunderbolt and void . . . ."

19. The bohemianesque Dill Pickle Club was located at 18 Tooker Alley, just east of Chicago's Bughouse Square. Dill Pickle operated as a combination coffeehouse, art gallery, and speakeasy. The clientele usually consisted of vagrants, professors, prostitutes, homosexuals, and every variety of nonconformist passing through Chicago. The club hosted weekend jazz dance parties and little theater productions of Strindberg, Ibsen, O'Neill, and local playwrights. In its early years, the Pickle, as it came to be known, was a meeting place for some of Chicago's most famous authors, intellectuals, and radicals, including Carl Sandburg, Sherwood Anderson, Floyd Dell, Clarence Darrow, Ben Reitman, Lucy Parsons, Ralph Chaplin, Ben Hecht, Harriet Monroe, and Vachel Lindsay. The *Chicago Daily News* journalist was a regular at the Dill Pickle Club during the early 1920s.

20. John Foster Dulles (February 25, 1888–May 24, 1959) served as secretary of state in the administration of President Dwight D.

Eisenhower, where he was instrumental in forming the Southeast
Asia Treaty Organization (SEATO). He resigned his office on April
15, 1959, after being diagnosed with cancer. He was awarded the
Medal of Freedom shortly before his death.

21. "I put "cut fingertips" instead of "mincing" to describe the effect of
inexperiencedly picking cotton (also, "mincing" sounds funny, like I
was a fairy)" Jack Kerouac to AGA, Jan 12, 1960.

22. "My shoes were 'clunkers', not clunkety-clunk, in Railroad Earth."
Jack Kerouac to AGA, Jan. 12, 1960

23. "I put in proper 'was' for football star, as clippings prove, and please,
Al, send the clippings back (one sports reporter on *Newsday*, Stan
Isaacs, doesn't believe I was a football star, and others too, like I suppose people wouldn't believe that Herman Melville was a whal-
ingman)" Jack Kerouac to AGA, Jan 12, 1960.

24. "Various inserts . . . singing to Frank Sinatra, 'up the stars', etc., are
obvious, and you should put them in for accuracy and tome of
article" Jack Kerouac to AGA, Jan 12, 1960.

25. Kerouac cut the word "Northport" and changed it to "Long Island."
"Yes, Sterling [Lord, Kerouac's agent] and I do not want mention of
Northport; you said that 'it should be left in the record that I once
lived there." I STILL live there; I do not want carloads of zen beatnik
hipsters scouting my yard and house? How'd you expect me to get
work done here? Have you no idea of the number of people who
would like to 'meet' me and visit me? Don't you know it runs in the
thousands and thousands, mostly teenagers full of insane desire to be
big Dean Moriarty's? And all kinds of people, even recently some of
Carl Solomon's friends from the nut-house got on my milk route and
what can you really expect from them? My mother is old and quiet
and needs her quietness at home. Well, now you understand. Jack
Kerouac to AGA, undated.

26. The last two sentences of that paragraph are an insert by Kerouac.
Jack Kerouac to AGA, Jan 12, 1960.

27. "A long insert about what I think about *Life* Magazine, etc. 'Brainwashed journalists who build their own hells.' If you don't put these
things in I'll know your article on the Beat Gen. was a hatchet-job
ordered by Wechsler . . . .but this volume is not for the *Post*, it's for
posterity" Jack Kerouac to AGA, January 12, 1960.

28. "When my mother said she liked 'one of them' in Calif. she meant
Whalen" Jack Kerouac to AGA, Jan 12, 1960.

29. "In the French-talking part, where I say *tu tutoye* you don't use an accent egue over the 'e' in '*tutoye*' (present tense) . . . And in French the name is Kerouac with the accent egue [sic]. And Michel Mohrt did say the French my mother and I spoke was pure 18th century Norman French, which was substantiated recently by visiting Quebecois scholar here at the house. In other words, 'French-Canadian' is a pure preservation of old pre-Louis XIV French before the influence of Moorish and Germanic on the French language which has now resulted in 'Parisia' guttural that you hear in French movies (however NOT in Jean Gavin and Maurice Chevalier, by the way, who are Normans). This is facts. Do you realize that everybody in Quebec is delighted with the French in *Doctor Sax*?" Jack Kerouac to AGA, January 12, 1960.

30. "Don't say that I read Henry Miller all my life, it just isn't true, I did read Louis Ferdinand Celine, from whom Miller obtained his style. I never could find a copy of the *Tropics* [Henry Miller's novels *Tropic of Cancer* (Obelisk, 1936) and *Tropic of Capricorn*, (Obelisk, 1939)] anyway. I think Miller is a great man but Celine, his master, is a giant." Jack Kerouac to AGA, Jan 12, 1960. Miller did not, as it turned out, write the introduction to *The Subterraneans*. (ed.).

31. "Allen Ginsberg did say 'I'd hate to be a poet in a country where Wechsler is the Commissar of Poetry' so there's no harm in that insert, factually, and are you afraid of Wechsler? I'm not and never will be." Jack Kerouac to AGA, Jan 12, 1960

32. "I didn't 'spit' talking about Columbia football, I wouldn't spit on my mother's floor . . . I went 'Pooh!' . . . I 'pooh-spit'" Jack Kerouac to AGA, Jan 12, 1960.

33. "Huncke was once bitter but isn't anymore . . . has sweetened completely . . ." Jack Kerouac to AGA, Jan 12, 1960.

34. "I repeat that James Wechsler accused me of not believing in Peace, which is a terrible thing to say about anybody who is not a munitions maker" Jack Kerouac to AGA, Jan 12, 1960.

35. "For 'beatific' paragraph I clarify about 'first confirmation' as my 'first vow'– this is extremely important and clear . . . that's why it doesn't apply to 'anyone else' in the beat gen." Jack Kerouac to AGA, Jan 12, 1960.

36. See note #1, Beat.

37. "Ronnie on the Mound" is published in *Good Blonde & Others* (Grey Fox Press, 1993).

38. Louis Milestone (1895–1980) was a Hollywood director of such films as *Two Arabian Nights* (1927), *Of Mice and Men* (1939), and *Mutiny on the Bounty* (1962).

39. Kerouac trained and served as a forest service lookout (or a "fire-spotter") in the Cascade Mountains of Washington State from June 1956 until September 1956.

40. Honore de Balzac (1799–1850) was a French journalist and writer, regarded as one of the creators of realism in world literature. Balzac's huge production of novels and short stories are collected under the name *La Comédie Humaine*. This inspired Kerouac to create his own autobiographical epic, *The Legend of Duluoz*.

41. Kerouac mentions to Robert Giroux in a letter dated February 19, 1963, that *Passing Through* was the sequel to *Desolation Angels*. Ellis Amburn, Kerouac's editor at Coward-McCann, who would ultimately publish *Desolation Angels*, advised Kerouac to merge the two smaller novels into one large novel. Part One, *Desolation Angels*, spanned the year 1956, with the second part, *Passing Through*, covering 1956 into 1957.

42. Kerouac was already planning as early as 1961 to rework his 1942 novel, *Vanity of Duluoz* (published 1968), and write another novel called *Memory Babe*. The former would have covered the years 1939 to 1943; the latter, 1926 to 1932 in his vast Duluoz Legend. *Memory Babe* was ultimately written in French and remains untranslated and unpublished.

43. Kerouac is quoting from the second part of Ginsberg's poem "Howl": "Moloch! Solitude! Filth! Ugliness! Ashcans and unobtainable dollars!"

44. James Jones (1921–1977), one of the major novelists of his generation, is known primarily as the author of fiction that probes the effects of World War II on the individual soldier. Born in Robinson, Illinois, Jones entered the U.S. Army and had the distinction of being the only major writer to witness the attack by the Japanese on Pearl Harbor. He wrote *From Here to Eternity* (1951) and *The Thin Red Line* (1962), among numerous other novels.

45. Kerouac had actually taken the taxi from Old Saybrook, Connecticut, from the home of John Clellon Holmes.

46. *Visions of Gerard* was written between December 27, 1956, and January 16, 1957. The "whole night's writing" that Kerouac rejected occurred on January 11: "seven successive benzedrine nights have

left me thought-empty and I cant get high no more—So I must lay off for 3 days and try again, Sat. night. Novel almost finished but the final funeral scene which I must do now, is a subject that wearies me" (Kerouac, *Some of the Dharma*, p. 378).

47. *An American Passed Here* was retitled *Passing Through* and incorporated as one of two "novels" that comprised a single book titled *Desolation Angels*.

48. *Fuck You: A Magazine of the Arts* was an independent publication founded in 1964 and edited by Ed Sanders. This publication featured poetry and addressed such issues as the legalization of marijuana.

49. President Lyndon B. Johnson initiated the Great Society during his 1964 presidential campaign. The Great Society was a "place where men are more concerned with the quality of their lives than the quantity of their goods." The Great Society had three central themes: abundance and liberty for all, an end to poverty, and an end to racial injustice.

50. "Beware of false prophets, which come to you in sheep's clothing, but inwardly they are ravening wolves" (Matthew 7:15).

51. Thomas Hayden, in 1962, drafted the famous Port Huron Statement expressing the idealism of the New Left. He was also cofounder of the Students for a Democratic Society. In the early sixties, Hayden participated in civil rights work in the South and in the black ghettoes of Newark. He later shifted his focus to efforts to end the Vietnam War, twice making trips to North Vietnam. After the Chicago Seven trial, Hayden married (and later divorced) activist actress Jane Fonda. Hayden also served as a state senator in California and attended the 1996 Democratic National Convention in Chicago as a delegate. Rennie Davis was, at the time of trial, the twenty-nine-year-old national director of community organizing programs for the Students for a Democratic Society. As a movement bureaucrat based in Chicago, Davis did most of the organizing for the Convention-week demonstrations.

52. The Blackstone Rangers (also known as the Black P Stone Nation) in the 1960s were Chicago's most famous gang. Started by a dozen twelve-to-fifteen-year-old kids from Blackstone Avenue in Woodlawn, the Rangers were led by Jeff Fort and came into existence on the heels of the Black Power movement.

53. The Progessive Labor Party fought for one working class, one party, and one world. Espousing communism over capitalism, the PLP

continue to believe that "communism can be won only through armed struggle by masses of workers, soldiers, students, and others to destroy the dictatorship of the capitalist class and set up a dictatorship of the working class."

54. The black flag was used by anarchists as a symbol at least from the early 1880s. The origin of the symbol is not clear, but it was adopted and bonded to anarchism during the latter half of the nineteenth century.

55. Writing to Allen Ginsberg on June 4, 1968, Kerouac describes a recent arrest and lashes out at Allen for his apparent loss of freedom due to the dissension of America's hippie youth: "I was in can month ago for carrying a bottle of beer (open) in street, in filthy cell in which I caught strep throat, and there was nothing in the papers about it. So you and your pals go to jail for disrupting society, and I go to jail for not disrupting anything at all . . . . I never was arrested in my life till the civil rights movement made the cops jittery and paranoid of everybody they see on the sidewalk."

56. Lawrence Sterne (1713–1768), English novelist and satirist, author of *Tristram Shandy* (1760) and *A Sentimental Journey through France and Italy* (1768).

Appendix

On March 15, Kerouac wrote his Lowell friend Sebastian Sampas from Lowell: "I failed to pass the Air Corps test, as you know I'm glad now I'm going to be a gob after reading about officers in your camp." The following Sunday, Jack was alone in his parents' Crawford Street home. Leo was working in Connecticut, and Gabrielle was visiting her stepmother in Brooklyn. Caroline had quit Sullivan Printers and joined the Women's Army Corps, leaving Jack isolated from his immediate family. At 4 A.M. on March 23, he wrote to Sebastian after Margaret Coffey had just left. After he kissed her goodbye and shut the door, he lit a cigarette and paced the house until he sat down to write: "Sunday morning. I shall go to church at 8 A.M. and kneel with the faithful, not for the church's sake, but for the sake of humanity. I am all alone in this silent house, tonight. The ghosts of those I love haunt me in the sorrowful stillness, not leering, capricious ghosts, but loving ghosts who touch my lonely brow with tender care." He recalled the times in Lowell when those now empty rooms had been filled with gaiety, when his friends crowded at his doorstep, when the future still glimmered with opportunity. Now that he was drafted, the outlook seemed grimmer than ever, and he wept. "I was alone. I don't know why, Sam, but tell me: Why did I begin to weep? I tell you I wept. . . . [M]y throat constricted, I sobbed, and tears went down my cheeks. I think it was the loneliness and the thought of humanity. I tell you, I had such a vision of humanity tonight, such a clear, powerful vision (tied up with me, my loved ones, and the human race), such a vision, I tell you, as I'd never expected to see, that it broke my heart and I cried." Closer to the truth may be that Jack realized he now was helpless to change the course of his life. Less than a week later, Kerouac entered basic training as a seaman's apprentice in the U.S. Navy.

At Newport, Kerouac had little in the way of an intellectual peer; luckily, he did have his hand-printed notebook of the third draft of "The Sea Is My Brother," which he worked on during off-hours. Not long after his arrival, Kerouac was straining against the incessant demands of military discipline. The violations of his "freedoms" initially were minor. He wanted to smoke when he chose to do so, not when an officer allowed it. There were other factors as well: the numerous work details like keeping barracks watch with a gun and holster around his waist and scrubbing latrines were, according to Jack, demeaning. Kerouac maintained a convincing front for his mother when he wrote home, leading her to believe that he was enduring all of this without conflict. She replied that she was "glad to know where you are and know that you are O.K. I'm also glad you like it, I was worried." Even toward Sebastian he kept his reserve and stuck to their discussions about philosophy, literature, and their shared Lowell past. In the barracks Kerouac continued to assert his disdain for the military. Sometimes he went to sick bay seeking aspirin for his headaches (which he told his mother in a letter were caused by his car accident in Vermont). On his nightly watch in the barracks—equipped with a pea coat, trousers, leggings, bow cap, and a club slung from his white belt—Kerouac would watch the rest of the men sleep. "I mind my own business," he told Sebastian, "they can have their peckers hanging out for all I care."

After a while, the basic training, with the navy's entrenched practice of dehumanization, disgusted him. He saw no sense in washing garbage cans and enduring the endless repetition of marching drills. One day, as the rest of the company went through its routines, Kerouac declined to handle any weapon designed to kill his fellow man. He put his gun down on the ground and walked away "from everybody forever more." He strolled to the base library to read, where military police accosted him. Kerouac surrendered, telling the guards that he simply was not equipped to complete basic training. They prodded him with questions, which Kerouac answered matter-of-factly. "You're off to the nuthouse, kid," one of the guards taunted as Jack was carted away in an ambulance. Kerouac fired off a letter to his parents telling them of his "condition," which he surmised might have stemmed from his frantic writing of "The Sea Is My Brother." While in the hospital, he was placed under psychiatric observation, given a neurological test, and administered a written IQ exam. (Kerouac claimed he had the highest intelligence quotient in the history of the Newport base.) Afterward, Kerouac suspected that they probably had thought him a Communist. But intuitively he knew that his behavior amounted to merely a "maladjustment with military life," a fact upon which both he and interviewing psychiatrist Dr. Conrad Tully seemed to agree. Tully noted in his report: "As one somewhat defiant in accordance with his beliefs as to the rights, duties, and behavior of human beings in an organized group, and as one who follows the promptings of his conscience, one might conceivably guide his conduct, in such cases, in accordance with principles unsafe to follow under military conditions. A member of the armed forces, whether enlisted or drafted, is not considered to have the right to act differently than the military unit; individuality is subordinated to obedience and discipline. Anyone not conforming to this regimen is of no use to the organization."

Kerouac, an avid reader of Henry David Thoreau, saw no shame in practicing passive resistance and, ironically, took pride in Dr. Tully's description of him as being afflicted with "extreme preoccupation." Trying to establish a prognosis by first inquiring into Kerouac's emotional attachments, the psychiatrist questioned him further. Kerouac revealed that he "wasn't in love with any girl," contradicting his emotional letters to Norma Blickfelt in New York City and a new girl named Edie Parker, whom he had first met briefly in the fall of 1942 when she was dating Henri Cru, Kerouac's Horace Mann classmate. Jack had no plans for marriage; callously he reduced his liaisons to either "mistresses" or "various promiscuous wenches." As noted in the published documents of recently declassified National Archive papers, Kerouac stated he was somewhat traumatized by a sexual experience with an older woman in Lowell when he was fourteen. Kerouac also stated that his relationships with his male friends made him feel more "closely attached," both spiritually and emotionally. In Kerouac's assessment, he was "pouring it on thick" to test the young doctor's reaction. However, Tully's thoughts about his patient's statements remained neutral.

With both children gone, Leo (fifty-four) and Gabrielle (fifty-eight) left Lowell for the last time as a couple and moved to New York City. However, their feuding and Leo's extended absences gave Gabrielle ideas of separating from him until he found a steady job—by no means a certain prospect, given her husband's age. Eventually, when Leo was securely employed, she moved into an apartment in Ozone Park, Queens, at 13301 Crossbay Boulevard, near her step-mother. After a while, Leo joined her and lived out the last three years of his life in fitful insolence and fractured pride. Initially, Jack's being drafted encouraged Gabrielle to buy into the Navy's patriotic, pro-war propaganda; she sent even more letters to boost his morale. But the underlying reality of Jack's personality could not be denied. Ultimately, she realized that Jack had not just temporarily run afoul of the military but that his "maladjustment" placed him firmly and entirely outside the conventions of military discipline. On May 3 Gabrielle wrote to her son inquiring, "What seems to be all the fuss out there?" In a letter Jack had asked her to attest to his "symptoms" (she had noted his hands shaking as he was drinking a cup of coffee) to the doctors.

It was Leo who relayed to her the news that Jack had refused to proceed with his training—or "in other words refuse to serve your country," as she stated bluntly in a letter to Jack.

Leo, however, sympathized with Jack's subversive defiance of authority and lauded his courage and convictions, while Caroline expressed concern for her brother's welfare. She felt that his enlist-ment would be a "lot safer" for him, rather than pursuing the reck-less path that he had been following for the past two years. Tired of his sister's incessant badgering, Jack did not bother replying. Ker-ouac was transferred to Bethesda Naval Hospital in Maryland. Iden-tifying himself with Dostoyevsky's Raskolnikov, a guilt-ridden Kerouac worked in his hospital room on "The Sea Is My Brother," which the naval doctors had already perused. However, Sebastian Sampas responded to Kerouac that he had "misunderstood" the novel *Crime and Punishment* and the foundation of its protagonist:

"At the beginning of the book, Raskolnikov is the over-refined, polished, finished product of the Western World. It is only through great suffering that he forgets himself—his own, Razumikhin's (who was a product of the Russian earth, a friend, a brother, and who never knew the Western World) and Sonya's. In this great suffering he forgets himself."

Influenced by literary and philosophical ideas that he had already encountered, Kerouac remained stoic in his decision to withdraw from the war effort. He said that it wasn't that he "[would] not accept discipline; I cannot." Ideas ranging from Thoreau's philosophy of passive resistance to Whitman's "Song of Myself" led him to delve into the core of his "extreme preoccupation." At Bethesda, Kerouac was surrounded by wounded vets and shell-shocked soldiers, and he sympathized greatly with those fallen comrades in black body bags unloaded onto the tarmac. Later in *Vanity of Duluoz,* he wrote that he "could have gained a lot out of loyal membership to that outfit." By war's end, when several close friends and casual acquaintances had perished, he would be haunted by the pall of death that seemed to plague him. (His later support for the military as embodied by the American soldier in both the Korean and Vietnam conflicts would find him once again out of step with his times.) Ultimately Kerouac realized he was in possession of "creative powers" and just needed, as he told Lowell friend John "Ian" Macdonald, "faith" in himself to fully realize his potential: "I must change my life, now, I have reached 21 and I am in dead earnest about all things. This does not mean I shall cease my debauching; you see, Ian, debauchery is the release of man from whatever stringencies he's applied to himself. In a sense, each debauchery is a private though short-lived insurgence from the static conditions of his society."

Kerouac, in his introspection, began to align himself with various writers of merit. In a letter to a Lowell friend (after giving himself a "searing self-analysis" from which he determined that "Fate closes portals to us and opens others; until all are closed at Death, Fate's master-stroke") he listed books he had read and his assessment of each: Joyce's *Portrait of the Artist as a Young Man* was "the Artist as an independent soul bending to nothing"; John Steinbeck's characters from his recent book *The Moon Is Down* were "conquerors conquered by the people"; Dostoyevsky's *Crime and Punishment* contained a "violent d.p. [dementia praecox] Raskolnikov—part schizoid—a Hamlet too destructively intelligent to live"; Hemingway's *Farewell to Arms* portrayed "War as it is—the price of love—the lost gene'rion" and *The Sun Also Rises* revealed a "sex-drive in life gone" with "bullfights for release." Kerouac's assessment of Hemingway was that he was a "supreme craftsman, investigation of American ideals on native grounds." His own novel "The Sea Is My Brother" Kerouac described as "Fate, the scheme of things, as a directing force in life."

Published for the first time are Kerouac's military medical record relating to his discharge.

National Archives and Records Administration

700 Pennsylvania Avenue, NW

Washington, DC 20408-0001

Jack Kerouac

Excerpts from official military personnel file

National Personnel Records Center

732-58-22 NAME KEROUAC, John Louis (SERVICE NO.) A. S. $50.00 (RATE) (PAY PER MONTH)

DATE 8 - 12 - 42 A FIRST ENLISTMENT ☒ REENLISTMENT ☐ IN THE UNITED STATES NAVY: (DAY) (MONTH) (YEAR)
AS REGULAR ☐ RESERVE ☒ CLASS V-1(G) FOR 4 YEARS; MINORITY ☐
ACCEPTED AT ONOP., No. York, N.Y. ENLISTED AT ONOP., New York, N.Y.
TRANSFERRED TO ACTIVE DUTY ☐ OR INACTIVE DUTY ☒
OCCUPATION Student *CITIZENSHIP U.S.
PLACE OF BIRTH Lowell, Mass. DATE OF BIRTH March 12, 1922 AGE 20 YRS. 9 MOS.

HOME ADDRESS 125 Crawford St. Lowell Middlesex Mass.
(STREET AND NUMBER) (TOWN) (COUNTY) (STATE)
NAME OF NEXT KIN OR LEGAL GUARDIAN Mrs. Gabrielle Kerouac Mother (RELATIONSHIP)
ADDRESS Same MARRIED ☐ SINGLE ☒
CREDITED TO 5th CONGRESSIONAL DISTRICT, STATE OF Massachusetts

PREVIOUS SERVICE - If none, check here ☒

**Continuous Service Certificate No. First enlisted in Regular Navy ☐ Navy Reserve ☐
Date Place Last Enlistment or Extension: Regular Navy ☐ Navy Reserve ☐
Date Term Was last discharged From
With Discharged as Service in Regular Navy (DATE)
Navy Reserve (YEARS) (MONTHS) (DAYS) Marine Corps (YEARS) (MONTHS) (DAYS) Coast Guard (YEARS) (MONTHS) (DAYS) Army (YEARS) (MONTHS) (DAYS)

PHYSICAL CHARACTERISTICS
Height 5 Feet 8.5 Inches; Weight 172 ; Eyes blue ; Sex male ; Hair bro ; Complexion med Color W US
(COLOR)
MARKS:

ANT: VSLA; Vertical scar outer surface right leg;

POST: mole over rt scapula region. Sc rt little finger.

I CERTIFY that I have carefully examined, agreeably to the Regulations of the Navy, the above-named recruit, and find that, in my opinion, he is free from all bodily defects and mental infirmity which would, in any way, disqualify him from performing the duties of his rating, or that he has stated he has not the has to be hereby allowed concealed or likely to be inherited.

G. E. LEE, LT. (jg)(MC)USNR, Examining Surgeon.

For and in consideration of the pay or wages due to the ratings which may from time to time be assigned me during the continuance of my service, I agree to and with D. K. WALKER, Lt. D-V(S), USNR of the United States Navy, as follows:
(NAME OF COMMANDING OFFICER)

First: To enter the service of the Navy of the United States and to report to such station or vessel of the Navy as I may be ordered to join, and to the utmost of my power and ability discharge my several services or duties and be in everything conformable and obedient to the several requirements and lawful commands of the officers who may be placed over me.

Second: I oblige and subject myself to serve 4 years from date of enlistment unless sooner discharged by proper authority, and on the conditions provided by the act of Congress of March 3, 1875, as follows:

SEC. 1422. That it shall be the duty of the commanding officer of any fleet, squadron, or vessel acting singly, when on service, to send to an Atlantic or to a Pacific port of the United States as their enlistment may have occurred on either the Atlantic or Pacific Coast of the United States, in some public or other vessel, all petty officers and persons of inferior ratings desiring to go there at the expiration of their terms of enlistment, or so soon thereafter as may be, unless, in his opinion, the detention of such persons for a longer period should be essential to the public interests, in which case he may detain them, or any of them until the vessel to which they belong shall return to such Atlantic or Pacific port. All persons enlisted without the limits of the United States may be discharged, on the expiration of their enlistment, either in a foreign port or in a port of the United States, as they may be detained in above provided beyond the term of their enlistment; and that all persons so enlisted shall be entitled, according to the provisions of this act, shall be subject in all respects to the laws and regulations for the government of the Navy until their return to an Atlantic or Pacific port and their regular discharge; and all persons so detained by such officer, or restricting to serve until the return to an Atlantic or Pacific port of the vessel to which they belong shall in no case be held in the service more than thirty days after their arrival in said port; and that all persons who shall be so detained beyond their term of enlistment, or who shall after the termination of their enlistment, voluntarily reenter to serve until the return in an Atlantic or Pacific port of the vessel to which they belong and their regular discharge therefrom, shall receive for the time during which they are so detained or shall so serve beyond their original term of enlistment, an addition of one-fourth of their former pay: Provided, That the shipping articles shall hereafter contain the substance of this section.

In the event of war or National emergency declared by the President to exist during my term of service, I oblige and subject myself to serve until six months after the end of the war or National emergency if so required by the Secretary of the Navy unless I voluntarily reenlist or extend my enlistment. I understand that when so detained the addition of one-quarter pay as specified in Section 1422, Revised Statutes, is not applicable.

I also oblige myself, during such service, to comply with and be subject to such laws, regulations, and articles for the government of the Navy as are or shall be hereafter established by the Congress of the United States or other competent authority, and to submit to treatment for the prevention of smallpox, typhoid (typhoid prophylaxis), and to such other preventive measures as may be considered necessary by naval authorities.

Third: I am of the legal age to enlist; I have never deserted from the United States Navy, Army, Marine Corps, or Coast Guard; I have never been discharged from the United States Service or other service on account of disability or through sentence of either civilian or military court; and I have never been discharged from any service, civil or military, except with good character and for the reasons given by me to the recruiting officer prior to enlistment. I am not a member of the Naval Reserve, Naval Militia, Marine Corps Reserve, National Guard, or Army Reserve.

Fourth: I understand that upon enlistment in the Naval Reserve, or upon transfer or assignment thereto, I may be ordered to active duty in time of war or when in the opinion of the President a National emergency exists, and that I may be required to perform active duty throughout the war or until the National emergency ceases to exist.

Fifth: I understand that if I become a candidate for the Naval Academy and fail to pass the entrance examination, I will be returned to general service.

Sixth: I have had this contract fully explained to me, I understand it, and certify that no promise of any kind has been made to me concerning assignment to duty, or promotion during my enlistment.

Oath of Allegiance: I, John Louis KEROUAC do solemnly swear (or affirm) that I will bear true faith and allegiance to the United States of America, and that I will serve them honestly and faithfully against all their enemies whomsoever, and that I will obey the orders of the President of the United States and the orders of the officers appointed over me, according to the rules and articles for the government of the Navy.
And I do further swear (or affirm) that all statements made by me as now given in this record are correct.

John Louis Kerouac
(SIGNATURE IN OWN HANDWRITING, SURNAME TO RIGHT)

Subscribed and sworn to before me this 8th day of December A.D. 1942 and contract perfected.

*CITIZENSHIP.—Native born, use initials U. S.; Naturalized, N. U. S.; Alien, intention declared, A. D. I.; Alien, A; Guam, Guam; Philippine Islands, P. I.; Samoa, Samoa; and Virgin Islands, V. I.
**For reenlistments with continuous service note Art. D-1002, Bureau of Naval Personnel Manual.

SHIPPING ARTICLES
PART 1 FOR BuPers ENLISTED MAN'S JACKET

Form H-8
(1940)

Page ....

MEDICAL HISTORY

⑧ KEROUAC
(Surname)

John   Louis
(Christian name(s))

Born: Place Lowell, Mass.   Date 3-12-22

STATE NAME OF PLACE   DATE EACH NEW ENTRY

U.S.N. HOSPITAL, NEWPORT, R.I.

RATE: 4-2-43

DIAGNOSIS: DU(DEMENTIA PRAECOX) #2122

NOT DUE TO MISCONDUCT.

HISTORY:

He complained of headaches and he asked
for aspirin instead "they diagnosed me
Dementia Praecox" and sent me here. I
was frank with them. I was in a series
of ventures and I knew they'd look them
up; like getting fired from jobs and
getting out of college".

F.H: Denied familial disease. Mother is
nervous and father is emotional.

Personal History: This 21 year old A.S.
USNR was born in Lowell, Mass on 3/12/22.
He is single, Catholic and enlisted in
N.Y.City on Dec. 1942, cannot recall the
date. Reported for active duty on March
22, 1943 at the N.T.S., Newport. Admitted
to the sick list March 30, 1943 having
had 8 days active duty before entering
sick list.

Developmental: Denies enuresis.

Educational: Two years of college.

Occupational: Not employed.

Military: Very poor adjustment. "I just
can't stand it; I like to be by myself".
He was in the Merchant Marine and was
fired because he was bucking everybody.

Sexual: He had a sex contact at age of 14
with a 32 year old woman which upset him
somewhat.

Habits: Smokes pack and a half a day.
Spree drinker.

Religious: Less religious.

Criminal: Denied ever being arrested.

500

Page _____

MEDICAL HISTORY

J. Kerouac J L

STATE NAME OF PLACE   DATE EACH NEW ENTRY

Clinical: Denied.

Mental: Denied.

Mental Exam: Appearance is neat.
Cooperative and inclined to exaggerate.
Emotionally he is not depressed.
He imagines in his mind whole symphonies;
he can hear every note. He sees printed
pages of words. Attention easily held,
gained and directed. Memory good. J.J.
O'CONNELL LIEUT. (MC) USNR

4-23-43: "My diagnosis is dementia
praecox" but as far as I'm concerned
I am nervous; I get nervous in an
emotional way but I'm not nervous enough
to get a discharge. I don't hear voices
talking to me from no where but I have
a photographic picture before my eyes;
when I go to sleep and I hear music
playing.I know I shouldn't have told the
psychiatrist that but I wanted to be
frank. J.J.O'CONNELL LIEUT. (MC) USNR

4-23-43: Patient's father, Leo A.Kerouac
states that his son has been "boiling"
for a long time. Has always been se-
clusive, stubborn, head strong, resentful
of authority and advice, being unreliable
unstable and undependable. B.L.ALLEN LT.
COMDR. (MC) USNR

5-4-43: Feels that he has improved.
His nervousness has decreased. The first
impression that the doctors got of him
was incorrect, he states, for he did not
take them seriously. Likes the sea and
will the jointhe Merchant Marine if he
can get out of the Navy. G.H.TARR LT.(JG)
(MC) USNR

5-8-43: Social Data:
"Interested in world affairs and political
theory. Is gregarious. Has many boy
friends. Mother believes him heterosexual but interest in girls shallow.
Somewhat stubborn. Broods when unhappy
or lonely.

5-8-43: Blood Kahn and urinalysis negative. B.L.ALLEN LT.COMDR.(MC)USNR

Form H-8
(1940)

Page ....

MEDICAL HISTORY

⑩   KEROUAC
(Surname)

John   Louis
(Christian name(s))

Born: Place Lowell, Mass.   Date 3-12-22

STATE NAME OF PLACE   DATE EACH NEW ENTRY

C 5-11-43: DIAGNOSIS CHANGED THIS DATE TO
39 DEMENTIA PRAECOX #1509. Reason establish-
& ed, not duty, not misconduct and E.P.T.E.
RA Recommend that he be brought before a
Board of Medical Survey for disposition
as he is unsuitable for Naval Service.
B.L.ALLEN LT.COMDR. (MC) USNR

5-14-43: Board of Medical Survey this
date found Dementia Praecox #1509.
Reason established, not duty, not misconduct and E.P.T.E. Recommends that he
be transferred to the National Naval
Medical Center, Bethesda, Maryland,
for disposition and treatment accompanied
by an officer and two hospital corpsmen.
B.L.ALLEN LT.COMDR. (MC) USNR

T 5-18-43: Transferred this date to the
7 National Naval Medical Center, Bethesda,
Maryland for disposition and treatment
in accordance with approved recommendation and COM One Dispatch #151449 dated
5/15/43.

B. Allen.
B.L.ALLEN
LT.COMDR. (MC) USNR

APPROVED:

C.C.Fuller.
C.C.FULLER
COMDR. (MC) USNR
CHIEF OF MEDICINE

16—9917

MEDICAL HISTORY

Kerouac J. L.

STATE NAME OF PLACE   DATE EACH NEW ENTRY

U.S. NAVAL HOSPITAL
Bethesda, Md.

RA   ADMITTED   5-20-43

DIAGNOSIS Dementia Praecox
#1509

DISABILITY not RESULT OF OWN
MISCONDUCT.

ADMISSION NOTE:

The patient was readmitted 4-2-43
to the sick list at the U.S. Naval
Training Station, Newport, R.I., because
at recruit re-examination he exhibited
vague, disconnected thoughts; he rambled
in a grandiose, philosophical manner;
displayed auditory and visual halluc-
inations. He had been placed on Trial
Duty Status on 3-22-43 due to his ab-
normal conduct. Before this trial period
expired, he was referred to the N.P.
unit for observation. He was transferred to the Naval Hospital, Newport,
R.I., on 4-2-43 with DU(Dementia Praecox).
At that hospital he was observed
for 5 weeks, and on 5-11-43 the diagnosis
Dementia Praecox, was established. Upon
the approved recommendation of a Board
of Medical Survey, he was transferred
to this hospital, arriving on 5-20-43.
Upon arrival here he was quiet and cooperative and courteous to the ward
personnel.

PAST HISTORY:

The patient is the older of two
children (a sister). He was the pet
of both his parents, especially his
mother.
Educational History: Bright in
school and a good all-around athlete.
He was outstanding in high school
football. He went to Columbia University (NY) on a football scholarship

10—9017

Form H-8
(1940)

hsm

Page ___3___

MEDICAL HISTORY

KEROUAC, AS 2-6 USNR 732-58-22
(13)
_____
(Surname)
John   Louis
_____
(Christian name(s))

Born: Place Lowell, Mass._____ Date 3-12-22____

STATE NAME OF PLACE   DATE EACH NEW ENTRY

U.S. NAVAL HOSPITAL, BETHESDA, MD.

in August 1940 to June 1941. He quit
college then due to fellow students'
critical attitude toward him and went
to Washington D.C. for three months.
His relations are heterosexual. He has
no shame, remorse or reluctance to discuss his affairs.

Religious: Although brought up
Catholic; he states that he is agnost-
ic, and has been such since 14 years of
age.

Occupational: Very unreliable.
He has been fired from every job he
had except newspaper reporting. The
latter was for a small paper at $15
per week, which he quit. He has been
discharged from steamship job, garage
job and waiter job. He is irresponsible
not caring.

SOURCE OF HISTORY:

The following was obtained from
the patient who is freely accessible and
cooperative and his statements are
considered reliable.

PRESENT ILLNESS: .

Patient arrived at the USNTS,
Newport, R.I. on 3-22-43. Shortly
afterwards began to suffer with headaches and went frequently to sick bay
and was given aspirin which he feels
only made the headaches more severe.
Prior to enlistment he had suffered with
occasional headaches and always obtained
relief by taking "aspirin." He found
it difficult to adjust to the recruit
training program "because of the reg-
imentation and discipline." He was
finally re-examined by the psychiatrist

Page _____

MEDICAL HISTORY

(13) Kerouac J. L.

STATE NAME OF PLACE   DATE EACH NEW ENTRY

at the end of his period of trial
duty and admitted to the dispensary.
He denies he was ill at the time or
that his headaches were very severe
and feels that the physician made a
mistake in labeling him as a case of
Dementia Praecox. He is no longer
bothered with headaches now.

FAMILY HISTORY:

Father, French-Canadian birth,
living and well, works as a printer,
and has always been a pal of the
patient's--"more like a big brother."
He has worked as a printer most of his
life. During the depression years,
was on WPA for a time. In 1941, lost
his job because his employers wanted
him to send his boy to Boston College
whereas the boy had already registered
at Columbia University. Since then
has obtained other satisfactory employment but according to the patient the
father feels that the whole town is
"against" the family.

Mother, 48, living and well,
closely attached to patient. Also
French-Canadian by birth.

Sister, 24, divorced just recently
joined the WAAC's. At 18 she married
a man of 30 but divorced him after one
year. Because of this she was considered the "black sheep" of the family.
Patient remarks that in years past
he was the favored child but that
recently his role has been reversed
so that he now looked upon as the
"black sheep." No history of mental
or nervous diseases.

PERSONAL HISTORY:

This patient is an AS (V-6)USNR
21 years old, born in Lowell, Mass.,
3-12-22, single, a Catholic, who en-
sted in class V-1 of USNR on   -8-42

Form H-8
(1940)

Page ___5___

hsm (14)

MEDICAL HISTORY

KEROUAC, ...AS V-6 USNR ...732-58-22...
(Surname)
John ....Louis
(Christian name(s))

Born: Place Lowell, Mass. .... Date 3-12-22

STATE NAME OF PLACE   DATE EACH NEW ENTRY

US. NAVAL HOSPITAL, BETHESDA, MD.

at New York City and reported for
active duty at USNTS, Newport, R.I.
on 3-22-43 having 10 days active
duty on admission to the sick list
and 1 month, 28 days active duty on
admission to this hospital.

DEVELOPMENTAL:

No significant data elicited.
Denies enuresis, sonnanabulism, temper-
tantrums, nailbiting, etc.

EDUCATIONAL:

During first 5 grades attended
French parochial school and finished
up in public high school with high
scholastic rating. Completed Lowell
High School with good records and
given scholarship to Horace Mann Prep
in New York where he attended for one
year, then given scholarship worth $500
per year to Columbia University.
Completed freshman year(1941) with
failure only in chemistry. Did not
return the following year but a year
later came back at behest of football
coach but left after 3 months (Dec.1942)
because funds ran out.

OCCUPATIONAL:

Merchant Marine, 3 months Northern
Greenland. Were attacked several times
by submarines. Worked in 1942, after
leaving Columbia, 3 months as a sports
reporter. While at Columbia had NYA
job, Private Secretary. Note also
patient's occupation as a writer.